Merleau-Ponty and the Art of Perception

Merleau-Ponty and the Art of Perception

Edited by
Duane H. Davis and William S. Hamrick

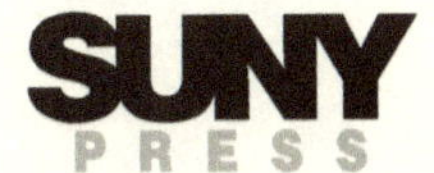

Cover Art: Marta Nijhuis, "(A Trip to) Newstead Abbey," 80 × 100 cm, mixed media on canvas, 2005.

Published by State University of New York Press, Albany

Printed in the United States of America

For information, contact State University of New York Press, Albany, NY
www.sunypress.edu

Production, Jenn Bennett
Marketing, Anne M. Valentine

Library of Congress Cataloging-in-Publication Data

Merleau-Ponty and the art of perception / edited by Duane H. Davis and William S. Hamrick.
pages cm
Includes bibliographical references and index.
ISBN 978-1-4384-5959-2 (hc : alk. paper)—978-1-4384-5958-5 (pb : alk. paper)
ISBN 978-1-4384-5960-8 (e-book)
1. Merleau-Ponty, Maurice, 1908–1961. 2. Perception (Philosophy) 3. Art—Philosophy. I. Davis, Duane (Duane H.), editor.
B2430.M3764M46823 2016
121'.34092—dc23 2015010179

10 9 8 7 6 5 4 3 2 1

Contents

Acknowledgments

I would like to express my thanks to Professor Ivan Kolev of the Department of Philosophy in the University of Sofía, Bulgaria, for hosting and helping to organize the 2008 conference celebrating the one hundredth anniversary of the birth of Maurice Merleau-Ponty. I would also like to thank many friends in the International Merleau-Ponty Circle—some of whom are represented in this volume—for their inspiration and support over the years. They and other members of the Circle incarnate and keep alive the ideal of peaceful, erudite conversations that actually take steps to the truth.

—William S. Hamrick

I wish to acknowledge my deepest gratitude to: Ivan Kolev for co-directing the conference in Sophia, Bulgaria, in 2008; to William S. Hamrick, who is a masterful collaborator—the finest one could work with, and who did much more than his share of editorial work on this volume; to Andrew Kenyon of SUNY Press who provided sage counsel and constant encouragement on the project; to the friendly staff at *The Universal Joint* in West Asheville, who make their patio a congenial place to work; to Pounce the cat, who probably co-authored some of my best work on the patio at home; to Cheryl A. Emerson and Cynthia J. Willett, each of whom carefully read drafts of *The Art of Perception*, each making suggestions that resulted in a much better essay; and, again, to Cheryl, who once showed me a new meaning of dehiscence in *Amarelli*—"*Aprimi il petto e vedrai scritto in core.*"

—Duane H. Davis

Abbreviations for Frequently Cited Merleau-Ponty Texts

AD 1973. *Adventures of the Dialectic.* Trans. Joseph Bien. Evanston: Northwestern University Press. Originally published in 1955 as *Les Aventures de la dialectique.* Paris: Gallimard.

C 2004. *Maurice Merleau-Ponty, The World of Perception.* Trans. Oliver Davis. London and New York: Routledge. Originally published in 2002 as *Causeries 1948.* Établies et annotées par Stéphanie Ménasé. Paris: Éditions du Seuil.

CAL 1973. *Consciousness and the Acquisition of Language.* Trans. Hugh Silverman. Evanston: Northwestern University Press. Published in 1964 as "La Conscience et l'acquisition du langage." *Bulletin de psychologie* 236: XVIII 3–6, 226–59.

E 1973. *In Praise of Philosophy.* Trans. John Wild and James M. Edie. Evanston: Northwestern University Press. Originally published in 1953 as *Éloge de la philosophie.* Paris: Gallimard.

IP 2003. *L'institution, la passivité, Notes de cours au Collège de France (1954–1955).* Textes établis par Dominique Darmaillacq, Claude Lefort, et Stéphanie Ménasé, Préface de Claude Lefort. Paris: Belin.

N 2003. *Nature: Course Notes from the Collège de France.* Trans. Robert Vallier. Evanston: Northwestern University Press. Originally published in 1994 as *La Nature, Notes, Cours du Collège de France.* Ed. Dominique Séglard. Paris: Éditions de Seuil.

NC 1996. *Notes de cours 1959–1961.* Préface de Claude Lefort et avertissement de Stéphanie Ménasé. Paris: Gallimard.

OE*	1964. "Eye and Mind" in *The Primacy of Perception and Other Essays*, pp. 159–190. Trans. Carleton Dallery. Retranslated in 1993 by Michael B. Smith in Galen A. Johnson and Michael B. Smith, eds. *The Merleau-Ponty Aesthetics Reader, Philosophy and Painting*. Evanston: Northwestern University Press. First published in book form in 1964 as *L'Œil et l'esprit.* Paris: Gallimard.
PC I	1997. *Parcours 1935–1951*, Ed. Jacques Prunair. Paris: Éditions Verdier.
PC II	2000. *Parcours deux, 1951–1961.* Ed. Jacques Prunair. Paris: Éditions Verdier.
PhP*	1962. *Phenomenology of Perception.* London: Routledge and Kegan Paul; New York: Humanities Press. Trans. Colin Smith. Retranslated in 2012 by Donald A. Landes. London and New York: Routledge. Originally published in 1945 as *Phénoménologie de la perception.* Paris: Gallimard.
PM	1973. *The Prose of the World.* Trans. John O'Neill. Evanston: Northwestern University Press. Originally published in 1969 as *La Prose du monde.* Paris: Gallimard.
PrP	1964. *The Primacy of Perception and Other Essays on Phenomenological Psychology, the Philosophy of Art, History and Politics*. Ed. James M. Edie. Evanston: Northwestern University Press.
Prim.Percp.	1964. "The Primacy of Perception and its Philosophical Consequences." Trans. James M. Edie. In *The Primacy of Perception and Other Essays*, 12–42. Originally published in 1947 as "Le Primat de la perception et ses conséquences philosophiques," *Bulletin de la Société française de philosophie*, XLI, (reporting on the meeting of 23 November 1946), 119–53.
RC	1970. *Themes from the Lectures at the Collège de France, 1952–1960.* Trans. John O'Neill. Evanston: Northwestern University Press. Originally published in 1968 as *Résumés de cours, Collège de France 1952–1960.* Paris: Gallimard.
S*	1964. *Signs.* Trans. Richard C. McCleary. Evanston: Northwestern University Press. Originally published in 1960 as *Signes.* Paris: Gallimard.

SNS 1964. *Sense and Non-Sense*. Trans. Hubert L Dreyfus and Patricia Allen Dreyfus. Evanston: Northwestern University Press. Originally published in 1948 as *Sens et non-sens*. Paris: Nagel. Reprinted in 1996. Paris: Gallimard.

VI 1968. *The Visible and the Invisible, Followed by Working Notes*. Trans. Alphonso Lingis. Evanston: Northwestern University Press. Originally published in 1964 as *Le Visible et l'invisible, suivi de notes de travail*. Ed. Claude Lefort. Paris: Gallimard.

*Different authors cite different editions of these works, which, unfortunately, have different paginations than the originals. The specific editions used in each article are noted at their first citations. Occasionally, a few authors cite other Merleau-Pontian texts. References to those works are appended to their articles.

Illustrations, Chapter 5

Preface

William S. Hamrick

In March 2008, at Sofía University, Professors Ivan Kolev and Duane H. Davis organized a centenary celebration of Merleau-Ponty's birth. The conference attracted a wide range of speakers from many countries, including some who have contributed to this volume. They explored the philosopher's views on perception, the body, art, science, and truth. In his remarks, Professor Kolev noted that, in "The Philosopher and His Shadow," Merleau-Ponty, citing Heidegger, writes about the "uncontemplated" that each thought outlines. That "uncontemplated" is a possibility and generates a task (S, 160/202).[1] Furthermore, in *The Visible and the Invisible*, a text substantially influenced by Heidegger, the author speaks about the "internal armature" of the visible (149/195). What belongs to that "internal armature" is "the possible which is not a shadow of the actual, but is its principle" (ibid., 152/199). That "internal armature" is the invisible in the visible, its "lining and depth" (Proust) (ibid., 149/195), its inherent and overwhelming meaningfulness that calls forth its creative expression across all levels of culture.

Merleau-Ponty's early and later works both stress the bodily foundation of this articulation of meaning, Professor Kolev continued. Whereas the early writings focus on the lived body's "I can" as powers for exploration and comprehension of the world and other people, the later texts take up these corporeal powers in the articulation of the chiasmatic reversibility of flesh, to which we shall return in a moment. Kolev went on to discuss Heidegger's phenomenological analysis of Dasein's possibilities by striving to disclose "a

1. Throughout this volume, when dual pagination is provided for Merleau-Ponty's texts, the English page number(s) will precede the original(s) and they will be separated by a "/". The editions of *Signs* cited in this Preface are, respectively, Evanston: Northwestern University Press, 1964, trans. Richard C. McCleary; and Paris: Gallimard, 1960.

phenomenon that shows itself." With regard to Merleau-Ponty's ontology, he continued, it is art, especially painting, that makes up one of the phenomena that most evidently disclose themselves and that most clearly reveal the structure and possibilities of the flesh. In art, as both *poeisis* and *contemplatio,* we see clearly that Possibilia constitute the metaphysical core of human existence. The essays that comprise this book articulate those possibilia.

In Part One of this volume, this Preface and the subsequent discussions of the art of perception and the relationship of art and science lay a foundation for the particular interpretations of art and perception in Merleau-Ponty's philosophy that follow in Part Two. Duane H. Davis's "The Art of Perception" closely follows Merleau-Ponty's philosophical development from his early to last texts. Davis's aim is to show that, at all stages along the philosopher's way, perception and art are so intimately intertwined and reversible that his view of perception is his account of art and vice versa. William S. Hamrick's "Concluding Scientific Postscript" converges on this thesis by showing that, contrary to the manner in which Merleau-Ponty contrasts science and art, they are more alike than the philosopher believed them to be.

Merleau-Ponty uses "reversibility" interchangeably with "chiasm," derivative from the Greek letter χ. Thus, the title of what proved to be the last chapter of the unfinished manuscript, *The Visible and the Invisible*, is "Intertwining—The Chiasm" (*L'entrelacs—le chiasme*). He arrived at this fundamental structure of flesh from at least three different sources, and it is significant for this volume that one of them was literary. It consists of the rhetorical figure in which the word order in the first part of two-part unit—say, a verse or sentence—is inverted in the second part. For this meaning, Merleau-Ponty is mainly indebted to Paul Valéry.[2] However, the poet himself applied the chiasm to perception and intercorporeity as the reversibility of self and other—as did Merleau-Ponty later.[3]

2. As Emmanuel de Saint Aubert points out, Merleau-Ponty first uses "chiasm" in "L'homme et l'adversité" (1951) (S 231/293). *Le Scénario cartésien, Recherches sur la formation et la cohérence de l'intention philosophique de Merleau-Ponty* (Paris: Librairie Philosophique J. Vrin, 2005), 169 (referred to hereafter as "ESA"). The term also appears at RC, 14/25, but with only a brief reference to the passage cited from Valéry quoted in full at S, 231–32/293–94.

3. For Valéry's text, see his *Choses tues*, VI, *Tel Quel*, I, in *Œuvres*, Vol. II, Bibliothèque de la Pléiade (Paris: Gallimard, 1960), 490–91 (ESA, 170, n. 1). In Merleau-Ponty's unpublished *Être et monde*, he again refers to Valéry as follows: "Thought = 'to mix oneself up with some object' and to be astonished at this confusion (*Mon Faust*): "La pensée = 'se confondre à quelque objet' et s'étonner de cette confusion (*Mon Faust*)" (ESA, 51), referring to Valéry's *Mon Faust* (Paris: Gallimard, 1946), 50.

The other two sources for the notion of chiasm are, first, physiological structures that intersect and cross over. The most common example, and one with which Merleau-Ponty was much taken, is the optic chiasm—the brain structure in which the two optic nerves intersect and at which half of the fibers of each nerve cross over to the other hemisphere. Second, he also used this structure as an analogue for the experience of touching and touched, which appears in several essays in Part Two of the present volume. The source for that sense of reversibility is Edmund Husserl's *Ideas II*, § 36. The latter pointed out that our experience of our own bodies is one of a sensory reflection. When one hand touches, say, another hand, the subjective body feels part of itself as object. Touching becomes touched. However, when the experience is reversed, the touched hand changes into a hand touching the previously touching one, which is now the touched. Merleau-Ponty's later published as well as unpublished texts reveal that this is how he began to think of the chiasm before generalizing it as one of the central meanings of flesh itself.

In 1993, there appeared what was and remains the most significant collection of Merleau-Ponty's writings about aesthetics and philosophy, *The Merleau-Ponty Aesthetics Reader*, edited by Galen Johnson. That volume contains Michael B. Smith's welcome retranslations of Merleau-Ponty's major writings on aesthetics—"Cézanne's Doubt," "Indirect Language and the Voices of Silence," and "Eye and Mind"—explanatory essays by the editor himself, and a number of interpretive, critical essays. All of the latter, with the exception of a well-known letter from René Magritte to Alphonse de Waelhens, come from the pens (or keyboards) of theoreticians instead of practicing artists. By contrast, the contributors to this book include not only philosophers, but also professionals in the fields of painting, photography, and architecture. All of these essays consist of particular illustrations and interpretations in different media of the reversibility of art and perception.

That diversity is immediately apparent in "Cohesion and Expression: Merleau-Ponty and Cézanne," by Jessica Wiskus. She follows the significant alteration in emphasis on depth in Merleau-Ponty's writings, and shows that "it comes to inform the way that Merleau-Ponty approaches other artistic questions articulated through the paintings of Cézanne—questions of movement, color, and style." Depth, in fact, "serves as a model through which Merleau-Ponty understands the notion of expression itself. This is singularly important for the latter because his philosophy is, from one end to the other, one of creative expression. Hence, there is a unity of style permeating all forms of expression, just as for Cézanne. As Wiskus phrases it, "There is a depth to his work through all canvases, as an orientation to painting—a resonance, an artistic movement, or a style. Thus the expression of a painter is not contained within some material work: his work, rather, coheres through (but in some way beyond) these canvases, as a style identifiable only in retrospect." The work of expression develops according to "a temporal dimension of depth"—in Merleau-Ponty's words, "a sort of existential eternity" (IP, 49/87).

As a musicologist, Wiskus writes about a philosopher, Merleau-Ponty who, in turn, writes about the painter, Cézanne. Marta Nijhuis's essay, "Echoes of Brushstrokes," inverts that order. She is a painter writing about her own creations in the light of a philosopher. She states that her own work and her readings of Merleau-Ponty have always run on parallel paths until this essay when she speaks of her art in relation to the latter's philosophy. She specifies that she does not seek to represent the philosopher in her paintings or to claim that his work is the "inspiring motif" of her own, but rather to create a dialogue between the two. On her view, philosophy maintains a dialogue with all artistic media.

To create this dialogue, she repairs to Gilles Deleuze's notion of a particular "image of thought," an "opening of a crack from which we are enabled to see the world differently." The connection between art and philosophy does not teach us "a mere transposition of thought into image, but rather the discovery of a certain 'image of thought' " (Deleuze). This constitutes "the inauguration of a new horizon of sense filling the world with an unexpected atmosphere-color, a new disposition of the eye and the mind at once." Behind this communicability between different forms of expression and fields of study lies "that invisible background embracing all things that Merleau-Ponty calls flesh." Magritte was partially correct, she goes on to say, that "our thought comprehends both: the visible and the invisible. And I use painting in order to make the thought become visible." This is a perception that echoes Oscar Wilde's pronouncement that what drives a painter to paint is the determination "to give visibility to an invisible." Nevertheless, Nijhuis sides with Merleau-Ponty's assertion that there is an invisibility and mystery about the world that can never be made visible. She also explores, with reference to Deleuze, the notion of contingency in artistic creation and the role of the body that painting "echoes." Part of this investigation consists of the exploration of symbols, and this leads her back to Baudelaire's poem, "*Correspondances*," discussed by Walter Benjamin and, in this volume, by Duane Davis.

Images comprise the central topic of Sara J. Northerner's essay, "From Edmund Husserl's *Image Consciousness* to Maurice Merleau-Ponty's *Flesh and Chiasm*: The Phenomenological Essence of Image." This paper presents certain philosophical concepts from Edmund Husserl and explores Merleau-Ponty's phenomenological project as rendered in a series of large-scale photographic artworks. As a visual artist, she discloses the possibilities of Husserl's image-consciousness as perceived through Merleau-Ponty's notion of the embodied viewer in intimate communion with the world. The overwhelming size of the photographic pieces, physical characteristics within the artwork, and corporeal relationship required for the viewing of an image, comprehensively emphasize the phenomenological theories as exemplified and illuminated by the artwork.

Northerner's artwork realizes photographically the diverse structures of a contemporary image-consciousness as detailed in Husserl's theories of the constitution of an object and his specific work with image-consciousness. His sketches, collected works, and lectures provide a foundation of knowledge beyond traditional and contemporary photographic theory. Furthermore, she holds, Merleau-Ponty's writings on phenomenology, perception, embodiment, and the visible/invisible, have strengthened her ability to create diverse structures of meaning in images throughout an installation of the artwork. His ideas of body schema, flesh, and chiasm are directly incorporated into the physical reality and aesthetic experience of her work. Within the photographic image and body of work, the deciphering of both image-consciousness and an aesthetic experience becomes a dialogue of flesh where all forms of perception intertwine. Through image, light, and translucency, the texture of the world visually makes itself known within the aesthetic, perceptual encounter with these specific images.

Bryan E. Norwood's essay, "Carnal Language and the Reversibility of Architecture: Modernism, Postmodernism, and Merleau-Ponty's Theory of Signs," turns our attention from photographic images to the linguistic intelligibility of a considerably different artistic medium. For modernist architects, language is extra-referential: it is indexical because its meaning is the structures to which it refers. For postmodern architects, language is infra-referential as a semiotics of signs: "all buildings and architectural elements act as signs" of themselves only. Postmodern architects, therefore, attempt to extract meaning from the "diacritical, infra-referential structure of immanent language." For modernists, therefore, meaning is transcendent, while for postmodernists it is immanent.

How can this gap between immanence and transcendence be bridged or, as Norwood puts it, "How can architecture both be about itself and about what it signifies?" With the aid of a plethora of examples, he seeks an answer in Merleau-Ponty's notion of flesh to "provide a conceptual structure . . . for *reversible architecture*—an approach that aims to redefine the architectural debate on language." "Architectural signs" turn out to be "not only ideals, but part of carnality that is able to affect and change the structure of the visible." Language and structure are not separate and distinct; rather, what is built "is built-spoken and a witness to Being."

In "Architecture and the Voices of Silence," Patricia Locke continues Norwood's discussion in the context of Merleau-Ponty's 1952 article, "Indirect Language and the Voices of Silence." She follows the latter as its author embraced both structuralism and phenomenology in his critical analysis of André Malraux's *musée imaginaire,* the museum without walls. In Locke's view, "Architecture refers only tangentially to itself through symbolic forms or through self-conscious narrative." Architecture is "more explicitly embodied" than language "because it both takes into account and creates a spatial world." However, like language, architecture "incarnates silence" because it is not simply a record of the past, but also "presents a future for embodied beings."

Taking as an instructive case study the Isamu Noguchi Garden Museum in Long Island City, New York, Locke shows that the meaningfulness of architecture emerges in the ways that it allows human beings—through the embodied architect, the "architect-as-inhabitant"—to orient themselves according to its "multidimensional organization of space-time" while at the same time demonstrating the ability to "fold back upon its resources" to illuminate "earlier ways of perceiving space." In both its past and future intentionalities, architecture consists of "a framing or structuring poeisis that makes vivid human embodiment possible."

A "structuring poesis" at the heart of "vivid human embodiment" lies at the heart of Duane H. Davis's "The Philosopher of Modern Life: Baudelaire, Merleau-Ponty, and the Art of Phenomenological Critique." In this paper, the author seeks to reveal the spirit of Charles Baudelaire that animates Merleau-Ponty's thought. The former's antiromantic critique of modernity, for Davis, discloses a social and political depth in the latter's work that has not yet been fully appreciated. The large background question of Davis's reflections posed by Baudelaire's critique and what it reveals in Merleau-Ponty's thought is, "What role or roles do philosophers and poets play in the critique of modernity?"

Davis approaches this question by reading Merleau-Ponty's later thought as an "ontological appropriation" of Baudelaire's concepts of "*réversibilité*" and "*correspondances,*" the latter being equivalent to Merleau-Ponty's key notion of the *écart.* Acknowledging these Baudelairean aspects of Merleau-Ponty's work reveals the latter's "critical (social and political) horizon and has implications for our own critical situation with respect to modernity."

Voices of silence and listening in depth have a double presence in Cheryl A. Emerson's "The Flesh Made Word: *As I Lay Dying* and Being Incarnate." The author uses Merleau-Ponty's phenomenology of embodiment to analyze William Faulkner's darkly comic tale of a family on a fool's errand in the sweltering heat of a Mississippi summer. They are transporting the decaying corpse of their mother and wife to a family grave plot many miles distant from their home. Emerson shows that the suggested alienation of the characters, through which they seem to be establishing isolated meanings on an incoherent, exterior world, is only apparent. The reader learns that, in the novel, each character "thinks" in relationship to his or her private physical world, but one that envelops the relationship of body to natural world and the gestural language of other bodies as expressed intent, even if the transfer of that intent goes wildly wrong. Furthermore, these relationships include the decaying corpse secreting its own nonverbal language, expressing its decay and humiliation to onlookers along the burial route. The idea of intercorporeality prolongs Merleau-Ponty's concept of language as embodiment, even with the dead. This unexpected reversible illumination is Faulkner's suggestion that the reversibility of carnal and even linguistic meanings works as well (or badly) with the dead as with the living.

What Merleau-Ponty teaches Emerson is that "literature, as with all art, is intercorporeal, not only in the 'involvement and lateral rapport of characters' (NC, 51) within the text, but through the reader's involvement as well, among 'the mist' of interior monologues. Our understanding is also one of embodiment, where we perceive the interior consciousness of the characters through a transfer of our own 'body schema' onto theirs." All of the descriptions of the book's characters are enriched and become more vivid "once we return to what lies 'beneath the noise of words' (PhP, 190/214)."[4]

Returning to "what lies 'beneath the noise of words'" requires an ability to listen appreciatively to them, and listening is the central theme of Galen A. Johnson's "Listening in Depth: Reading Merleau-Ponty Alongside Nancy." Johnson reflects on Merleau-Ponty's late texts together with Jean-Luc Nancy's *Listening* and *Corpus* in order to produce "something like a counterpoint harmony," but with some dissonances. Merleau-Ponty uses the terms *auscultation* (listening) and *palpation* for a kind of attentive, conscious experience that is different from (mere) hearing.

For both Merleau-Ponty and Nancy, in the latter's words, listening is "an intensification and a concern, a curiosity or an anxiety." To listen is to

4. The editions cited in this Preface are, respectively, London and New York: Routledge, 2012, trans. Donald A. Landes; and Paris: Gallimard, 1945.

be on the edge of meaning and push toward it, and both prefer to conceive the philosopher as a listener rather than seer. The philosopher effects a "close transition from hearing to touching and from touching to a certain mode of seeing" without collapsing all differences between them.

Nor are they equal in their effects. As Nancy puts it in *Corpus*, "The sound that penetrates through the ear propagates throughout the entire body something of its effects, which could not be said to occur in the same way with the visual signal." Sound can both stroke and strike us and affect the entire body.

An "auscultation or palpation in depth" that is involved in listening is also a key factor in intercorporeity and participation in community. Listening deeply touches the body/spirit that is the other. It opens one to the other through its pregnant silence. It is also essential to opening ourselves to the work of art in order to let it speak to us. Johnson notes that listening "is like an art of drawing, and in a double sense: drawing out the other at the same time as the listener is drawn into the space of the question, and it means that listening to the other also becomes a listening to oneself and a relation to oneself." This kind of listening does not achieve a perfect concordance with the other, as there is always a difference or gap (an *écart*) between our different situations, joys, and sufferings, but it can provide enough commonality to draw us together.

Finally, Johnson discusses the connection between listening in depth and Merleau-Ponty's ontology of flesh as well as Nancy's charge that that ontology is "infected with the legacy of the Christian doctrines of incarnation (the Word made Flesh) and the cross (chiasm) insufficiently deconstructed in the age of the death of God"—in other words, "onto-theology." Nancy, by contrast, construes the body medically and technologically, "as suffering and survival, an exscription of Being—body written and imprinted from the outside rather than, or at least in addition to, signifying inscriptions written from the inside." This is a significant difference from Merleau-Ponty's reliance on poetry—particularly that of Paul Claudel and Paul Valéry—to offer a vision of the body and its relation to nature that is one of the fullness of silence and "listening in depth" to the world as poem and "total harmony" (Claudel).

Communicative intercorporeity and the body's relation to nature also figure prominently in William S. Hamrick's "Art and the Overcoming of the Discourse of Modernity." The author sets Merleau-Ponty's view of the body and its relationships with nature against the modernist view that descended from the Galilean-Cartesian physics. For the latter, nature is purely quantitative, all purposes and values, including the good, are exiled from it, and this "mechanistic despiritualization" (E. A. Burtt) results in nature being conceived as standing over against us as subjects or spectators. This is what Merleau-Ponty rejects as "the ontology of the object."

Hamrick offers an aesthetic critique of all three of these modernist beliefs based on two main sources. The first is the nature and significance of art in German Romanticism, especially that of F. W. J. Schelling, who substantially influenced Merleau-Ponty. The second source is Merleau-Ponty's own discussions of art, mainly painting, in which, as we have seen, his final and nascent ontology of flesh is situated. With regard to the latter source, the paper demonstrates different ways in which Merleau-Ponty's treatment of modern art—discussions that "illuminate vital connections between the good, the real, and the intelligible" aid in understanding his ontology of flesh. Films, sculpture, music, painting, and poetry all exhibit the fundamental reversibility of flesh in which we are implicated in art works and they in us. As Gaston Bachelard observes of the chiasmatic experience of poetry, when a "poem possesses us entirely," when "a single poetic image" reverberates in our souls," it "takes root in us . . . expressing us by making us what it expresses."[5]

The article also reprises certain themes from other contributors about reversibilities in painting and architecture, in Cézanne's search for depth, and the significance of color in that investigation. The paper concludes with a discussion of the ways that various artistic media reveal values, how these modes cohere with Merleau-Ponty's early "thesis" of "the primacy of perception, and the type of humanism that Merleau-Ponty thought they made possible."

Robert Switzer, in "Tactile Cogito: Horizons of Corporeity, Animality and Affect in Merleau-Ponty," also uses Merleau-Ponty's writings on the body and flesh to overcome the longstanding "philosophical idol" of the separation of mind from body (and the rest of reality), and of the superiority of the former over the latter. He wants to redeem "the place of the body at the heart of both truth and art"—i.e., to repair the "metaphysical fissure" at the heart of the "human animal." There is an "ineliminable bond with the natural world around us—its texture and feel, the resonant sonority of its surfaces and depths—and with the animals with which, in our own animal being, we share, as Heidegger wrote, a fundamental 'kinship.' "

5. Gaston Bachelard, *The Poetics of Space*, trans. Maria Jolas, Foreword by Etienne Gilson (Boston: The Beacon Press, 1969), xviii, xix. Published originally as *La poétique de l'espace* (Paris: Presses Universitaires de France, 1958).

The author positions Merleau-Ponty's writings about art and the body over against Heidegger's and Hegel's reflections on artworks and aesthetic experience. As against these thinkers, Switzer demonstrates that Merleau-Ponty had no wish to attempt to bridge "metaphysical divides" between human and animal, soul and body, form and matter, the invisible and the visible. Rather, he replaced the "divide" with the notions of intertwining and chiasm—"carnal implication." A human being, and therefore the artist, is "embodied by the physical insertion of the human animal into . . . the environing natural world." The artist thus becomes a special case of what we all are—a "tactile cogito"—while art itself gets grounded not on "ideality, but on our corporeal insertion into the real, in a mutually dependent dance." Merleau-Ponty's emphasis on a tactile cogito, together with his account of "incarnate artistic realization in the work of Cézanne and others," encourages us to continue the exploration of perception "uncorrupted by dualistic metaphysical myths."

Finally, in "The Chiasm as a Virtual: A Non-Concept in Merleau-Ponty's Work (With a Coda on Theatre)," Marcello V. Rosati argues that we should think of Merleau-Ponty as a philosopher of the virtual, not because of his explicit use of the term, but rather because of its ability to articulate the meaning of the chiasm. Moreover, he advances the hypothesis that Merleau-Ponty's notion of the virtual can "resolve a theoretical problem raised by the Aristotelian concept of *dunaton*" (the possible), and which is "at the heart of the modern notion of the possible." Rosati divides the question into conflicting pre- and post-actualization possibles. To understand the former, he relies on the notion of possible worlds as developed by Saul Kripke in *Naming and Necessity*, and which, for Rosati, do not differ substantially from Leibniz's concept of possible worlds. As opposed to those possibles, those that follow actualization are dependent on the action and are, thus, not contingent. Spinoza, Hegel, and Bergson are interwoven in the author's analysis of this notion of *dunaton*, and to resolve the conflict between the two types of possibles and answer the question, How does what happens happen?, Rosati seeks a solution in the idea of the virtual.

To do this, he returns to the "plurivocity of the word *dunaton* in Aristotle's work to try to find a meaning that avoids the logical concept of the possible." The concept of *kinesis* is the desired "middle course" via which the *dunaton* achieves "tension, strength, and transition from before to after." It is "what explains the transition from past to present, from what is not yet existent to what is." The notion of transition "leads to the creation of pre-actualization before a completely novel post-actualization." This move also entails understanding the *dunaton* not as the possible, but as something virtual. Its advantage is that it can avoid the before-and-after polarity because the "virtual and the actual constitute both parts of the real object. The virtual is an interstitial principle from which existence is produced." The virtual is not identical with the before because it also adheres to the produced object, the after.

Further remarks on virtuality follow in the light of, among other things, Deleuze's *Difference and Repetition*. However, Rosati wants to go beyond Deleuze's work with Merleau-Ponty's notion of the chiasm, in order to understand how the virtual and the actual can belong to each other. To illustrate this relationship, the author discusses at length Merleau-Ponty's account of Proust's description of the actress, Berma, playing the role of Phèdre, and significance of the theatre in Merleau-Ponty's thought.

It is also worth noting that both Switzer's and Rosati's essays form a capstone for the collection and, as such, can well be considered an effective "anchor" for the volume. They can therefore significantly increase readers' sense of the integral character of the collection.

As noted above, all of these interpretive essays are particularizations in diverse artistic media of the central theme of this work—the intertwining of art and perception. As such, they themselves form a chiasmatic unity with the foundation established in Part One: the groundwork extends through them as a connecting thread, while they exemplify and illustrate it, thus uncovering ever deeper and richer layers of meaning inherent in Merleau-Ponty's fascinating philosophy. Before our players take the stage, however, we must lay the scene.

References

Bachelard, G. 1969. *The Poetics of Space*. Translated by Maria Jolas, Foreword by Etienne Gilson. Boston: The Beacon Press. Originally published in 1958 as *La poétique de l'espace*. Paris: Presses Universitaires de France.

Husserl, E. 1989. *Ideas Pertaining to a Pure Phenomenology and to a Phenomenological Philosophy, Second Book, Studies in the Phenomenology of Constitution*. Translated with an Introduction by Richard Rojecwicz and André Schuwer. Dordrecht: Kluwer Academic Publishers. Originally published in 1952 as *Ideen zu einer reinen Phänomenologie und phänomenologischen Philosophie. Zweites Buch: Phänomenologische Untersuchungen zur Konstitution*, Husserliana IV. The Hague: Martinus Nijhoff.

Saint Aubert, E. de. 2005. *Le scénario cartésien. Recherches sur la formation et la cohérence de l'intention philosophique de Merleau-Ponty*. Paris: Librairie Philosophique J. Vrin.

Valéry, P. 1960. *Œuvres*, Vol. II. Bibliothèque de la Pléiade Paris: Gallimard.

Part One

Context and Orientation

1

The Art of Perception

Duane H. Davis

We pose a thesis, which is the organizing principle of this volume: in Maurice Merleau-Ponty's works, art and perception emerge as an intertwining. And we do not mean that they simply overlap or happen to be featured in some of the same works: they are ineluctably intertwined throughout his work—topically and methodologically. They can be distinguished only by an abstract analysis. His account of perception and his account of art are organic, interdependent, and dynamic. His account of perception *is* his account of art, and vice versa. We maintain that any reading that ignores this principle examines an abstraction of his positions on art or perception.

The essays included in this volume examine aspects of this intertwining in a variety of artistic media, each author ingeniously revealing an original perspective upon this intertwining. The five sections that comprise this essay offer a short account of how art informs Merleau-Ponty's account of perception as well as how perception informs his account of art. We shall accomplish this by looking at the way the interaction appears at five different moments of his philosophical development.

Merleau-Ponty's phenomenology of perception is not only the title of his most famous book, but also describes his philosophical *parcours*. He depicts phenomenology as a *problem* for understanding in the broadest and most genuine and open senses of inquiry rather than as a dogmatic program to secure or provide some apodictic grounding for all knowledge and reality. Of course, to depict phenomenology as a problem is not to concede the impossibility of solutions; but these solutions will not be like ones sought after by other philosophers, nor even like those pursued by some other phenomenologists. Phenomenology is a *style* of inquiry for Merleau-Ponty.

Its solutions are creative, disciplined responses that are stylized to open up areas of inquiry rather than attempts to pronounce the last word on any given subject. And this open-ended interrogative approach bespeaks a unique aesthetic style of rigor and discipline. As we will see, for Merleau-Ponty, phenomenology itself is more of an art than "the science of sciences."[1]

As such, perception and art are inextricably bound together throughout Merleau-Ponty's work. It is less the case that he associates art and perception as two disparate topics than that he calls our attention to what we have called *the art of perception.* As befitting Merleau-Ponty's celebration of the fundamental ambiguities of human existence, the double genitive phrase *the art of perception* signifies that Merleau-Ponty uses art in association with his discussions of perception—that some art is especially germane to his discussion of perception, and it also implies that there is something essentially aesthetic about perception. Both connotations are crucial.

More specifically, art is indispensable to Merleau-Ponty's phenomenology of perception in at least two senses. First, it is essential insofar as his account of art restores art (and aesthetics) to its proper status, befitting serious philosophical inquiry, even within the philosophical examination of perception.[2] Merleau-Ponty shows us over and over how much we can learn about perception and the perceptual world from art, artists, and artworks. Second, phenomenology as an art effectively re-prescribes new lines of inquiry for perception—available only because of its creative engagement

1. Edmund Husserl, indisputably acknowledged to be the founder of the phenomenological movement, conceived of phenomenology as the science of sciences—the rigorous method that secured the philosophical foundations necessary for scientific inquiry to be possible and productive. Cf. Edmund Husserl, "Philosophy as Rigorous Science," in *Phenomenology and the Crisis of Philosophy*, trans. Quentin Lauer (New York: Harper Torchbooks, 1965), 71–147.

2. Gentle readers will perhaps find it difficult to believe, but there have been many philosophers who delegate aesthetics to some secondary status as a footnote, like this, or at least not unlike this, in the philosophical pantheon. Allow me to relate a brief anecdote to illustrate this point. Once upon a time, at a lovely conference in Cork, Ireland, many of the invited speakers were gathered for informal conversation late in the evening. The conversation turned to the dire job market all young philosophers face upon graduation, and how fortunate it was to be able to call philosophy one's profession as well as one's love. Eventually this led to a related topic: What if things had not worked out? What would each philosopher gathered there do for a profession if it had been impossible to continue in philosophy? One person said she would probably be a chef. One person said he would try to write songs. But then, one recent Oxford graduate wryly said, "If I were not able to continue in philosophy, I think that I should try aesthetics."

within the perceived world. We call Merleau-Ponty's unique style of phenomenology an *aesthetic phenomenology*. Merleau-Ponty's aesthetic phenomenology re-prescribes the conditions of the possibility of perception, because the conditions of the possibility for experience emerge within experience as potentials reconstructed after the fact. With all of this in mind, we can pose again our main thesis concerning the intertwining of art and perception: in both senses of the double genitive locution, Merleau-Ponty's entire philosophical project of a phenomenology of perception calls us to consider *the art of perception*.

Merleau-Ponty's foregrounding of the art of perception can be seen as a philosophy of perception's (re)turn to art. On the one hand, a philosophy of perception ought not to be innocent of aesthetics. Moreover, it ought not to suffer the pretense of escaping aesthetics toward the aim of achieving purity. Merleau-Ponty repeatedly *turns* our attention to the myriad ways that art figures in the creative role we play in perception. In this first sense, the art of perception instructs us about how we embody lived space and lived time. Thus, there is disclosed an aesthetic component of what Calvin O. Schrag (echoing Aristotle) has termed a "hermeneutic of everyday life."[3] This refers to the interpretation involved in the myriad aspects of the matrix of the intentional relation of art: the relation of the artist to the artwork; the relation of the observer to the artwork; the relation of the artwork to the world; the relation of the artist to the world; the relation of the artist to the observer; and the relation of the observer to the world, (among others). We see perceptual worlds emerging in these accounts of the techniques of art.

On the one hand, the art of perception returns our attention to the *aesthetic* essence of *aisthêsis*. And inversely, it returns our attention to the *aisthetic* essence of *aesthêsis*.[4] Merleau-Ponty's account does not aim to be reductive one way or the other.[5] His *aisthetic/aesthetic* phenomenology is an

3. Calvin O. Schrag, *Radical Reflection on the Origin of the Human Sciences* (West Lafayette, IN: Purdue University Press, 1980). Cf. chapter 5 "Understanding and Reason: Towards a Hermeneutic of Everyday Life," 97ff.

4. *Aisthêsis* connotes perception, while *aesthêsis* connotes appreciation of beauty. Jenny Slatman has produced an important inquiry into this relation in great detail in her excellent thesis, *L'expression au-delà de la representation: Sur l'aisthêsis et l'esthétique chez Merleau-Ponty*, Faculteit der Geesteswetenschappen, 2001, University of Amsterdam. More recently, Jacques Rancierre has played on these terms, but in very different ways than I imply here.

5. No matter what the aim may be, it seems clear that there inevitably must be something *thetic* in both *aisthêsis* and *aesthesis*.

attempt to illustrate the possibility of experience and the experience of possibility without reducing one to the other. In all of these ways, Merleau-Ponty calls us to consider *the art of perception*. Now let us consider *the art of perception* at five moments in Merleau-Ponty's philosophical development, though we maintain that he holds this position throughout his career.

1. The Phenomenology of Perception and Its Aesthetic Primacy

In this section, we will try to show how the art of perception is central to Merleau-Ponty's *Phenomenology of Perception*. In this work, Merleau-Ponty announces a new direction for phenomenology, an explicitly aesthetic orientation to his analysis of perception. In order to establish this, we will discuss the following topics: (1) how the art of perception provides Merleau-Ponty a different sort of rigorous analysis from modern science; (2) how Merleau-Ponty's phenomenology of the art of perception differs from Husserl's scientific model of phenomenology; (3) how there is an important reflexivity at the heart of Merleau-Ponty's aesthetic phenomenology; (4) how Merleau-Ponty's project of a phenomenology of perception is centered on expression in two senses—as an account of works of art as expression, as well as portraying perception in the context of the expression of phenomena; (5) how Merleau-Ponty attends specifically to the artist Paul Cézanne in his *Phenomenology of Perception* to provide a rigorous analysis of the art of perception.

In the Preface to his *Phenomenology of Perception*, Merleau-Ponty described phenomenology as "a problem and a promise,"[6] making room to redefine phenomenology in his own style (PhP, lxxi/ii).[7] Merleau-Ponty noted here how it might seem peculiar that one still needs to ask "What is phenomenology?" some fifty years on in the movement.[8] But he points out that the indeterminacy of what phenomenology is or where it is going are not signs of phenomenology's failure to establish its own identity, but

6. Perhaps the English "promise" does not quite to capture the French sense of avowal in the French *voeu*.

7. The editions cited in both this essay and in my paper in Part Two are, respectively, London and New York: Routledge, 2012, trans. Donald A. Landes; and Paris: Gallimard, 1945.

8. It is our position that we would do well to pose this question once again now that we have passed a century of phenomenology.

its very hope for a viable future. At the very end of the Preface, he likens this hope to that of art.

> Phenomenology is as painstaking as the works of Balzac, Proust, Valéry, or Cézanne—through the same kind of astonishment and wonder, the same demand for awareness, the same will to grasp the sense of the world or of history in its nascent state. (PhP, lxxxv/xvi)[9]

This conspicuous allusion to artists is featured as the grand conclusion of the anthemic Preface to his *Phenomenology of Perception*. Merleau-Ponty's aesthetic phenomenology is essentially an intertwining of art and perception. Here, at the very onset of his phenomenology of perception project, he calls our attention to the rigor and discipline of art—thus laying claim to that sort of "painstaking" labor to announce his vision of a new style of phenomenology. It is an acknowledgment of another sort of rigor and discipline more befitting the understanding of perceptual phenomena quite apart from that of the rigor of science.

This appeal to art is not to dismiss science *tout court*; nonetheless, Merleau-Ponty makes it clear by his invocation of these artists as paragons of another form of discipline that art provides more than just examples for his phenomenology. Also in the Preface, Merleau-Ponty appropriates from Husserlian phenomenology a critical standpoint in relation to modern science. "Phenomenology involves describing, and not explaining or analyzing" (PhP, lxxi/ii). The "promise" (*voeu*) of phenomenology is at once "a disavowal [*désaveu*] of science" (ibid.). As we pledge ourselves to the revealing of phenomena as phenomena, we detach from our scientific orientation, with its theoretical presuppositions about phenomena. But while we notice Merleau-Ponty's disparaging remarks about objective modern science in the Preface—and they are presented in stark contrast to his vision for phenomenology, we also see him in dialogue with psychologists and other scientists throughout the text, and indeed throughout his career. When we describe Merleau-Ponty's position as an *aesthetic phenomenology*, in sharp contrast not only to objective modern science but also in contrast to Husserl's vision of phenomenology as "the science of sciences," this is not to foreswear science altogether or to offer some forced choice between art and science. It may be helpful here to remember that there is an ancient common root of art and science: *technē*. And while Merleau-Ponty draws the aforementioned

9. Translation corrected.

contrasts between his vision for an existential phenomenology from modern objective science or Husserl's scientific phenomenology, he also calls our attention to the commonality of all three standpoints: *expression*. Phenomena *are* expressions. Phenomenology is a reflexive awareness of perception, which is the first-order expression of phenomena; science is a second-order expression (PhP, lxxii/iii).[10] But what if phenomenology were to assume a different style of reflexivity than science such that it makes no claim to purity or certainty? What if this aesthetic phenomenology showed us that there is no awareness of the self except as ambiguity (ibid., 360/397)?

Science proceeds by making theoretical assumptions about the world that have the effect of qualifying its claims about the world. It is tantamount to a conditional statement, where if the condition of the antecedent clause is not met, the statement has nothing to say about the consequent. And that is precisely the way Merleau-Ponty puts it. "Everything I know about the world, even through science, I know from a perspective that is my own or from an experience of the world without which scientific symbols would be meaningless." (More literally translated: without which scientific symbols would mean to say nothing—"*sans laquelle les symboles de la science ne voudraient rien dire*" [PhP, lxxii/ii].) They would have nothing to say.

Our modern epoch is defined by its inability or unwillingness to recognize this conditionality of scientific knowledge. It is repressed—we live in denial of it. We might well say that science's uniqueness lies in its status as the art that wants to forget that it *is* an art. Instead, science is treated as if it unconditionally presented the truth of the real world. But this duplicity is achieved by the pretense of positing an objective and universal standpoint for science: the disinterested observer. This same pretense is to act as if it severs rather than serves the connection between the scientific observer and the world—in effect discounting the value of our own lived perspectives. This makes it impossible to affirm the aforementioned antecedent condition for scientific knowledge. Thus, modern objective science has nothing to say about the world, unless we acknowledge the usually unacknowledged conditions and contingency of its manner of understanding. Science has a human face that tries to remain expressionless—as if science itself were not an expression.

---

10. It is unfortunate that, according to Don Landes, Merleau-Ponty's 1929 thesis, *La Notion de multiple intelligible chez Plotin* [*The notion of the Intelligible Multiple in Plotinus*], is lost. Merleau-Ponty produced this under the direction of the great historian of philosophy, Émile Bréhier. Cf. Don Landes, *The Merleau-Ponty Dictionary* (London: Bloomsbury Academic Publishers, 2013), 2.

And, as we noted above, Merleau-Ponty's aesthetic phenomenology differs from Husserl's scientific phenomenology. Just as art differs from science insofar as it recognizes, acknowledges, and trades upon its conditionality, an aesthetic phenomenology makes no claims to apodictic knowledge. While phenomenology always seeks the essences of phenomena, Merleau-Ponty says that his version of phenomenology "puts the essences back into existence" (PhP, lxx/i).[11] Likewise, Merleau-Ponty famously tells us that phenomenology does not exhaust the meaning of phenomena once and for all. "The most important lesson of the reduction is the impossibility of a complete reduction" (ibid., lxxvii/viii). Merleau-Ponty contrasts art and the objective ideals of modern science by celebrating art's candor—owning up to its conditionality and recognizing its situation within the contingent perceptual world.

> Scientific perspectives according to which I am a moment of the world are always naïve and hypocritical because they always imply, without mentioning it, that other perspective—the perspective of consciousness—by which a world first arranges itself around me and begins to exist for me. (PhP, lxxii/iii)

So Merleau-Ponty's aesthetic phenomenology differs from Husserl's scientific phenomenology not only by distinguishing itself from science, but also by distinguishing itself from scientific ideals. Merleau-Ponty's aesthetic phenomenology celebrates its conditionality and recognizes its situation within the contingent perceptual world. It does this by disclosing its own status as an expression of phenomena rather than denying it and claiming to provide the truth of the real world. But by owning up to its own status as expression, it enjoys a new style of verisimilitude with regard to the ways phenomena disclose themselves.

While Merleau-Ponty's aesthetic phenomenology differs from Husserl's scientific phenomenology in this regard, it does not differ from Husserl's insofar as both are accounts of phenomena. Furthermore, Merleau-Ponty's phenomenology is also transcendental and reflective, in a sense. However, it

11. It is important to note that the context of this passage is to contrast phenomenology in general with other philosophical approaches rather than to separate his view from Husserl's. However, we are not being tendentious here, since: (1) Merleau-Ponty's position diverges from Husserl's due to its situation in the contingent world of experience; and (2) Merleau-Ponty's strategy in the Preface and elsewhere is to offer creative readings of various figures, often articulating his own position under their name.

is better thought of as *reflexive* rather than reflective, since a phenomenology of perception is situated within the perceptual world. The difference between a modern scientific orientation and an aesthetic orientation is that aesthetic phenomenology in no way claims to be disinterested, pure, or innocent of conditionality and contingency, nor does it hold this as its ideal.

This reflexive aspect of Merleau-Ponty's phenomenology is profound. "As the disclosure of the world, phenomenology rests upon itself, or rather, founds itself" (PhP, lxxxv/xvi). Perception is the disclosure or expression of the world, and phenomenology is itself a disclosure or expression of the world. A phenomenology of perception is a disclosure of disclosure, an expression of expression.[12] Phenomenology is only accessible via phenomenology (ibid., lxxi/ii)—not because it gives some pure vista upon phenomena, but precisely because it does not succumb to such pretenses. We are mired in phenomena even as we reflect upon them. Thus we ad-mire and are ad-mired in the world wherein we are mired. The world is meaningful and it matters because we are of the world. This engaged reflexive aspect of Merleau-Ponty's phenomenology marks it as an aesthetic phenomenology expressing the value of the world quite apart from sterile scientific factual knowledge. Recalling our earlier gesture, perhaps what is unique about objective scientific facts is that they are values in disguise.

"Perception is not a science of the world" (PhP, lxxiv/v), nor should a phenomenology of perception be so construed. Perception is a disciplined, stylized, and creative expression of the world. A phenomenology of perception is itself a reflexive expression—not a reflection upon some distant world "out there," but the reflexive, situated, engaged expression of the truth of being within being.

> The phenomenological world is not the making explicit of a prior being, but rather the founding of being; philosophy is not the reflection of a prior truth, but rather, like art, the actualization of a truth. (PhP, lxxxiv/xv)

Merleau-Ponty's phenomenology of perception seeks truth as an achievement or actualization by acknowledging itself as expressing truth within its domain of the perceptual world. "Rationality is measured exactly

12. In each case, with the disclosure of disclosure as well as with the expression of expression, we mean to emphasize not only the reflexivity but also to complicate the reflexivity with the double genitive.

by the experiences through which it is revealed" (PhP, lxxxiv/xv).[13] The achievement or actualization of the expression bespeaks our engagement within the world rather than pretending to overcome it.

> With regard to consciousness, we must no longer conceive of it as a pure being-for-itself, but rather as a perceptual consciousness, as the subject of a behavior, as being in the world or existence, for only in this way will another person appear in control of his phenomenal body and receive a sort of "locality." (PhP, 367/404)[14]

This expression is an intentional relation: revelation, disclosure, and expression involve our intentional correlates of astonishment before the world.

"The problem . . . is to make explicit our primordial knowledge of the 'real' and to describe the perception of the world as what establishes, once and for all, our idea of truth" (PhP, lxxx/xi). This primordial understanding is contingent and situated. This is why, at the end of the Preface, it is of such great significance that Merleau-Ponty lists artists as paragons of the discipline and rigor appropriate to his model of phenomenology. Art does not simply provide examples for Merleau-Ponty's phenomenology of perception; rather, art is its heart.

We have stressed that Merleau-Ponty's style of phenomenology is an aesthetic phenomenology as opposed to a scientific orientation toward phenomena. Once again, this in no way entails an abject dismissal of science. Much of his *Phenomenology of Perception* is written in dialogue with psychologists and psychophysiologists in order to articulate his own position.[15] As we will discuss below, it is important see that Merleau-Ponty was always a scientist, albeit without presupposing the objective idealism that he often attributes to modern scientists (rightly or wrongly). Nonetheless, our main concern here is that we see him constantly attending to artists as he engages in his phenomenology of perception. And though Merleau-Ponty focuses much of his philosophy of art upon painters, he does not restrict his account solely to painting. On the contrary, he makes many references to literature, poetry, photography, film, sculpture, architecture, theater,

13. Translation corrected.

14. Translation corrected.

15. He begins to define his own phenomenological project where Husserl's late manuscripts end—especially the *Krisis* and *Ideen II* and *III*.

and music.[16] Indeed, Merleau-Ponty intercalates his accounts of linguistic expression and painting, most notably in the essay *Indirect Language and the Voices of Silence*, as we shall see below in section 4. For our purposes here, we must emphasize that all of these aesthetic media are expressions, just as perception is expression. This is not an ex-pression in the sense of pressing something from inside to the outside, but an engaged emergence of the differences between inside and outside, the expression of a world. Merleau-Ponty is engaged in an aesthetic phenomenology—*he is expressing the art of perception.*

In the discussion following Merleau-Ponty's 1946 presentation at the *Société française de philosophie*, "The Primacy of Perception," the famous historian of philosophy and Merleau-Ponty's thesis director from his early days at the *École normale Supérieure*, Émile Bréhier, sharply criticized his former student, Merleau-Ponty, for his novel transcendental position (Prim. Percp., 30). Bréhier rejected Merleau-Ponty's attempt to fashion a phenomenology of perception that valued lived experience while also engaging in reflective philosophy. In effect, Bréhier maintained that Merleau-Ponty's position was fundamentally self-contradictory and untenable. From Merleau-Ponty's perspective, of course, Bréhier is mandating a fallacious forced choice.

Bréhier wryly asked Merleau-Ponty whether such a phenomenological position that puts a premium upon lived experience "must remain unformulated, only lived" (Prim. Percp., 30). Merleau-Ponty somewhat impatiently reminded his former thesis director that he had indicated that phenomenology was not calling for some naive return to immediate experience—that the philosophical access to prereflective experience could be accessed only through reflection as an to attempt to understand it. While Merleau-Ponty insisted that this paradox was essential to philosophy and to human existence itself, Bréhier dismissively quipped, "It is to betray immediate experience" (ibid.). Merleau-Ponty was no doubt agitated, and his rejoinder is both direct and profound. "It is to begin the effort of *expression* and of what is *expressed*; it is to accept the condition of a beginning reflection" (ibid.).[17]

16. For example, cf. PhP 271/300–301 and PhP 332–33/357–58, where Merleau-Ponty explicitly proceeds through a series of examples from various media, including writing, photography, film, and theater. Despite Merleau-Ponty's famous emphasis on painting, he is engaged with literary figures throughout his career. As Cheryl Emerson pointed out in conversation one evening, note that at the end of the Preface his pantheon of artists comprises three writers and only one painter.

17. My emphasis.

Once again, Merleau-Ponty explicitly described his phenomenology of perception as focusing upon *expression.* Earlier in the presentation itself, he had described the perceptual world as a *style* (ibid., 16).[18] The apparent relativism, the invocation of aesthetic terms such as *expression* and *style* were apparently too much for the grand historian to tolerate in a serious philosophical discussion. In essence, Bréhier dismissed Merleau-Ponty's work as unphilosophical (despite the conciliatory gesture to the contrary that follows). But it is the way Bréhier dismissed Merleau-Ponty that is most relevant to our work here.

> I see your ideas as being better *expressed* in literature and in painting than in philosophy. Your philosophy results in a novel. This is not a defect, but I truly believe that it results in that immediate suggestion of realities which we associate with the writings of novelists. (Prim.Percp., 30)[19]

While we do not accept many aspects of Bréhier's unsympathetic attack, nonetheless we want to say that, in an important way, Bréhier was correct in his diagnosis.[20] Merleau-Ponty's phenomenology of perception is an aesthetic phenomenology; that is what sets it apart from Husserl's vision of phenomenology as a science of sciences. Of course we do not accept that it is in any way unphilosophical—quite the contrary! The position is of greater value because Merleau-Ponty's philosophy of art and his phenomenology of perception are ineluctably intertwined. For our purposes here, however, we need only note the intertwining marking this moment along Merleau-Ponty's pathway.

---

18. My emphasis.

19. My emphasis.

20. I want to extend my thanks, once again, to my excellent former colleague at the Pontificia Universidade Católica do Paraná, Dr. Ericson Fallibretti, for his interesting question at my colloquium presentation there on August 5, 2008, which in part inspired this discussion. Ericson was surprised to hear me argue that Merleau-Ponty's phenomenology could be read best as an art rather than the Husserlian vision of a science of sciences. Cf. also Marcos Muller's brilliant and influential work, *Merleau-Ponty acerca da expressão*, Porte Allegre, EDIPUCRS, 2001, which correctly treats expression as the central theme in Merleau-Ponty's philosophical development. Indeed, Muller has shown through his own original work on Gestalt therapy how expression does not preclude scientific thought—it resituates it entirely.

Galen Johnson, in *The Merleau-Ponty Aesthetics Reader*, also noted the importance of Merleau-Ponty's phenomenology of art, especially of painting, for the development of his phenomenology of perception.[21] Indeed, Johnson pioneered the direction we are heading in this volume, albeit along a slightly different route. We can see that our paths diverge somewhat in the following passage, where Johnson constructs tension between Merleau-Ponty's account of perception and his use of Cézanne in Merleau-Ponty's account of art.

> In the preface to *Phenomenology of Perception*, Merleau-Ponty had written that "the most important lesson which the reduction teaches us is the impossibility of a complete reduction" (PhP lxxvii/viii), *yet* Merleau-Ponty found in Cézanne a paradigm of the phenomenological epochē and achievement of a prescientific perception of the visible. Merleau-Ponty quoted Novotny's analysis of Cézanne's art as the attempt to paint the "pre-world" (PhP 337/372–3), the physiognomy of things in their sensible configuration as they effortlessly arise in nature. (Johnson 1997, 9)[22]

While we admire that Johnson associates Merleau-Ponty's use of Cézanne with his phenomenology, we think that the contrast Johnson established with the word *yet* is unfortunate. It implies that, on the one hand, Merleau-Ponty unequivocally stated that it would be impossible to complete the phenomenological reduction. Presumably it would be wrong even to hold that as an ideal. And Johnson implies that, on the other hand, Merleau-Ponty seems to portray Cézanne as one who has done exactly that as the painter's career developed. However, Merleau-Ponty says that Cézanne was engaged in the *attempt* to paint the "pre-world." As his career developed, Cézanne stopped trying to do this and focused on material, situated—i.e., enworlded—techniques. In the sentence preceding the passage Johnson quoted, Merleau-Ponty wrote that Cézanne "gradually learned that *expression* is the language of the thing itself, and is born of its configuration"[23] (PhP,

21. Johnson's most recent work has dealt with Merleau-Ponty's literary figures. Cf. the forthcoming work: Mauro Carbone, Galen Johnson, and Emmanuel de Saint-Aubert, eds., *Merleau-Ponty's Poets and Poetics*. We will soon be able to redeem Johnson's promissory note from his earlier work calling for a work on Merleau-Ponty's poets and writers.

22. My emphasis. Also, the English pagination has been adjusted to the Landes translation. Finally, we corrected the transliteration of *εποχη*.

23. My emphasis.

337/372). We want to stress that just as in his discussion with Bréhier in the 1946 presentation, Merleau-Ponty emphasized here Cézanne's *expression* of the things themselves rather than some return to the thing-in-itself. When Merleau-Ponty sees in Cézanne's later work the "achievement" of a prescientific perspective or a "pre-world," this achievement is surely a process and not a *fait accompli*. That is why Cézanne's work is so appropriate for Merleau-Ponty's phenomenology: Cézanne paints phenomena appearing: the appearance of phenomena as the phenomenon of appearance.

In a parallel passage earlier in *Phenomenology of Perception*, Merleau-Ponty also emphasizes how Cézanne gradually came to see that he needed to focus on the situated phenomenon in his painting of a scene Balzac described, "a tablecloth white as a bed of freshly-fallen snow, on which the places were laid in orderly array, crowned with honey-colored rolls" (PhP, 204/230).

> All of my early life I wanted to paint that, the tablecloth of fresh snow. . . . Now I know that one must want to paint merely "the places laid in an orderly array" and "honey-coloured rolls." If I paint "crowned" I'm done for. . . . Do you understand? And if I truthfully balance and relate my places and my rolls as they are in nature, you can be sure that the crowns, the snow, and all the excitement will be there. (PhP, 204/230)

Merleau-Ponty clearly stated that the "problem of the world . . . consists in the fact that everything resides within the world (PhP, 204/230). As usual, our "problem" turns out to be the basis of our hope as well: when Cézanne said he wanted to paint them as they were in nature, he made progress in his painting by focusing on the materiality and the concrete. He gradually came to see that his goal needed to be on the *expression* of phenomena. *The expression of phenomena is nothing other than the art of perception.*

Let us continue our discussion of Merleau-Ponty's early interest in Cézanne and the intertwining of art and perception in Merleau-Ponty's phenomenology by proceeding to a second moment in his development.

2. Merleau-Ponty's Sketch of Cézanne as Phenomenologist

We now turn our attention from Merleau-Ponty's attention to Cézanne in his *Phenomenology of Perception* to the 1945 essay, *Cézanne's Doubt*, where

Merleau-Ponty focuses on the artist in a much more sustained manner so as to develop his aesthetic phenomenology of perception, to reveal more of the art of perception. It is roughly contemporaneous with his work in *Phenomenology of Perception*, though surely the latter, much larger work emerged over a longer period of time, and its publication was delayed by World War II. At any rate, the positions in these works are mostly consistent, with a strong intertwining of art and perception resting on expression. Merleau-Ponty depicted Cézanne as an artist who was offering a very careful description of moments of the world—phenomenological descriptions, although he worded with paints. Merleau-Ponty said that Cézanne's painting was "the exact study of appearances" (SNS, 11/16). That is, Cézanne was seeking the *essence* of the moment in an important new sense of that term shared by Merleau-Ponty.[24] Indeed, the account of Cézanne's artistic expression is so phenomenologically saturated that the sketch of Cézanne Merleau-Ponty produces almost seems to be a self-portrait. Let us pursue this line of thought.

Our point of departure is again Galen Johnson's pioneering investigations of Merleau-Ponty's aesthetics. Johnson notes the divergence between Cézanne's assessments of the meaning and significance of his own work over against the harsh remarks he faced from his contemporary critics.

> This discordance between Cézanne's own interpretation of his efforts and the question of [Émile] Bernard and attacks by the critics provoked Merleau-Ponty to invoke his own phenomenological theory of "lived-perspective" and the primacy of perception as a philosophy of painting that could give philosophic credence both to the works of Cézanne and Cézanne's own words. (Johnson 1997, 11)

As the author correctly notes, Cézanne's doubt manifests this irreducible tension as does Merleau-Ponty's response.[25] And Johnson goes far in the right direction when he describes the reaction as Merleau-Ponty's response

---

24. One should recall the Preface of *Phenomenology of Perception*, where the idea of essence in phenomenology turns out to be a rejection of idealism and the basis of an existential philosophy (PhP, lxxviii–lxxxi/ix–xii).

25. Merleau-Ponty had highlighted a similar irreducible tension at the heart of phenomenology at the beginning of the Preface of *Phenomenology of Perception* (PhP, lxx–lxxi/i–ii). His point there was, in his usual style of making lemonade out of a sour fruit, that this irreducible tension was more the promise of phenomenology than its peril.

as an invocation of his phenomenology of perception; it would not do to speak as if it were a matter of applying a theory of perception to the aesthetic situation. As we have seen, Merleau-Ponty's phenomenology was already essentially aesthetic in style. To speak of applying it like a theory would not go far enough in indicating the organic, interdependent, and dynamic intertwining of art and perception at work in Merleau-Ponty's position.

Painting was an adventure for Cézanne.[26] Merleau-Ponty described this kind of radical artistic expression as "a step taken in the fog—no one can say where, if anywhere, it will lead" (SNS, 3/8). Such expression was an achievement, a project in process that was risky and precarious, something to be accomplished. From Merleau-Ponty's point of view, quite unlike some art critics of Cézanne's day, this radical expression was very successful. Indeed, this risky endeavor was characteristic of what Merleau-Ponty described as the development of a new rationality that would recognize that the highest form of sense always entails contingency and necessarily borders on non-sense. Authentic artistic expression is not some failed representation; it is an original presentation of a phenomenon.

We have already seen that Merleau-Ponty's aesthetic phenomenology expressed a world, and that this was a matter of actualization and realization, not representation. And this was true not only for phenomenology, perception, and art, but for ethics and politics as well. So according to Merleau-Ponty, Cézanne was doing something no less audacious and dangerous than revealing the value of the world anew, and without any certain or guaranteed outcome.[27] How would we live if the most intense reflection did not guarantee certain results? How could we bear to live if every time we make sense of the world (which is always to value the world), after taking great pains to put out of play all of our bias—commonsensical, theoretical, and ideological—we realized that we could not lay claim to any certain and necessary truths? That is, of course, our situation, according to Merleau-Ponty. And rather than the advent of nihilism, it is the dawning of the new adventure of existential phenomenology. We are describing a new sense of rationality when we realize that "the most important lesson of the reduction is the impossibility of a complete reduction" (PhP, lxxvii/viii). As we have already seen, it should come as no surprise that Merleau-Ponty

26. I hardly need to mention that ad-venture is a sort of expression.

27. "In morality as in art there is no solution for the man who will not make a move without knowing where he is going and who wants to be accurate and in control at every moment" (SNS, 4/8).

concludes the famous preface to *Phenomenology of Perception* with a reference to Cézanne, among others artists, as an exemplar of a new vista upon the world. Everything is at stake here.

Merleau-Ponty tells us that Cézanne's art teaches us that the work of art requires embodiment, but that his radical, creative artistic expression cannot be explained away as an epiphenomenon, derivative from physiology or psychology. This was a point he had already made in *The Structure of Behavior* with regard to El Greco, and in *Cézanne's Doubt* he reiterates this point with regard to Van Gogh (Johnson 1997, 375, n.2). Some critics alleged that these artists' unique styles were pathological symptoms of astigmatism or schizophrenia.[28] In his *Notes from Underground*, Dostoevsky mused darkly that consciousness might be a disease. And Merleau-Ponty will develop this theme as well without reducing the creativity of the artist to be the effect of some physiological cause. For there is a strangeness about the expression of the artist that makes his or her work stand out.[29] This strangeness must be understood within the perceptual world as the expression discloses the world.

And, Merleau-Ponty points out that often it is useful to look at the pathological, the disordered, the nonsensical, in order to understand the world meaningfully. For Merleau-Ponty, if this strangeness of creative expression is pathological, it is best seen as a matter of style, not a reduction to some physiological cause. The style implicates the artist as the artist—a new invocation of *by thy works I shall know thee*. And although this style of expression is ineluctably situated in the carnal, it is not a byproduct of an inert organism. It is the manifestation of embodied empirical consciousness.

Merleau-Ponty describes Cézanne's artistic expression as a struggle against "chance," or a struggle toward expression against an "accident of his body" (SNS, 9 /13). Indeed, the title of the essay, *Cézanne's Doubt*, refers to Cézanne's worry in old age, looking back over his career, whether his achievements were only the result of "accidents of his body" (ibid.). The body is not a collection of parts for Merleau-Ponty. It is not the body treated by the psychophysiologists, who are forever solely in search of external and internal objective causes for behavior. That is to treat the body mechanically, as if it were a corpse. Indeed, one can say that modern

28. (SC 202ff/218ff). And he likewise dismisses similar reductive allegations regarding Cézanne, Van Gogh, and da Vinci (SNS, 9–11, 20, 22–25/14–17,26, 29–33).

29. Cf. Heidegger's analysis in *Einführung in die Metaphysik* of the line from the chorus in Antigone, "nothing surpasses man in strangeness" (Heidegger 1957, 112–26).

medicine treats the body as if it were a corpse until it succeeds.[30] Instead, Merleau-Ponty sketches Cézanne as a model for the possibility of recognizing the limitations of his body without pretending to explain his creativity at the exclusion of them. Expression is achieved *through* the accidents of the body. Merleau-Ponty describes this authentic achievement when describing an aspect of Simone de Beauvoir's work as "actively being what we are by chance."[31] Merleau-Ponty also puts it this way: "Cézanne won out against chance" (ibid., 5/9).

In addition to Cézanne's doubt, Merleau-Ponty speaks of Cézanne's *ennui,* Cézanne's terror, Cézanne's mistrust, Cézanne's faith, Cézanne's uncertainty, Cézanne's difficulties, Cézanne's solitude, Cézanne's adventure, Cézanne's schizophrenia, Cézanne's schizoid temperament, and even Cézanne's suicide.[32] Merleau-Ponty depicts Cézanne as engaged in a constant autocritical project of expression, where the artist sought to present works of art that at once present the world and call our attention to how we perceive and value it. Once again, this is as much an articulation of Merleau-Ponty's phenomenological project as it is a sketch of Cézanne. Insofar as Merleau-Ponty's phenomenology is an aesthetic phenomenology, his sketch of the artist at work bears as much resemblance to himself as to Cézanne.

One aspect Merleau-Ponty sketches of this autocritical project of expression is the way Cézanne wanted to restore the weight and depth of the object in his work by foregoing the use of outlines of objects, opting instead for the juxtaposition of patches of color to create contours (SNS, 15/20–21).[33] These contours are portrayed indirectly as an "ideal

30. Of course, we do not mean to imply that physicians do not have any compassion or that they consciously conceive of the human body as a cadaver when practicing medicine. Yet the mechanistic and instrumental problem-solving standpoint assumed by modern medicine is tantamount to seeing the body in its space as *partes extra partes*—just one damned thing after another, both among its components and in relation to other things—for it is surely a thing in this worldview.

31. SNS, 52/40.

32. The "suicide" was not literal, but referred to a worry of Cézanne's friend Émile Bernard, who thought that the paradoxical relation between Cézanne's obsession to portray reality while eschewing the traditional techniques artists used to attain the effect of realism was so self-contradictory it was tantamount to self-annihilation (SNS, 12/17).

33. Though he did this in a different way than some Impressionists, whose work he thought lacked weight and depth.

limit" (ibid., 15/21). This limit emerges within our engagement with the object, the *lived-object*, rather than the *fait accompli* of a circumscribed object. There is a precision here, but not an objective precision—a discipline without a program. And here in this particular aspect of Merleau-Ponty's sketch of Cézanne's technique we see the familiar "painstaking" discipline characteristic not only of Cézanne, but of Merleau-Ponty's own aesthetic phenomenology. The lived object is "an inexhaustible reality, full of reserves" (ibid., 15/20–21). The lived object is a source from which sensations radiate interdependently. That is, we perceive its texture, its weight, its color all at once through our engagement with the lived-object. This is to present the *reality* of the lived-object. Thus, it is not only the proliferation of things that keeps the artist from completing the task of expression; it is that "expressing what *exists* is an endless task" (ibid.). Its essence is disclosed through the phenomenon in transcendence.

Now let us make even more explicit some aspects of artistic expression in Merleau-Ponty's self-portrait of Cézanne that depict the artist as phenomenologist (and at once depict the phenomenologist as artist). According to Merleau-Ponty, the artist accomplishes this presentation by attending to the *intentional* relations with the object rather than positing some gulf between artist and world to be overcome. Since Husserl taught us that "consciousness is always consciousness *of* something," we can exploit the pre-given relatedness of the artist within his or her world. That is, we can see that (Merleau-Ponty's) Cézanne was concerned with the world as *intended.* The meaning Cézanne gave to objects and faces in his paintings presented itself in the world as it appeared to him. Cézanne simply released this meaning: it was the objects and faces themselves as he saw them that demanded to be painted, and Cézanne simply expressed what they *wanted* to say (SNS, 27/21).[34] According to Merleau-Ponty's sketch of Cézanne, Cézanne can release this meaning in his paintings by disclosing disclosure, by expressing expression—by engaging in the presentation of a world rather than the re-presentation of an object.

Phenomenology is an account of appearances as they achieve meaning in intentional relations. Cézanne's artistic expression, framed by Merleau-Ponty, is an illustration of this process. When Merleau-Ponty stresses the passivity of Cézanne's creative process in this passage, he is not

34. In personal correspondence, Cynthia Willett poses another interesting way of framing this: Is there an *eros* in nature?

denying Cézanne's originality or creative ingenuity. On the contrary, it is only Cézanne who could "release" the objects and faces. Again, this is not a process of representation; it is a process of presentation. Only Cézanne could present these objects and faces through his intentional relation with them in the world.

Now, Merleau-Ponty's phenomenology stressed more than anyone heretofore, going well beyond Husserl, that this intentionality of consciousness was no intellectual relation, but embodiment itself. So Cézanne's passionate, physical struggles we have described here are manifestations of the intentional matrix *by which* his artistic expression is achieved. His body does not get in the way of his art; rather, it is the sine qua non of his original stylistic expression.

Merleau-Ponty's self-portrait of Cézanne also manifests the bracketing of the natural attitude and theoretical biases, laying bare a reduced intentional relation with the essence through the phenomenon. Merleau-Ponty is quite explicit about this. He speaks of Cézanne's "way of seeing the world reduced to the totality of frozen appearances with all expressive values suspended" (SNS, 20/27). We see Cézanne portrayed as engaging in the *epochē* when he brackets the natural attitude during his artistic expression. We live in the midst of manmade objects, among tools, in houses, streets, cities, and most of the time we see them only through the human actions that put them to use. We become used to thinking that all of this exists necessarily and unshakably; but Cézanne's painting suspends these habits of thought and reveals the base of inhuman nature upon which man has installed himself (ibid., 16/22). And this bracketing reveals the essence of the phenomenon by putting out of action the usual ways we are accustomed to seeing things in order to present them in a fresh way. By "suspending these habits of thought," Cézanne can call our attention to the essential aspects of what is intended. He also brackets theoretical biases, but this aesthetic phenomenology goes very differently than Husserl's foundational phenomenology as a science of all sciences.

The task before Cézanne was, according to Merleau-Ponty's self-portrait, first, to forget all that he had ever learned from science; and, second, *through* these sciences, to recapture the structure of the landscape as an emerging organism (SNS, 17/23). We recall that Merleau-Ponty described phenomenology as a "disavowal" of science, yet he worked through various scientific positions to articulate his own position throughout his career. Merleau-Ponty was, after all, a scientist of a sort himself, though not one of the kind criticized earlier: soon he would be named Chair in Child

Psychology at the Sorbonne.[35] Cézanne's discipline achieves through artistic expression a rigor of a different sort than scientific rigor. Just as it is through Cézanne's expression that we come to understand expression, we saw that Merleau-Ponty claimed that it is only through the *praxis* of perception that we understand perception—because perception is situated expression. According to Merleau-Ponty's sketch of Cézanne, Cézanne's painting calls our attention to this *praxis* through a phenomenology of perception. This phenomenology of perception is affected not by some withdrawal to a foundational, pure transcendental reflection, but by the artist's engagement within the world. Furthermore, when we keep in mind Merleau-Ponty's own creative expression in constructing this self-portrait of Cézanne, his own unique posture of transcendental phenomenological reflection is properly recognized as contingent engagement within his world.

As Merleau-Ponty presents it, through Cézanne's phenomenological *epochē* and phenomenological reduction, the intentional relations of perception are explored within the realm of perception, not in spite of it. This is achieved as transcendence. Thus, the transcendence of expression in Cézanne's work is a phenomenology that "puts the essences back into existence" (PhP, lxx/i). And this is accomplished, as might be suspected, by a conflation of the phenomenological and eidetic reductions.[36] In Cézanne's work, the contours emerge, as we have seen, as *ideal* limits. It is the *essence* of the appearance that is presented. Yet this essence is an "inexhaustible" resource for the artistic images, so the reduction is never complete.

That transcendence of creative engagement within one's world is a movement within the intentional relations described above. In fact, it is a double movement, since as Cézanne paints what the world wanted to say, he creates himself with the same brushstrokes. In this sense, Cézanne as well

---

35. So while it is understandable that he would not abandon all hope for the sciences—albeit enlightened sciences—to provide their own phenomenological understanding without appealing to an independent phenomenology, that is certainly not what Husserl had in mind. Indeed, I used to have a bit of fun in graduate school when speaking with Thomas Seebohm, an orthodox Husserlian in some matters. I used to say things such as, "But Professor Seebohm, don't you think that a science like psychology can only be effectively grounded *by its own praxis*?" There was a little vein that would pop out on the side of his temple whenever I would say something like that.

36. For a clear critical account of these different aspects of reduction in Husserl's thought as they emerged over his career, cf. Herbert Speigelberg, *The Phenomenological Movement, A Historical Introduction*, Third Revised and Enlarged Edition, with the Collaboration of Karl Schuhmann (The Hague: Martinus Nijhoff, 1982), 104–23.

as his works remains unfinished, as he and his works beckon us to present them anew. And Merleau-Ponty's aesthetic presentation of Cézanne is itself an unfinished self-portrait, revealing his own phenomenological project without circumscribing or overdetermining it.

We all know well how it is sometimes much easier to show someone how to do something rather than to explain to him or her how to do it. It is as if (Merleau-Ponty's) Cézanne were saying, "I cannot tell you how we perceive, but I can *show* you." His work is a presentation—a unique showing of perception in the world. Cézanne's vivid descriptions presented the world. His *Mont St. Victoire* looms luminously. When he paints a river, he reduces it to its essence, allowing the river to present itself in such a way that, through the miracle of intentionality, we are *there. Cézanne* takes you down to a place by the river. You can hear the boats go by. And yes, if you carefully attend to the art of perception, you can hear the river answer . . .[37] We can see a face emerging in Merleau-Ponty's sketch of Cézanne; and this visage looks suspiciously like someone engaged in a phenomenology of perception.

3. Causeries: Art and the Perceptual World

In his 1948 radio lectures, published as *Causeries 1948*, Merleau-Ponty developed a phenomenology of perception for a general audience.[38] He devotes each these seven lectures to different aspects of his account of perception. As Stéphanie Ménasé noted in her *Avertissement* for the work she

37. Apologies to Leonard Cohen. Cynthia Willett wondered, in private correspondence, whether Merleau-Ponty would have been even more sensitive to affect if he had made music as central to his aesthetic account as he did painting. For an illuminating and challenging answer to Willett's question, see Jessica Wiskus, *The Rhythm of Thought, Art, Literature, and Music after Merleau-Ponty* (Chicago and London: The University of Chicago Press, 2013).

38. Maurice Merleau-Ponty *Causeries*, (Paris: *Éditions de Seuil*, 2002). The English translation is: *Maurice Merleau-Ponty: The World of Perception*, trans. Oliver Davis, with a foreword by Stéphanie Ménasé and an introduction by Thomas Baldwin (London and New York: Routledge, 2008). Since it is intended for a general audience, Merleau-Ponty attempts to make the case for his phenomenology of perception while trying to avoid the jargon and technical language characteristic of academic philosophical discourse. Hence, throughout the lectures, Merleau-Ponty refers to the position he advocates as a "philosophy of perception" rather than a phenomenology of perception.

labored over, "By way of illustration, we have chosen three of the artists alluded to [*évoqués*] in these *causeries*" (C, 10).[39] She does not say this, but we think it is fitting to have selected some artworks to preface the *Causeries* because Merleau-Ponty's philosophy of perception and his philosophy of art are ineluctably intertwined—it illustrates (literally) the main thesis of the present volume.

Merleau-Ponty has been criticized for an overemphasis of painting in his accounts of art. There is no doubt that his most extended and frequent analyses are of painting. One could debate this charge of an overemphasis, of course: certainly his writing on art was not about painting exclusively. For example, his work—and especially his course notes and his working notes—is rife with references to literary figures, especially Proust and Valéry. Also, there are innumerable musical metaphors throughout Merleau-Ponty's works (despite the apparently obtuse things he sometimes says about music).[40] He occasionally makes reference to sculptors as well. And there are many other oblique references to other literary figures "between the lines" of his work where one can see the inspiration of Baudelaire, Mallarmé, Claudel, and many others.[41] It is almost as if Merleau-Ponty were presciently aware of this later line of criticism of his work when he crafted the sixth *causerie*, "Art and the Perceived World." For though he begins on familiar turf by

39. "*En guise d'illustration, nous avons choisi trois des artistes évoqués dans ces causeries.*" We provide the original text here because the sentence has been left out of the English translation (at p. viii).

40. The apparently obtuse remarks occur in *Causeries* and in *L'Oeil et l'esprit*, where he says that music is outside of *sens*—which implies that it is meaningless. I hope that he did not mean that. It seems to be in stark contrast to the general sensitivity of his work as well as to his usual penchant for employing musical metaphors. Cf. Merleau-Ponty's multiple references to music in the section of *Phenomenology of Perception*, *The Spatiality of One's Own Body and Motricity* (PhP, 100–48/114–72). A charitable hermeneutic posture could allow that Merleau-Ponty was trying to preserve the uniqueness of music and prevent its reduction to linguistic meaning. However, he surely did not explain this, if that was what he had in mind. He did say that painting and music were analogous in another working note from 1959 (*Chiasmi International* 3, [2001]: 17–18). Regarding Merleau-Ponty's constant invocation of musical metaphors throughout his work, cf. Jessica Wiskus, op. cit.

41. Cf. Duane H. Davis, "The Philosopher of Modern Life," *Natureza Humana: Revista de Philosophia e Psicanálise* 11, no. 2 (Julho-Dezembro 2009). http://www.centrowinnicott.com.br/grupofpp/modules/mastop_publish/?tac=106.

This text is also available in Portuguese as: "O filósofo da vida moderna: Baudelaire, Merleau-Ponty e a arte da crítica fenomenológica," *Aurora—Revista de Filosofia*

referencing the painters Cézanne, Gris, Picasso, and Braque, in these few pages he extends his discussion to address film, music, poetry, and literature. And, as we noted above, Merleau-Ponty seemed to be going out of his way to include references to a variety of arts in his *Phenomenology of Perception.* Merleau-Ponty elucidates certain aspects of each of these arts that complement and illustrate his phenomenology of perception. More accurately, he uses each aesthetic area to reveal the means whereby a phenomenology of perception can be accomplished and to disclose the cultural horizon essential to perception.

Merleau-Ponty begins the chapter by reframing the previous five causeries as sharing a common purpose: to "revive" the perceived world (C, 69/53). He builds on this trajectory to point out that art does not offer some creative misrepresentation of the perceived world of which science represents the truth of the real world—a point he will elaborate upon later in *l'Oeil et l'esprit.* Nor does art offer a misrepresentation as if truth had been abducted and held hostage by science. The work of art is not a misrepresentation because it is best seen to outstrip its representative function. That is, once again, the work of art is simply not a misrepresentation because it is not essentially a representation. And although for two centuries almost all philosophies of art and artists themselves have rejected mimetic theories of art, the best way to account for this is phenomenologically.

Merleau-Ponty stresses that we should not separate things from the means whereby they appear to us (C, 70/54). This applies bidirectionally to his phenomenology—subjectively as well as objectively. To say the least, his analyses of artists are consistent with his philosophical position; they adumbrate the

---

(Curitiba, Paraná, Brazil) 21, no. 29) (jul./dec. 2009*):* 503–29, translated into Portuguese by Richard Simanke.

I would be remiss if I did not mention Merleau-Ponty's own explicit salute to William Faulkner (S, 225/367). The editions used here and in my paper in Part Two are, respectively, Evanston: Northwestern University Press, 1964, trans. Richard C. McCleary; and Paris: Gallimard, 1960, 2003. I would like to thank Ms. Cheryl Emerson for calling my attention to Faulkner's connection to French thought and to Dr. Emmanuel de Saint-Aubert for reminding us of this particular passage. Ms. Emerson's original work develops a powerful reading of Faulkner through a Merleau-Pontyan frame. Cf. her "*A Carne Feita Palavra*: *Enquanto Agonizo* e o Ser Encarnado"/"The Flesh Made Word: William Faulkner's *As I Lay Dying* and Being Incarnate," trans. Dr. Wagner Felix. *Prólogos–Revista de Filosofia* [*Prologos—Journal of Philosophy*], EDUEM—Editora da Universidade Estadual de Maringá [State University of Maringá Press], vol. 1, no. 1 forthcoming. An original English version of her essay is included here below.

means whereby the phenomenological account of perception can be accomplished. Regarding the new ways we see everyday objects in art, Merleau-Ponty writes that artworks "bizarrely communicate their secret substance" (ibid., 69/53). The artist "redirects us toward vision of the things themselves" while the phenomenologist of perception restores art to its "true place" of "dignity" (70/53). "The perceived world is not the ensemble of natural things; it also includes paintings, music, books, and all . . . the 'cultural world' " (76/61). Thus, art is included in the proper horizon of phenomena even as it reveals phenomena. And just as artworks are restored to their proper place as being worthy of serious philosophical reflection, likewise a phenomenology of perception is possible because art, properly construed, "retraces" the horizon of phenomena, disclosing "the *means* to contemplate works of art in their autonomy and in their original richness, of language and culture" (ibid.).[42]

Since consciousness is intentional, the appearance of a phenomenon at once calls into question the *means* of its appearance. "It is impossible to separate the things from their manner of appearance" (C, 70/54). The cultural richness of phenomena is disclosed through phenomenology *as the art of perception* rather than as a science of sciences. This allows for the uniqueness of phenomena as well as Merleau-Ponty's own unique stance within the phenomenological movement. On his view, in perceptual experience, I cannot remain "disinterested" from the particularity manifest through the accidents of phenomena (ibid.). Phenomena are "revived" and situated properly in a "cultural world" in all of their fragility, ambiguity, contingency, and uncertainty.

4. Indirect Language and the Voices of Silence: Structure, Advent, and Latency

In 1951–52, Merleau-Ponty began a project with a working title, *The Prose of the World*, which he abandoned unfinished.[43] *Indirect Language and the Voices of Silence* is a revision of a chapter from the unfinished work.[44] It is

42. My emphasis.

43. For some fine disparate discussions regarding the provenance of this essay and some brief indication of the significance that *The Prose of the World* was abandoned, cf. Johnson, 14–18; M. C. Dillon, *Merleau-Ponty's Ontology*, (Bloomington: Indiana University Press, 1988), 177–223; Hugh J. Silverman, *Inscriptions between Phenomenology and Structuralism* (New York: Routledge and Kegan Paul, 1987), passim; and James M. Edie, *Merleau-Ponty's Philosophy of Language: Structuralism and Dialectics* (Washington, DC: University Press of America, 1987), passim.

44. Cf. Johnson, 15 for a very brief but clear account of the differences between the original chapter and the published revision.

an amazingly wide--ranging essay, even for Merleau-Ponty, who is prone to meander; for it deals with art, expression, art history, language, and history in general.

Since this particular essay is especially rhapsodic, let us carefully orchestrate our response for this section. Merleau-Ponty continued to explore the intertwining relation of perception and art here, albeit in several new interesting ways. He continued to revel in his fascination with Cézanne, but now he has expanded his focus to include modern art, especially abstract modern art. Expression is mired in perception here in a new way, with a greater emphasis upon expression as *style*. Furthermore, he uses this interest in abstract art to decenter his account of expression. He turns to linguistics to expand the discussion of expression well beyond painting—explicitly including poetry and novels in both his account of perception as well as the literary uses of language. He uses his interest in linguistics to explore the diacritical opposition of signs—be they painted, spoken, gestured, or written—and the grounding of this diacritical opposition in silence. This profound account of silence allows Merleau-Ponty to develop his account of the latency of meaning that he began earlier in terms of an inexhaustible reserve of all meaning. Finally, he considers the cultural and historical horizon of all forms of expression.

He began to turn his attention toward the work of Klee and other abstract artists.[45] He defends abstract modern art here against André Malraux, who thought that such art had consciously severed its own umbilical cord, arriving stillborn, bereft of history or future cultural significance—lacking any truth. On the contrary, Merleau-Ponty insists that there is truth in these works, but that the truth of modern painting does not lie in the resemblance to things (S, 51/82–83). Rather, the truth of modern painting is once again described in terms of perception and the expression of a world. Now, in a sense, this is nothing new for Merleau-Ponty. As we have seen, he was always adamant about the meaning of painting exceeding representation. But in Merleau-Ponty's earlier work, part of his admiration for Cézanne was for Cézanne's ability to present *things* as they were intended, replete with weight, texture, etc. Abstract art, however, does not rely upon things—except insofar as abstract art is itself an abstraction. Literally, it is *drawn out* of the world of things, negatively defined over against them. Nonetheless, in one sense, the analysis of this kind of painting is unfettered by some vestiges

45. I will not dwell on this fascinating essay at length in this context. To see a careful explication of the aesthetic dimensions of the essay, cf. Gary Madison's account of painting in his important *The Phenomenology of Merleau-Ponty*, (Athens: Ohio University Press, 1981), 73–107.

of representational thinking. It is not surprising, then, that Merleau-Ponty begins to speak more of the *process* of artistic expression than the specific images produced. We are still engaged in a phenomenological account of the art of perception, but the phenomenological account is expressed in new ways. The new link here is the mediation of *style*; and the account of style is given in terms of the diacritical opposition of signs.

Style mediates the account of artistic expression and perception in *Indirect Language and the Voices of Silence*. Merleau-Ponty now refers to the style of an artist as a "system of equivalences" (S, 61/98). Painters can be seen to create meaning in their art by constructing differences in their media. This allows another way for the meaning of the artwork to be discussed without reducing it to the conscious goal of the artist. Each painter's style emerges as a system of equivalences within the work that evoke a new structure of meaning as a coherent deformation of the existing meaning structure. A new self-propagating style emerges through artistic expression in the context of, and through the deformation of, the existing meaning structure.[46] Each written phrase or brushstroke calls for the next one allowing the artist and the artwork to emerge. These systems express an "allusive logic of the perceived world" (ibid., 57/92).[47] There can be no question that the work of the writer or painter is articulated as the art of perception.

The mediation of style at once also allows Merleau-Ponty to decenter his account of expression. "Style has to be detached from the philosophy of the individual" (S, 52/84). "The painter does not put his immediate self . . . into his painting, he puts his style there" (ibid.). The recognition

46. Cf. Merleau-Ponty's interesting notion of institution developed in his 1954–55 course at the *Collège de France*, *L'institution dans l'histoire personnelle et publique*, (Paris: Belin, 2003). Cf. also Mauro Carbone's very interesting work, *An Unprecedented Deformation: Marcel Proust and the Sensible Ideas*, (Albany: State University of New York Press, 2011). No one has gone farther than Carbone in exploring the rich Proustian dimension of Merleau-Ponty's work. The term "coherent deformation" is very Proustian, but it is actually a phrase taken from Malraux's *La creation esthétique*, 152 (S, 54/88). Cheryl Emerson develops this line of thought in an original way in her discussion of the "surface destruction of narrative" in the essay included below.

47. This is an important presentiment of his discussion of the *logos prophorikos*/*logos endiathetos* opposition in the working notes of the posthumously published incomplete work, *The Visible and the Invisible*. For an extended discussion of this opposition, cf. William S. Hamrick and Jan Van Der Veken, *Nature and Logos, A Whiteheadian Key to Merleau-Ponty's Fundamental Thought* (Albany: State University of New York Press, 2011), 103–22.

of style is intersubjective in the same manner that meaning is diacritical. There is a lateral relation among us wherein style becomes meaningful.[48] Style is "the system of equivalences," which implicates the writer or painter as artist and "manifests the world he sees" (ibid., 54/88). The artist stylizes and recognizes style through others, since the meaning of the artwork is not up to the artist. The painter "is no more capable of seeing his paintings than the writer is capable of reading his work. It is in others that the expression takes on its relief and really becomes signification" (52/84). And this style is not something complete as subjective or interior, merely ex-pressed in the manner of a representation. Instead, the painter or the writer must learn to recognize his or her own style as it becomes "legible" (53/85). The style implicates the artist as that unique artist as it discloses a perceived world shared with others. And it is not the case for Merleau-Ponty that style is some accoutrement of perception. As an artist's style emerges, not only as some technique but the *life* of the artist, this life "emerges from its inherence, ceases to be in possession of itself . . . and is thus not shut up in the depths of some mute individual but diffused throughout all he sees" (ibid.). Indeed, for Merleau-Ponty, "perception already stylizes" (54/87). Once again, we are not conjoining two disparate fields of inquiry in what we have called the art of perception.

> Since perception itself is never complete, since our perspectives give us a world to express and to think about which envelops and exceeds those perspectives, a world which announces itself in lightning signs as a spoken word or as an arabesque, why should the expression of the world be subjected to the prose of the *senses* or of the concept? It must be poetry. (S, 52/83–84)

Perhaps he makes the intimacy of art and perception most clear in this essay when he writes, "[T]here is not simply a question of an *analogy* . . . ; it is the expressive operation of the body, begun by the smallest perception, which is amplified into painting and art" (S, 70/112).

So, in *Indirect Language and the Voices of Silence*, both the artwork and the work of the artist are decentered. This is an important step in Merleau-Ponty's

48. Cheryl Emerson notes a parallel reference in the *Notes de cours* of this lateral relation—this time Merleau-Ponty mentions a "lateral involvement" and a "lateral rapport" of the characters in a novel (NC, 49, 51). Cf. Emerson's essay included below where she discusses this in the context of Faulkner's style.

philosophical development, since it is this new account of the art of perception whereby his phenomenology steps away from a philosophy of consciousness. But this is not tantamount to stepping away from phenomenology. Attending to the intertwining of art and perception is essential to understanding this.

In this transitional essay, he describes the emergence of meaning from diacritical opposition of signs in linguistics; but contrary to some accounts, Merleau-Ponty never embraced structuralism uncritically—nor did he abandon phenomenology to do so.[49] Just as Merleau-Ponty's position trades upon a kind of ambiguity between phenomenology in the Husserlian and Hegelian senses, it exploits an ambiguity between the notion of structure in Gestalt psychology (and the early work of Husserl, via Dilthey) and the notion of structure in Saussurean linguistics to develop his own original position. And in each case, Merleau-Ponty's position is not a middle ground in between two extreme opposites, but a dialectical and critical appropriation of aspects of the opposed positions. As usual, Merleau-Ponty proceeds in a neither/nor logic: he adopts neither the relation of parts and wholes intrinsic to Gestalt psychology and Husserl, nor the diacritical opposition of signs in the relation of the signifier and the signified characteristic of structuralism.

One sees that Merleau-Ponty has not jumped ship from phenomenology to structuralism most clearly when one attends to what we have called the art of perception. Some passages, especially when taken out of their dialectical context, seem to imply that Merleau-Ponty is denying any extralinguistic reference and occupying a position that Martin Dillon infamously described as "semeiological reductionism."[50] Merleau-Ponty, adum-

49. For accounts that commit this sort of violence and feature Merleau-Ponty's gesture toward structuralism as a radical departure from his earlier phenomenology, cf. James Edie 1987, op. cit.; Hugh Silverman, op. cit.; and James Schmidt, *Maurice Merleau-Ponty: Between Phenomenology and Structuralism* (New York: St. Martin's Press, 1985). Cf. also James M. Edie, "The Triumph of Dialectics over Structuralism," *Man and World* 24 (1984): 299–312. Edie claims here and in many other places that the influences of structuralism caused Merleau-Ponty to abandon phenomenology and that *The Prose of the World* is "the pivotal work in his development" (299). As one of the pioneers in Merleau-Ponty scholarship in the United States, Edie has enjoyed tremendous influence on how Merleau-Ponty has come to be read for decades.

Joseph J. Kockelmans once objected to Edie's assertion that Merleau-Ponty's proximity to Lévi-Strauss in the halls of the *Collège de France* accounted for a complete change of direction in Merleau-Ponty's thought. Edie implied that Merleau-Ponty would constantly run across the hall to follow Lévi-Strauss. Kockelmans dryly said, "Presumably one could walk both ways across these halls."

50. Cf. Martin C. Dillon, *Merleau-Ponty's Ontology*, 178–86 and at greater length in his rather bellicose *Semiological Reductionism* (Albany: State University of New York Press, 1995). Dillon varies his spelling of the term among these works.

brating Saussure's position, describes the "lateral liaison of sign to sign as the foundation of an ultimate relation of sign to meaning" (S, 40/65). He reiterates this point two pages later. "As far as language is concerned, it is the lateral relation of one sign to another which makes each of them significant, so that meaning appears only at the intersection of and as it were between words" (ibid., 42/68). He even goes on to say that the meaning of the sign "is entirely involved in language" (ibid.). "Nowhere does it stop and leave a place for pure meaning; it is always limited only by more language and meaning appears within it only set in a context of words" (ibid.). Finally, Merleau-Ponty states forcefully that "language is only understood through the intersection of signs"(42/69).

One could easily conclude, relying only upon phrases like these, that Merleau-Ponty would endorse the view that language refers only to itself and that there is nothing outside of language. But this would be a rather violent misreading of the text. The violence of this reading lies in the isolation of these quotable quotes bereft of the context wherein they interact. Merleau-Ponty might be seen to speak presciently of this misreading when he says that isolated signs are "equivocal or banal," making sense "only by being combined with others" (S, 42/69).[51] Context is the emergent site of the interaction of signs.

First, one must always take great care when reading Merleau-Ponty's texts, since he argues dialectically. Here Merleau-Ponty, as he often does, is articulating a position that is not his own—one he is working through *as if* it were his own. He adopts positions like this throughout his work, trying them on for size, as it were, pushing them to their limits, often disclosing untenable assumptions that he brackets out in the articulation of his own original position.[52] This is most clear a little later in the essay:

---

51. Merleau-Ponty is actually speaking of individual signs here, but the point holds for this larger hermeneutic context as well.

52. We can further complicate this by noting that Merleau-Ponty's reading of Saussure is controversial. Merleau-Ponty's readings are always imaginative and creative. Marilena Chauí has written brilliantly about this, suggesting that Merleau-Ponty's hermeneutic style is itself an artistic venture essential to preserving the mystery of the world. Cf. *Da Realidade sem Mistérios ao Mistério do Mundo: Espinosa, Voltaire, Merleau-Ponty*, (São Paulo: editora br-brasilienese, 1981). Another way to say this is that "Merleau-Ponty tailors de Saussure's structural linguistics very much to his own purposes, and, indeed, as has been pointed out, manages to misrepresent structuralism in the process." Laurie Spurling, *Phenomenology and the Social World* (London: Routledge and Kegan Paul, 1977), 59. For more on this, see William S. Hamrick, *An Existential Phenomenology of Law: Maurice Merleau-Ponty* (Dordrecht: Martinus Nijhoff, 1987), 58–61.

"Signs do not simply evoke other signs for us and so on without end, and language is not like a prison we are locked into" (S, 81/131). Saussurean linguistics provides Merleau-Ponty a powerful analytic once he appropriates it within his aesthetic phenomenological account. And as we have seen, while Merleau-Ponty does not dismiss such sciences as linguistics, they must be recognized as conditional and contingent endeavors in order to avoid reductivism.

Yet this surely marks an important development in his thinking. We remind the reader of a passage from *Phenomenology of Perception* by way of contrast to show this development as he decenters his aesthetic phenomenology.

> Scientific perspectives according to which I am a moment of the world are always naïve and hypocritical because they always imply, without mentioning it, that other perspective—the perspective of *consciousness*—by which a world first arranges itself around me and begins to exist for me. (PhP, lxxii/iii)[53]

Now, in *Indirect Language and the Voices of Silence*, while Merleau-Ponty consistently rejects reductive science in favor of the perceptual world, he no longer centers on consciousness in his aesthetic phenomenology. When he described the activity of the painter, Merleau-Ponty writes of a "cohesion" in a painting, "the presence of a unique principle in it which affects each means of expression . . . [which] replaces the object *not with the subject*—it is the allusive logic of the perceived world." (S, 57/91–92)[54]

Secondly, he is adopting the Saussurean position to reiterate in a new way his position that he had already articulated clearly in his earlier work, that language is not primarily representative but instead presents a world. So when Merleau-Ponty writes here in *Indirect Language and the Voices of Silence* that there is "no language prior to language" (S, 43/69), or "painting does not exist before painting" (ibid., 54/86), one must hear echoed from his earlier work the prohibition of any metaphysical appeal

53. My emphasis. Even though we make the case for the decentering of Merleau-Ponty's aesthetic phenomenology here, it would be inaccurate and grossly unfair to imply that Merleau-Ponty's early philosophy naively equated consciousness with the Modern sovereign subject, as if consciousness were not already intersubjective in his early works. Nonetheless, Merleau-Ponty will no longer equate the perceived world with consciousness.

54. My emphasis. The parallel in language would be when he speaks of "matrices [*sic*] of ideas" (S, 77/125).

to a preestablished *Logos* as well as the emphasis upon the contingency of our experience. Language is not a tool used to represent the world; it is the expression of the being of the world. "Language does not *presuppose* its table of correspondence; it unveils its secrets itself" (ibid., 43/69). To us, this bears striking resemblance to his earlier assertions that "the phenomenological world is not the making explicit of a prior being, but rather the founding of being" and that "the only *Logos* that pre-exists is the world itself" (PhP, lxxxiv/xv).

Far from renouncing his phenomenological approach, the appropriation of Saussurean linguistics complements his account of the art of perception. The intertwining of art and perception is manifest when Merleau-Ponty writes, "Perception already stylizes"; and that painting begins in perception (S, 54/88). For the artist, the painting emerges within an orientation toward the world that begins "as soon as he perceives" (ibid.). For, as Merleau-Ponty noted, "How would the painter or poet express anything other than his encounter with the world?" (ibid., 56/91). It could not be clearer that Merleau-Ponty was still engaged in a phenomenology of the art of perception when he wrote that "language speaks peremptorily when it gives up trying to express the thing itself" (44/71).

It is at the end of the essay, where Merleau-Ponty muses on the "museum" of language, where we see him most clearly taking his distance from Saussure—or at least from his version of Saussure. Here, Merleau-Ponty links language with Hegel and with the museum as analogs, insofar as each claims to preserve spirit. Language tries too hard sometimes.[55] Merleau-Ponty says that there is a kind of paralyzing self-consciousness about language that we overcome at every instant we speak, write, or gesture. And language also has its own artistic dimension—what Merleau-Ponty calls the "literary use of language."[56]

55. Sometimes language tries too hard; and sometimes so do we. To illustrate the important correlate, Cheryl Emerson has pointed out that the frustrating phenomenon of writer's block is often the author trying too hard and not letting language speak. It is very important that these are differences in perspective of the same phenomenon of an intrusive silence, when overdetermined intentions confound intentional relations. However, as we shall see immediately, silence can be seen to play a *founding* role as well as a *confounding* role in language, and in expression in general.

56. Merleau-Ponty adapted material from this essay, in its various forms of revision, for his 1953 course at the *Collège de France*: *Recherches sur l'usage littéraire du langage*, ed. B. Zaccarello and E. de Saint Aubert (Geneva: Metis Presses, 2013).

> Literary language fills the same kind of office [as other great works of art]. . . . And as our body guides us among things only on condition that we stop analyzing it and make use of it, language is literary . . . only on condition that we stop asking justifications of it at each instant and follow it where it goes, letting the words and all the means of expression of the book be enveloped by that halo of significations that they owe to their singular arrangement. (S, 78/125–26)

However, Merleau-Ponty completes this last sentence by saying that the literary use of language "*almost* rejoins the mute radiance of painting" (S, 78/126).[57] Here he contrasts language to art, which is more intimately linked to the perceptual world—not because of what it *says* about the world, but by its affinity with silence. The *spirit* of art only exists in the museum: by transitivity, it exists in linguistic accounts *about* art—and in the science of linguistics' accounts about language. "The marvel is that before Saussure we did not know anything about this [lateral relation of signs], and that we forget it again each time we speak—to begin with when we speak of Saussure's ideas" (ibid., 81/131). According to Merleau-Ponty, painting and "the mute arts" do not suffer this conceit. Saussure's diacritical opposition and the synchronic nature of speech he (falsely) attributes to Saussure are not a structuralist foundation displacing phenomenology, but a useful analytic to articulate the art of perception in a new way.[58]

One place to see how Merleau-Ponty's gesture toward structuralism is consistent with his phenomenological project is in the profound account of silence that Merleau-Ponty provides in this essay. Silence preserves the account of latency Merleau-Ponty began in his earlier work and allows him to focus more explicitly upon the latency of meaning, and in a way that is no longer based on a model of individual consciousness.

Merleau-Ponty's philosophy could just as well be described as a philosophy of latency as a philosophy of ambiguity. Expressions of latency run through his work and are an important component of his thought. Here we can only address the theme as it bears upon his account of the art of perception. The philosopher who maintained that we are "condemned to sense" also has a subtle and complicated relation with non-sense—not only in the manner of a stark opposition to meaning and direction, but in the

57. My emphasis.

58. The reader will note that we make no attempt to resolve these inconsistencies in Merleau-Ponty's account. This would be to constrain his artistry with analysis. . . .

more nuanced ways he consistently describes the sense of the world as latent. Merleau-Ponty's works are rife with a variety of expressions of latency: sense is tacit, allusive, inexhaustible, hidden, secret, indirect, pregnant, oneiric, secret, magical, invisible, etc. Here, as one sees immediately from the title of the essay, Merleau-Ponty's choice expression of latency is *silence,* though he also expresses latency here with the metaphors of *halo* (as we just saw above) and *advent.* Silence and its latency is a theme he will continue to explore later in his career, as we will discuss in the next section.[59]

One of the memorable sentences from this essay is, "In short, language speaks, and the voices of painting are the voices of silence" (S, 81/130). In the preceding few pages, Merleau-Ponty contrasts the way speech (and presumably all language) has a spirit that carries itself along, for better or for worse; it explains itself in its own terms in a way that painting does not. We can write about writing, but we cannot paint painting.[60] He speaks of a "dreaming eternity" and a "hypocrite eternity" germane to painting but not to language (ibid., 80/129–30). Painting does not aim to sum up or propagate a spirit of painting in the way that language perpetuates itself in its self-reference. However, earlier in the essay, he provocatively and perhaps inconsistently claimed, "Now if we rid our minds of the idea that our language is the translation or the cipher of an original text, we shall see that the idea of *complete* expression is nonsensical, and that all language is indirect or allusive—that is, if you wish, silence" (ibid., 43/70).

We have seen that Merleau-Ponty used the metaphors *silence* and *halo* to express the latency of meaning.[61] He also cites Paul Ricoeur to invoke the notion of the *advent* of meaning in language (S, 68/109). Merleau-Ponty speaks of a "primordial expression" presupposed by every substitution of signs (or "derivative" expression), which, "far from exhausting itself in the instant at which it occurs—inaugurates an order and founds an institution

59. I have in mind his invocation of *logos endiathētos* in the working notes to *The Visible and the Invisible.* Cf. our brief discussion of this below. For an excellent full-length study on the theme of silence across the thought of several philosophers, including Merleau-Ponty, cf. Bernard P. Dauenhauer, *Silence: The Phenomenon and Its Ontological Significance* (Bloomington: Indiana University Press, 1980). The finest discussion of two *logoi* and their relationship with silence is in Hamrick and Van Der Veken, op. cit.

60. This seems patently false to us; but this is what Merleau-Ponty says. Perhaps we cannot paint painting as literary expression; but then we cannot say saying adequately, either (thankfully).

61. When we say that these are metaphors, we do not mean that they are *merely* metaphors, but the only means whereby this can be expressed.

or tradition" (ibid., 67/108).[62] Primordial expression seems to be, and to be in, the perceptual world whose meaning is inexhaustible. There is a latency associated with this inexhaustible reserve, which is itself expression; and we see this latency as the *advent* of meaning. "We propose . . . to consider the order of culture or meaning an original order of *advent*, which should not be derived from that of mere events" (S, 68/109). So it is the advent of meaning rather than some specific particular event of meaningfulness that allows for artistic expression. Artistic expression is not the representation of primordial expression, it is its presence, or, more accurately (even if the phrase is unbecoming), the becoming-present of primordial expression. This advent is always situated. "Speech always comes into play against a background of speech; it is always only a fold in the immense *tissue* of language" (ibid., 42/68).[63] Here the tissue of language is analogous to primordial expression with its latency in the advent of meaning. This is also the basis for the historical and cultural significance of works of art.

It is also interesting to compare this constellation of terms with which Merleau-Ponty expresses the inexhaustible latency of meaning (silence, halos, advent, and tissue) to his "halos of Being," invisibility," secrecy," and "flesh of the world" as he articulates his situated ontology in *Eye and Mind* (EM, 164/OE, 23).[64] This gives some vague indication of the direction his thinking takes as it develops from his early phenomenology toward an indirect ontology.[65] But as we shall see, even though he has been making explicit a

62. Merleau-Ponty investigates the important idea of institution at length in his 1954–55 course at the *Collège de France*, *L'institution dans l'histoire personnelle et publique*, (Paris: Belin, 2003).

63. Translation corrected and my emphasis. The metaphor *tissu* is ambiguous in French: it can be a cloth or an expanse taken as a whole—or it can have a biological sense. We propose to preserve this important ambiguity here in this passage, especially since we have the cognate term in English. The important thing to see here is the latency of that which allows for meaningful artistic expression and in that sense situates or unites each artistic expression. Cf. note 74 below.

64. Though it is important to note that we have two different words at work here in French.: *aureoles* and *nimbes*. Nonetheless, one might playfully describe an aspect of the difference between the accounts of situatedness in Husserl's and Merleau-Ponty's phenomenological styles as a progression from horizons to halos. In addition to halos, Merleau-Ponty will have a new constellation of terms to express latency in his ontology, as we shall discuss below in the next section.

65. Emmanuel de Saint-Aubert discusses the indirect nature of Merleau-Ponty's ontology at length, drawing upon many unpublished resources, in his masterful work, *Vers une Ontologie_Indirecte* (Paris: VRIN, 2006).

concern with ontology from the beginning of his work,[66] this development is not tantamount to a simple shift in terms from signification to being, nor is it a simple matter to conceive of this shift.

5. Eye and Mind: Art Situates Ontology

We have seen in the previous four sections of this Preface how the art of perception is essential to Merleau-Ponty's philosophical development. In this final cross-section of Merleau-Ponty's career, we turn our attention primarily to the essay, *l'Oeil et l'esprit* (*Eye and Mind*), where the art of perception situates the indirect ontology he was beginning to develop.

In this section, we have two main goals: we will briefly indicate how this ontology is consistent with his lifelong project of a phenomenology of perception; and more extensively, we will show how the art of perception situates the new ontology. Gary Brent Madison and Martin C. Dillon have already established the former point regarding the continuity of Merleau-Ponty's phenomenological project. Our new contribution to this topic here lies only in reminding the reader of our work above to indicate the aesthetic axis upon which Merleau-Ponty's phenomenological project turns here, as well. The aesthetic phenomenology of perception provides the bridge to accomplish the second (and larger) task of showing how the art of perception situates the new ontology. We will accomplish this in several steps: (1) contrasting the promise of art and science for revealing the ontological aspects of the inquiry; (2) discussing Merleau-Ponty's central theme of his ontology, *the flesh of the world*—especially with regard to its reversibility and divergence; (3) focusing upon the latency of the ontological account; (4) finally, turning our attention to how Merleau-Ponty's account of the artist Paul Klee is crucial to the articulation of this ontology. As we saw above with Merleau-Ponty's account of Cézanne, the sketch of Klee Merleau-Ponty provides is Merleau-Ponty's "self-portrait" of Klee. It reveals an artist at work; but the artistry reveals Merleau-Ponty's aesthetic phenomenology as much as Klee's work.

In *Eye and Mind*, Merleau-Ponty expresses his ontology in terms of his philosophy of art. This nascent ontology is also expressed in *The Visible and*

66. At the end of the Introduction to *The Structure of Behavior*, his first major work, Merleau-Ponty writes that we need to investigate "the meaning and the mode of existence of these structures" (SC, 5/SC, 3). That Merleau-Ponty is slowly throughout his work making explicit an ontology that was implicit, if not fully formed, is the central thesis of Martin C. Dillon's influential *Merleau-Ponty's Ontology* (op. cit.).

the Invisible, the Preface to *Signs*, and various working notes and course notes from the period of the last three years of his life, from 1958–1961. Gary Brent Madison, in his groundbreaking work, *Merleau-Ponty's Phenomenology*, observed well that the insights of Merleau-Ponty's phenomenological account lead directly toward his ontology. Madison makes this point regarding the latter's earliest work.

> Although they are not yet fully unraveled, Merleau-Ponty is already in possession of the guiding threads of his thought in *The Structure of Behavior*; the rest of his work will be a following up of these clues, a philosophical adventure which will finally direct him to their ultimate source [in his ontology]. (Madison 1981, 14–15)

This point is prefigured at the very end of the Introduction of *The Structure of Behavior*, where Merleau-Ponty says that it will be necessary to inquire further into the *existence* of the structures he discloses in that first major work (SB, 5/SC, 3).

Martin C. Dillon has also argued convincingly that the ontology of Merleau-Ponty's later works is a continuation of his phenomenology of perception. More specifically, Dillon holds that the later works make explicit an ontology that was implicit to the early works. Dillon defines the "reversibility thesis" of Merleau-Ponty's later explicit ontology as "the *de facto*—phenomenal—interwovenness of things, [which] is primordial, elementary, irreducible" (Dillon 1988, 156). Like Madison, Dillon argues forcefully that this later work is indicated by his phenomenological project.

> [The] antecedents of the reversibility thesis are clearly evident in the *Phenomenology of Perception*, and . . . the ontology of the later work explicates the ontology implicit in the earlier work. . . . [There] is a consistent development of a unitary standpoint rather than a turn or break in the continuity of Merleau-Ponty's thought. (Dillon 1988, 153–54)

Alongside Madison and Dillon, we want to stress that Merleau-Ponty's ontology unfolds from his project of a phenomenology of perception. Of course, there are changes in the later work. Indeed, in several working notes to *The Visible and the Invisible*, he draws a sharp contrast between his earlier approach in *Phenomenology of Perception*, which was based in a philosophy of consciousness, and his new ontological approach.[67] There are important developments in Merleau-Ponty's philosophical position at this point in his career, and we will address some of these below. However, Madison and Dillon correctly indicated that the phenomenology of perception is the prevailing project throughout Merleau-Ponty's career. We find some evidence for this continuity in a working note from February, 1959: "I must show what one might consider to be 'psychology' (*Phenomenology of Perception*) is in fact ontology" (VI, 176/230). Certainly this passage marks a difference in orientation between his early and late work; but it does so by implication of a common trajectory upon which to appreciate that difference. The psychological consciousness-based account of perception in his earlier work is clarified and grounded in his later ontological work. We see this clearly in another working note from August 1959:

> The information theory applied to perception, and operationalism applied to behavior—is, in fact, confusedly glimpsed at, the idea of meaning as a view of the organism, the idea of flesh. (VI, 200/254)

Merleau-Ponty is criticizing psychology as modern science, with its operationalist and functionalist traits. Psychology could be approached differently; and Merleau-Ponty has tried to indicate this at various stages of his career. Nonetheless, even the best approach to pose psychological problems—through phenomenology—reveals ontological answers (S, 98/159).

Of course, Merleau-Ponty's aesthetic phenomenology, as we have described it above, is especially rooted in the art of perception. Merleau-Ponty's ontological account of the flesh of the world takes the phenomenology of perception project in new directions. He continues to revolutionize phenomenology, transforming it through an interrogation of the art of perception. Merleau-Ponty is developing a new perspective on his account of expression with this nascent ontology. We can draw upon this aesthetic continuity in his philosophical development as we turn our attention to how the art of perception situates his ontology.

The first line of Merleau-Ponty's last published work states that "science manipulates things and gives up living in them" (PrP, 159/OE, 9). Modern science is expected to provide the truth of the real world. Worse

67. "The problems posed in Ph.P. are insoluble because I start there from the 'consciousness'-'object' distinction" (VI, 200/254).

yet, it purports to do so. Still worse, it threatens to succeed. This success would come at the price of the reduction of value to objective fact, the extrication of scientific value from culture and history such that the truth of the real world is achieved *soi-disant*. Science understands the world not as we perceive it, but from the perspective of the no-place of the disinterested spectator. The modern scientist is not even a *flâneur*. Science defines the truth of the real world bereft of its culture and history.

Artists live with the things they understand. Artists, unlike scientists, dwell among the phenomena they study. The attention artists devote to these phenomena allows phenomena to show themselves as themselves even as the showing of phenomena simultaneously implicates the artists as artists. Science provides an often useful abstraction, whereas art grounds us in "the soil of the sensible and opened world" (EM, 160/OE, 12).

Modern science attempts to illuminate all space with the light of reason; but this illumination nearly results in the elimination of lived space. Science seeks a meaning with no secrets. The truth is that science deals with abstract constructions of reality rather than providing the truth of the real world. These abstractions, functions, deprive us of culture and history (EM, 159–61/OE, 9–12). Our bodies are not information machines—that is not how we are condemned to sense or meaning. Our bodies are not isolated disinterested observers. Rather, we are intertwined, "haunted by one sole actual being," situated within a "primordial historicity" (ibid., 161/13). It is important to note that, in the very next sentences, Merleau-Ponty illustrates the art of perception. "But art, especially painting, draws upon this fabric [*nappe*] of brute meaning which activism [or operationalism] would prefer to ignore. Art and only art does so in full innocence" (ibid.). Contrary to the conventional wisdom that art is a capricious misrepresentation of the real world about which science give us truth, Merleau-Ponty advocates that we should turn to art for the truth of the world which science presents via various distorted, albeit often useful, abstractions.

At the same time, unlike the stereotype of continental thinkers, Merleau-Ponty never eschewed science. His first work, *La Structure du comportement* (*The Structure of Behavior*), is fashioned in dialogue with scientific research in his contemporary psychology. He continues this dialogue throughout his career, but most especially during his tenure at the Sorbonne (1949–1952).[68] Indeed, one must remember that, as noted earlier, his appointment at the Sorbonne was as Professor of Child Psychology—the

68. Cf. Maurice Merleau-Ponty, *Psychologie et pédagogie de l'enfant: Cours de Sorbonne 1949–1952* (Paris: Verdier, 2001). Cf. Talia Welsh, trans., *Child Psychology and Pedagogy: The Sorbonne Lectures 1949–1952*, (Evanston: Northwestern University Press, 2010). For

chair subsequently held by Jean Piaget. His Sorbonne lectures are replete with references to psychophysiological research, Gestalt psychological research, psychoanalytic research, and psychological and sociological research in general.[69] But Merleau-Ponty's scientific concerns were not limited to the social sciences. His three-year series of courses at the *Collège de France* on the topic of nature, collected and published posthumously as *La Nature*, contain perhaps his most sustained engagement with research in the natural sciences.

However this is not a matter of "either/or" logic; even though cultural biases may present it as a fallacious forced choice between accepting or rejecting science. Merleau-Ponty's position is best seen as a return to the aesthetic dimensions of experience in an age that has undervalued them rather than an "aestheticism" per se. Modernity favors efficient, objectively certain, and instrumental thought at the expense of the aesthetic dimension of experience. We still suffer this bias in our everyday lives, from the decided emphasis on math and science over the humanities and the arts in our education programs, to locutions such as "It's not rocket science" to indicate the highest standard of complex knowledge.[70] This is the context that requires an affirmative action on behalf of the neglected or at least undervalued aesthetic dimension of experience.

Merleau-Ponty emphasizes that science and its Cartesian world forecloses the source of value and virtue in two other places in *Eye and Mind*. "At one swoop, then, he [Descartes] removes action at a distance and relieves us of that ubiquity which is the whole problem of vision (as well as all its virtue)" (EM, 170/OE, 37).[71] The purported amorality of modern science, which achieves the separation of fact and value only by pretending that facts are not values, is a contrivance of which art is innocent. Merleau-Ponty is pointing out that art, unlike science, is innocent of this conceit—not that art pretends to stand aloof and innocent of its involvement in the world of value it presents. To point out that art reveals a multiplicity of perspectives

a thoroughgoing and insightful discussion—surely the most informed critical discussion of the material presented by Merleau-Ponty in the Sorbonne lectures, cf. Talia Welsh, *The Child as Natural Phenomenologist: Primal and Primary Experience in Merleau-Ponty's Psychology*. (Evanston: Northwestern University Press, 2013).

69. For an interesting original sociological approach drawing upon Merleau-Ponty's work on the social sciences, cf. John O'Neill, *The Communicative Body* (Evanston: Northwestern University Press, 1989).

70. Indeed, I recommend that academia should adopt a new commonplace, "Well, it's not phenomenology," in its place.

71. Translation corrected.

within the flesh of the world rather than seeking to dogmatically assert one is not to abnegate morality or politics.

> There are, in the flesh of contingency, a structure of the event and a virtue peculiar to [*propre du*] the scenario. These do not prevent the plurality of interpretations but in fact are the deepest reasons for this plurality. They make the event into a durable theme of historical life and have a right to philosophical status. (EM, 179/OE, 61–62)

So, at the end of *Eye and Mind*, when Merleau-Ponty acknowledges that in art "no painting ever comes to be *the* painting," he is showing how the art of perception discloses the source of value: "each creation changes, alters, enlightens, deepens, confirms, exalts, re-creates, or creates in advance all the others" (EM, 190/OE, 92).[72]

He continues the trend we saw in the previous sections, moving toward a decentered account of expression. However, Merleau-Ponty now moves his account away from the expression of meaning to the expression of being, so in this ontological account latency is a transition from the advent of meaning to the advent of being.[73] This advent of being is fundamentally tied to the central theme of his later ontology, *the flesh of the world.*

He calls our attention to the ways painters have always understood being. Merleau-Ponty described painting as a "secret science" that reveals what is, the "*il y a,*" instead of pretending to absent itself from its opening upon the world we "haunt" and by which we are haunted—a world Merleau-Ponty describes as "one sole actual being" (EM, 161/OE, 13). Merleau-Ponty's name for this "one sole actual being" is the flesh of the world. He makes occasional reference to this—directly with the term *chair* [flesh], and indirectly with the term *tissue*[74]—in several places in *Eye and*

72. "It is all the others." Merleau-Ponty elided this sentence from the final draft of the essay when he edited it for published form. Cf. Maurice Merleau-Ponty, notes on reserve at the *Bibiothèque nationale* in Paris, Vol. V, 53.

73. It is important to note that Merleau-Ponty always had a decentered notion of subjectivity. As we have seen, expression was never the labor of an isolated individual. And as we shall discuss below, even though he surely changes his position throughout his career, there is much continuity to Merleau-Ponty's philosophical development.

74. The French word is *tissu,* which often has been translated as "fabric" throughout his work. In English and in French, as noted above, *tissu* can carry the connotation of living tissue. Systematically rendering it as fabric carries only one sense of the term—which is an especially important matter in the work of the philosopher whose work pioneered work on embodiment in the twentieth century and whose central ontological term is *flesh.*

Mind; but the idea is described mainly in *The Visible and the Invisible* and in various working notes and course notes from this period.

We cannot do justice here to this complex and profound ontology. We offer only a few words describing some of Merleau-Ponty's unique terminology in this period.[75] *The flesh of the world* (*la chair du monde*) is the central term in Merleau-Ponty's ontology. The emphasis he previously put on embodied consciousness as his phenomenological account of embodiment based upon the consciousness of *le corps propre* is maintained but decentered—revealing an organic intertwining in which we participate and by which we are who we are. The flesh of the world has two main aspects: *écart* (divergence, differentiation) and *réversibilité* (reversibility). The flesh of the world involves difference as well as commonality: our being is reversible, though never completely so. There is thus a latency in this reversibility of the flesh—an inexhaustible reserve of being-in-the-world.

This latency associated with reversibility is a direct outgrowth of the latency of meaning we discussed in the previous section, which focused upon *Indirect Language and the Voices of Silence*. The reader will recall that in that work, Merleau-Ponty discussed an "advent of meaning" that seemed to disclose the voices of silence through the art of perception.[76] Here, in the explicitly ontological later work, Merleau-Ponty describes an advent of being—"an advent to the body of a visible world" (VI, 147/193). "This new reversibility and the emergence of the flesh *as expression* are the point of insertion of speaking and thinking in the world of silence" (ibid., 190/144–45).[77] There is a direct connection of the latency and the advent being of reversibility with the world of silence from *Indirect Language and the Voices of Silence*. It is through expression and the art of perception that we can best see how Merleau-Ponty's ontology is a continuation of his account of meaning; and, more to the point here, how this ontology is situated by the art of perception.

Another aspect of this ontology is that reversibility is at once the divergence of our being as beings. The flesh of the world is not a meta-

75. For an outstanding resource explaining Merleau-Ponty's position in his later work very carefully, and including a great deal of heretofore unpublished work, cf. Emmanuel de Saint-Aubert, *Vers une ontologie indirecte*. For a systematic and clear presentation of Merleau-Ponty's ontological position as it developed throughout his career, cf. Martin C. Dillon, *Merleau-Ponty's Ontology*.

76. Cf. the advent of ultimate historical meaning in the brilliant *bon mot,* "History never confesses" (S, 4/10). The implications for political philosophy are profound when one approaches these issues from an aesthetic phenomenological perspective.

77. My emphasis.

physical substrate: it is our *style* of being. It is perhaps best thought of as an implied horizon of differentiation and divergence manifest in our intertwining within the world. And this divergence and intertwining implicates us as finite creatures. What might have been assumed as the identity of a transcendental ego in Husserl's phenomenological account of intentional relations is revealed in Merleau-Ponty's ontology as "differentiations of the tissue" (VI, 231/284).[78] The flesh of the world is living tissue, but it is also contingent and moribund. It is of *this* world. All flesh dies.[79]

Galen Johnson notes that Merleau-Ponty's account of art and the work artists do is even more reverential in *Eye and Mind* than in his earlier work. Indeed, Johnson notes that there is almost a "spiritual tone" in this ontological work (Johnson 1997, 52). And he is not alone in this observation. Some twenty years after Johnson's observation in passing, Jacques Derrida, in his *Sur le toucher, Jean-Luc Nancy*, deconstructs Merleau-Ponty's account of the flesh of the world. Derrida notes with acute interest the choice of metaphors throughout Merleau-Ponty's project of a phenomenology of perception. Merleau-Ponty consistently invokes metaphors that trade upon Christian ontotheology: communion, incarnation, and transubstantiation, for example.

More generally, Derrida notes three traits of Merleau-Ponty's phenomenological account: "God, death, and flesh," which he describes as "the triple name of all ontotheology" (Derrida 2000, 211). Derrida situates Merleau-Ponty's account squarely in the legacy of transcendental phenomenology when he asserts that Merleau-Ponty is less interested in accounting for touch than the conditions of touching (ibid., 213). The flesh of the world is situated within an account of *Einfühlung* (sympathy), the means by which we feel and share the world together (ibid., 216ff.). *Einfühlung* is "an echo of my incarnation" (ibid, 220).

Derrida correctly sees here the connection between Merleau-Ponty's ontological account of the flesh of the world and the earlier account of embodiment. And Derrida beautifully and sensitively captures the ambigu-

78. Translation corrected. To be fair to the translator, Alphonso Lingis, although this working note is clearly referring to the reversibility of the flesh, and Merleau-Ponty once again chose the ambiguous word *tissu*, he also was referring to "intentional threads" in the same sentence.

79. Cf. Galen A. Johnson, *The Retrieval of the Beautiful* (Evanston: Northwestern University Press, 2010), 125–26, in which he relates an episode at the Fondation Beyeler in Basel. Heidegger paused before Paul Klee's small gouache *Ein Tor* (The Gate) and was transfixed by the way that the gate symbolized death.

ity of the flesh of the world by virtue of its *écart*: "the syncopated non-coincidence of its rapport with itself" (Derrida 2000, 218).[80] He also captures well the notion of latency and advent intrinsic to reversibility (ibid., 235). What Derrida does so provocatively, for better or for worse, is to stress the frequency with which Merleau-Ponty relied upon these onto-theological metaphors in the earlier work in order to present the flesh of the world in the same light. According to Derrida, in order to account for this intertwining, its noncoincidence, and its advent, Merleau-Ponty will need to appeal to a term that is "a little religious," the flesh (ibid., 231). Derrida makes a clear association in his account of Merleau-Ponty's flesh of the world as the messianic flesh that is yet to come, whereby all meaning is to be revealed (ibid., 214).

Anyone who employs a metaphor trades upon its polysemy. And it will get us nowhere to pick and choose among these to crown one as the "true" meaning or what the author "really meant." So we would not defend Merleau-Ponty in this way against the observations Derrida brilliantly makes regarding the onto-theological metaphors Merleau-Ponty employs. Derrida is correct that Merleau-Ponty trades upon these meanings—one merely needs to read the texts in question and allow these words to live as metaphors. But is that what Derrida's foregrounding does; or does it tendentiously limit the resonance of the metaphors?

Any reading that reveals a meaning or meanings of a text is partial (in both senses) and tendentious insofar as it tends to some senses of the text. So we do not pretend to be innocent of the domain of the sense(s) of the texts. However, inspired by Merleau-Ponty, it might be possible to be a little less "scientific" in our hermeneutic posture than Derrida here. We might let the metaphors "muse." We might interpret the text "in full innocence" of such conceits. Another reading, one that we offer, accepts Derrida's astute and careful observations while better respecting the polysemy of these profound metaphors. Merleau-Ponty indeed trades upon the onto-theological senses of the flesh of the world; yet, while this cannot be defended here, one can read him to be demythologizing these metaphors and leaving them room to live rather than to redefine their lives, albeit within new parameters. That is not to say that we are claiming that Merleau-Ponty empties them of the onto-theological sense Derrida emphasizes; it is to acknowledge that, while

80. Cf. also pp. 224 and 226, where Derrida carefully discusses the noncoincidence of *écart,* albeit mainly in the context of a universality of the flesh and a privileging of vision that he wants to criticize.

no reading "comes to be *the*" reading, if no reading "is ever absolutely over and done with," the meanings of these metaphors "have almost all their life still before them."[81]

We can best see how the ontology is situated through the art of perception by Merleau-Ponty's discussion of painting, and most especially of his use of the account of the artist Paul Klee. Just as we saw Merleau-Ponty produce a sketch of Cézanne that turned out to be a "self-portrait"—a portrait of someone offering a phenomenology of perception—likewise, we can see Merleau-Ponty's sketch of Paul Klee in *Eye and Mind* as another self-portrait. Artists are preoccupied with self-portraits. Paradoxically and predictably, artists like to attempt the impossible—to catch themselves in immanence. These two "self-portraits," styled as Cézanne and Klee, bear a similarity to one another; but like any artist's series of self-portraits, they are far from identical. Merleau-Ponty's situated ontology is related to, perhaps implicitly contained, or at least called for in his previous phenomenology of perception. Likewise, his sketch of Klee and his use of Klee's art to situate his explicitly ontological reflections present a different profile of the artist still engaged in a project of a phenomenology of perception.

Yet Merleau-Ponty was acutely aware of Klee's adage, "I cannot be caught in immanence."[82] Merleau-Ponty reminds us that these words from Klee's journal are also his epitaph—inscribed on his tomb. Merleau-Ponty also tells us that these words "give the ontological formula of painting" (OE, 188/87).[83] They will also provide a sketch of his indirect ontology. This analysis, in *Eye and Mind*, is done nearly fifteen years after *Cézanne's Doubt*. And while Cézanne was "never at the center of himself" (SNS, 25/32), according to Merleau-Ponty, the account of expression is different here. He was not looking for an ontological formula before, though, as we have seen, it seems clear that much of what he said was consistent with the ontology he began to articulate later. In many ways the ontology is meant to be a justification, but not a foundation, for expression and transcendence.

---

81. Obviously, in this paragraph we appropriate several passages already cited above from *Eye and Mind* and translate them, and thus resituate them from their original context of painting within a hermeneutic context. Our difference with Derrida here is only to insist that "every *c[h]rist*alization is illusory in some respect" (VI, 214/267, mutatis mutandis).

82. Paul Klee, as cited in OE, 87/188.

83. The editions cited here and in my paper in Part Two are "Eye and Mind," trans. Carleton Dallery, in *The Primacy of Perception and Other Essays on Phenomenological Psychology, the Philosophy of Art, History, and Politics*, ed. James M. Edie (Evanston: Northwestern University Press, 1964), 159–90; and Paris: Gallimard, 1964.

One can see immediately that there is overlap between the earlier and later portraits when one observes that the narrative of *Eye and Mind* begins with a quote from Cézanne: "What I am trying to translate to you is more mysterious; what is entwined in the very roots of being, in the impalpable source of sensations" (EM, 159/OE, ix). And yet there is something decidedly new here, so we must attend to the stylistic changes in Merleau-Ponty's artistry. In *Eye and Mind*, Cézanne is portrayed as plumbing the depths of the meaning of not only our intentional relations, but of existence itself. Thus, although he does cite Cézanne extensively, it is the abstract artist that will be the most important model for Merleau-Ponty in this essay.

As we have seen, Merleau-Ponty makes clear that the problems science has explaining the lived-world can only be addressed by recognizing the expression of embodied perception. Just as in his portrait of Cézanne as phenomenologist, Merleau-Ponty portrays the artist Klee as painting in such a manner that we can learn much about how we perceive from the artistic expression. That is, the abstract art of Klee not only makes present images for visual perception, but also his paintings call that process of expression into question. Again, Merleau-Ponty claims that only the painter, not the scientist, can present the world "in full innocence" (EM, 161/OE, 13).

One way of reading this is to see the phenomenological dimensions of Klee's work as artist—and in Merleau-Ponty's work in presenting his "self-portrait" of Klee. The *epochē* is transforming the attitude of the artist—something we have already seen in his self-portrait of Cézanne. The work provides a reduction of perceptual experience. And once again, Merleau-Ponty makes a great deal of the fact that art is not degenerate perception. As we have seen, the goal of painting is not to represent, but to present. The goal of art is not adequation. Painters celebrate the enigma of visibility by being in the world of the visible.

But there is something new here in the account. In the early work, Merleau-Ponty stressed that painting and perception were expression and transcendence. This guaranteed that the meaning of the painting was never complete, like the phenomenological reduction involved in vision or any other mode of experience. In the early work, Merleau-Ponty spoke of the meaning of the artwork. Then, especially in *Indirect Language and the Voices of Silence*, he spoke of the signification process. But in *Eye and Mind*, Merleau-Ponty is trying to account for that expression and transcendence in a new way by making explicit a new situated ontology. And that situation occurs through Merleau-Ponty's account of the art of perception, and most clearly in his "self-portrait" of Klee. So now when he stresses the open-ended hermeneutic situation of seeing art or seeing the world, he wants to account for the inexhaustibility of meaning by speaking of the "fission of being." He speaks of the "deflagration of Being"—which is at once a conflagration we experience as the expression of meaning. The "interrogation" of painting also reveals the fire burning within us—"the feverish secret genesis of things in our body" (EM, 167/OE, 30). The expression and transcendence that accounted for the meaning of the artwork is now seen ontologically as *écart,* or divergence, the emergence of being as an interval whereby meaning can occur. Merleau-Ponty does not become Klee by writing these words. The ontological interval is manifest here in the divergence intrinsic to Merleau-Ponty's self-portrait of Klee.

Perhaps the place to see this most clearly is disclosed when Merleau-Ponty asks *where* the art is when we see a painting. Merleau-Ponty inquires, when he looks at the ancient cave paintings at Lascaux, where the art is. In a sense it is on the wall; but the meaning of the art involves him—indeed it involves a world. Thinking about Klee's work shows us that when we look at art, we do not only see a painting, we are looking for the impossible—we are looking to find *seeing.* We can't see seeing even though all seeing is situated in the realm of the visible. But according to Merleau-Ponty, Klee's art shows us seeing—especially in his abstract art that is not representational. Seeing is manifest as expression most clearly by the abstract artist's refusal to ground the expression in things seen.

Merleau-Ponty points out that depth is, as he has said earlier, not a *trompe l'oeil*—it is the primary dimension of painting (EM, 180/OE, 65). He showed this in his early work on Cézanne, and he reiterates it here in *Eye and Mind* in the context of a discussion of Cézanne. It was Cézanne who showed us how the enigmatic depth comes because things "eclipse one another and are rivals before my sight" (ibid., 180/65). And it was Cézanne, the phenomenologist, who showed us that this depth comes in an intentional relationship where expression occurs. But how can there be depth in a painting that is not representational? Where is the depth? But there is no doubt that it is *there.* Immediately, in *Eye and Mind,* Merleau-Ponty goes farther and says that this depth is a "reversibility of dimensions," and immediately Merleau-Ponty turns to Klee, the ontologist, to say what he wants to say. Merleau-Ponty's Klee, the "artisan of Being," shows us how painting deals with "identities" and "differences," which gets us to "the heart of things" (ibid., 181/67). Merleau-Ponty says that, unlike in a traditional ontology, Klee's depth is "internal animation" and it reveals how painting is "autofigurative" (181/69). Colors for Merleau-Ponty's Klee are "the inspiration and expiration of Being" (167/31–32), "exhaled at the right place" (182/70). Klee is portrayed as "letting a line muse" so that the line can be an "animating axis" and "render the visible" (183/74). Klee's interrogation of painting shows us that the expression we saw in Cézanne's phenomenology is now explained in as "the fission of Being," (186/81) the "dehiscence of Being" (187/85).

Much of *Eye and Mind* is devoted to a critique of the scientific understanding of the meaning of space, but most importantly, of the Cartesian ontology of traditional science. It is not only a matter of the objectified knowledge of the world it seeks, now it is also vilified for the manner in which Cartesian modern science "builds certain properties of beings into a structure of Being" (EM, 173/OE, 47). Merleau-Ponty's Klee, the ontologist, has shown us the error of this ontology as a forgetting of the *Seinsfrage*. Through an interrogation of painting, we see Descartes's space as something the properties of which are known with certainty, but it is not the space we live in. In order to understand lived space, we need to attend to expression as differentiation, the divergence of beings within the flesh of the world.

So Merleau-Ponty's self-portrait of Klee provides an explanation of what was revealed about expression in his self-portrait of Cézanne. Interestingly, Merleau-Ponty remarks that artists are always fascinated with self-portraits because they want to do the impossible—to see seeing. We are reminded of Camus's short story "The Artist at Work," where a newly famous artist is to be the object of a portrait of the title of the story.[84] Camus points out how it is easy to paint the painter, the canvas, and the studio, but it is impossible to paint painting. But for the analogy to be apt here, Camus should have had the artist attempting to paint himself. The self-portrait allows the artist to show himself or herself as seer and seen, as vision within the visible, as the latent reversibility of the flesh of the world.

Merleau-Ponty's self-portrait of Klee shows Klee's painting as an interrogation of painting, the art of perception disclosing a new ontology. This notion of being as the reversible flesh of the world, but whose reversibility is never complete, depicts the expression of his earlier work as a state of being, *écart*. This is a new and richer account of the phenomenologically described expression of the earlier work, but it is not inconsistent with it.

An unpublished working note from the preparation of *Eye and Mind* points out how Merleau-Ponty will look to an interrogation of painting to show a situated ontology.[85] He is looking at a concrete engagement within

84. Cf. Albert Camus, "Jonas, or The Artist at Work," in *Exile and the Kingdom*, trans C. Cosman (New York: Vintage International, 2007), 87–123.

85. Maurice Merleau-Ponty, notes on reserve at the Bibiothèque nationale in Paris, Vol. V, 148.

the world to articulate his ontology. Merleau-Ponty does not want to risk developing a fundamental ontology akin to Heidegger's early work, with its risk of a new transcendental idealism. In this note, Merleau-Ponty shows how when we attend to the art of perception, as the artist radicalizes our understanding of picture, transcendence of images, light, color, embodiment, and space, the art of perception situates painting in the history of being and discloses the artwork as an interrogation of being from within being—what he calls in *The Visible and the Invisible* an "endo-ontology" (VI, 226/279) with its "endotime" and "endospace" (ibid., 265/318).

But this note can also show the procedure of a phenomenologist at work, just thinking through the problems of the art of perception to their ontological substance. For we see here the *epochē* and reduction at work. When we bracket our biases for picture, transcendence of images, light, color, embodiment, and space, we disclose the reduced phenomenon as that which is a realization of the dehiscence of being.[86] Then, we can see the historical horizon of being in the concrete activity of the artist.

Merleau-Ponty's self-portrait of Klee illustrates the importance of Merleau-Ponty's project of making explicit an ontology at the end of his unfortunately brief career. Perhaps the passage we cited above from the last lines of *Eye and Mind*, among the last of his own words published during his lifetime, can be seen as a self-portrait as well, showing the latency of the ontology he was articulating given the recent swell of interest in his work.

> If no painting comes to be *the* painting, if no work is ever absolutely completed and done with, still each creation changes, alters, enlightens, deepens, confirms, exalts, re-creates, or creates in advance all the others. If creations are not a possession, it is not only that, like all things, they pass away; it is also that they have almost all their life still before them. (EM, 190/OE, 92)

Like the creations and re-creations of a painting, the philosophy of Merleau-Ponty has many possibilities today that were unforeseeable in his time. An important prerequisite to appreciate his work is to recognize it as a process of articulating the art of perception—from a phenomenology of perception to a situated ontology. Each contribution in this anthology is an important contribution to realizing the latent possibilities of Merleau-Ponty's

86. *Dehiscence* is a term Merleau-Ponty borrowed from the natural sciences to express the violent eruption or expression of being in his ontology. In botany, a milkpod dehisces its seeds; in thoracic surgery, one dehisces the rib cage.

philosophy; each essay included in this volume provides a significant and original account of the art of perception.

References

Camus, Albert. 2007. "Jonas, or The Artist at Work." In *Exile and the Kingdom*, translated by C. Cosman, 87–123. New York: Vintage International.

Carbone, Mauro. 2011. *An Unprecedented Deformation: Marcel Proust and the Sensible Ideas*. Albany: State University of New York Press.

Chauí, Marilena. 1981. *Da Realidade sem Mistérios ao Mistério do Mundo: Espinosa, Voltaire, Merleau-Ponty*. São Paulo: Editora br-brasilienese.

Dauenhauer, Bernard P. 1980. *Silence: The Phenomenon and Its Ontological Significance*. Bloomington: Indiana University Press.

Davis, Duane H. 2009a. "The Philosopher of Modern Life." *Natureza Humana: Revista de Philosophia e Psicanálise* 11, no. 2 (Julho–Dezembro). http://www.centrowinnicott.com.br/grupofpp/modules/mastop_publish/?tac=106.

———. 2009b. "O filósofo da vida moderna: Baudelaire, Merleau-Ponty e a arte da crítica fenomenológica." Translated by Richard Simanke. *Aurora—Revista de Filosofia* (Curitiba, Paraná, Brazil) 21, no. 29 (Julho-Dezembro): 503–29.

Derrida, Jacques. 2000. *Le Toucher, Jean-Luc Nancy*. Paris: Éditions Galiléi.

Dillon, M. C. 1988. *Merleau-Ponty's Ontology*. Bloomington: Indiana University Press.

Edie, James M. 1984. "The Triumph of Dialectics over Structuralism." *Man and World* 24: 299–312.

———. 1987. *Merleau-Ponty's Philosophy of Language: Structuralism and Dialectics*. Washington, DC: University Press of America.

Emerson, Cheryl A. "A Carne Feita Palavra: Enquanto Agonizo e o Ser Encarnado." Translated by Wagner Felix. *Prólogos—Revista de Filosofia* 1, no. 1 (forthcoming).

Hamrick, William S. 1987. *An Existential Phenomenology of Law: Maurice Merleau-Ponty*. Dordrecht: Martinus Nijhoff.

———, and Jan Van Der Veken. 2011. *Nature and Logos*. Albany: State University of New York Press.

Heidegger, Martin. 1957. *Einführung in die Metaphysik*. Tübingen: Max Niemeyer Verlag.

Husserl, Edmund. 1965. *Phenomenology and the Crisis of Philosophy*. Translated by Quentin Lauer. New York: Harper Torchbooks.

Johnson, Galen A., ed. 1993. *The Merleau-Ponty Aesthetics Reader*. Evanston: Northwestern University Press.

———. 2010. *The Retrieval of the Beautiful*. Evanston: Northwestern University Press.

Landes, Don. 2013. *The Merleau-Ponty Dictionary*. London: Bloomsbury Academic Publishers.

Madison, Gary B. 1981. *The Phenomenology of Merleau-Ponty.* Athens: Ohio University Press.

Merleau-Ponty, Maurice. 2001a. "Deux notes inédites sur la musique/Two Unpublished Notes on Music." *Chiasmi International* 3: 17–18.

———. 2001b. *Psychologie et pédagogie de l'enfant: Cours de Sorbonne 1949–1952.* Paris: Verdier.

———. 2010. *Child Psychology and Pedagogy: The Sorbonne Lectures 1949–1952.* Translated by Talia Welsh. Evanston: Northwestern University Press.

———. 2013. *Recherches sur l'usage littéraire du langage.* Edited by B. Zaccarello and E. de Saint-Aubert. Geneva: Metis Presses.

Muller, Marcos. 2001. *Merleau-Ponty acerca da expressão*, Porte Allegre: EDIPUCRS.

O'Neill, John. 1989. *The Communicative Body.* Evanston: Northwestern University Press.

Saint-Aubert, Emmanuel de. 2006. *Vers une Ontologie Indirecte.* Paris: J. Vrin.

Schmidt, James. 1985. *Maurice Merleau-Ponty: Between Phenomenology and Structuralism.* New York: St. Martin's Press.

Schrag, Calvin O. 1980. *Radical Reflection on the Origin of the Human Sciences.* West Lafayette, IN: Purdue University Press.

———. 1986. *Communicative Praxis and the Space of Subjectivity.* Bloomington: Indiana University Press.

Silverman, Hugh J. 1987. *Inscriptions between Phenomenology and Structuralism.* New York: Routledge and Kegan Paul.

Slatman, Jenny. 2001. *L'expression au-delà de la representation: Sur l'aisthêsis et l'esthétique chez Merleau-Ponty. Faculteit der Geesteswetenschappen*, University of Amsterdam.

Speigelberg, Herbert. 1982. *The Phenomenological Movement: A Historical Introduction.* 3rd Revised and Enlarged Edition. With the collaboration of Karl Schuhmann. The Hague: Martinus Nijhoff.

Spurling, Laurie. 1977. *Phenomenology and the Social World.* London: Routledge and Kegan Paul.

Welsh, Talia. 2013. *The Child as Natural Phenomenologist: Primal and Primary Experience in Merleau-Ponty's Psychology.* Evanston: Northwestern University Press.

Wiskus, Jessica. 2013. *The Rhythm of Thought, Art, Literature, and Music after Merleau-Ponty.* Chicago and London: The University of Chicago Press.

2

Concluding Scientific Postscript

William S. Hamrick

Merleau-Ponty's last and most important study of art and perception was "Eye and Mind." It appeared in the first issue of the journal *Art de France* in January 1961—four months before the philosopher's untimely death. It was apparently meant to be the first expression of ideas to be elaborated in the second half of his unfinished work later titled *Le Visible et l'invisible*.

Merleau-Ponty wrote the essay during the summer of 1960. Its immediate context and orientation consisted of the third of his three years of lectures at the Collège de France on the subject of Nature, which he finished in May.[1] He wrote "Eye and Mind" the next month. As Jan Van der Veken and I have pointed out,[2] readers of Merleau-Ponty's works have not sufficiently appreciated that linkage and that it accounts for the fact that the first section of "Eye and Mind" is dedicated to the contrast of science and art. In truth, the first section of the essay is simply a continuation of the last of the Nature lectures. The first word of "Eye and Mind" is "science," and the rest of the sentence claims, "Science manipulates things and gives up living in them" (OE, 121/9).[3] Merleau-Ponty contrasts art with both the

1. "Le Concept de Nature" (January–May 1957), "Le Concept de Nature (suite). L'animalité, le corps humain, passage à la culture" (January–May 1958), and "Nature et Logos: le corps humain" (January–May 1960).

2. William S. Hamrick and Jan Van der Veken, *Nature and Logos, A Whiteheadian Explanation of Merleau-Ponty's Fundamental Thought* (Albany: State University of New York Press, 2011), 1. This text will be referred to hereafter as "NL."

3. The editions cited here are, respectively, "Eye and Mind," in *The Merleau-Ponty Aesthetics Reader*, ed. with an introduction by Galen A. Johnson and Michael B. Smith, translation editor (Evanston: Northwestern University Press, 1993), 121–60; and Paris: Gallimard, 1964.

heritage of seventeenth-century mechanistic physics that still hung over his own time (RC, 67/97) as well as some scientific developments of his own era in psychology, physics, biology, and information theory.

Since our contributors do not deal with the relationship of art and science in Merleau-Ponty's writings, I want to sketch a brief remedy for this lacuna in order to show that the relationship is closer than Merleau-Ponty took it to be, and to encourage additional thinking about this intimate connection.

A rapid summary of the major developments of his view of science reveals that, to begin with, his early texts—especially *The Structure of Behavior*, *Phenomenology of Perception*, and *Sense and Nonsense*—used the experimental and experiential results of Gestalt psychology to argue against the prevalent scientific view of mechanistic causality. On that view—characteristic of both Galilean-Cartesian physics, the behaviorism of Merleau-Ponty's own time, and the Gestaltists' own theories (undermined by their research)—human actions are nothing but determined effects of previous chains of causes and effects: *f* (x).

Phenomenology of Perception also advanced the view that "scientific perspectives" that interpret me as a "moment of the world" are inevitably "naïve and hypocritical because they always imply, without mentioning it, that other perspective—the perspective of consciousness—by which a world first arranges itself around me and begins to exist for me" (PhP, lxii/iii).[4] This is the pre-known world, anterior to scientific explanations, and with respect to which every scientific proposition is "abstract, signitive, and dependent, just like geography with regard to the landscape where we first learned what a forest, a meadow, or a river is" (ibid., lxii/iii). "The natural-scientific attitude" is, as Husserl expressed it, "a theoretical attitude" in which nature becomes a "*bloße* Sache"—a "pure thing" stripped of value- and use-references.[5]

Both Merleau-Ponty's early and late discussions of science rest on the rejection of two main doctrines of seventeenth-century physics. The first one, termed the "ontology of the object," interprets nature is a full and com-

4. The English translation used in these comments is by Don Landes (London and New York: Routledge, 2012). The French pagination is from *Phénoménologie de la perception* (Paris: Gallimard, 1945).

5. Edmund Husserl, *Collected* Works, Volume III: *Ideas Pertaining to a Pure Phenomenology and to a Phenomenological Philosophy*, Second Book: *Studies in the Phenomenology of Constitution*, trans. Richard Rojcewicz and André Schuwer (Dordrecht: Kluwer Academic Publishers, 1989), 6 and 27.

plete object over against us as subjects. (Jean-Paul Sartre's early writings also argue for this ontology.) Consciousness, subjectivity, values, and purposes are all excised from nature that, for seventeenth-century thinkers, consists of objective matter known only quantitatively. Human beings become spectators, or surveyors, of nature, and that is the second doctrine. This surveying activity is what Merleau-Ponty describes as a "*pensée de survol*" (OE, 122/12; VI, 222/276).[6] In "Eye and Mind," the author describes scientific thinking as this kind of cogitation that "must return to . . . the [preceding] site, the soil of the sensible and humanly modified world such as it is in our lives and for our bodies" (OE 122/12–13)—and one to which the artist is a privileged witness. In other words, science must return to its origins.

That "soil of the sensible and humanly modified world" includes nature as an essential component. Indeed, already in the *Phenomenology* the author stated, "The natural world is the horizon of all horizons . . . which ensures my experiences have a given, not a willed, unity beneath all of the ruptures of my personal and historical life" (345/381). Yet, operating still under the shadow of Cartesianism, Merleau-Ponty continued to interpret science as committed to the ontology of the object. Thus, he complained of an attitude "particularly true" in France that science states the truth about the world while the perceptual life of the lived-body finds itself "at a single stroke devalued" (C, 32/11).

For example (his), if I wanted to understand what light is, the prevailing mindset would send me to a physicist in order to listen to explanations of particle- and wave-theories. What perception would give me—"the colors, reflections, and the things that bear them"—would be interpreted as "only appearances" (C, 32/12). In this way, nature becomes an object-in-general, stripped of value, divorced from the experient. The physicist's explanation defines what light really is, as opposed to my subjective experiences of it or, for that matter, the way that the magical glow of a painting by Rembrandt or Vermeer has captured it. Inverting this relationship, Merleau-Ponty construes the scientific object as an abstraction in the literal sense of the word: something pulled out of, derivative from, our original experiences of the world around us that it presupposes.

Two concepts in the preceding paragraph require explanation. The first is "object-in-general," one that is seen from no one's perspective. The phrase

6. Benita Eisler, in her translation of Volume IV of Jean-Paul Sartre's *Situations*, coined the translation "high-altitude thinking" for this type of thought. Smith translates it as "a thinking that looks on from above" (122).

has the Husserlian sense of the *bloße Sache* that, as we have seen, consists of the intentional correlate of a theoretical consciousness from which value- and use-predicates have been bracketed. By the time that Merleau-Ponty reaches "Eye and Mind," it turns out that the *pensée de survol* is not only the correlate of the ontology of the object, but also characterizes all scientific thought. Thus, in the sentence partially quoted earlier from "Eye and Mind," he writes: "Scientific thought—*pensée de survol,* thought of the object in general—must be replaced in a previous 'there is' [*il y a*], to the site, the soil of the sensible and humanly modified world such as it is in our life, for our body" (122/12–13; translation altered). Either this is evidence of the long shadow of Cartesianism hanging over his conception of science and nature, or it amounts to a confusion between the objects of scientific thought and the referent of the "ontology of the object." In the latter, nature is something from which consciousness is completely excluded and cut off. For the former, so far from being cut off from consciousness, they are products of a certain type of it.

The second concept to clarify is the meaning of abstraction. This is quite important because Merleau-Ponty sometimes oscillates between two senses of the word. In addition to the first meaning of being "taken from" ordinary perceptual life, the second sense is something like "deficient in truth" or "deficient in reality" as compared to that life in which it is grounded. The first meaning does not imply the second, and statements such as "Science does not describe the real world" rely on the second meaning alone. All that does follow is that science provides a partial account of nature and our place within it, and it is only in that weak sense that scientific propositions are lacking in truth or reality. We shall return to this ambiguity.

Beyond Merleau-Ponty's early writings, his view of nature changed considerably during the nature lectures at the Collège de France. From 1956 or so on, he is clear that a new understanding of the subject is essential to his "new" ontology, which he describes as an "ontological rehabilitation of the sensible" (S, 166–67/210). Henceforth, "Nature is not only the object, the partner of consciousness in the tête-à-tête of knowledge, but also an object from which we have emerged" (RC, 64/94). Therefore, "the concept of Nature is always expression of an ontology—and privileged expression" (N, 204/265). It is neither arbitrary nor one among other equals. In that regard, Rudolf Bernet is correct that the concept of nature as "an object from which we have emerged" "presents at the same time the sizeable stakes [*les grands enjeux*] of the philosophy of nature outlined since *Phenomenology of Perception.*"[7]

7. Rudolf Bernet, *La vie du sujet, Recherches sur l'interprétation de Husserl dans la phénoménologie* (Paris: Presses Universitaires de France, 1994), 168.

In the "new" ontology, science is not "naïve and hypocritical" because it has forgotten its foundation in consciousness. There are two reasons for this. First, the primacy of consciousness is decentered and recentered in "the flesh," and constitution by institution and reversibility. Second, Merleau-Ponty wants to think Being in the light of science (NC, 148). One example is his utilization of relativity theory to counter the ontology of the object because the theory shows that "each particular observation is strictly linked to the location of the observer and cannot be abstracted from this particular situation; it also rejects the notion of an absolute observer" (C, 36/16). For the same reason, he criticizes "the radical opposition traced by Heidegger between ontic science and ontological philosophy [that] is only valid in the case of Cartesian science that posits Nature as an object laid out before us and not in the case of a modern science that places in question its own object and its relation to the object" (N, 85/120). *Pace* Heidegger, he writes, we must give up a direct approach to Being in favor of one that is indirect—"to show Being across the *Winke* [signs, indications] of life, of science, etc." (NC, 148). The "new" ontology aimed to find a way to think Being in the light of, among other things, modern physics and biology, and to pursue this knowledge while maintaining our "astonishment before the world" that expresses "the true philosophical outlook" (ibid., 78). This attitude had earlier been the "best formulation of the [phenomenological] reduction" (Eugen Fink) (PhP, lxxvii/viii) (substituting "astonishment" for "wonder"; *étonnement*).

Merleau-Ponty made it clear that nature outside of us and nature in us are intimately intertwined. "It is necessary," he wrote, that "Nature in us has some relationship with Nature outside of us, [and] it is even necessary that Nature outside of us be revealed by the Nature that we are" (N, 206/267; translation altered). The philosopher, therefore, wanted to focus on "the nexus" of both (ibid.). This is why he endorsed, and repeated, Bergson's assertion that, whatever be the ultimate nature of what is, "we are of it" (E, 16/25–26). Nature in this sense is what Cézanne's paintings tried to express, "the depth of inhuman nature on which man is installed," a depth one can feel in Cézanne's paintings as he magically depicts the seismic upheavals of forests [59] and rocks. Nature is "the autoproduction of meaning" (N, 3/19).

Merleau-Ponty's second and third Nature courses explore in great detail the process of evolution. It is the human body in which "evolution makes the transition to human being" (N, 214/276). Therefore, his rationale for this long, complex treatment of it was "to give this depth to the human body, this archeology, this natal past, this phylogenetic reference, to restore it in a fabric of preobjective, enveloping being, from which it emerges and which recalls to us its identity as sensing and sensible at every moment" (N, 273/341).

Among other things, Merleau-Ponty analyzes Edward S. Russell's experiments with flatworms and Adolf Portmann's studies of animal appearances and mimicry that leads to the emergence of the expressive body in higher animals. He discusses Konrad Lorenz's work with chimpanzees and the relationship of body and consciousness, and Jakob von Uexküll's notion of the Umwelt in animal life. He finds in their work, as in Evelyne Lot-Falck's study of Eskimo masks, our *Ineinander* relationships with (other) animals and a confirmation of Husserl's contention that a fundamental empathy (*Einfühlung*) with (other) animals is a necessary condition for the development of zoology (NC, 383–92).[8] Human beings make up "another corporeity" (N, 214/276) shared with animals with different degrees of mentality. We "co-exist with animality instead of rashly refusing it any kind of interiority" (C, 58/39).

It is in light of these investigations that Merleau-Ponty criticizes operational thinking in physics, biology, and cybernetics. Operational thinking amounts to defining the essences of things in terms of the operations necessary to explain them. Merleau-Ponty's immediate target is Percy W. Bridgman's *The Logic of Modern Physics*,[9] though Bridgman himself credits the American pragmatists—especially Dewey—for the concept. For example (Bridgman's), the meaning of the concept of length must be determined by the operations required to measure it. To measure the distance from my keyboard to my coffee cup, I would use a ruler. But if I desired to know the distance between Earth and the far edge of the Milky Way, I would have to use very different measurements and that "length" would then take on new meaning in terms of measurements of light rays.

Merleau-Ponty considered biology controlled by operational thinking to be a "technical science" that considers a "living being as an artifact, as physicochemical composite" (NC, 90). This is to see an organism as a "*bloße Sache*" in contrast to a living being that exists in *Einfühlung* relationships with others. These relations are not a "residue of pre-science in science"

8. Merleau-Ponty translates and comments on Husserl's *Beilage* (Supplement) XXIII of the *Krisis* (not included in the English translation), which concerns biology. For both thinkers, biology is just as universally true as physics (NC, 386). There is an "*Ineinander* of intersubjectivity [that] extends to our relationship with our body, with animals, [and] plants—universal Ontology" (ibid., 89).

9. Percy W. Bridgman, *The Logic of Modern Physics* (New York: Macmillan, 1927).

(ibid.). Rather, they reveal "a reference to the *Umwelt* and to the *world* that cannot be reconstituted starting from *bloße Sachen*: it is the universe of physics that is *enveloped* in that of life and not the inverse"[10] (ibid., 90–91).

This is the conception of science in the first section of "Eye and Mind" that animates the strong contrast with art. The objects of that kind of thinking are abstract in both senses, though it would be wrong to say that its referents are not the real world. They are, rather, a partial aspect of the real and, for that reason, are ontologically relevant. This is why Merleau-Ponty even says, "The information theory applied to perception, and operationalism applied to behavior—is, in fact, confusedly glimpsed at, the idea of meaning as a view of the organism, the idea of flesh (VI, 200/254). Rather, what Merleau-Ponty objects to is the absolutization, or totalization, of such thinking: "To say that the world is, by nominal definition, the object x of our operations is to treat the scientist's knowledge as if it were absolute, as if everything that is and has been was meant only to enter the laboratory. Thinking 'operationally' has become a sort of absolute artificialism, such as we see in the ideology of cybernetics" (OE, 122/11–12).[11]

Nonetheless, even when absolutized, operational definitions still refer to the real world and thus retain their ontological pertinence. Thus, Merleau-Ponty writes, "an organism is, in a sense, only physico-chemistry" (N, 206/267). No nonnatural entelechy, consciousness, can intervene in it or be imposed on it. Rather, consciousness emerges from the "physic-chemistry." In other words, the *bloße Sache* of the physic-chemical unity is less false than abstract, and abstract in both senses.

Now, this conclusion leads to a puzzle similar to the one suggested by Galen Johnson, which Duane Davis discussed above. That puzzle consists of two seemingly incompatible claims: Merleau-Ponty asserts that (1) it is

10. There is a strong parallel here with the way that F. W. J. Schelling situates mechanism within the life of organisms rather than the other way around. See NL, 130ff.

11. Another implication of this absolutization is the fear that human beings themselves will be reduced to a set of functions and operations—in other words, "the *manipulandum* he thinks he is . . . [in which case we enter] into a sleep, or nightmare from which there is no awakening" (OE, 122/12). There is more than a faint echo here of Gabriel Marcel's identical fears in *On the Ontological Mystery* (1933), which he would have known, and Marcel's later work, *Tragic Wisdom and Beyond* (1968), published after Merleau-Ponty's death. In the latter work, the author states that the contemporary saint is the naturalist, the person for whom there is no insignificant life form and who has transcended the rift between humanity and nature.

impossible to complete the phenomenological reduction; and (2) in effect Cézanne did it by reaching a "prescientific perception of the visible." The conundrum about science is that (3) the philosopher holds that biological explanations are abstract in the sense of being taken from the richness of embodied life as well as in the sense of presenting only partial truths. Yet (4) there is not the slightest suggestion of abstractness in either sense as he traces the complex history of evolution on the way to the realization of the human body and consciousness emerging from nature. Nor is there any qualification of his reality claims when he appeals to relativity theory for support for his "new" ontology (e.g., at RC, 91/128; cf. VI, 166/222). Nor, finally, is there any concern about abstractness and lack of truth or reality in the empathic relationships inscribed in the lives of zoologists and their subjects. Thus, in the case of both Cézanne and science, there is a certain dissonance between theory and practice, and it is simply mistaken to say that sciences (and which ones?) deal with abstractions while art provides us with the truth of the real world.

This is the point to return to the first part of "Eye and Mind." As noted earlier, the author distinguishes art from science because the latter "manipulates things and gives up living in them" (OE, 121/11). Yet, on his view, philosophy and even perception give up living in things. Philosophy is not a repetition of life. Rather, it provides the necessary reflection without which "life would probably dissipate itself in ignorance of itself or in chaos" (Prim. Percp., 19/127).[12] He also tells his listeners in his sixth radio lecture, "Art and the Perceived World," that perception often ignores the details of what we see day in and day out, whereas art has the distinction of making us see what we usually take for granted (C, 69/53).

As we have seen, Merleau-Ponty also states that science gets farther and farther away from the everyday world (*le monde actuel*), and "must return . . . to the soil of the sensible and humanly modified world" (OE, 122/12). This claim raises a number of unanswered questions: What would such a return mean? Why and how should science return? Does it need to? Phrased otherwise, how would science be improved by such a return, whatever that might mean? What ontological or epistemological value or reality would be gained? And is science, at least in some sectors, much closer to that "soil" than others? The answers have to be a bit complex because Merleau-Ponty often makes universal statements about "science" that do not

12. The French pagination is from "Le Primat de la perception et ses conséquences philosophiques," *Bulletin de la Société française de philosophie* XLI (December 1947): 119–53.

apply to all sciences. Owing to space limitations here, I will confine myself to the natural sciences.

In the first place, data collection and the manipulation of variables constitute only part of scientific research. It is not true that all of the sciences attempt to define the truth of the real world while excluding its culture and history, as operational thinking by itself does. For examples, it is certainly not true of primatologists studying intertwining histories of humans and primates. It is equally not true of marine biologists studying the effects of climate change and human negligence and recklessness on coral reef destruction. Nor, finally is it true of scientists studying climate change by correlating tree ring growth with human history and prehistory.

Second, some scientists, and perhaps many, dwell among the phenomena they study just as much as artists do. Primatologists such as Dian Fossey and Jane Goodall come easily to mind, just as do Marie Curie, paleontologists on digs, and immunologists trying to find causes of diseases. I think that Merleau-Ponty would have realized this if he had followed out the full implications of Husserl's remarks about empathy and the science of zoology. Except in the case of Cézanne, Merleau-Ponty pays much more attention to the artist at work—usually painting—than he does to the work of art itself. If he had paid similar attention to scientists at work, he could have grasped the reversibility of flesh present in their efforts as well. No one who has seen films of Fossey and Goodall can truly doubt this. In other sciences, the same mutual implication manifests itself for seismologists in active earthquake zones, for immunologists working with patients in the midst of epidemics, marine biologists in thrall with the magnificent diversity of sea life, and astronomers' passion for understanding cosmology—the same complex and stunning order of the universe that led Kant to express a special respect for the cosmological argument for the existence of God, even though he held the proof to be fallacious. In sum, rather than undervaluing or neglecting the aesthetic dimension of experience, the scientific articulation of nature is often motivated by and expressive of its beauty, complexity, and order. And not just for scientists, either. Witness the stunning pictures of supernovas and other celestial phenomena beamed to us from the Hubble telescope that inspire such wonder. In all of these cases, the same structures of perceptual reversibility in the experience of art can also be present—indeed, if Merleau-Ponty is right, *must* be present in these fleshly interactions with Nature.

One might object at this point that, although it is unquestionable that scientists are engaged with the world they study, it is still the case that they operate with metaphysical pretensions of being disengaged even while they claim to be engaged. The best answer to this objection, I think, is that offered by Charles Hartshorne. In "Perception and the Concrete Abstractness of Science," he begins by observing, "It is a truism that science gives us an abstract description of reality."[13] Yet, it is also true that "science does not simply abstract from, omit, certain of the *positive* features of the perceived world; it also adds enormously to those features" (CE, 33). For examples, "To the obvious macroscopic organisms in nature it adds microorganisms, a whole subworld to itself, including the cells of which all visible plants and animals are composed. . . . To the obvious stones, bodies of water, and diaphanous air it adds molecules, atoms, and particles" (ibid.). There is no pretension, metaphysical or otherwise, of being disengaged from the world in doing such work.

Further, Hartshorne correctly points out that, as Merleau-Ponty noted, "[I]t is not only science that abstracts; our very sense perceptions do this for us" (ibid., 34). That is because "Sense experience is an enormous *simplification of* the perceived world. Where there are billions of individuals (cells, molecules), direct experience gives us only gross outlines of quasi-individual groups of these individuals" (ibid.). Finally, "Science and perception are both abstract; but there are two forms of abstractions" (ibid., 35). In perception, as just described, "details, special cases of some general property, are left out of account." In science, there is a willful setting aside of "the entire class of what are often called secondary and tertiary qualities and [science] substitutes the so-called primary qualities, which are really structures rather than qualities in the distinctive sense" (ibid.). It is this willful setting aside that can be misinterpreted as a metaphysical pretension of disengagement.

The upshot of this discussion is that science, like art, may truly, if partially, increase our understanding of what is real. Both are ontologically relevant and important, and one is not to be denigrated to the profit of the other. Further, as they are carried out, they are much more similar than Merleau-Ponty appears to believe. To say that science is a human activity is a double-edged sword. The direction of one side leads to development of new knowledge about nature, including ourselves. The other side opens us to appreciate that the work of scientists as well as artists opens us to deeper reversibilities between the flesh of the world and our own flesh.

---

13. Charles Hartshorne, *Creative Experiencing, A Philosophy of Freedom*, ed. Donald Wayne Viney and Jincheol O (Albany: State University of New York Press, 2011), 33 (referred to hereafter as "CE"). He also states, "Merleau-Ponty was right to reject the notion that minds could operate without bodies, and his "generalized idea of 'flesh' has truth in it" (24).

References

Bernet, Rudolf. 1994. *La vie du sujet, Recherches sur l'interprétation de Husserl dans la phénoménologie*. Paris: Presses Universitaires de France.

Bridgman, Percy W. 1927. *The Logic of Modern Physics*. New York: Macmillan.

Hamrick, William S., and Jan Van der Veken. 2011. *Nature and Logos, A Whiteheadian Explanation of Merleau-Ponty's Fundamental Thought*. Albany: State University of New York Press.

Hartshorne, Charles. 2011. *Creative Experiencing, A Philosophy of Freedom*. Edited by Donald Wayne Viney and Jincheol O. Albany: State University of New York Press.

Husserl, Edmund. 1989. *Collected Works*, Volume III: *Ideas Pertaining to a Pure Phenomenology and to a Phenomenological Philosophy*, Second Book: *Studies in the Phenomenology of Constitution*. Translated by Richard Rojcewicz and André Schuwer. Dordrecht: Kluwer Academic Publishers.

Part Two

Interpretations

3

Cohesion and Expression

Merleau-Ponty on Cézanne

Jessica Wiskus

Merleau-Ponty's engagement with the visual arts, and in particular with painting, spans the whole of his career. And, as is well known, from *The Phenomenology of Perception* through "Eye and Mind," Cézanne stands as a key figure in Merleau-Ponty's work. What is interesting, therefore, is to follow the development that his consideration of Cézanne undertook. This can be traced not only through his well-known essays in aesthetics, "Cézanne's Doubt" and "Eye and Mind," but also through the course notes written in the last decade of his life, *Institution and Passivity* (1954–55), "La philosophie aujourd'hui" (1958–59), and "L'ontologie cartésienne et l'ontologie d'aujourd'hui" (1960–61). What one gathers from these sources is a subtle but important change in emphasis, underlining *depth* as a philosophical notion. For it is not only that depth, from a phenomenological perspective, serves as a principal theme of interrogation in these works, but that it comes to inform the way that Merleau-Ponty approaches other artistic questions articulated through the paintings of Cézanne—questions of movement, color, and style. Indeed, depth serves as a model through which Merleau-Ponty understands the notion of expression itself.

Depth in Cézanne

In "Eye and Mind," Merleau-Ponty writes, "Four centuries after the 'solutions' of the Renaissance and three centuries after Descartes, depth is still new, and it insists on being sought" (OE, 140/64).[1] But how might depth—a matter of technique approached by painters at least, as we might be reminded, from the time of the caves at Lascaux—be "still new"? What, according to Merleau-Ponty, is the particular depth that Cézanne was seeking?

Clearly, it is not the illusion of depth presented upon a canvas by the *perspectiva artificialis* (as the " 'solutions' of the Renaissance"). Cézanne paints not a depth that would simply present another dimension—a dimension equated with breadth or height but in another direction; one could not take a ruler to the landscape and calculate the coordinates of this depth.[2] For Cézanne's depth is not simply a kind of object that one could grasp, look at from several points of view, or see deployed in transparency. As Merleau-Ponty envisions through the work of Cézanne, depth serves rather as that through which the measurable dimensions of breadth and height come forth. In the phenomenological sense, depth serves as an opening—a "voluminosity" through which the visible world is expressed (OE, 140/65).

Moreover, Merleau-Ponty writes that there is a certain "enigma" associated with depth, which "consists in the fact that I see things, each one in its place, precisely because they eclipse one another, and that they are rivals before my sight precisely because each one is in its own place—in their exteriority, known through their envelopment, and their mutual dependence in their autonomy" (OE, 140/64–65). The place (or opening) that depth gives to the things manifests a principle of *Ineinander* ("in their exteriority, known through their envelopment, and their mutual dependence in their autonomy"). And so, for Merleau-Ponty, depth is a volume of space that

1. The editions cited here are, respectively, "Eye and Mind," in *The Merleau-Ponty Aesthetics Reader*, edited with an introduction by Galen A. Johnson and Michael B. Smith, translation editor (Evanston: Northwestern University Press, 1993), 121–60; and Paris: Gallimard, 1964.

2. Indeed, in "Eye and Mind," Merleau-Ponty writes that, contrary to our ordinary conception of depth, "we can no longer call it a third dimension. In the first place, if it were a dimension, it would be the *first* one; there are forms and definite planes only if it is stipulated how far from me their different parts are. But a *first* dimension that contains all the others is no longer a dimension, at least in the ordinary sense of a *certain relationship* according to which we make measurements. Depth thus understood is, rather, the experience of the reversibility of dimensions, of a global 'locality' in which everything is in the same place at the same time, a locality from which height, width, and depth are abstracted, a voluminosity we express in a word when we say that a thing is *there*" (OE, 140/65). It is a voluminosity that, as we shall see, participates not only in space but also in time.

allows for things not only to be seen (as an opening for breadth and height), but that allows for things to have an *unseen* side ("because they eclipse one another"); it is thanks to depth that the *unseen* side is constitutive of the things themselves. This is how perceptual depth operates according to an intertwining: it provides an expressive opening not only for the visible but also for the invisible, other side of objects.

Yet this intertwining through the perception of depth is not to be thought as a mere alternation between the visible and the invisible; what is important about depth is not that one could imagine changing one's position such that an object (perhaps an apple resting upon a table) would then reveal its *unseen* side. The *unseen*, through depth, is not an illusion to be stripped away through the adoption of a different point of view, or (better yet) an omniscient point of view. For the perceptual experience of depth does not arise according to a vision that would strive to see everything displayed in positivity, according to a vision that would act as a pure mind by synthesizing different points of view. The perceptual experience of depth is rooted within the body schema; depth arises, in particular, only because we have two eyes that see the same object *differently*. Divergence stands at the heart of the experience of depth. What we see through depth, then, is not equivalent to one or another of the images that the left or right eye would offer, nor a calculated layering of one image upon the other. It is not alternation but cohesion that characterizes depth, which unites, at once, otherwise contradictory elements (e.g., the image of the left eye and the image of the right eye). Perceptual depth is, in a sense, a field that unfolds from this divergence. As a field, what we see as depth is *something else*—something that the gaze of neither eye alone could see—*something of another order* that the total body effects.[3] It is not simply something

3. Merleau-Ponty writes: "The unity of binocular vision, and with it the depth without which it cannot come about is, therefore, there from the very moment at which the monocular images are presented as 'disparate.' When I look in the stereoscope, a totality presents itself in which already the possible order takes shape and the situation is foreshadowed. My motor response takes up this situation. Cézanne said that the painter in the face of his 'motif' is about 'to join the aimless hands of nature.' The act of focusing at the stereoscope is equally a response to the question put by the data, and this response is contained in the question" (PhP, 305/311). The editions cited here are, respectively, revised ed., trans. Colin Smith (London and New York: Routledge, 1981); and Paris: Gallimard, 1945. Thus, already in the *Phenomenology of Perception*, the idea of depth—exemplified through the stereoscope—is linked with Cézanne's "motif." That is to say, the artistic vision of Cézanne is here placed in relation to the phenomenon of depth.

that we see; nor is it the unveiling of the *unseen* itself. Depth discloses the fact that *there is* an *unseen*. Indeed, Merleau-Ponty writes that depth "is pre-eminently the dimension of the hidden" (VI, 219/268). It is not, Merleau-Ponty clarifies, that painting merely "renders present to us what is absent" (OE, 132/41). For it does not render present what is occasionally absent—absent for us and otherwise present to others in space or time (as in Descartes's theory of vision). It "renders visible," Merleau-Ponty writes, citing Klee (OE 143/74), the fact that the invisible is constitutive—that absence is fundamentally intertwined with presence. "The hallmark of the visible is to have a lining of invisibility in the strict sense, which it makes present as a certain absence" (OE, 147/85). In this way we must think of depth, in accordance with the working notes of *The Visible and the Invisible*, as a "negativity that *comes to the world*" (VI, 250/298).

It is this ontological sense of depth that informs much of Merleau-Ponty's last work: depth as that through which oppositional pairs (visible-invisible, sensible-ideal, present-past, activity-passivity) cohere. In another working note of *The Visible and the Invisible*, entitled "The Invisible, the negative, vertical Being," Merleau-Ponty writes that there is "[a] certain relation between the visible and the invisible, where the invisible is not only non-visible (what has been or will be seen and is not seen, or what is seen by an other than me, not by me), but where its absence counts in the world (it is 'behind' the visible, imminent or eminent visibility, it is *Urpräsentiert* precisely as *Nichturpräsentierbar*, as another dimension) where the lacuna that marks its place is one of the points of passage of the 'world.' It is this negative that makes possible the *vertical* world, the union of the incompossibles" (VI, 227–28/277). Thus, in understanding depth as "the union of the incompossibles"—as the cohesion (and not synthesis) of divergence—one begins to trace its ontological significance.

For the illusion of depth given through the *perspectiva artificialis* of Renaissance painters, according to Merleau-Ponty, discloses an attendant philosophical system that depends upon the positing of a "zero point of Being" (VI, 113/150). This "zero point" (in painting, the *punta della fuga*) would be timeless, unchanging, and omniscient—the point from which all things would be arrayed in positivity. In the course notes to *L'ontologie cartésienne et l'ontologie d'aujourd'hui*, Merleau-Ponty sketches out this relation between Renaissance perspective and ontology, writing, "Descartes: idea of a universal language where the signs would have an exactly circumscribed meaning—It is the equivalent of the theory of perspective" (NC, 183). Therefore, we might say that, on the one hand, in structuring their canvases around the placement of the *punta della fuga*, the Renaissance masters attempted to portray depth as the synthesis of a totalizing, immaterial mind; on the other hand, insofar as Cézanne rejects the technique of *perspectiva artificialis,* we might say that his work thematizes the modern rejection of Cartesian thought. It is thus that Merleau-Ponty writes, as we have seen, that modern painting gives "a transformation in the relationship between humanity and Being" (OE, 139/63).

And so, following Merleau-Ponty, it appears that Cézanne's paintings search for the expression of a new ontology. But such a quest—not unlike that of Merleau-Ponty's own work, proceeding in stops and starts, progressions and revisions—is not undertaken easily. "This is the reason," writes Merleau-Ponty, "for his difficulties and for the distortions one finds in his pictures between 1870 and 1890" (SNS, 12–13/17). In particular, this is the reason, in the paintings of this period, for Cézanne's curious treatment of the line. In order to portray cohesion of "incompossibles" as depth, Cézanne liberates the line, and in so doing he transforms the foundations of the Renaissance technique of perspective.

For one could consider the traditional function of the line in a drawing or painting to be that of containment. The line works to keep an object within bounds, as if it were an actual property of an object: the object's own separate end or beginning. Merleau-Ponty writes, "There has been, for example, a prosaic conception of the line as a positive attribute and property of the object in itself. Thus, it is the outer contour of the apple or the border between the plowed field and the meadow, considered as present in the world, such that, guided by points taken from the real world, the pencil or brush would only have to pass over them" (OE, 142/72). Here, the line has the effect of defining the edge between the object and the general volume of space. Such an object seems to be placed within space, but is not *of* space; it is in some way set apart from the voluminosity of the world. Through this line, there is no *Ineinander*—there is not *exteriority known through envelopment* nor *mutual dependence through autonomy*. Rather, the traditional line separates the object from the space that surrounds it.

Yet, in the work of Cézanne, there is no hard edge, finite boundary, or fixed outline. The line, contrary to its traditional function of circumscription, does not merely delineate the surface; it inaugurates depth. In many of his still life canvases from the 1880s and 1890s, for example, Cézanne traces not just one line around a specific plate, ginger jar, or piece of fruit, but paints several lines of different shades of blue, as if the line were the string of a violin seen as it vibrates. The repetition of the line has the effect of generating a rhythm upon the canvas, lending a plate, a ginger jar, or fruit the sense of a kind of movement. Merleau-Ponty writes that in Cézanne's paintings, there is "the impression of an emerging order, of an object in the act of appearing, organizing itself before our eyes" (SNS, 14/20). There is a kind of dynamicism at work in the paintings. In Cézanne's resonant lines, there is no fixed edge and no static *beginning* to objects; in place of a synthesis of views (as in *perspectiva artificialis*), there is cohesion of incompossibles (as in depth). Merleau-Ponty describes Cézanne's technique:

> If one outlines the shape of an apple with a continuous line, one makes an object of the shape, whereas the contour is rather the ideal limit toward which the sides of the apple recede in depth. Not to indicate any shape would be to deprive the objects of their identity. To trace just a single outline sacrifices depth—that is, the dimension in which the thing is presented not as spread out before us but as an inexhaustible reality full of reserves. That is why Cézanne follows the swelling of the object in modulated colors and indicates *several* outlines in blue. (SNS 14–15/20)

And so Cézanne's employment of "*several* outlines in blue" does not work to circumscribe or contain space; rather, his technique offers the line as a membrane—as "the inside of the outside and the outside of the inside" (OE, 126/23). Thus, the line articulates a certain permeability or reversibility. This resounding of line seems to exert an expressive force through which the colors and forms of objects gather up—not separate out—the fullness of space. For the "inexhaustible reality" of the world is not *out there,* as if there were an absolute separation between our flesh and the flesh of the world. Like the apples on Cézanne's canvases, we, too, are bound by quivering edges or membranes. Our every gesture—our very breath—repeats the plenitude of this world. "We speak of 'inspiration,'" writes Merleau-Ponty, "and the word should be taken literally. There really is inspiration and expiration of Being" (OE, 129/31–32). Thus, the artist creates according to a certain resonance with this vital rhythm: a creative cohesion between the sensible and its other side, as a "carnal essence" (OE, 126/22). In speaking of the genesis of a work of art, Merleau-Ponty writes:

> Things have an internal equivalent in me; they arouse in me a carnal formula of their presence. Why shouldn't these correspondences in turn give rise to some tracing rendered visible again, in which the eyes of others could find an underlying motif to sustain their inspection of the world? Thus there appears a

> "visible" to the second power, a carnal essence or icon of the first. It is not a faded copy, a *trompe l'oeil*, or another *thing*. (OE, 126/22)

It is thus the performance of vision that the painter is called upon to repeat and transform into art; and it is the sensible world, in all of its tangled, complex individuation, that calls for this transformation. When Cézanne follows the curve of the fruit or the extension of the table in not one but several lines of blue, his response is not to a vision that only sets out objects before him; his response is to an intertwining of vision and visibility, such that, through his brushstrokes, as Merleau-Ponty writes, "there appears a 'visible' to the second power." His radiant blue lines serve as gestures of resonance, for precisely their reinstatement—their repetition—opens up a realm of depth: indeed, of time as well as space. We perceive this repetition as a kind of vitality or movement, as if the plate of fruit were tipping toward the edge of the table. We see something that is not there, yet precisely according to that which is there: the pigment, proportions, and texture. There is the *Ineinander* of presence and absence.

Depth of Movement and Color

What is this "motion"—this movement of the line? The repetition of the line—the "outlines in blue"—cannot effect an actual, physical dislocation within space or time, not even if it were to inspire a movement of the eye within the gaze of the viewer. Such movement would be purely mimetic, like that of an eye that follows a sequence of lights appearing to "move" along a screen. This mimetic movement is not the type of movement made present through Cézanne. For, as Merleau-Ponty says, the work of art is not *there* in the same way that the canvas is there. And so the work of art elicits a particular kind of movement—a resounding movement—a depth of movement. Here, it is not a matter of mimesis but always a question of the cohesion of the visible and invisible. The "mutual confrontation of incompossibles" (that is to say, of the seen and unseen or the present and past) gives rise to *motion*—in time as in space (OE, 145/79). In an important passage from "Eye and Mind," Merleau-Ponty writes:

> Movement is given, says Rodin, by an image in which the arms, the legs, the trunk, and the head are each taken at a different instant, an image which therefore portrays the body in an

> attitude which it never at any instant really held and which imposes fictive linkages between the parts, as if this mutual confrontation of incompossibles could—and alone could—cause transition and duration to arise in bronze and on canvas. The only successful instantaneous glimpses of movement are those which approach this paradoxical arrangement—when, for example, a walking man or woman is taken at the moment when both feet are touching the ground; for then we almost have the temporal ubiquity of the body which brings it about that the person *bestrides* space. The picture makes movement visible by its internal discordance. Each member's position, precisely by virtue of its incompatibility with that of the others (according to the body's logic), is dated differently or is not "in time" with the others; and since all of them remain visibly within the unity of one body, it is the body which comes to bestride duration. (OE, 145/78–79)

The *body* (in a sculpture, the work of art itself) bestrides space and time because it serves as that through which the "fictive linkages"—the "incompossibles"—cohere. It is thus, Merleau-Ponty makes clear, that such a body appears to show movement; *movement is this very cohering of noncoincidence.* Movement is not simply *from* some position in space *to* another position in space—nor *from* one instant in time *to* another instant in time. It is not Cartesian. There is no external movement—no movement outside one thing and another. One must think this movement through the flesh: movement "by a sort of folding back, invagination" (VI, 152/197). For here, there is a *rendering visible* of movement that works not through a principle of revealing (as if absence had merely to come forth through the presence of appearance) but through a principle of resounding—through the concatenation of "internal discordance" or divergence that Merleau-Ponty cites in Rodin. This is movement as depth. Indeed, Merleau-Ponty writes, in "Eye and Mind," that painting makes "for itself a movement without displacement, a movement by vibration or radiation" (OE, 144/77)—a movement that arises not through external relation but through itself by means of the cohesion of noncoincidence. Like the resounding string of an instrument, all this is accomplished as resonance. For, as Merleau-Ponty writes, "Painting searches not for the outside of movement but for its secret ciphers, of which there are some still more subtle than those of which Rodin spoke. All flesh, and even that of the world, radiates beyond itself" (OE, 145/81).

And so just as this movement could not be considered a property of an object upon the canvas, neither is it even quite a moment in time. For it cannot be frozen or captured as a singular image; this depth-movement is indeed lost, according to Merleau-Ponty, within a photograph. Merleau-Ponty relates, "Rodin said profoundly, 'It is the artist who is truthful, while the photograph lies; for, in reality, time never stops.' The photograph keeps open the instants which the onrush of time closes up forthwith; it destroys the overtaking, the overlapping, the 'metamorphosis' [Rodin] of time" (OE, 145/80). This overtaking, overlapping, and metamorphosis—that which Merleau-Ponty also describes as a "coiling up or redoubling" (VI, 114/150) of noncoincidence—is precisely what painting shows as movement. And so when we speak of a kind of radiance—resonance—that arises through the cohesion of incompossibles, we must understand that there are many ways, beyond Rodin's formula, for art to effect this transformation. Indeed, for as eloquently as Rodin speaks of movement in sculpture, Cézanne the painter turns to investigate what could not be of concern to a sculptor in marble and bronze: Cézanne turns to color.[4] For the challenge posed by depth and movement is "equally," Merleau-Ponty claims, "the problem of color" (OE, 141/67). Writes Merleau-Ponty, "This inner animation, this radiation of the visible, is what the painter seeks beneath the words *depth, space,* and *color*" (OE, 142/71). Yet again, as with the sense of movement or "inner animation," Cézanne's work upon the canvas never simply poses a problem of mimetic color; painting interrogates color as depth. Merleau-Ponty writes, "Thus the question is not of colors, 'simulacra of the colors of nature.' The question, rather, concerns the dimension of color, that dimension which creates—from itself to itself—identities, differences, a texture, a materiality, a something" (OE, 141/67). That is to say, what Cézanne pursues is a style—a carnal essence—of color, not color merely as a property of an

4. Thus, Merleau-Ponty writes, "Cézanne already knew what cubism would restate: that the external form, the envelope, is secondary and derived, that it is not what makes a thing to take form, that that shell of space must be shattered—the fruit bowl must be broken. But then what should be painted instead? Cubes, spheres, and cones—as he said once? Pure forms having the solidity of what could be defined by an internal law of construction, forms which taken together, as traces or cross-sections of the thing, let it appear between them like a face in the reeds? This would be to put Being's solidity on one side and its variety on the other. Cézanne had already made an experiment of this kind in his middle period. He went directly to the solid, to space—and came to find that inside this space—this box or container too large for them—the things began to move, color against color; they began to modulate in the instability. Thus we must seek space and its content *together*. The problem becomes generalized; it is no longer solely that of distance, line, and form; it is also, and equally, the problem of color" (OE, 140–41/65–67).

object. For in this sense, an object does not *contain* color; it radiates color as a resonance—shimmering through "identities, differences, a texture, a materiality, a something." Color, precisely like movement, coheres in this way without subordination to a concept, for its sense depends precisely upon that ever-open dimension of divergence—that which we perceive within the realm of the sensible. Also as in movement, it arises not *from* somewhere or something *to* somewhere or something, but "from itself to itself": it is not a representation but an upsurge of expression through the fold of the flesh.

In a curious way, then, operating not according to a positive being but as a cohesion of incompossibles, color serves as an emblem of what Merleau-Ponty describes as the "universality of the sensible" (VI, 218/268)—a universality that would be not removed from the particularity of the world but would arise in relation to it, through a transformative dimension as depth. Merleau-Ponty writes:

> Now this particularity of the color, of the yellow, and this universality are not a *contradiction*, are *together* sensoriality itself: it is by the same virtue that the color, the yellow, at the same time gives itself as a *certain* being and as a *dimension*, the expression *of every possible being*—What is proper to the sensible (as to language) is to be representative of the whole, not by a sign-signification relation, or by the immanence of the parts in one another and in the whole, but because each part is *torn up* from the whole, comes with its roots, encroaches upon the whole, transgresses the frontiers of the others. It is thus that the parts overlap (transparency), that the present does not stop at the limits of the visible (behind my back). (VI, 218/267)

There is "overlap" and there is the unseen ("behind my back") precisely because there is depth. There is not "contradiction" but cohesion; there is a dimension of the *Ineinander* of particularity and universality. In this sense, the particularity and universality of color, according to Merleau-Ponty, "can present us with things, forests, storms—in short the world" (OE, 133/43). And so we must not think of color—just as we must not think of the line—as a thing; it arises as a radiance of things. In *The Visible and the Invisible*, Merleau-Ponty writes:

> A naked color, and in general a visible, is not a chunk of absolutely hard, indivisible being, offered all naked to a vision which could be only total or null, but is rather a sort of straits between

> exterior horizons and interior horizons ever gaping open, something that comes to touch lightly and makes diverse regions of the colored or visible world resound at the distances, a certain differentiation, an ephemeral modulation of this world—less a color or a thing, therefore, than a difference between things and colors, a momentary crystallization of colored being or of visibility. Between the alleged colors and visibles, we would find anew the tissue that lines them, sustains them, nourishes them, and which for its part is not a thing, but a possibility, a latency, and a *flesh* of things. (VI, 132–33/173)

Color, like movement and depth, effects a "momentary crystallization" through the cohesion of differentiation or divergence. It awakens a transformative view of the world; it "comes to touch lightly and makes diverse regions of the colored or visible world resound at the distances." What arises, then, through the lines, colors, and depths of a canvas is something that would not belong solely to the canvas as a material object (for it is "a possibility, a latency, and a *flesh* of things"). What arises is a style of expression: a work of art.

Artistic Style and Expression

Certainly, Cézanne's late paintings bear this out, and particularly those of Montagne Sainte-Victoire. It is estimated that Cézanne painted more than twenty-five canvases (oils and watercolors) on the theme of Mont. Sainte-Victoire, most between 1902 and 1906. Taken together, however, the canvases do not form a series that might systematically explore a single subject within different parameters of daylight and season (like that of Monet's paintings of the Rouen Cathedral). Such an approach, self-aware and carefully controlled, does not suggest the spirit of Cézanne's paintings. Rather, one has the sense that these paintings emerge from a compulsion on the part of the painter—a certain demand of the "carnal essence" of the landscape to which only Cézanne could respond. The painter's vision is permeated by the mountain. "It is the mountain itself which from out there makes itself seen by the painter," writes Merleau-Ponty (OE, 128/28). There is an intertwining of world and expression. Cézanne's vertical hatches of color—ochre, green, and rich violet—perform an interrogation of the landscape through which a style of space forms itself. There are no "objects" placed "within" spatial boundaries of the near and the far or the extensive and expansive; these landscapes, as we can observe particularly with respect to those canvases that appear to have been left unfinished by the painter, come together all at once. There is *crystallization* of the trees, the plains, the houses, and the mountain. The paintings resound, composing their own harmony of color.

Merleau-Ponty writes:

> Motivating all the movements from which a picture gradually emerges there can be only one thing: the landscape in its totality and in its absolute fullness, precisely what Cézanne called a "motif." . . . [A]ll the partial views one catches sight of must be welded together; all that the eye's versatility disperses must be reunited; one must, as Gasquet put it, "join the wandering hands of nature." "A minute of the world is going by which must be painted in its full reality." His meditation would suddenly be consummated: "I have my *motif*," Cézanne would say, and he would explain that the landscape had to be centered neither too high nor too low, caught alive in a net which would let nothing escape. Then he began to paint all parts of the painting at the same time, using patches of color to surround his original charcoal sketch of the geological skeleton. The picture took on fullness and density; it grew in structure and balance; it came to maturity all at once. (SNS, 17/22–23)

Like the movement of a musical melody that expresses a unity—something more than simply the arrangement of sounds in sequence—this *motif* offers a depth that holds together the divergent colors of the landscape. What Cézanne sees in the *motif,* therefore, is not the illustration of some particular view or another—what he sees is that through which it all coheres. For Cézanne in these later paintings, it is not the actual, physical limestone but the ungraspable, looming presence of Mont. Sainte-Victoire—a sense of the gravity of the mountain that far exceeds its visible quality—that orients the whole of the landscape. One could compare, for example, Cézanne's configuration of the mountain *motif* to Renoir's treatment in *Montagne Sainte-Victoire* (c. 1888–89). Despite its essential role in the title of the painting, the mountain for Renoir bears an almost insignificant presence in the landscape, dwarfed by the blues of the broad and open sky that harmonize with the blues of the olive trees in the foreground. While, for Cézanne, the mountain similarly presides over the canvas in deep blues and purples, yet the way that Cézanne employs the mountain as a *motif*—the way that his depth of blue discloses a depth that is not visual but ontological—is extraordinary: that blue somehow does not make the mountain retreat into the background. Despite its distance, the mountain exerts a kind of gravitational pull over the landscape. For Cézanne, Sainte-Victoire wields a presence beyond that which merely appears—it serves as a *motif* around which ranges not only the elements of the canvas but (one could say) also an eloquent question on the nature of painting itself. For in work after work, is it not the *same* mountain that asserts itself upon the canvas? Yet, for Cézanne, it must never have been the same; for Cézanne, the mountain called for a reiteration—a renewed vision. It never could be exhausted by its representations; there could be no beginning or ending to this *motif*. Merleau-Ponty writes, "The 'world's instant' that Cézanne wanted to paint, an instant long since passed away, is still hurled toward us by his paintings. His *Mont. Sainte-Victoire* is made and remade from one end of the world to the other in a way different from but no less energetic than in the hard rock above Aix" (OE, 130/35). The presence of the mountain—a force of cohesion "different from" that visible, "hard rock above Aix"—could not be endured by the painter except by a repeated summoning.

Between such making and the remaking emerges the expressive sense. "Art is not imitation," writes Merleau-Ponty, "nor is it something manufactured according to the wishes of instinct or good taste. It is a process of expressing" (SNS, 17/23). It is the engagement of this process—not the production of a completed canvas per se—that Mont. Sainte-Victoire demands of Cézanne.[5] "What we call his work was, for him, only an essay, an approach to painting": a movement of expression (SNS, 9/13). It is for this reason that Cézanne paints the mountain again and again, piling canvas upon canvas with harmonies of blue and ochre. What we now call his work—the material production of paintings—was not, for Cézanne, an end; rather, each individual work formed as a moment of crystallization within a more total encounter of the sensible realm. The value of this work, therefore, is not to be determined according to any single canvas, or even according to the sum of several canvases. Rather, there is a depth to

5. Merleau-Ponty writes: "[There is] motivation that comes simultaneously from colors, light, substance, movement, a call from all of that to the movement of the hand which resolves the problem while being unaware of it just as when we walk or gesture" (IP, 47/86). This movement of the hand is not *from* somewhere *to* somewhere else; there is no beginning or ending to this motivation. Such a call can never be exhausted—no more than can the sensible world itself be empty or barren. For artistic expression is a response, as Merleau-Ponty writes, to "the vibration of appearances which is the cradle of things" (SNS, 18/23).

his work through all canvases, as an orientation to painting—a resonance, an artistic movement, or a style. Thus, the expression of a painter is not contained within some material object; his work, rather, coheres through (but in some way beyond) these canvases, as a style identifiable only in retrospect. For, Merleau-Ponty writes:

> How do we know what we are making in painting? We do not work by chance. And yet, the entire field of *the* art of painting, and, for each painter, the field of *his* painting, is not truly given. History is retrospective, metamorphoses, and in this sense painters do not know what they are making. (IP, 41/78)

That is to say, the painter, not unlike the performing artist who is subject to the unfolding of time, cannot convey the essence of his style *until he paints*. The expression is not formulated in advance, only to spring forth, Athena-like, upon the canvas. "The meaning of what the artist is going to say *does not exist* anywhere—not in things, which as yet have no meaning, nor in the artist himself, in his unformulated life" (SNS, 19/25). The meaning is an absence. Only in *retrospect* does it appear that the painter, at each moment, made the one, singular choice necessary for the creation of a particular canvas.

In a lengthy but important passage from "Indirect Language and the Voices of Silence," Merleau-Ponty writes about a film that was made of the painter, Matisse, at work. The film was recorded in slow motion, and Merleau-Ponty relates that thanks to the augmentation of the overall temporal pace:

> That same brush which, seen with the naked eye, leaped from one act to another, was seen to meditate in a solemn and expanding time—in the imminence of a world's creation—to try ten possible movements, dance in front of the canvas, brush it lightly several times, and crash down finally like a lightning stroke upon the one line necessary. (S, 45/73)[6]

The film seemed to reveal an almost divine power of foresight on the part of the artist, since at each brushstroke Matisse, faced with an infinite number of choices, selected "the one line necessary" to the formation of the final painting that would emerge. Yet, according to Merleau-Ponty, "there is something

6. The editions cited here are, respectively, trans. Richard C. McCleary (Evanston: Northwestern University Press, 1964); Paris: Gallimard, 1960; 2003 reprint.

artificial in this analysis" (S, 45/73). Such an analysis does not attend to the experience of the painter in the moment of his creative engagement; rather, the analysis is dependent upon subsequent knowledge—knowledge of the end or completion of the work. That is to say, only in retrospect—only in relation to the final painting anticipated by the viewers of the film (including Matisse himself)—does it seem that Matisse exercised a kind of divine artistic foresight. But it was not in advance of the expressive process itself that Matisse battled an infinite set of possibilities in an attempt to secure the final work; nor did he experience his process of artistic choice at the expanded pace conveyed by slow motion. "He did not have in his mind's eye all the gestures possible, and in making his choice he did not have to eliminate all but one" (S, 45/73). The slow motion of the film effected a retrospective analysis that belies the emergent and embodied process of painting. And so Merleau-Ponty concludes:

> Matisse, set within a man's time and vision, looked at the still open whole of his work in progress and brought his brush toward the line which called for it in order that the painting might finally be that which it was in the process of becoming. By a simple gesture he resolved the problem which in retrospect seemed to imply an infinite number of data. (S, 45–46/74)

Similarly, in "Cézanne's Doubt," Merleau-Ponty writes, "Each brushstroke must satisfy an infinite number of conditions. Cézanne sometimes pondered hours at a time before putting down a certain stroke, for, as Bernard said, each stroke must 'contain the air, the light, the object, the composition, the character, the outline, and the style.' Expressing what *exists* is an endless task" (SNS, 15/21). Expressing what exists is endless and difficult, for each stroke of the brush will not only articulate certain technical parameters (color, texture, form)—each stroke of the brush will alter the composition as a whole. Painting does not proceed linearly from conception to execution, as merely a matter of filling in certain outlines with various shades of pigment. The work of art is never determined in advance.[7]

---

7. In the labor of artistic expression, as Merleau-Ponty tells us, "'Conception' cannot precede 'execution.' There is nothing but a vague fever before the act of artistic expression, and only the work itself, completed and understood, is proof that there was *something* rather than *nothing* to be said. Because he returns to the source of silent and solitary experience on which culture and the exchange of ideas have been built in order to know it, the artist launches his work just as a man once launched the first word" (SNS, 19/24–25).

On the contrary, it is only thanks to the "execution" that one could look back and begin to designate anything like a "conception," as confirmation that, through the "vague fever" of the artistic process, "there was *something* rather than *nothing* to be said" (SNS, 19/24–25). The work of art makes present the fact that there was going to have been a generative absence—a *something*—all along.

Painting is a temporal art, in which there is cohesion of incompossibles. In this sense, what we might call the *beginning* of expression—that "there was *something*"—comes to be known through the *end*. Each brushstroke that appears to the viewer in retrospect as a singular choice leading to the logical conclusion of a work, indicates in fact, for the artist, an ever-open process of initiation, since the end of the work was not, at the moment of the brushstroke, yet determined. Yet just as, thanks to the depth of space, the *unseen* side of things is constitutive, the (unseen) *end* (in time) of a painting is not merely hidden from the artist, waiting to be discovered; it clings to the other side of the *beginning*, for it is implicated in the creative recentering and surpassing of each reinitiation. The end and beginning are *Ineinander*; the present and the absent flow into one another. Time, for the painter, is a membrane, and the work of art has always to be performed. Merleau-Ponty writes:

> Each partial act reverberates upon the whole, provokes a deviation which is to be compensated by others. Rather than choice, it is necessary to say *labor*. The choices are the trace of this labor of "germination" (Cézanne) (along with nature, along with other pictures). Each choice remakes painting by inheriting it. Each work re-creates the entire work of a painter by inheriting it if it is truly a work. (IP, 47/86)

Thus, this movement of artistic labor, for both the painter and the history of painting, operates according to a kind of "subterranean logic," not according to a logic that would proceed linearly (in the traditional sense) from one decision to the next decision. This "subterranean," deep logic creates a sense "as open sense, which develops by means of proliferation, by curves, decentering and recentering, zigzag, ambiguous passage, with a sort of identity between the whole and parts, the beginning and end. A sort of existential eternity by means of self-interpretation" (IP, 48–49/87). The labor of expression unfolds according to a temporal dimension of depth—a cohesion of incompossibles. There is not absolute identity of beginning and end—not absolute coincidence—but, as Merleau-Ponty states carefully, "a sort of identity . . . a sort of existential eternity." Artistic expression is the movement through which the noncoincident hesitations, approaches, and experiments cohere as a meaning that exceeds what is merely present. It is a resonance—a radiance–through the membrane of time.

4

Echoes of Brushstrokes

Marta Nijhuis

A painting makes its charm dwell from the start in a dreaming eternity.

—Maurice Merleau-Ponty

As I was asked to write a paper about Merleau-Ponty's aesthetics and my own art, I felt I was facing a most difficult challenge.[1] To me there is nothing as hard as talking about my art. An Italian historian of art once asked me to talk to him about the way I paint. "You are not obliged to answer"—he said—"for I know that to ask a painter about how he or she paints is like asking someone how he or she makes love." Indeed, he knew painters well. I never answered his question; I had no words to answer such a question, for the reason why I paint is that I have no words to say what I am nevertheless urged to express. Everything is just there: in the colors, in the lines, in the texture of the brushstroke, or, more appropriately, *between* them, in the gaps of invisibility that they secretly disclose. I have often experienced the

1. When reading this essay, you may find that the language I used is a bit too literary for a scientific work. However, by writing this way, not only did I consider the point of view I was asked to assume when I was invited to write—i.e., the point of view of a painter rather than that of a philosopher—but I also made a specific philosophical choice, which keeps me nonetheless within the philosophical field. Indeed, to use metaphors in philosophy is to let images penetrate the field of theoretics, that is to say, to take our senses with us. I consider this indispensable, especially in an essay on Merleau-Ponty. "Merleau-Ponty leans towards a philosophical language which shall consciously assume a metaphorical value: the metaphor *makes visible* the idea as a sensible idea" (Carbone 1990, 196).

feeling that concerns the painter Basil in Oscar Wilde's *Picture of Dorian Gray*: to have expressed so much about himself in his newborn painting that he fears someone may, by observing his painting, see *through him*.

Yet, the challenge intrigued me, for here I had the opportunity to talk about my art *in relation* with the philosophy of Merleau-Ponty, to talk about my art in the only possible way: by letting its invisible sides softly emerge in a non-self-referential context, precisely through an indirect *relationship*. My philosophical reflection and my artistic research have—until this day—run over parallel paths. As a painter, obviously I never tried to *represent* Merleau-Ponty's nor any other philosopher's thought in colors. It would have been useless. Not only because representation is no longer possible in an epoch in which the Platonistic concept of Model has lost its value,[2] but also because Merleau-Ponty's thought, and his theory of painting in particular, already constitutes a wonderful artwork itself, the colors being the vivid and sparkling invisible of its words. Therefore, my attempt here is not to provide a representation of Merleau-Ponty's thought through my art, nor to move backward such a thought as the inspiring motif of my painting, but rather to make his thought and my artistic experience talk together. For it is precisely within a dialogue that my painting and my philosophical research always found a mutual nourishment. I am a painter who has chosen to study philosophy. This is not very unusual, as any artist needs to establish a dialogue with different fields of human expression. Some find their interlocutor, for instance, in music, or in literature, or in photography, and some—like me—in philosophy, perhaps because philosophy holds a dialogue in its turn with each of these subjects.

What the relationship between art and philosophy offers is not a mere transposition of thought into image, but rather the discovery of a certain "image of thought," as Gilles Deleuze would call it; that is to say, the opening of a crack from which we are enabled to see the world differently. In other words, the inauguration of a new horizon of sense filling the world with an unexpected atmosphere-color,[3] a new disposition of the eye and the mind at once. Even if art and philosophy communicate differently, even

2. On the loss of value of the concept Model and of the notion of representation, see Deleuze 1969. On the convergence between Merleau-Ponty and Deleuze concerning this topic, see Carbone 2004.

3. See Merleau-Ponty's working note about yellow becoming "a universe or an *element*" (VI, 218/ 272).

if—as Visual Culture Studies teach us, in the case of images we cannot strictly talk of a "language"[4]—such different fields can communicate with one another in virtue of that invisible background embracing all things that Merleau-Ponty calls flesh—a unitary texture in which each body and each thing only presents itself precisely through its *difference* with regard to any other body or thing (see Carbone 2002, 49). No need to undress my painting and the mystery that always accompanies painting, then; no need to reveal how it works: the secret will be secretly shown through the variably becoming *veil* that the relationships interweave or, in a word, through the multicolored *flesh* of the world. As Nietzsche wrote in the well-known "Preface to the Second Edition" of the *Gay Science*, "We no longer believe that truth remains truth when one pulls off the veil; we have lived too much to believe this" (Nietzsche 1882, 8). And "we artists" (ibid., 70) know very well that "art is a veil, rather than a mirror" (Wilde 1891, 89–90), a veil that—let me say it with the words that Merleau-Ponty refers to the visible and the invisible—denounces in the act of concealing (see S, 20/29).[5]

As an artist, I find it particularly interesting to read a comment on Merleau-Ponty's aesthetics in a letter to Alphonse de Waelhens by a most remarkable painter of the twentieth-century, René Magritte: "Merleau-Ponty's very brilliant thesis is very pleasant to read, but it hardly makes one think about painting—which he nevertheless appears to be dealing with" (Magritte 1962, 336). Still, elsewhere, when talking about his art, Magritte declares: "Visible things can be invisible. . . . However, our thought comprehends both: the visible and the invisible. And I use painting in order to make the thought become visible."[6] Indeed, it is the will to give visibility to an

4. Since the 1990s, several scholars belonging to different scientific areas—from philosophy to psychology, from history of art to anthropology—have reflected on the question of images trying to establish a new way to study this topic. They have sought a way of accounting for the specificity of images, avoiding their reduction to the terms of language. The fact of talking about a "pictorial turn" (Mitchell) or an "*ikonische Wende*" (Boehm) witnesses precisely the will to abandon the path to which the "linguistic turn"—codified by Rorty in the 1960s—had led, by inaugurating a field exclusively devoted to Visual Culture Studies. [See the following essay by Sara Northerner—eds.]

5. The editions cited here are, respectively, trans. Richard C. McCleary (Evanston: Northwestern University Press, 1964); Paris: Gallimard, 1964.

6. Magritte referred such a statement to his painting *Le blanc-seeing*. See Magritte quoted by Marcel Paquet in Paquet 1993, 45.

invisible that urges the artist to paint. "No great artist ever sees things as they really are. If he did, he would cease to be an artist," Oscar Wilde writes in *The Decay of Lying* (Wilde 1891, 97).

According to Merleau-Ponty, the painter's "eye sees the world, and what it would need to be a painting, sees what keeps a painting from being itself, sees—on the palette—the colors awaited by the painting, and sees, once it is done, the painting that answers to all these inadequacies just as it sees the paintings of others as other answers to other inadequacies" (OE, 127/25).[7] No man—we shall say, paraphrasing Wilde—ever sees things as they really are. Indeed, is there a way "things really are"? In the horizon of flesh the way things are changes continuously according to the becoming relationships that constitute each vision, each ensemble of visions and the interactions that occur between the visions themselves. Yet, the artist has the gift of expressing the invisible that constitutes his own vision, even if—of course—partially, for it shall not be forgotten that "no thing, no side of a thing, shows itself except by actively hiding the others" (S, 20/29). The artist's gift allows him to express such an invisible for others as well as for himself. Not because he expresses something *for* others to contemplate it, but—as, again, Deleuze would say—because he expresses certain things *in place of* the people who are not able to express them as effectively. Thus, the vision of the artist—always self-constituting anew through the interaction with more visions, more eyes, more thoughts—becomes somehow "universal." I place this term in quotation marks to signal a desire to reach a new sense of the term: with the precaution of inverted commas, so that their characteristic wing shape may allow this old concept, to which "we have lived too much to believe," to fly away toward new destinations of sense—like those of a "universal" becoming of all things and a "universal" difference, which, by differentiating all things, unifies them. This is "a conceptless universality" (OE, 133/43), the sense supported by the notion of flesh.

Getting back to Magritte, I partly agree with him when he says that painting is a way to make an invisible—the thought—turn into visibility—the painting. However, I have a feeling that Magritte's paintings go much farther than his words: according to his above-mentioned declaration, one may argue that any thought can become *totally* visible through its artistic expression. Still, is there anything in the world capable of being *totally*

7. The editions cited here are, respectively, "Eye and Mind," in *The Merleau-Ponty Aesthetics Reader*, ed. with an introduction by Galen A. Johnson and Michael B. Smith, translation editor (Evanston: Northwestern University Press, 1993), 121—60; and Paris: Gallimard, 1964.

visible? Indeed, if the invisible could really turn into visible without any residue, without any latent trace of invisibility, art would lose its mystery and the painter would turn into a sort of carnival magician. Yet, mystery is what painting, according to Magritte, is all about. In the letter quoted above, he writes: "The only painting worth looking at has the same *raison d'être* as the *raison d'être* of the world—mystery" (Magritte 1962, 336).

Here is the point: Magritte accuses Merleau-Ponty of trying to reveal the secret of painting, and blames him for not sticking to the *question* of painting instead (ibid.). However, by conceiving the visible itself as inseparable from the invisible, by stating that what is invisible will never completely turn into visible and that what is visible will always exceed its visibility, Merleau-Ponty preserves both the mystery of the world and the mystery of art that mattered so much to Magritte who, on the other hand, by binding the co-presence of the visible and the invisible to the field of thought only, metaphysically separates the thought from the vision, depriving the latter of its mystery.[8] If painting turns an invisible into a visible keeping a constitutive halo of invisibility, the painter's meaning can do no more. As Merleau-Ponty writes in "Indirect Language and the Voices of Silence," once the painting is finished, its significance always exceeds "the painter's intended meaning" (Merleau-Ponty 1952, 105/S, 85).[9] In my experience as a painter, the intended meaning is indeed just a mere pretext for expressing something—i.e., the vision—which was not intended at all, but happened in virtue of a contingency of encounters. The importance of such a contingency shall never be forgotten when producing a work of art. In fact, as Merleau-Ponty remarks, "personal life, expression, understanding, and history advance obliquely and not straight towards ends or concepts. What we strive for too reflectively eludes us, while values and ideas come forth abundantly to him who, in his meditative life, has learned to free their *spontaneity*" (ibid., 120/S, 104; my emphasis).

The spontaneity Merleau-Ponty talks about is precisely the creative contingency inaugurating each vision, a contingency thrown in the work

8. As I said, this can be true for what Magritte wrote on Merleau-Ponty, but surely not for what he painted, as I strongly think that his paintings wonderfully account for a nonmetaphysical perspective, perhaps due to the mysterious fact I am going to discuss in a moment, that the painter's intended meaning is often exceeded by the painting itself.

9. The references to the English version can be found in *The Merleau-Ponty Aesthetics Reader*. However, the pages referring to the French edition shall be found in *Signes*. Therefore, the abbreviation "S" refers only to the pages of the French edition.

of art by the act of painting, as well as by the encounter, through which more visions are produced, with other artworks and other gazes. Art clearly shows how necessity, far from being opposed to contingency, is propitiated by contingency. As Deleuze remarks when commenting on the work of Nietzsche, the good dice player knows that the number that matters to win the game is not that of the times the dice are thrown: the number that matters appears in just one throw when the right combination is produced. "The dice which are thrown once," Deleuze writes, "are the affirmation of *chance,* the combination which they form on falling is the affirmation of necessity. Necessity is affirmed of chance in exactly the sense that being is affirmed of becoming and unity is affirmed of multiplicity" (1962, 24). Think of Picasso's famous statement according to which he would put everything he loved in his pictures (a single throw of the dice—the affirmation of chance/contingency). It would then be up to the things to find a way to arrange themselves with one another (the falling of the dice—affirmation of necessity). As a new visible born from the invisible of other visible things and mediated by the act of painting, the work of art secretly discloses its own invisible, which surprises the painter him/herself. In fact, the painting's invisible is constituted by the relationships between the canvas and the colored shapes, between the colors themselves, between the color and the brushstroke, between the brushstroke and the artist's body, between the artist's body and its own memory. Thus, not to be eluded, the painter doesn't have to search too much: with Picasso, all he or she does is to find.[10]

I am in front of a canvas, my brush in my hand. The canvas is in front of me. As soon as I approach its immaculate surface following the invisible sketch that my vision of the world traces upon it, something unexpected happens. Depending on the quality of my first touch—strong or delicate, shy or dashing, circumspect or confident—the canvas suggests to me, in a play of activity and passivity, where to move my next step. A vision is not a preliminarily given idea patiently waiting to be transposed on the canvas. A vision is the continuously changing condition of painting, which makes it a way of expressing, but also a way of listening—to the smooth *voices of silence.*

As Merleau-Ponty observes in *Eye and Mind,* "The painter 'takes his body with him,' says Valéry. Indeed we cannot imagine how a *mind* could paint. It is by lending his body to the world that the artist changes the world into paintings. To understand these transubstantiations we must go back to the working, actual body—not the body as a chunk of space or a

10. Remember another famous Picasso statement: "I do not search: I find!"

bundle of functions but that body which is an intertwining of vision and movement" (OE, 124/16). The pressure of my hand on the canvas, its evolutions over the surface of the emerging picture, the exhaustion of my back after hours of work, the rhythm of my breathing, my eyes' perception of color, my hesitation and my inspiration converge as the invisible depths of the painting, the brushstrokes of which stand as the visible traces of my body's "*quasi* presence."[11] The painting *echoes* my body.

Yet, what is an echo? According to the Greek mythology, the nymph Echo, loved by the god Pan, was in love with a satyr who neglected her. Irate and jealous, Pan decided to punish Echo and asked the shepherds to slaughter her. Although her body was quartered, her voice remains—repeating each last word—to remind us of her grief. Echo's voice, however, is not a voice simply *remaining*, as it is not the voice she might have had when she was alive. In fact, it is a voice interweaving many voices,[12] each coming from a different direction, as if each voice felt the new dismembered condition of Echo's body, of its disseminated flesh still throbbing as flesh of the world. Only speaking when entering in relation with other sounds or voices, emerging from the silence as the trace of a "*quasi* presence," Echo's voice continuously constitutes itself anew. Hence, instead of being considered in terms of the mere *repetition* of a preliminarily given *origin*, the echo can be interpreted as the manifestation of an origin that is not relegated "behind us," but, on the contrary, never ceases *originating*: in a word, that which Merleau-Ponty calls *originaire*. "The 'originating' is not of one sole type, it is not all behind us; the restoration of the true past, of the pre-existence is not all of philosophy, the lived experience is not flat, without depth, without dimension, it is not an opaque stratum with which we would have to merge. The appeal to the originating goes in several directions: the originating breaks up" (VI, 124/165).

The painting echoes my body, I said. And it does precisely in the just mentioned "originating" way. It is not an echo intended as a repetition, then, but rather a creative movement inaugurated by the interaction of differences

11. "What Merleau-Ponty calls "Visibility," rather than being circumscribed by the ensemble of the visibles, comprehends the dimensions, the lines of force, the gaps that the visibles obliquely suggest as their invisible glow, a glow which turns out being not an absolute absence, but a '*quasi* present' absence" (Carbone 1999, 11; my translation).

12. "The subject towards which Merleau-Ponty's phenomenology leads us is . . . a collection, a *legein* of many voices" (Levin 2003, 70; my translation). "It is the voice of no one, since it is the very voice of the things, the waves and the forests" (VI, 155/204).

constituting the unitary although heterogeneous texture of flesh. In one of the working notes of *The Visible and the Invisible*, Merleau-Ponty remarks: "For me it is no longer a question of origins, nor limits, nor of a series of events going to a first cause, *but one sole explosion of Being which is forever*" (ibid., 124/165; my emphasis). To me, such is art: "one sole explosion of Being which is forever."

The painting echoes my body as well as the body of others, the glances of whose eyes will be touched by the painting's colors, so that such colors will then be born again in a new vision, for "it is in others that expression takes on its relief and really becomes signification" (Merleau-Ponty 1952, 89/S, 66). In their turn, however, their glances shall pin upon the painting, which will then see the world from a new point of view, opening up to more eyes and more encounters, for it is not just we who look at things: the world sees us in its turn in virtue of the flesh that we both are. Indeed, as Merleau-Ponty remarks, "The world is made of the very stuff of the body" (OE, 125/19).

It took me a long time to remember when it was that I first felt the eyes of the world staring at me. The more I kept thinking of it, the less I could remember. Then, like an unexpected shine that surprises the eye with its clearness, the memory came in no time at all, when I was thinking about something completely different and I had forgotten my attempts to remember. The tomb of Agamemnon was proudly standing, securely guarded by two severe stone lions unconcerned by the embarrassing clangs that my children's camera mercilessly produced with each of the inexperienced shots of my early years. Jorghos, an archeologist who accompanied us, diverted our gazes from the ancient site and invited us to look just in the opposite direction. A mountain was lying there, like a massive dead warrior, his long hair softly spread on the ground, his powerful hands joined on the large motionless breast, his straight Greek nose recklessly facing the horizon, his noble feet enveloped in the shroud. "According to the legend, Heinrich Schliemann discovered Agamemnon's tomb after looking at the peculiar shape of this mountain, which can be seen this way from this very point only." Jorghos's voice came muffled to my ears: that grand mountain *demanded* all my attention, cast on me its petrified gaze calling for my respectful look, and so did the surrounding landscape. Each tree, each shrub, each grain of sand seemed to be bathed in an aura. That is to say, each seemed to outstretch toward me and toward the mountain at once, demanding the gazes of those who were there looking, precisely in the same way one demands the gaze of another by insistently staring at him or her. I don't know what the other people who were with me thought in that moment, nor what they felt, but as for me, as fascinated as I was, I could not help believing the legend. It was actually only many years later that I fully realized the reach of the emotions and thoughts by which I was then overwhelmed. It was only when, by observing a series of drawings I had done in different moments of my life, I noticed that whenever I'd drawn a mountain it would always have the same shape—the rocky shape of the dead warrior. The recognition of that shape among its variations and the memory of that day's emotion came at once, as involuntarily as I had involuntarily kept that vision stuck in my head.

"L'homme y passe à travers des forêts de symboles / Qui l'observent avec des regards familiers," Baudelaire writes in the poem entitled "*Correspondances*" (1857, 19). In his essay concerning Baudelaire, Walter Benjamin reflects on the problem of the aura, explaining that "to experience the aura of an object we look at means to invest it with the ability to look back at us" (Benjamin 1940, 204). This kind of auratic experience, according to Benjamin, is an involuntary experience (*Erfahrung*) and is therefore strictly related to that of the Proustian involuntary memory. In this sense, Benjamin assimilates the *réminiscences* Proust accounts for in the *Recherche* to the auratic *correspondances* (see Carbone 1998, 37) that Baudelaire intended as a kind of experience trying to establish itself despite the crisis introduced by modern technology (see Benjamin 1940, 199). The most evident characteristic of involuntary memory is that it does not come forth when consciously searched, but happens to emerge in virtue of a fortunate sensible encounter with the world. And it emerges in a powerful, essential way: when involuntarily remembering, we do not remember things just as they happened: we remember them in a more essential way, which is unrepeatable precisely because, in its turn, it is not a mere repetition, but rather the never-lived essence of our past experiences.[13] As for me, this was exactly what happened: I only realized the importance of my experience when it was long since gone, forgotten by my voluntary memory. Then the experience was created again by my fortunate encounter with the series of my drawings and the memory of it came as clear and fresh as my experience itself had probably never been, suggested by the creative repetitions of the mountain shape, the differences among which referred to a unitary

13. On the creation of essences through the emergency of involuntary memory, see Mauro Carbone's *Introduction* to his book on sensible ideas (see Carbone 2004).

texture: a texture like that of flesh.[14] Within the peculiar domain of involuntary memory, within its dynamics of correspondences, activity and passivity switch and become undistinguishable. The same seems to happen with vision, and with the correspondence between what sees and what is seen. As Merleau-Ponty writes in *Eye and Mind*, "Inevitably the roles between the painter and the visible switch. That is why so many painters have said that things look at them" (129/31). Then he quotes a testimony by André Marchant, which somehow echoes Baudelaire: "As André Marchant says, after Klee, 'In a forest, I have felt many times over that it was not I who looked at the forest. Some days I felt that the trees were looking at me, were speaking to me . . . I was there listening . . . I think that the painter must be penetrated by the universe and not want to penetrate it . . . I expect to be inwardly submerged, buried. Perhaps I paint to break out' " (ibid.).

It is interesting that, like Benjamin, Merleau-Ponty also reflected on both Proust and Baudelaire.[15] Sometimes his remarks tend to converge with

14. According to Platonism, the model comes before its copies, which we call images. However, with Deleuze's reversal of Platonism, it is the deformated copies (*simulacra*) that constitute the model, a model that, therefore, far from being preliminarily given, emerges from the gap drawn by the differences *among* deformations. In other words, those of Mauro Carbone (2004, ch. 3), the model emerges from the relationships that its deformations mysteriously interweave. It is in this gap, in *this* "among," and not in the comparison between a previously given model and its deformations, that the effects of similitude are produced. Thus, the model is not a preliminary condition, but rather a *simultaneous* effect of the resonance among its deformations (see Deleuze 1969). On the *recognition* of a model emerging "among" its deformations, see Carbone 2004, ch. 3, §2 and ch. 5, n. 5. Moreover, by reinterpreting the notion of *chôra* in relation to that of "flesh," Carbone refers such a newly significated *chôra* to the Deleuzian notion of "chaosmos," which accounts precisely for the question of differences producing effects of similitude (again, see Deleuze 1969). In this way, Carbone institutes an indirect relationship between Deleuze's similitude through differences and Merleau-Ponty's *chair* as a "unitary texture of differences in continuous differentiation" (see Carbone 2008, 127–31).

15. As Mauro Carbone—whom I take here the opportunity to thank—pointed out in one of our conversations, an example of Merleau-Ponty's interest in Baudelaire's relation with Proust can be found in a working note of *The Visible and the Invisible*, where Merleau-Ponty explicitly quotes Proust ("There is an architectonic past. cf. Proust") and implicitly refers to Baudelaire ("This 'past' belongs to a mythical time, to the time before time, to the prior life [*la vie antérieure*], 'farther than India and China' ['*plus loin que l'Inde et que la Chine*']" [VI, 243/296]). "*La vie antérieure*" is the title of a poem (Baudelaire 1857, 36–37), while "*plus loin que l'Inde et la Chine*" is a line from the poem entitled "*Mœsta et Errabunda*" (Baudelaire 1857, 131).

those of Benjamin;[16] the switch of activity and passivity is one of these cases. Merleau-Ponty continues: "We speak of 'inspiration' and the word should be taken literally. There really is inspiration and expiration of Being, respiration in Being, action and passion so slightly discernible that it becomes impossible to distinguish between who sees and who is seen. Who paints and what is painted. We say that a human being is born the moment when something that was only virtually visible within the mother's body becomes at once visible for us and for itself. *The painter's vision is an ongoing birth*" (OE, 129/31–32).[17] Such an "ongoing birth" reminds me precisely of that "one sole explosion of Being which is forever." If one looks deeper, "One reason why the painter takes up his brush is that in a sense the art of painting still remains to be created. . . . Painting as a whole presents itself as an abortive effort to say something which still remains to be said" (Merleau-Ponty 1952, 116/S, 99). Each time we try to communicate something through painting, we end up expressing something unexpected, and our intention changes continuously. But then again, remember what Picasso once said: If one already knows what he is going to do, where is the point in doing it?

Merleau-Ponty wrote about painting assuming the fascinated eyes of a painter. But he used words that no painter would ever have found. The colors of his intuitions continue to explode in the indefinite shape of a newborn life, breaking out in thoughts that never cease to surprise us. More than a hundred years ago Maurice Merleau-Ponty started being born.

References

Baudelaire, Charles. 1857. *Les fleurs du mal.* Paris: Poulet-Malassis et de Broise.

Benjamin, Walter. 2006 [1940]. "On Some Motifs in Baudelaire." In *The Writer of the Modern Life: Essays on Charles Baudelaire*, translated by Howard Eiland et al., 170–210. Cambridge: Harvard University Press.

Carbone, Mauro. 1990. *Ai confini dell'esprimibile*, Milan: Guerini.

———. 1998. *Di alcuni motivi in Marcel Proust.* Milan: Edizioni Libreria Cortina.

———. 1999. "Presentazione." In Merleau-Ponty, *Il visibile e l'invisibile*, translated by Andrea Bonomi and Mauro Carbone. Milan: Bompiani.

16. On convergencies and divergencies between Merleau-Ponty and Benjamin on Proust, see Carbone 1998, 23–41.

17. This description of a "respiration in Being" related to the act of painting, a description culminating with the metaphor of birth, beautifully accounts for the reason why, in the beginning of my essay, I agreed with the historian of art who once told me that, for an artist, painting is a way to make love.

———. 2002. "Flesh: Towards the History of a Misunderstanding." In *Chiasmi International N. 4, Figures and Grounds of the Flesh*, 49–64. Milan-Paris-Memphis: Mimesis-Vrin-Memphis University.

———. 2008. *Sullo schermo dell'estetica. La pittura, il cinema e la filosofia da fare.* Milan: Mimesis.

———. 2010. *An Unprecedented Deformation: Marcel Proust and the Sensible Ideas.* Translated by Niall Keane. Albany: State University of New York Press.

———, and David Michael Levin. 2003. *La carne e la voce.* Milan: Mimesis.

Deleuze, Gilles. 2006 [1962]. *Nietzsche and Philosophy.* Translated by Hugh Tomlinson. London and New York: Continuum Press.

———. 1990. "The Simulacrum and Ancient Philosophy." In *The Logic of Sense*, edited by Constantin Boundas, translated by Mark Lester with Charles Stivale, 253–79. New York: Columbia University Press. The first section of this essay was originally entitled "Renverser le platonisme" and published in *Revue de Métaphysyque et de Morale* 71, no. 4 (Oct.-Dec. 1966). Subsequently, it has been revised and included, under the title "Plato and the Simulacrum," in "The Simulacrum and Ancient Philosophy," which is the first appendix to *The Logic of Sense.*

Johnson, Galen A., ed. 1993. *The Merleau-Ponty Aesthetics Reader. Philosophy and Painting.* Translation Editor Michael B. Smith. Evanston: Northwestern University Press.

Levin, David Michael. 2003. "Verso l'origine etica della voce." In Carbone and Levin, *La carne e la voce*, 67–115. Milan: Mimesis.

Magritte, Réné. 1962. "Letter to Alphonse de Waelhens." In *The Merleau-Ponty Aesthetics Reader. Philosophy and Painting*, edited by Galen A. Johnson and Michael B. Smith, Translation Editor, 336. Evanston: Northwestern University Press.

Merleau-Ponty, Maurice. 1952. "Indirect Language and the Voices of Silence." In *The Merleau-Ponty Aesthetics Reader. Philosophy and Painting*, edited by Galen A. Johnson and Michael B. Smith, Translation Editor, 76–120. Evanston: Northwestern University Press.

Nietzsche, Friedrich. 2001 [1882]. *The Gay Science.* Edited by Bernard Williams. Translated by Josefine Nauckhoff. Cambridge: Cambridge University Press.

Paquet, Marcel. 1993. *Réné Magritte 1898–1967. La pensée visible*, Paris: Benedikt Taschen Verlag.

Wilde, Oscar. 2007. *The Complete Works of Oscar Wilde.* Edited by Josephine M. Guy. Oxford and New York: Oxford University Press.

5

From Edmund Husserl's *Image Consciousness* to Maurice Merleau-Ponty's *Flesh* and *Chiasm*

The Phenomenological Essence of Image

Sara J. Northerner

In the current range of postmodern art discourse, attention to the complexity of the perceptual experience of contemporary works of art remains absent. Earlier aesthetic theories that privilege the art object as perceived are insufficient when applied to the explosion of genres and elaborate installation environments produced today. The validation of contemporary art often resides in the complex statement or theoretical momentum of the artwork rather than the creative impact, aesthetic intent, or unique visual qualities an image holds. With postmodernism, the cultural result of the artwork became more important than the approach of the artist or the impression of the viewer. Current artworks often rely on difference, plurality, and paradox where the artist is less concerned with what one sees *in* the art object than with the relationships into which one enters in reaction to it as a cultural object. To this end, artists neglect the truth or essence found in the numerous layers of visual interaction or perceptual experience possible within any contemporary genre of art.

As an artist searching for an alternative to postmodern art theory, I have come to realize that through phenomenology I can clarify the entire visual field of awarenesses required to work successfully in multiple genres of contemporary art. An application of the "lived body" as a definitive aspect of perceptual/artistic/aesthetic experience can function as an artistic and critical approach to a wide range of new media, including installation. I utilize phenomenology as a philosophical foundation to confront the photographic image or artwork as a focus of perceptual experience given through its mediating body. The role of embodied viewer in translating the intangible moment found in an aesthetic perceptual encounter cannot be denied. Unlike other applications of theory, which often function as external viewing devices for artworks, through phenomenology the embodied viewer is communally intertwined with the artwork to determine his or her perceptual experience. Since the spectacle has become a norm for most postmodern visual experiences and the simulated visual world as presented represents what reality has become, a basis for truth can only be found in examining one's directed perception of their immediate environment. The placement of perceptual consciousness within the viewer's mind/body provides for an acceptance of an art installation as a controlled world through the use of provisional bracketing and the projection or co-intention of possible meanings as co-constituted on a horizon pre-delineated by the artist.

This paper presents the philosophical concepts of Edmund Husserl on phenomenology and image consciousness and explores the phenomenological project of Maurice Merleau-Ponty as rendered throughout an installation of creative visual artwork. By building upon Husserl's theories on the phenomenological constitution of an object and his specific work with image consciousness, the diverse structures of a contemporary image consciousness are realized photographically in the artwork. His sketches, collected works, and lectures provide a foundation of knowledge beyond traditional and contemporary photographic theory. Furthermore, Merleau-Ponty's writings on phenomenology, perception, embodiment, and the visible/invisible have strengthened the creation of diverse structures of meaning in the images as seen throughout an installation. His ideas of body schema, flesh, and chiasm are directly incorporated into the physical reality and aesthetic experience of my work. As artist, I disclose the possibilities of Husserl's image consciousness as perceived through Merleau-Ponty's concept of the embodied viewer in intimate communion with the world.

Traditionally accepted as an objective record of reality, photographic portraits within society are usually measurements of our existence in the world. The creative work associated with this project consists of a series of eleven images, most of which are larger than life-sized portraits. These images, while photographically captured and digitally produced, do not result in what are considered conventional photographs. Ranging from twenty-eight to forty-two inches in width to eighty-four inches in length, the large, mixed-media prints are suspended throughout an installation space so as to physically confront the viewer. Additionally, the method of their production, surface treatments, and multilayered technique of integration, makes each image a unique entity. These technical aspects additionally allow a degree of translucency and image depth to be manipulated within the work through a changing quantity and variable quality of light. The increased scale of the pieces, physical characteristics, and amount of movement required for the viewing an image and the entire installation comprehensively places emphasis on the phenomenological theories as embedded within or illuminated by the artwork. Whether it is one image or the entire body of work, all must be considered as part of a predetermined horizon or world that can only be constituted by the embodied viewer as his or her consciousness and world are synthesized or intertwined.

Of all visual works, photographic images, or perceptual re-presentations, are considered the most complex as examples of image consciousness in regard to their phenomenological constitution. In the *Collected Works, Volume XI*, entitled *Phantasy, Image Consciousness and Memory*, Edmund Husserl's sketches and collected writings and lectures on image consciousness provide multiple examples of his thought on a variety of visual images, including specific and numerous references to photographic images. A substantial number of the writings on image consciousness resulted from Husserl's work on intuitional and conceptual presentations where he examined how "high-

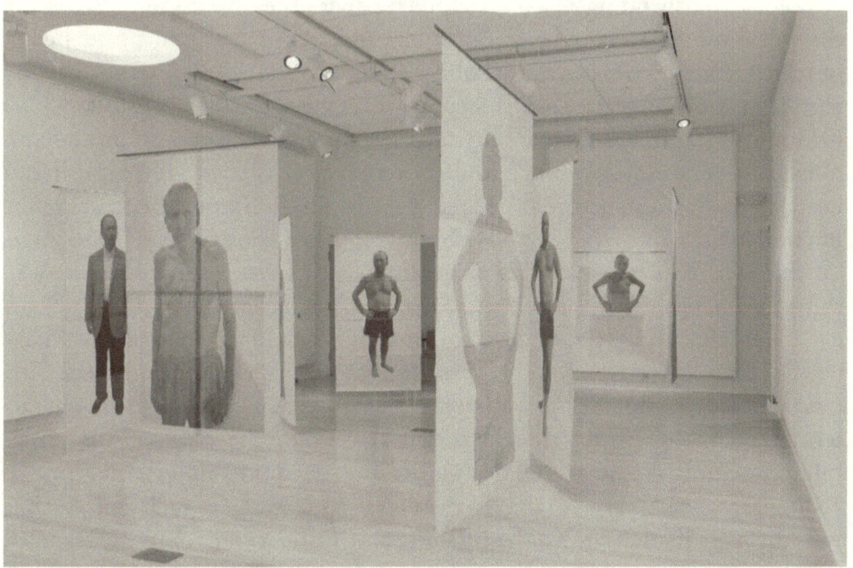

Figure 1. Installation View, East.

er-level, conceptual acts and categorical acts of intending . . . are founded in the sensuous, intuitive acts of perception and their modifications" (Bernet 1993, 141–42). One of the key features in this analysis was Husserl's interest in how picturing apprehension, in regard to phantasy, memory, and expectation, differs from the perception of an evidentially given object. He connected this same conceptual presentation with image consciousness, but also distinguished the act when picturing apprehension is concerned with "ordinary picture-consciousness which requires mediation of something appearing perceptually in the present" such as a photograph (ibid., 144). By investigating image apprehension and image presentation as qualities of both types of sensuous, intuitive acts, Husserl sets the foundation for his three levels of perception required for image consciousness. In a photograph, he established that image consciousness had a complex relationship involving three separate types of apprehensions: perceptual, sensing, and constituting. Additionally, it was the tension between each of these apprehensions that made image consciousness phenomenologically distinctive.

To break down the formal structure of image consciousness, Husserl divides the description of the experience into three levels. The first would be the physical foundation or object of our perception. As a physical entity, it is constituted as a thing itself. Normally, a photograph exists as a glossy, thin stratum of phenomena that maintains a minimal physicality as layers of polyester suspending ink on a support paper. The object grounds itself in the world by the rectangular proportions and a certain amount of depth or weight. However, as a perceptual object, the reason for being extends beyond that of a mere object. Our perceptual apprehension of a photograph, as held in our hands, phenomenologically becomes a horizon with an unfixed, nonspatial yet linear, temporal mode of experience. We cannot escape, in our need to develop a structure of meaning for its physical existence, placing the physical object into the cultural context of what constitutes a *photograph*. To this fact, Husserl states, "as printed paper . . . we say that the *image* in this sense hangs askew, is torn, and so forth" (Husserl 2005, 118).

For Husserl, the next level of intuition would be that of the image object. The object or physical foundation presents the image object. The image object is significant because it "bears a new apprehension-characteristic because it is fused in a certain way with the original" or physical foundation (Husserl 2005, 31). As the depicting object, he tries to distinguish "the image as the *image object* appearing in such and such a way through its determinate coloration and form" (ibid., 20). To be more specific: the colors, shapes, lines, or shaded forms that give the illusion of having depth or perspective generate the image object. By only exhibiting or making the next level intuitable, we perceive or sense the image object without acknowledging its moments or parts. It cannot constitute itself as actual and is therefore dependent on the image subject. As Husserl states, "We look *into* the image object, we look at that *by means of which* it is an image object" in order to arrive at the next level of image subject (ibid., 33).

The constitution of the image subject involves an inactual perception of the image subject or represented thing in that, where the image object directly appears, the image subject is "meant" or sensed by the viewer. The presentation of image object gives rise to the re-presentation of the image subject bringing forth a consciousness of *presentiation* of a subject not actually present. Phenomenologically, we have a doubling of apprehension in seeing the image object in the physical image and seeing the image object in the depicted "state of affairs" or image subject. A new object relation or new apprehension that "points beyond its primary object" is created in the re-presentation of the image subject as grounded upon what it resembles (Husserl 2005, 27).

The constitution of a photograph of a person or body-object requires that consciousness reflect upon these three conflicting levels of perception. The three conflicting levels of perception—physical foundation of the image, image object, and image subject–work together to make image consciousness possible. The multiple perceptions cannot exist separately but fuse, in reflection, to become its own horizon of multiple intertwined apprehensions within one image subject. A tension between both physical image and image object sets itself against a second tension between image object and image subject. Within the strata of mental processes that constitute the re-presentational image, these tensions reinforce the belief that one is experiencing an image and not reality. This is due to the fact that, unlike ordinary perceptual intending, Husserl's re-presentational consciousness can apprehend what presently exists, yet, not as evidentially given.

As the structure of image consciousness transitions from a straightforward perception of an object to a re-presentation of an image, as an artist, I am able to intensify a certain degree of ambiguity at the points where the image is not inherently a traditional photograph. For example, the viewer can sense or feel as well as perceive the physical image "which yields the appearing image, the appearing re-presenting image object but with the constitution of this appearance, however, the relation to the image subject has not yet become constituted" (Husserl 2005, 24). In the intending of a photograph, the viewer sees and feels the paper substrate as object and perceives the visual elements as presented in the image as separate apprehensions prior to completing the perception of the image subject. The apprehension of the image subject is not the reality as given within the first two apprehensions. As for the image subject, Husserl states: "The perceptual appearance depicts a nonperceived object" (ibid., 27). He finds within image apprehension, another apprehension or a new act of meaning based on a perceived sensation. This is the "characteristic of re-presentation by means of resemblance, the characteristic of seeing-in an image" (ibid., 28). The image presents itself in itself while pointing to something external through itself. The viewer completes the perception of a photograph of an individual by apprehending the subject of the image as a human being or person.

My objective is to exaggerate the tension essential to Husserl's interpenetration of these three levels of perception that are found in image consciousness. Certain characteristics of each artwork were created to challenge the overlapping of the multiple dual apprehensions necessary for image consciousness. In developing each artwork, I began in the same manner as

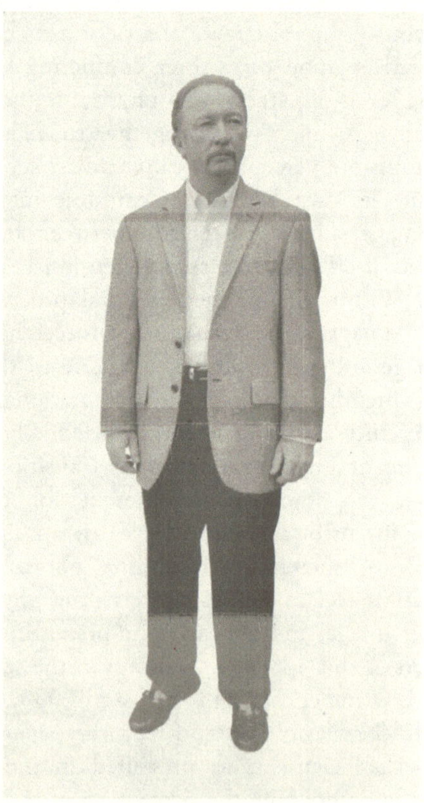

Figure 2. Richard, Full Image.

Husserl's unbuilding of the structure of image consciousness, at the level of physical object. While each piece is unique, the physical foundation of each, or that which is given perceptually through direct observation, does not exhibit the same attributes as a traditional photograph. The work intentionally presents a dichotomy in regard to classification as a tangible object where there is an added physicality in some respects and a diminished material substratum based on other perspectives. The increased size of the images, averaging three and one-half feet in width to more than six feet in length, must be considered initially. By creating the work on a dimension comparatively similar to or, in some manner, overwhelming to the viewer, the physical object constituted is not co-intended as a traditional, hand-held photograph. In every artwork, my attention to the overlaps or layering and segmenting of the pieces of substrate to generate such size reinforces the physicality of the paper as object. The hand-sewn stitches, as essential in the formation of size and in regard to their presence as part of the physical object, are integral to manipulating the viewer's direct observation. These small details demand a fluctuation of perception, similar to the Gestalt concept of the figure/ground, between the individual stitch or knot and overall piece. In the same manner, the surface treatment of each work strengthens the physicality of the paper substrate while providing unique opportunities for directed observation of drips or thickening of the veneer.

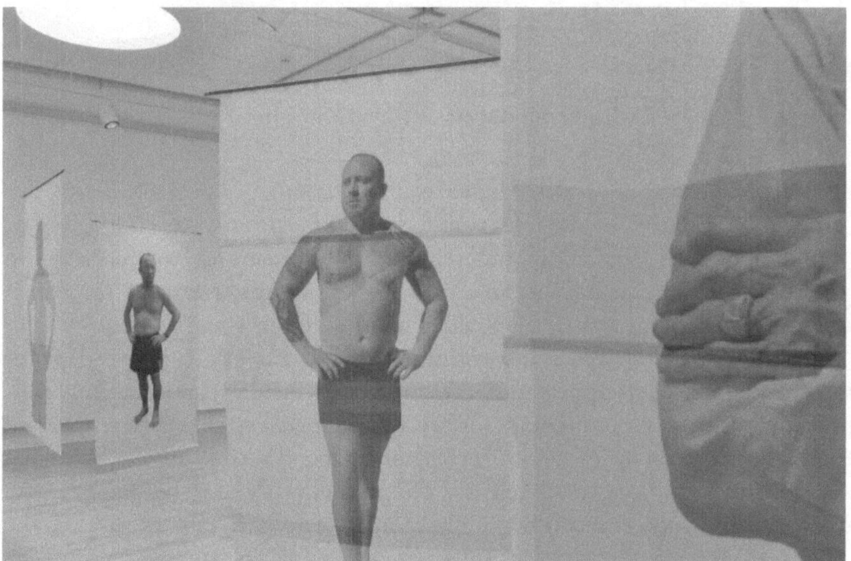

Figure 3. Installation View, West, Robert W. Reverse.

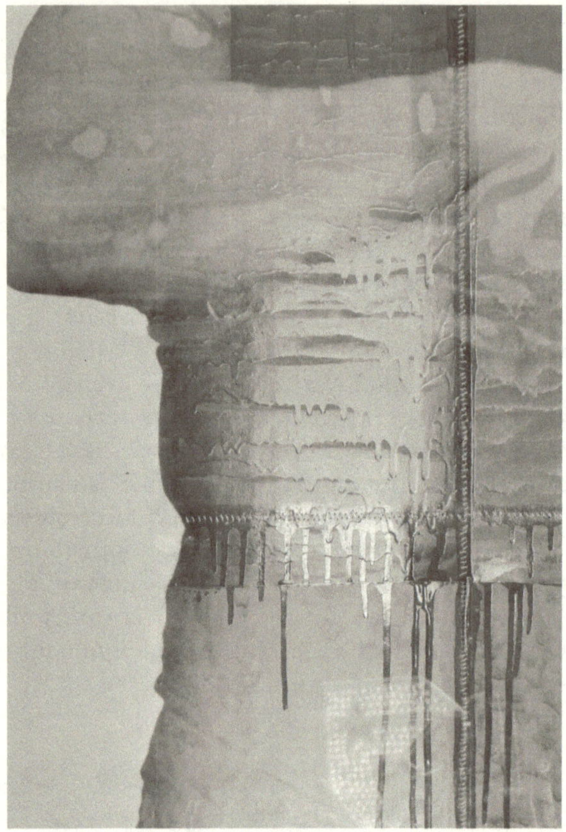

Figure 4. Robert W., Detail of Drips.

It is crucial to realize, however, these same physical elements also provide a disparity in the observable strata of existence of the object or foundation when viewed in different lighting situations. My decision to create pieces that are translucent allows for a constant change in the physical properties of the work depending on the amount and quality of light available. For the viewer, the constitution of the artwork as object depends on the manner of its appearance. Several factors such as paper choice, layering methods, or amounts and surface treatments, are all selectively varied throughout the body of work. The quantity and direction of the light that illuminates each work can determine the perceptibility of the different materials. Additionally, the contrast and color of the light source can alter the ability to discern the physical substrate altogether in some situations. By exhibiting different tangible qualities depending on the main light source or combinations of light sources available, each artwork maintains a unique physical existence from many viewpoints. Because of the translucency of pieces, multiple images of the same individual, when exhibited together, directly display the "seeing in" or "seeing through" of an image toward the subject to which it refers (Husserl 2005, 188). In other words, the image object or physical image displays the image subject throughout all of the work, yet neither has a distinct content. The same properties can generate two different apprehensions intertwined to create an understanding of the image subject. Together, the intertwining of different apprehensions is directed toward something outside of its content, to wit, the depicted individual. A comparison of more than one image brings forth, immanently, another doubling apprehension available only through the constitution of each image subject, as generated by image consciousness, originally experienced separately.

The importance of perceptual intentionality and image consciousness, as defined by Edmund Husserl, sets the foundation of my project but does not explain the complexity and depth of my application of phenomenology. Further research into the role of the body, pertaining to both viewer and within the images, as well as research into phenomenological perception, has

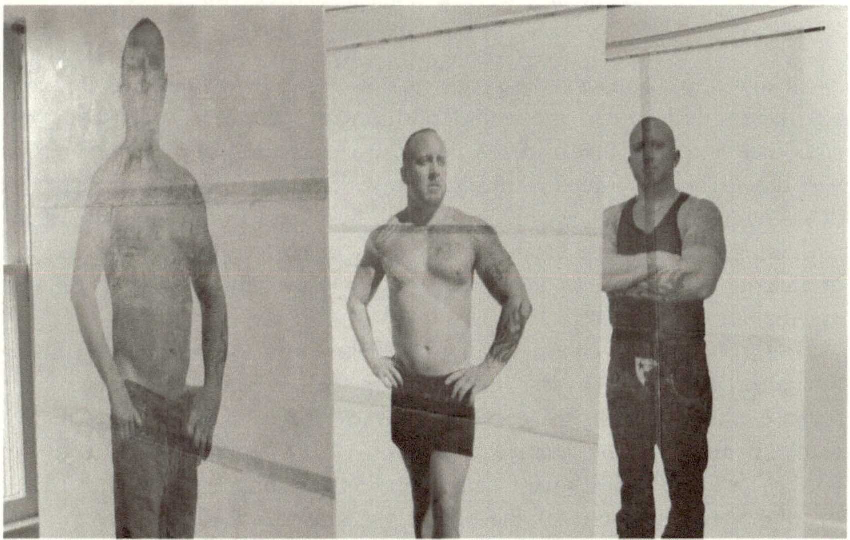

Figure 5. Three Print Comparison, Robert W.

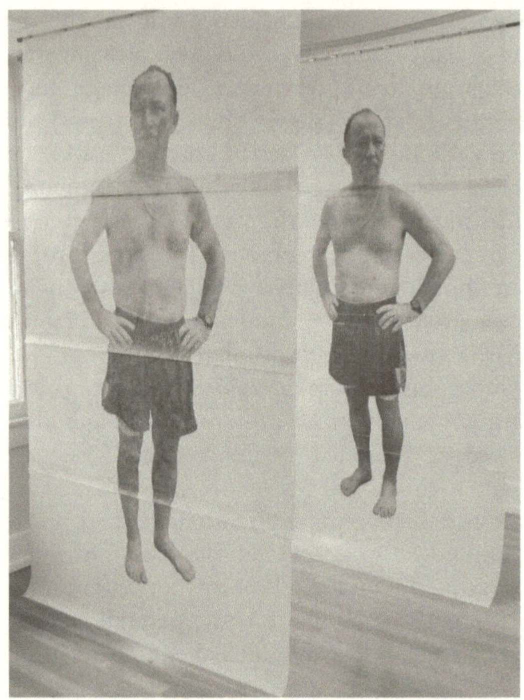

Figure 6. Two Print Comparison, Richard.

had a significant impact on the construction of meaning presented throughout the exhibition. The theoretical position of Maurice Merleau-Ponty on embodied intentionality and the perceptual unfolding of all experience as part of our bodily embeddedness in the world must also be considered. A direct connection between his ideas of a "lived" perception and the essential connectedness with what one perceives in the world exists in relation to viewing each image in this body of work, especially when they are seen together in an installation.

Throughout all of his writing, Merleau-Ponty puts forth the fundamental premise that it is the "body" that perceives. The significance of this statement defines a starting point in my own artistic vision and creative work. As an artist, my creative interaction with the world begins with the body. Merleau-Ponty asserts, "I regard my body, which is my point of view upon the world, as one of the objects in that world" (Prim. Percp., 70). The two-sided aspect of perceiving, that we maintain both subjective and objective views, also allows for our evidential experience of the world to be self-directed and self-aware. With this, perception is both intentional and bodily. But in reflection on such experience, Merleau-Ponty retains the awareness that, "In so far as it sees or touches the world, my body can therefore be neither seen nor touched. What prevents it ever being an object, ever being 'completely constituted' is that it is that by which there are objects" (ibid., 92). Thus, in contrast to Husserl's fundamental idea that intentionality is an awareness of our consciousness as based in thought, Merleau-Ponty's concept of perception stems from the body at a pre-predicative level of awareness. We are oriented in our world via the body and perceive as a mode of existence or being in the world. There is an "ordinary intuitive understanding we have of ourselves as embodied perceivers," which serves as a starting point for his phenomenological method (Carman 2008, 94).

In regarding a work of art, for example, as an object of direct experience, my immediate judgment of the object is dependent on perception as stemming from my body's one-sided point of view. I am aware of the space inhabited by my body in contrast to the existence of the artwork. The act of perception can cross the divide or threshold of depth between my body and the object/artwork. An inseparable active and passive perception allows for my embodied constitution of the object/artwork as part of the world and myself as part of that same world through movement over time. As I reflect on my understanding of the image as given to me, this reflection includes my multiple awarenesses of my body and the world. The predelineated horizon that Husserl establishes as the spatial and temporal synthesis of all of our mental processes of experience, Merleau-Ponty redefines as continuously constituted through a synthesis or moving flow stemming from our bodily nature of perception.

As Merleau-Ponty states, reflection "watch[es] the forms of transcendence fly up like sparks from a fire; it slackens the intentional threads which attach us to the world and thus brings them to our notice" (PhP, xiii). He embeds reflection as part of a lived experience of the world. Our lived horizon fuses how we are essentially interwoven with the world we perceive, and each feature of the perceptual field is interwoven with others throughout space and time. In other words, as I interact or move in the world over time, I accept a unified yet constantly restructured, embodied perception that both automatically and thematically constitutes the world and the objects/subjects within that world. For Merleau-Ponty, a "lived-through" world encompasses a transcendental field that can never be fully disclosed because it exists prior to the phenomenal field or any possible reduction (ibid., 60). Whereas Husserl speaks of a transcendental reduction in which my reflective position allows me to understand my role in the constitution of objects, Merleau-Ponty puts forth that this concept "is included in and transcended by" itself within all reflection (ibid., 213). I reflectively constitute the world as part of the phenomenal field in which I exist. Furthermore, all bodily movement or lived experience takes place within the "domain of the phenomenal" because it connects the "intentional threads" that intertwine our body and the world (ibid., 106).

Because of the range of materials and physical applications throughout the project, I approached the creation of each artwork with Merleau-Ponty's notion of a unified structuring of perception. As Merleau-Ponty placed emphasis on the concept that "perception is essentially interwoven with the world we perceive, and each feature of the perceptual field is interwoven with others," the essential interconnectedness stems from the body's sensory relation with the world (Carman 2008, 46). Within this idea, the intertwining of sensing and sensible is not isolated but creates a framework in which the body is already oriented in the world. For Merleau-Ponty, this structuring or bridge between the body and the world as perceived grounds his notion of body schema. The body schema serves as the position from which and against which the world is perceived in flux and over time/space. The body schema provides "the crux or reference point that establishes a

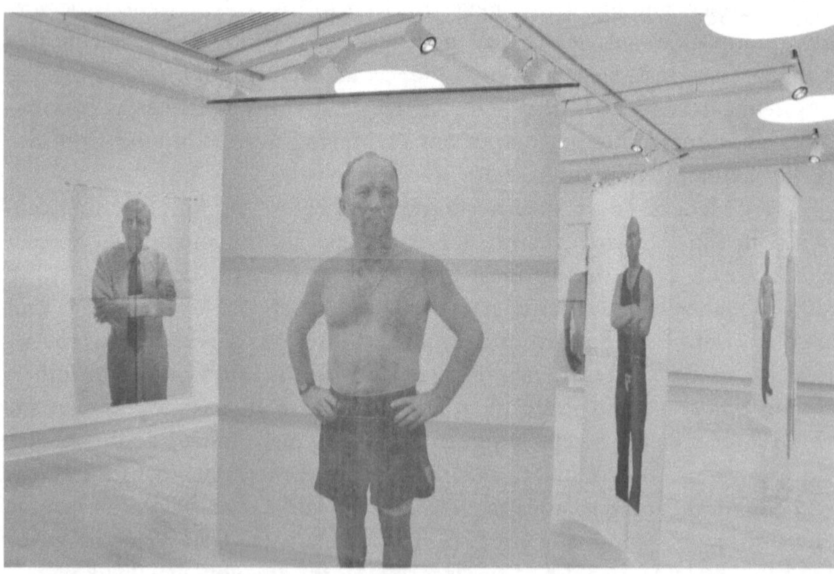

Figure 7. Installation View, West, Richard W. Reverse.

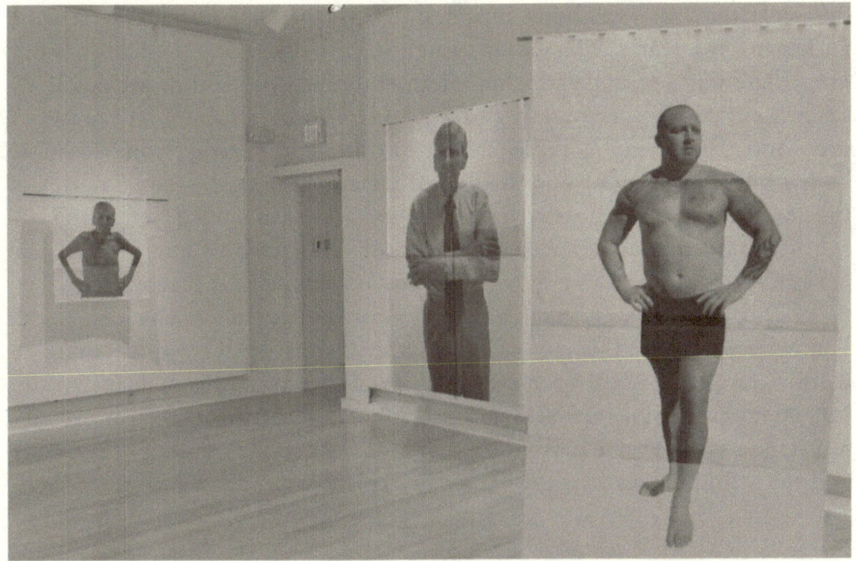

Figure 8. Installation View, Comparison, Robert W.

stable background against which I perceive and respond to changes and movements in my environment, at thereby opens me onto a world of other selves" (Carman 1998, 220). This concept is crucial to how the viewer relates to the images as placed throughout the installation and moves in regard to image subjects within the exhibition environment.

Throughout the *Phenomenology of Perception*, it has been argued in different writings by Shaun Gallagher, there are mixed references and mistranslations of the specific term for body schema. Merleau-Ponty's use of the term *schema corporel,* translated by Colin Smith as both body image and body schema, needs specific definition depending upon the relation to consciousness. Most sources claim that body image can only be identifiable when the body is mentally represented. For the purposes of this project, I recognize the implicit image when "the body makes its appearance as an appearance only, as an intentional object, as the body image" (Gallagher 1995, 231). This descriptive analysis places the role of the body as image in Husserl's model of intentionality. With body image, "the body can be described in its noematic appearance" only and does not constitute the body as a body for an embodied subject (ibid., 231). When Merleau-Ponty utilizes body image he references only the body as an object of awareness or concrete particular (Carman 2008, 106). This is vitally important when differentiating between body image and body schema since body schema anticipates the world prior to an awareness or perception. It establishes our immediate sense or understanding of an embodied perception because body schema structures our awareness of the body as both a subject and object in the world. Furthermore, our awareness of other bodies stems from this same bodily understanding of ourselves. As the viewer interacts with or moves in the installation (of images) over time they accept a unified yet constantly restructured, embodied perception that both automatically and thematically constitutes the world and the art objects/subjects within that world.

Our knowledge unfolds along the horizon as we perceive the world. For Merleau-Ponty, this unfolding or opening up to the world comes to us through perception or sense experience. As we move through the world, judgments of sensible qualities emerge from an observing and thinking subject. Understanding the perception that inheres with the crossing of the body and the world allows Merleau-Ponty to explain what he means by a "flesh"

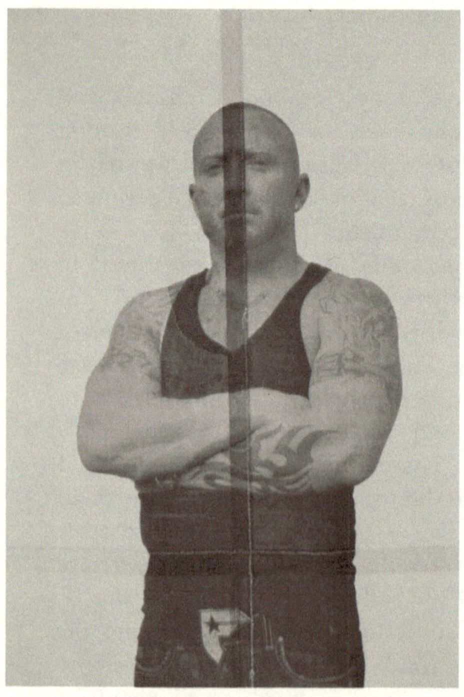

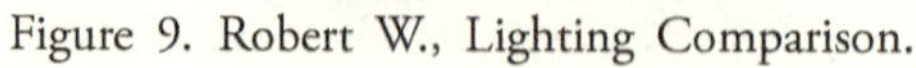

Figure 9. Robert W., Lighting Comparison.

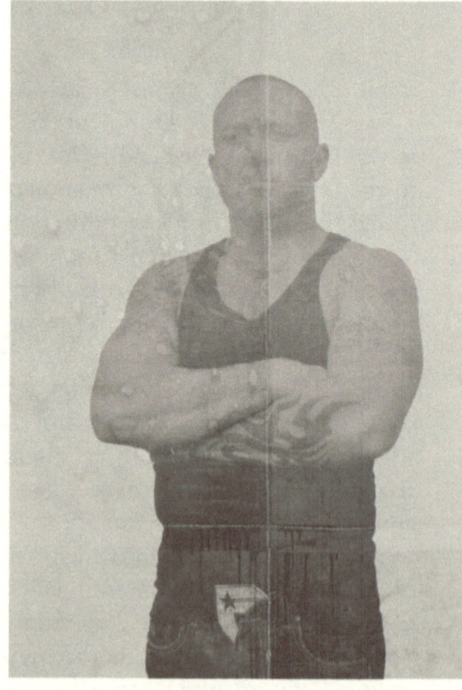

Figure 10. Robert W., Lighting Comparison.

of existence (VI, 127). Perception intertwines with all that is sensed and each object perceived is interwoven with all other aspects of the perceptual field. The place of body schema or *hinge* enables the overlap or intertwining of existence. This weaving together or fabric of existence has significance because of our place within it. We must be both subject and object of our own perception, a seer and the seen. Additionally, we are an embodied viewer embracing this perceptual field, at both visible and invisible levels. As Merleau-Ponty tells us, "He who sees cannot possess the visible unless he is possessed by it, unless he *is of it* (flesh)" (VI, 135). This interwoven tissue is not an object or thing but a "flesh of things" that maintains and cultivates all aspects of the phenomenal field (ibid., 133). The modulation of visibility springs from a mutual relation of the embodied viewer and the world but does not belong to either. Merleau-Ponty believes this modulation to be the "means of communication" connecting the seer and the seen, even if the object of perception is the body itself or a "sensible for itself" (ibid., 135). It creates a texture to the fabric of the visible. Thus, the perceiver is not the origin of flesh but finds himself/herself/itself immersed within the connective flesh of existence.

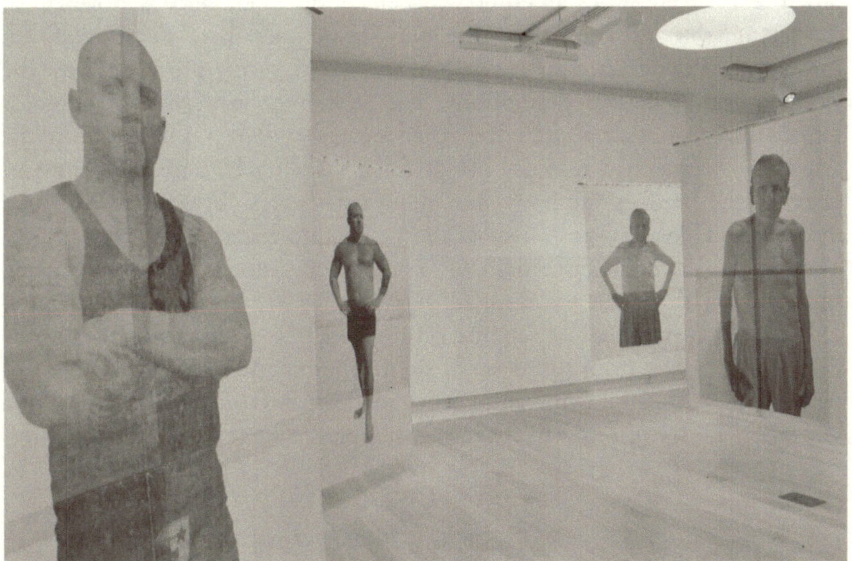

Figure 11. Installation View, South, Robert W. Reverse.

My application of Merleau-Ponty's concepts within this creative work has numerous manifestations. His writings have influenced the manner in which I understand and integrate the role of the body throughout my artwork and in an installation environment. The embodied self as the point of orientation on the world is crucial whether considered in regard to the artist themselves and the creation of the work or how another individual perceives a work of art. In a Husserlian phenomenological reduction, the point of view comes from outside of the object and world. A distancing exists for the purpose of objectivity as in art when the viewer takes an aesthetic critical perspective on something. However, the reflective awareness that transpires in Merleau-Ponty's embodied experience of an object occurs in intimate communion with the world. A dialogue of flesh where all forms of perception intertwine is already established.

In Merleau-Ponty's three major essays on visual art, "Cézanne's Doubt," "Indirect Language and the Voices of Silence," and *Eye and Mind*, painting and the nature of representation provide him with the means to clarify his phenomenology of perception with respect to the body, mind and world. Of these three, the last work, *Eye and Mind*, is most significant in explaining how "the meaning of our experience comes from our bodily and perceptual confrontation with the world, from within it" (Gilmore 2005, 296). Recognizing these qualities in Cézanne's paintings, Merleau-Ponty discusses how the artist embraces an embodied perception to enhance the overlap of the seeing/seen and the visible/invisible. He believes that artists give form, through direct contact with the flesh of the world, to the process of how the world opens up to our perceptions. The phenomenon of visibility unfolds for the artist so that a prereflective awareness can be realized within the artwork. Ultimately, the artist brings forth visuality because the center or place of the "eye" is the body, and the artist creates "by lending his body to the world" (Valéry) to transpose the world into the artwork" (OE, 162).[1] The idea of the connective flesh of existence does not separate the sensing subject from that which is sensed.

For the visual artist, an interaction with the world primarily occurs through or results from the sense of sight. The texture of the world perceptually makes itself known to the artist so that they can seize the multiple sensible qualities in order to make them apparent in an artwork. The inter-

1. "Eye and Mind," trans. Carleton Dallery, in *The Primacy of Perception and Other Essays*, ed. James M. Edie (Evanston: Northwestern University Press, 1964), 159–90, at 162.

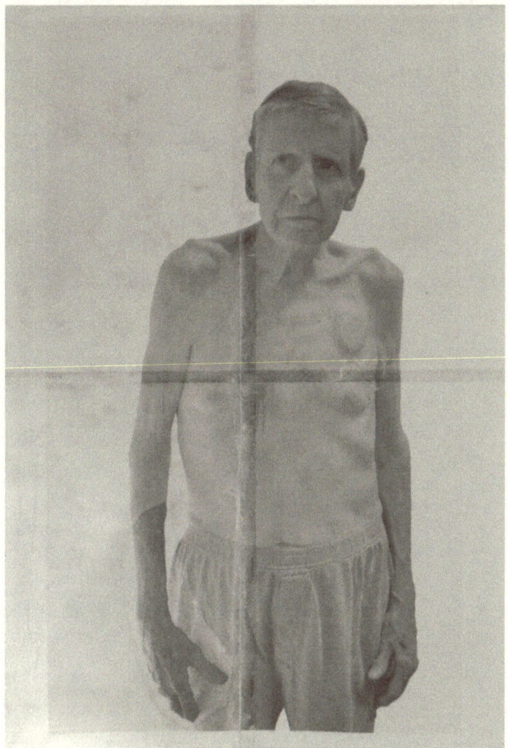

Figure 12. Robert N., Full Image.

twining of visibility creates a chiasm that exists both in the work and as a result of the work. To enhance and strengthen an awareness of the visible or sensed between an embodied viewer and the object of which they are aware or to augment the possibility of perceiving something of which they were never aware previously has been my goal. Artworks inherently generate a space of perceptual exchange where the viewer looks for significance beyond the art object as exclusively given. With my pieces, I challenge the viewer's perceptual relation to the image on multiple levels. The artwork, as expressive object, does not function in the same manner as other objects in the world because it articulates a network of visibility that structures our perception of it and the world. As primarily photographic in nature, the artwork mirrors yet questions the line of visuality that exists between reality and the image.

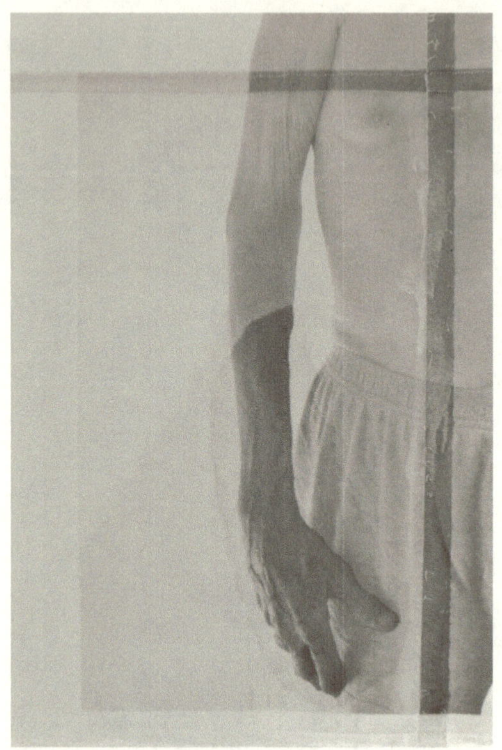

Figure 13. Robert N., Detail of Quadrant.

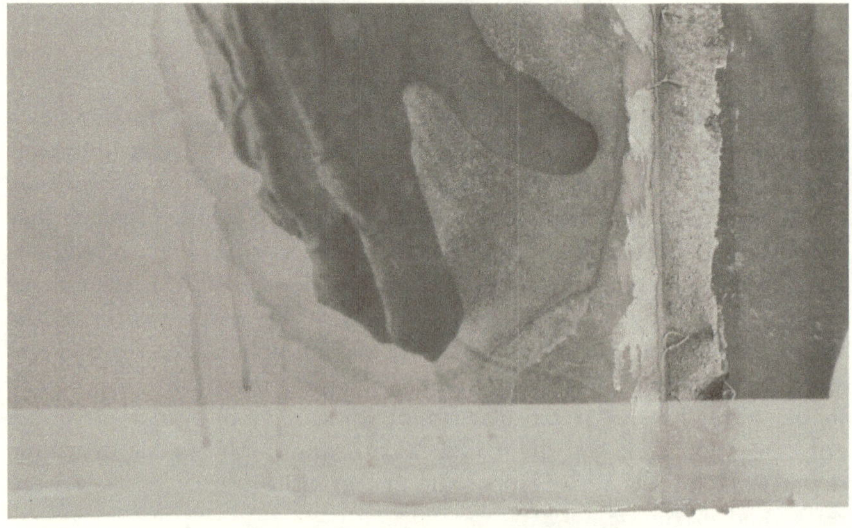

Figure 14. Robert N., Detail Overlay, Drips.

For the photographic image, a network of visibility is the structure of Husserl's image consciousness. As explained earlier, the physical foundation, image object, and image subject each establish the construction of meaning on which the image is constituted. A threshold of the visible/invisible exists within the intertwining of intuitions necessary for image consciousness. The overlapping of the multiple dual apprehensions essential to image consciousness is Merleau-Ponty's "undividedness of the sensing and the sensed" (OE, 163). By increasing the tension that resides between the layers of the physical foundation, image object, and image subject in my artwork, I call attention to the field of difference in which visibility fluctuates.

Again, Merleau-Ponty places this intertwining of visibility or chiasm within the body. As a "strange system of exchanges" between flesh or my body and the world, "vision must somehow take place in them; their manifest visibility must be repeated in the body by a secret visibility" (OE, 164). In other words, as we experience the artwork "a tracing which arises out of the concatenation of things and my body" allows us to see beyond the thing itself (Silverman 1982, 372). This secret visibility or tracing establishes the culmination of image consciousness or seeing through the image itself to that person or object to which the image refers. Merleau-Ponty explains, "it is more accurate to say that I see according to it, or with it, than that I *see* it" (OE, 164). His concern is that visuality emanates from the perspective of the body and encompasses more than merely the visible. The "quality, light, color, depth, which are there before us, are there only because they awaken an echo in our body and because the body welcomes them" (ibid., 164). For the embodied viewer, the apprehension of each level of image consciousness toward a re-presentation of image is through the unity of body image, body schema, and world. In each piece, I have intentionally accentuated the connection and contrast between the tangible sensory (texture of different surface treatments, stitching, paper choices, overlapping/layering of images) and the intangible sensory (lighting as changing appearance, visual relationships between images) to enhance the "system of exchanges" (ibid., 164).

The tangible sensory qualities of the work were created to directly make evident Merleau-Ponty's concepts of flesh and chiasm. He places the identity of perception and perceptibility within flesh because it is the shared tissue between our consciousness and the world. His choice of this term, as an interwoven fabric of the visual, obviously unites the surface of the body with the sensed/sensible relation to the world. As part of the physical foundation, I have endeavored to simulate, in different ways, flesh on the surface of each piece. A skin-like substance has resulted in multiple forms by varying and building the layering of the surface treatments applied to each image. For all the work, the flesh or skin of the piece holds the image

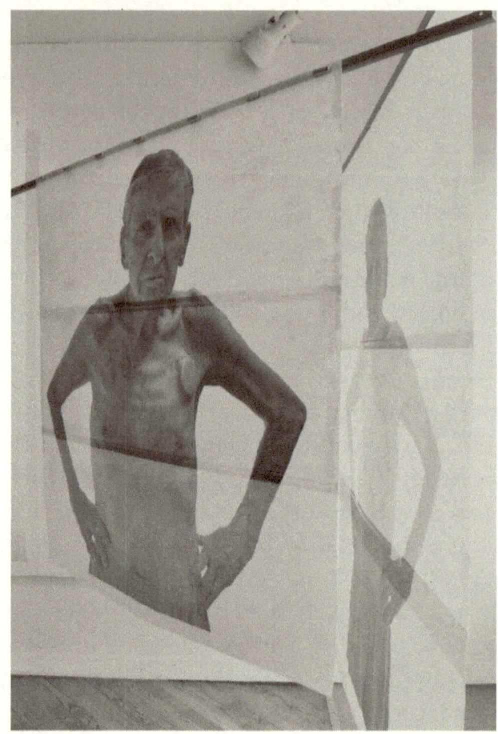

Figure 15. Installation View, Window Comparison.

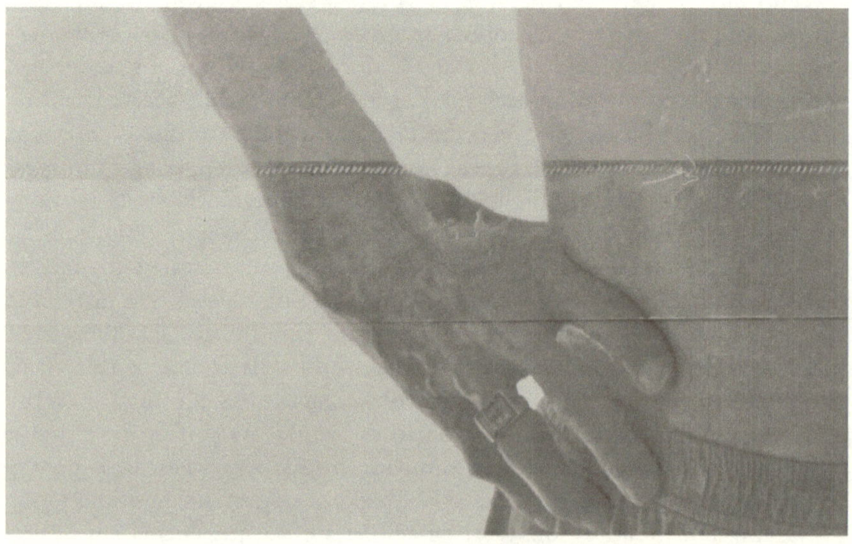

Figure 16. Robert N., Detail of Surface Treatment.

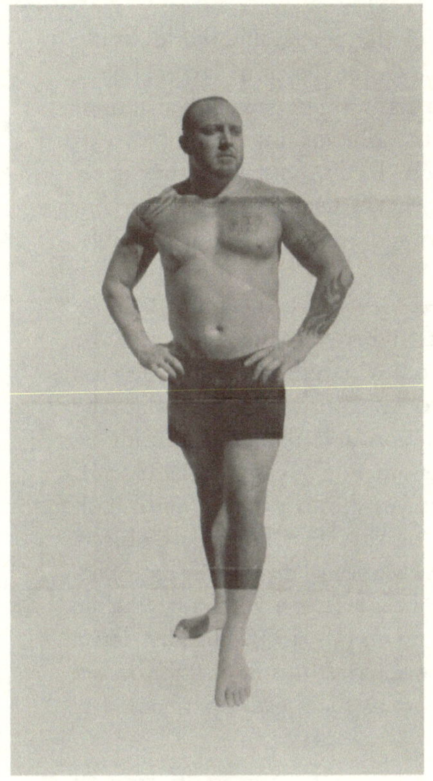

Figure 17. Robert W., Full Image.

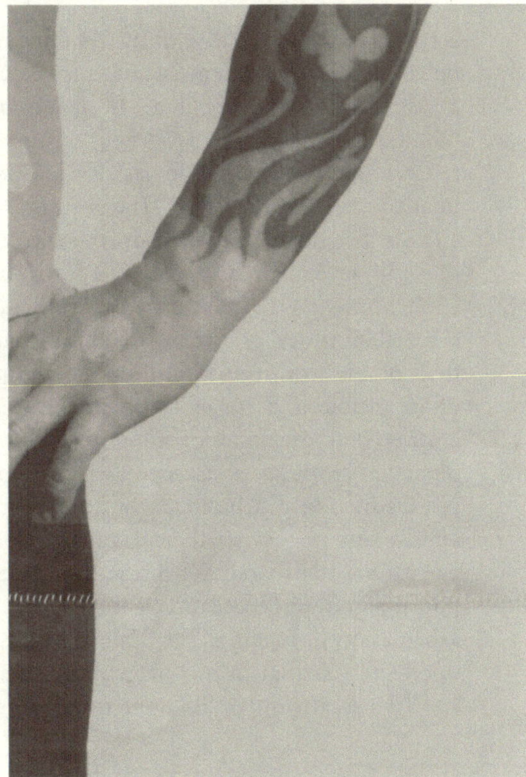

Figure 18. Robert W., Detail of Layers.

within it to replicate the manner that our flesh is seen/senses as the surface of our own bodies. While only distinguishable in certain sites or in specific instances, the layering together of multiple prints to create one image reflects the "thickness of flesh" or invisible connective fabric of existence (VI, 135).

The body as connective tissue or, with the prints, paper as connective tissue is fused by the skin or surface treatments and joined with the world through a binding thread. In hand sewing together the sections of the image, I reference the action or motility of the body as the hinge, which weaves together the fabric of existence and establishes our place within it. The binding thread or chiasm literally interlocks the body and world. The tactile sense breaks the structuralization of vision by negotiating with the sensing and becoming of it, as sensible. As chiasm, the threads unite the differences in the sensible/sensed to construct a divergence or crossing over of perception.

While a clear relationship to the binding of flesh in the technique of stitches can be made with regard to the sewing together of the image, a stronger reference to wound or opening of the perceivable world would be the bubbles or inconsistencies that occur within the print layers. Like a chiasm of flesh that separates from inside of itself, often gaps or separations within the images are produced through the adhering together of two or more prints. These unique vesicles can be seen in different works but never in any pattern or regularity. The perceptibility of the inconsistencies, overlaps, and surface details depends on the direction and amount of light available.

In several of his texts, Merleau-Ponty uses light as a metaphor and a phenomenon in relation to an embodied viewer. He develops light as a sensible entity or thread of communication between the body and the flesh of the world into light having an embodied nature of its own because of its visible and invisible qualities. In another contrast of meanings, he "insists that the light of conscious illumination and reflection cannot be separated from its experience as a lived phenomenon" (Vasseleu 1998, 33). No distinction can be made in how light weaves through the fabric of flesh amidst our phenomenal field and variables of light that illuminate objects or create a transparency from within objects. Merleau-Ponty gives light corporeal significance because it intertwines or becomes one with our sensible articulation in making "the flesh of things" known (VI, 133). His idea draws upon the fact that in our perceptual experience, constitution of light occurs at all levels. In order for light to become part of the sense experience that

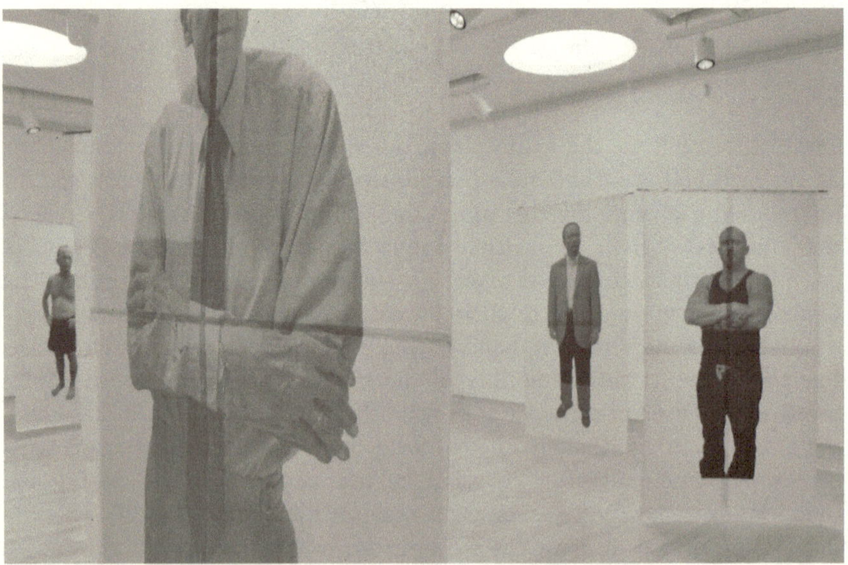

Figure 19. Installation View, South, Robert N. Reverse.

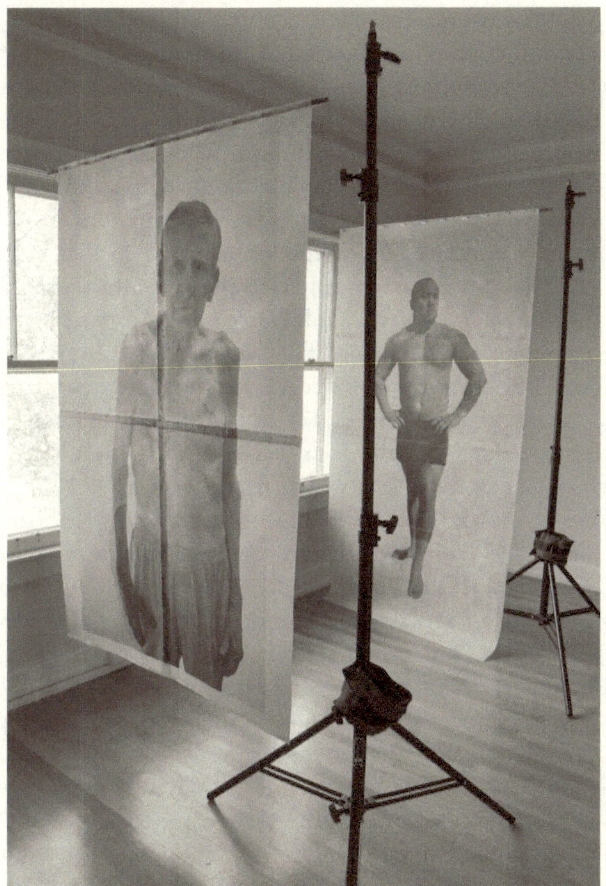

Figure 20. Two Print Comparison.

"spreads beyond our visual domain" it must be interwoven with all of the perceptual field (PhP, 211). I want the changes in the intensity or spectrum of light to become an integral part of the pieces and create different variations of the same images. A viewer's sensing of the light should intertwine with the perceptual experience of the artwork. In this installation, light works to illuminate and/or hide what is visible and/or invisible in the work.

These examples of flesh and chiasm within the artwork also establish the images as a place of interweaving of an inner and outer visibility. Moreover, the subjects within the images also demand a crossing of visible/invisible to contribute to the fabric of existence. Attention to the flesh of the pieces as revealed or hidden corresponds to the surface of the bodies as seen within the images. The choice of clothed/unclothed for each figure represented is an obvious distinction. A comparative study of the body throughout the artworks exhibits the cultural relationship of the body as seen/unseen in reference to each individual as clothed/unclothed. A more engaging distinction can be found in comparing the visible/invisible on/beneath the surface of the flesh. For example, in the three images of the young man, various tattoos or body marks are visible on the skin but it is the detail of the heavily muscular structure underneath that gives weight or strength to the body. In contrast, in two of the three images of the old man the flesh hangs in folds against a vulnerable skeletal structure. The hidden or invisible comes to the surface of flesh yet remains beneath the body. To understand the implications of these details, namely, the pacemaker and defibrillator raised on each side of his chest, the viewer must extend "the bond between the flesh and the idea, between the visible and the interior armature which it manifests and which it conceals" (VI, 149). The devices and their wires are not immediately known to the viewer (and sometimes are concealed due to the lighting situation) but can recognizably be perceived as something foreign to the body and flesh.

In considering an artwork, perception of the embodied viewer "allows us to see the world as something separate from us, as independent of our point of view on it, as fully and genuinely real" (Carman 2008, 191). In this case, the "real" means the image or object of our perception. It is important to realize this distinction, as the body in a photograph is not an embodied being. Nevertheless, the artwork increases our awareness or makes visible the viewer's embodiedness. The disparity between body image and body schema demanded definition in the last section for similar reasons. In the manner that the constitution of body image depends on the reflection of body as represented rather than body as subject of perception, the photograph as the object of perception culminates in Husserl's third level of image consciousness with the image subject as reflected upon separate from the photograph as presented. As Gallagher points out, perception (such as reflecting upon, imagining, conceptualizing) of a body as "the content of intentional consciousness" would be considered body image (Gallagher 1995, 226). Body schema performs the functions that render the body image possible at both the conscious and unconscious level (ibid., 234). Both reside in the viewer, yet the body schema, which establishes the interaction of the body and world, is rarely controlled by body image (ibid., 235). In my artwork, however, I intentionally call into question the role of body image and manipulate the performance of the body schema by means of body image within the viewer.

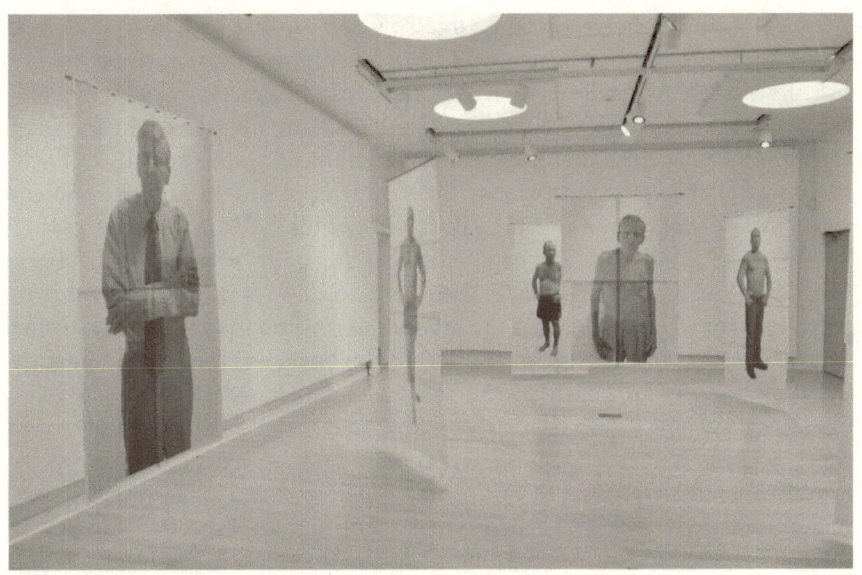

Figure 21. Installation View, West.

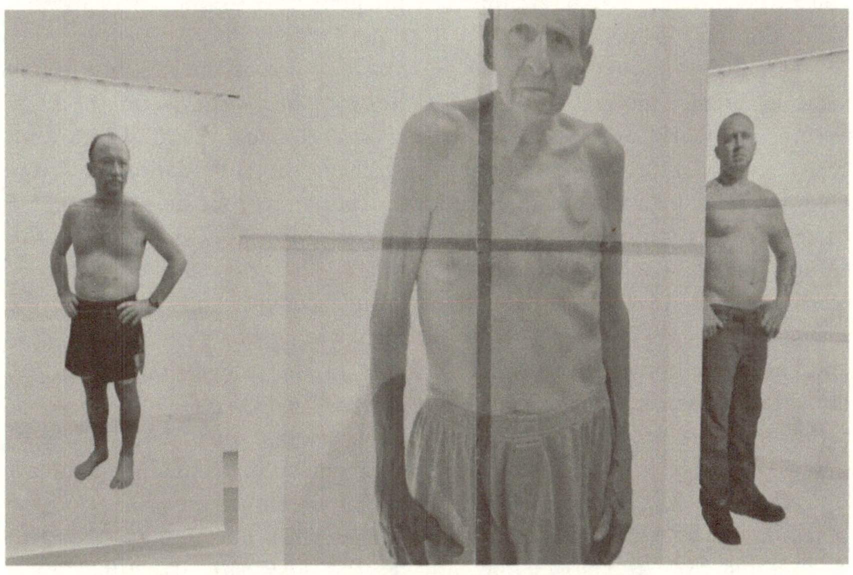

Figure 22. Three Print Comparison, Robert N.

For each of the works, the large size and varying scale of the figures, from almost life-sized to larger-than-life, exist in direct relation to each other and the viewer. As Merleau-Ponty discusses in *Phenomenology of Perception*, the body schema moves in contrast to important objects or figures that are prominent against the background structure of bodily spatiality (Prim. Percp., 101). Next to the images, the viewer is placed in an environment where "every figure stands out against the double horizon of external and bodily space" and must be negotiated by the body schema (ibid., 101). But where mere objects in our horizon are not always subject to conscious reflection, the viewer perceives the artwork as an intentional object creating an awareness of body image in relation to the image subject. By eliminating the background from each of the images, I have deliberately isolated the figure against any possible horizon within the image. The result of image consciousness, a mental representation of a body, occurs communally (as intertwining flesh) with the perceptual experience and conceptual understanding of the viewer's own body image. Furthermore, the translucency of the pieces allows for the overlapping of figures in other images and regarding other viewers within an exhibition environment to establish a perceptual horizon interweaving external, image, and bodily space together. In this, I force the embodied viewer, the one that "straddles the boundary between subject and object, visible and invisible, conscious and unconscious," to constitute an image that attempts to integrate these same characteristics along the same perceptual horizon (Carman 2008, 185).

In the unfolding of knowledge, which comes to the viewer through sense experience along this perceptual horizon, he or she is "of the same flesh as the world one inhabits and perceives" (Carman 2008, 123). With each artwork, I present a figure that, through the culmination of image consciousness, parallels the constitution of "otherness" but only with regard to the viewer's (self) body image in contrast to other beings in the world. In other words, I acknowledge that the chiasm that exists in the "transitivity from one body to another" cannot be formed between the viewer and the image (VI, 143). However, because the intertwining of an embodied viewer and the other bodies in the world is based in the recognition that others also exist as perceiver/perceived, knowledge of the viewer's body image is transformed in reference to the perceived representation or body image of other. My images compel the viewer, in their reflection on the image subject or as part of the perceptual awareness between an embodied viewer and the object/figure of which they are aware, to recognize meaning as related to or differing from their own body image. The chiasmatic structure creates a crossing of different perceptual modes where the consciousness moves between levels of body image, body schema, and world. A naive perception makes way for a reflective perception where the expressive body opens to the events that occur within image consciousness because the artwork immerses the viewer within the flesh of the world.

References

Bernet, Rudolf, Iso Kern, and Eduard Marbach. 1993. *An Introduction to Husserlian Phenomenology*. Evanston: Northwestern University Press.

Carman, Taylor. 2008. *Merleau-Ponty*. London and New York: Routledge.

———. 1999. "The Body in Husserl and Merleau-Ponty." *Philosophical Topics* 27, no. 2: 205–26.

———, and Mark B. N. Hansen, eds. 2005. *The Cambridge Companion to Merleau-Ponty.* Cambridge and New York, Cambridge University Press.

Frings, Manfred. 1970. "Max Scheler: Rarely Seen Complexities of Phenomenology." In *Phenomenology in Perspective*, edited by F. J. Smith, 32–53. The Hague: Martinus Nijhoff.

Gallagher, Shaun. 1995. "Body Schema and Intentionality." In *The Body and the Self*, 225–44. Cambridge: MIT Press.

Gilmore, Jonathan. 2005. "Between Philosophy and Art." In *The Cambridge Companion to Merleau-Ponty*, edited by Taylor Carman and Mark B. N. Hanson, 291–317. Cambridge and New York, Cambridge University Press.

Gurwitsch, Aron. 1966. "On the Intentionality of Consciousness." *Studies in Phenomenology and Psychology*. Northwestern University Studies in Phenomenology and Existential Philosophy. Evanston: Northwestern University Press.

Husserl, Edmund. 1977. *Cartesian Meditations: An Introduction to Phenomenology.* Translated by Dorian Cairns. 11th impression. Dordrecht; Boston: Kluwer Academic Publishers.

———. 1969. *Ideas I; General Introduction to Pure Phenomenology*. Translated by W. R. Boyce Gibson. London; New York: Allen and Unwin.

———. 2005. *Collected Works XI: Phantasy, Image Consciousness, and Memory (1898–1925)*. Translated by John B. Brough. Dordrecht: Springer.

Silverman, Hugh J. 1982. "Cézanne's Mirror Stage." *The Journal of Aesthetics and Art Criticism* 40, no. 4: 369–79.

Smith, F. J., ed. 1970. *Phenomenology in Perspective*. The Hague: Martinus Nijhoff.

Vasseleu, Cathryn. 1998. *Textures of Light: Vision and Touch in Irigaray, Levinas, and Merleau-Ponty*. London; New York: Routledge.

6

Carnal Language and the Reversibility of Architecture*

Modernism, Postmodernism, and Merleau-Ponty's Theory of Signs

Bryan E. Norwood

> Language is a life, is our life and the life of the things . . . what is lived is lived-spoken . . . born at this depth, language is not a mask over Being, but—if one knows how to grasp it with all its roots and all its foliation—the most valuable witness to Being.
>
> —Maurice Merleau-Ponty, *The Visible and the Invisible*

The Architectural Language Problem: Modernism and Postmodernism

Twentieth-century architects, historians of architecture, and theorists who treated design as a problem of language tended to reduce the problematic to either one of transcendence or one of immanence. Language understood

*I would like to thank Rachel McCann of Mississippi State University's School of Architecture for her insightful comments on this paper. I would also like to thank Iris Aravot for a helpful discussion at the annual meeting of the Society for the Study of Existential and Phenomenological Theory and Culture, June 3–5, 2008, at the University of British Columbia, where portions of this paper where presented, and Chris Monson, in whose fourth-year architectural studio course this paper originally began. An earlier version of this paper was also presented at 100 Years of Merleau-Ponty: A Centennial Conference held March 14–16, 2008, at Sofia University in Sofia, Bulgaria.

as a relationship of transcendence, of signifier to the objective thing in the world that transcends the signifier, can be characterized as system of extra-referentiality, a structure that creates a correspondence between the signifier and the signified to generate meaning and speak truth about the world. Language understood as systematic immanence, as a subjective and internal construct, can be characterized as a structure of infra-referentiality, a diacritical set of differences in which a signifier has meaning in relation to all other signifiers. Architectural language understood as either only extra-referential or only infra-referential thus treats signifiers as either an impediment to the clarity of the visible, material practice of architecture or as a superstructural playground of architectural signifiers untethered from the encumbrances of the materiality and immediate functionality of the built environment, which allows theoretical speculation and reflection.

The reduction to transcendence is best exemplified by the extreme of functionalist modernism, which aimed at a sort of referential clarity in which the signifier makes clear the signified—form clarifies function. The reduction to immanence, best exemplified in the extremes of the postmodernism linguistic turn, essentially redefines architectural meaning as a diacritical product, separating signifying potential from materiality and functionality and attempting to free architectural language from being merely a tool for functional clarity. However, both extremes have something in common. For the functionalist or the postmodernist, architectural language is a construct that works, for better or for worse, in disjunction from the architectural real, from the being of architecture. For the modernist, the disjunction of language is a gap to be overcome in the adequate presentation of true architectural being, while for the postmodernist, the loosened connection of the signifier and the signified liberates architecture from the demands of the project of essentialist representation.

One may immediately object that that this dichotomization of modernism and postmodernism is an anachronistic generalization, a difference invented post hoc by the modern critics of classicism and the subsequent postmodern critics of modernism, and this is no doubt true to a degree.[1] But here I want to speak about conceptual, theoretical positions. I want

1. A number of books on architectural language have been written as a sort of progressive or polemical critique of the past (and quite often the recent past). For example, after the historian John Summerson, in *The Classical Language of Architecture* (1963), described classicism as the "Latin" of architectural language that, through conceptions of rationality, continued to have profound effects on modernism, the historian-polemicist Bruno Zevi responded in a series of writings in the early 1970s, translated together in the volume

to use this purposeful extremism in the rhetoric of architectural history and theory to make clear the architectural potential of Merleau-Ponty's theory of language as the *reversibility* of the transcendence and immanence of meaning. In fact, if the Merleau-Pontian theory of language presented below is correct, architecture has never and will never be practiced only in the extremes. While an architect may gear practice or theory toward one of the limits, she will invariably be pulled back toward the center. With this caveat in mind, I will first give a brief characterization of the theoretical limits, before moving into a Merleau-Pontian theory.

Modernist architects, with characteristic concern for intelligibility and rationality, attempted (and still attempt) to treat the signifying aspects of the built environment as extra-referential signs. Architectural signifiers at their best refer immediately and only to the fundamental being of architecture, avoiding the ultimately meaningless infra-referential signification of ornament or other signs only internal to the symbolic discourse of architecture.[2] While the immediate contrast of modernism with the ornamented orders of classical architecture is clear enough (although the contrast is not nearly as clear in terms of proportionality), the question of what for the modernist constitutes the being of architecture that architectural signifiers should map is not immediately obvious.

As has been pointed out with fervor in contemporary architectural history, there was not just one modernism, as some of the early historian-promoters of modern architecture would have had it, there were (and are) in actuality many modernisms. For example, Le Corbusier's moving account of architectural language in *Towards an Architecture* sets the ground as mathematical ideals: "A thought that clarifies itself without words or sounds, but only through prisms that have relationships with one another. . . . These relationships don't necessarily have anything to do with what is practical or descriptive. They are a mathematical creation of your mind. They are the language of architecture. With inert materials, based on a more or less utilitarian program that you *go beyond,* you have established relationships that move me. It is architecture" (Le Corbusier 2007, 195). This quasi-classical mysticism about the fundamental role of mathematics in architecture that

---

The Modern Language of Architecture (1994), that described modernism as the anticlassical language of architecture. Charles Jencks followed not long after, in 1977, with *The Language of Post-Modern Architecture* (New York: Rizzoli), describing postmodernism "as a partial inversion and modification of the former language of architecture" (6).

2. Adolf Loos's famous critique in *Ornament and Crime* is perhaps one of the most forceful examples of this position.

collapses the distinction of the language of architecture and architecture itself (a belief that is once again deeply at work in architectural culture with developments in digital production and parametricism) is much different than the fully developed rhetoric of modernist functionalism that I want to identify as the limit condition of its language. The limit is in the famous catchphrase, "Form follows function." The limit is in architectural form, the shape that its signifiers take, being grounded in an extraformal signified that is in the material world.

The character and specificity of the function in which architectural form is grounded and which it attempts to clarify varied for modernists. The historian Sigfried Giedion, in his famous *Space, Time, and Architecture*, saw the grounds of modern architecture in a new, modern conception of space-time that architecture was to express. Reyner Banham, in *Theory and Design in the First Machine Age*, saw the grounds in the potentials of standardization and technological development which modern architecture was to embody. Manfredo Tafuri's more cynical and pessimistic historical analysis in *Architecture and Utopia* saw the grounds of modernism in the totalizing planification of capital. Although there is great variety in these attempts to ground modern architecture's form in the function of the real world, I want to suggest there is a constant within architectural modernism as wide ranging as the harsh functionalism of Hannes Meyer and Ludwig Hilberseimer to the universal logic of vision of Walter Gropius, and even to the expressionism of Le Corbusier and Alvar Aalto, at least when it comes to understanding architecture as a language.

The modern constant is precisely the goal of extra-referential clarity. This is to say that modernist architecture, as Charles Jencks pointed out, primarily treats signs as indexical semantics (Jencks 1977, 52–54). Modern architecture strives for signs that are didactic and transparent. Signs are to be at the very least icons, but ideally indexes—signs that directly relate the signifier (in typical language, the word, e.g., "cat"), the signified (the idea, e.g., the idea of cat), and the referent (the thing, e.g., the actual furry thing that sits in my lap).[3] Modernist architectural signs are to explain immediately

3. I will be using Charles Jencks's terminology for different kinds of signs as laid out in *The Language of Post-Modern Architecture*, 52–54, and Geoffery Broadbent's elaboration in "A Plain Man's Guide to the Theory of Signs in Architecture" (1978, 480). This approach classifies three basic kinds of architectural signs: symbolic, iconic, and indexical. The meaning of symbolic signs is set by conventional usage (such as the word *cat* being attached to the idea of a cat); the meaning of an iconic sign is set by shared characteristics between the signifier and the signified (such as a structurally shaped bridge or Robert Venturi's famous duck drawing). The form of the indexical sign directly indicates its content (such as a linear corridor).

and ultimately architectural being—and this being at its most reductive limit is function, whether timeless and universal or historically determined.

As another caveat, it should be noted that when architecture is treated as a language the elements of a sign never remain separate and distinct to the degree that they can be in spoken or written language, a condition that Merleau-Ponty notes also breaks down the symmetry of language and painting (S, 78–81).[4] As Geoffrey Broadbent pointed out, a building can act as a signifier, a signified, and/or a referent (Broadbent 1978, 478–79). This difference between spoken and written language and architectural language is one of the main sources of the critique of the consideration of architecture as language in the first place. But if we set aside the complete dismissal of the problematic for the purposes of this paper, the modernist idea for architectural language can be understood as an attempt to collapse all the aspects of the sign together in each architectural element to make architecture self-illuminating. The building and its elements are to act as signifiers, signifieds, and referents for themselves, rather than for or to another work of architecture in history. Architectural signifiers do not merely refer us to function; they are one and the same as function. Architecture doesn't just represent space-time, technology, or capitalist planification; it also embodies it. The formal signifier is one and the same as the functional signified. The language of modern architecture thus uses signifiers to refer extra-referentially to the reality of which it is an index, not infra-referentially to other signifiers within the larger body of architectural language.

A paradox emerges within the modernist position. Although architectural signifiers are always transcended by what they signify—e.g., reality is not the signifier but goes beyond the signifier—modernism also attempts to fix the relationship of transcendence within the architectural work. While signifiers are about something that transcends the system of signifiers, the signified and the signifier (and ultimately the referent itself) are bound up into the same form. Language is nothing but a transparent and perhaps even visually sharpening membrane over the real. At the extremes of functionalism: a column should represent only what a column does; a door represents only what a door does. A linear hallway is both the sign for and the actual thing that one uses to proceed to or come from some place. Architectural language illuminates how architecture came into being, how architecture works, and how it is to be used.

The ultimate shortcoming of modernist language, according to the postmodernist critic, is the refusal to acknowledge that all buildings and

4. The edition used here is Evanston: Northwestern University Press, 1964, translated by Richard C. McCleary.

architectural elements act as signifiers of more than just themselves and their function.[5] Architectural signs are, in practice, always Janus-faced. While these signs are no doubt partially constituted by the connections of signifiers and signifieds—a door should be legible as a door to at least some degree to function properly—a complete interpretation of architectural signs must also acknowledge the fundamental role of the immanent diacritical system of architectural conventions. Form always greatly exceeds function in the meanings that it carries. Pure indexical semantics in architecture are not permanently attainable at a large scale, as even the basest functionalism is quickly imbued with a multitude of meanings. Architectural form always has various denotations and connotations, as Umberto Eco analyzed in "A Componential Analysis of the Architectural Sign /Column/" and Robert Venturi, Denise Scott Brown, and Steven Izenour famously found in the Vegas Strip (Eco 1972; Venturi, Scott Brown, and Izenour 1977). And further, while the most devout of the functionalists passed their architecture off as concerned with form only insofar as it was dictated by real function, in reality their architecture often was as much rhetorical and symbolic of functionalism as it was an actual index of function. As Broadbent and other critics often pointed out, many supposedly "functionalist" buildings are in fact paradigms of nonfunctionality (Broadbent 1978, 474).

The initial movement of explicitly textually based architecture attempted to construe meaning in the built environment in the structuralist terms of Ferdinand de Saussure and the pragmatic terms of Charles Peirce, with a notable semiotic shift visible in a variety of architectural writing beginning in the 1960s, from the influential writing of Roland Barthes, to the architectural theory and practice of figures such as Peter Eisenman, Venturi, Scott Brown, Mario Gandelsonas, and Diana Agrest.[6] Postmodernism in theory and practice is as diverse and multivariate as modernism and is as difficult to reduce to any core concern. However, from the fight between

---

5. Broadbent writes, "Like it or not, *all* buildings symbolize or at least 'carry' meaning. . . . There is no getting away from it; just as Chartres Cathedral carries meaning, so does the meanest garden shed" (1978, 474–75). And Jencks contends that, "People invariably see one building in terms of another, or in terms of a similar object; in short as a metaphor. The more unfamiliar a modern building is, the more they will compare it metaphorically to what they know" (1977, 40).

6. Geoffrey Broadbent, Richard Bunt, and Charles Jencks, eds., *Signs, Symbols, and Architecture* (Chichester: John Wiley and Sons, 1980) collects a number of essays related to the turn toward thinking architecture in terms of a language.

the so-called whites and grays, to Mario Gandelsonas's distinction of the semantic "neorealism" practiced by Venturi and Michael Graves and the syntactic "neorationalism" practiced by Eisenman, Aldo Rossi, and John Hejuk (Gandelsonas and Morton 1972; Gandelsonas 1976), all the work of what I am broadly labeling postmodern architecture is concerned fundamentally with the complexity of the process of signification that takes place within architecture.

However, at its extreme, postmodern architectural practice not only acknowledges that the built environment is a system of complex and contradictory signs but further essentializes this conception by grounding architecture in the meaning derivable from the diacritical, infra-referential structure of the language immanent to architecture. The extreme of postmodern approaches to architecture can be characterized by what M. C. Dillon terms *semiological reductionism,* a view that claims that there is no escape from the chain of signifiers and thus no access to the transcendent world because all meaning is defined in relation to other signs (Dillon 1997, 183). The meaning of a sign is derived diacritically from its relation to other signs in the immanent structure of language. Postmodern architecture at its extreme turns this weakness into a supposed strength, through an architectural idealism that posits the deep structure of the immanent system of signifiers as the true location of architectural meaning, an attitude for which some of the work of Peter Eisenman stands as a strikingly clear example.

While Eisenman's various early house projects and his later Arnoff Center at the University of Cincinnati and Wexner Center at The Ohio State University all embody a concern with diacritical signifiers, as the idea of the grids that generate the buildings clearly takes priority over the stuff that makes up these grids, it is in paper projects such as his 1978 project for Cannaregio in Venice that the wish comes out most clearly.[7] The practice of architecture begins and ends with iterative, self-reflexive formalism of the syntactical play of cubes, planes, lines, and points. The elements are signifiers that no longer signify anything beyond the internal system of architecture, and with Cannaregio even the human scale seems to be abandoned as a referent. Architecture, constituted as a diacritical system of signs, finds its essence in the inability to fundamentally signify something real—it becomes

7. See K. Michael Hays's *Architecture's Desire* for an account of Eisenman's Cannaregio project (2010, 59–86). On my last visit to Eisenman's Arnoff center with an architecture studio, we were each handed a 190-page booklet of critical essays explaining the building; this is the epitome of an architecture of immanence.

a process of exploring the structures of signifiers that mark the absence of an architectural signified.

The neorealist grays, in contrast, relied on more semantic relationships to historical architecture or extra-architectural objects—as with Graves's Portland Building or his Swan and Dolphin hotels at Disney World or Venturi and Scott Brown's study of the Vegas Strip and their Guild House. But the signifiers again remain largely ideational, so that the materiality of the made object is at best insignificant and at worst a hassle. Architecture is understood as something that is fundamentally to be interpreted, and the process of interpretation is understood through the conception of the building as something to be read like a text. The infra-referential reduction is made not by necessarily denying that there is a real world or that architecture has functionality or might have some sort of fundamental being as the modernist thought but rather in insisting that architecture has no unmediated recourse to this world outside of language, and thus must fundamentally be treated as a system of signs. While there certainly could be something transcendent called Architecture itself—Architecture with a big "A"—the language of architecture has no way to guarantee access to it.

Since the 1980s, the attitude toward architectural semiotics could be, for the most part, characterized as one of waning interest. Certainly poststructuralist and deconstructionist critiques undermined much of the presupposed stability in early approaches to architectural language, and more recent pluralizations in the scope of architectural practice have changed the nature and content of theorization. However, as so often happens in architectural culture, movement to new theoretical grounds results as much from perceived creative exhaustion in a paradigm and the changing fashions of studio culture as it does from paradigmatic failure. In what follows I will argue there is a way to formulate a robust conception of language that is relevant to contemporary practice and that navigates between the limits of extra-referential certainty about architecture's being and infra-referential semiological reductionism that abandons hope of architecture's ability to say anything meaningful about this being. The way between, I will argue, is Merleau-Ponty's conception of reversibility.

Between Modernism and Postmodernism: Saussure and Perception

Before developing the language of the flesh in *The Visible and the Invisible*, Merleau-Ponty writes in *Consciousness and the Acquisition of Language* that "language is neither thing nor mind, but it is immanent and transcendent at the same time" (CAL, 6). As is characteristic of much of his philosophy, Merleau-Ponty describes language not as an either-or, but rather as a both-and. The modernist and the postmodernist architect are both right, but they are also both wrong. As he develops his notions of flesh, chiasm, and reversibility, Merleau-Ponty continues this inclusive conception of language as being caught up in both transcendent silence and immanent speech. In *The Visible and the Invisible*, he writes, "Philosophy is the reconversion of silence and speech into one another" (VI, 129). The task of philosophy is the thinking of reversibility—immanence and transcendence at the same time. An intertwined conception of the relationship of language and the world resists reductions and unidirectional movement from language to the world or from the world to language.

After encountering Saussure, Merleau-Ponty appropriates the terminology of structural linguistics as a tool to describe both language and perception. Saussure's distinction of *la langue* and *la parole* plays a vital role in Merleau-Ponty's thought on the structure of the infra-referential relationship between language and meaning (Saussure 1966, 14–15). *La langue* is conceived of as the system of rules and conventions that underlies all of spoken language. It is a necessary condition for speech but cannot be spoken as a whole and thus is not sufficient. *La parole,* the individual speech act, is the situational use of language that takes place against the backdrop of *la langue,* which acts as an ordering structure that enables *la parole* to express a new and original act of meaning.[8] Merleau-Ponty develops a correlation between the functions of language and perception in *Consciousness and the Acquisition of Language*: "Language functions with respect to thought as the

8. See James Edie's forward to *Consciousness and the Acquisition of Language*, xxiii. For a careful examination of Merleau-Ponty's reading of Saussure, see James Schmidt's *Maurice Merleau-Ponty: Between Phenomenology and Structuralism* (New York: St. Martin's Press, 1985).

9. CAL, 91–92. Merleau-Ponty also writes that "thought inhabits language and language is its body" (CAL, 102). In *Phenomenology of Perception*, the act of thought is directly connected to the individual speech act of *parole* through Merleau-Ponty's gestural theory of language. He writes, "A thought limited to existing for itself, independently of the constraints of speech and communication, would no sooner appear than it would sink into the unconscious, which means that it would not exist even for itself. . . . The orator does not think before speaking, nor even while speaking; his speech is his thought" (PhP, 206–209). The edition used here is London: Routledge, 2002, translated by Colin Smith.

body does with respect to perception."[9] *La langue* is characteristically similar to the body, a structure of which we are often not conscious, while *parole* is characteristically similar to the act of perception:

la langue : *la parole* :: body : perception[10]

In addition to the distinction of *la langue* and *la parole,* Merleau-Ponty adopts a second of Saussure's ideas. Saussure writes, "in language there are only differences" (Saussure 1966, 120). Language is created by a series of divergences in which each word gets its meaning from all the words that it is not. Saussure's structuring of language as a diacritical system becomes a springboard from which Merleau-Ponty is able to connect Gestalt theories of perception with a structural theory of language. As he writes in *Consciousness and the Acquisition of Language*: "In truth, language is not made up of words, each of which is endowed with one or several meanings. Each word has its meaning only inasmuch as it is sustained in this signification by all the others. . . . The only reality is the *Gestalt* of language. In order for a word to endure in its meaning, it is necessary that it be supported by others" (CAL, 92). Just as an object (figure) must be seen in relationship to its background, so must a word be considered in relationship to all other words. Merleau-Ponty elaborates on the diacritical structure of phenomena: "The color is yet a variant in another dimension of a variation, that of its relations with the surroundings: this red is what it is only by connecting up from its place with other reds about it" (VI, 132). Colors are differences among things, just as the infra-referentiality of language is determined by relations among words (Edie 1973, xxv–vi). The ideal of a color, such as "red" as compared to a red phenomenon is the same as the ideal laws of *la langue* versus the raw phonetic use of *la parole*. This extends the analogy from simply a relationship between the act of perception or *la parole* and the body or *la langue* to parts of the world:

word : language :: percept : world horizon

From this construct, a spoken word or perceived thing can be defined more clearly: "A naked color, in general a visible, is not a chunk of absolutely

10. This analogy is similar to the one Dillon writes as "language : thought :: body : perception" (1997, 217).

hard, indivisible being, offered all naked to a vision which could be only total or null, but is rather a sort of straits between exterior horizons and interior horizons ever gaping open . . . less a color or a thing, therefore, than a difference between things and colors, a momentary crystallization of colored being or of visibility" (VI, 132).

In moving from Saussure's linguistics to the reversibility thesis, the correlation of the diacritical nature of perception and phenomena with that of language becomes the turning point from which Merleau-Ponty is able to go beyond Saussure and allows infra-referential language to move outside of itself and be affected not only by meaning, which is the infra-referential first reversibility of language, but also by the world, which is the extra-referential second reversibility. Language becomes an intertwined system of reversibilities between itself and meaning and between itself and the silent, sensible world (VI, 118; Dillon 1992, 132–33). In the first reversibility, the diacritical structure of language is a way of binding together finitude (immanence) and infinity (transcendence), for both are defined in relation to the other: "Transcendence is identity within difference" (VI, 225). Words are both able to be spatio-temporally finite ("this cat") and diacritically infinite ("cat" is not "dog," "bear," "wall," "cheeseburger," ad nauseam). The diacritical structures of language and perception amount to a dehiscence, an *écart*; words and precepts are defined through divergences. In the second reversibility, "the possibilities of speech" are bound to "the structure of the mute world" (VI, 155).

The chiasmatic structure of the first reversibility of language and meaning—signs as a series of divergences—keeps language from simply being the thing that controls us. Merleau-Ponty, in an idiosyncratic reading of Saussure, suggests that, in addition to *la langue* being the structure for acts of *la parole,* the "synchronic linguistic of speech" (*la parole*) also modifies the "diachronic linguistics of language" (*la langue*) (S, 86; Edie 1973, xxiii). *La parole* can affect the structure of meaning because both have a spatio-temporal character, a character that for *La parole* derives from primal expression, the singing of the world, in which the sign is bound up with its context (Dillon 1997, 190). Merleau-Ponty writes, "The look, we said, envelops, palpates, espouses the visible things . . . as though it knew them before knowing them it moves in its own way with its abrupt and imperious style, and yet the views taken are not desultory—I do not look at chaos, but at things—so that finally one cannot say if it is the look or if it is the things that command" (VI, 133). The reversibility that takes place in perception where one does not know whether the perceiver or the perceived is in command is analogous to the reversibility in language (*la langue*) and meaning (*la parole*) in which one does not know whether the speaker or the spoken is in command.[11]

While the reversibility between language and meaning accounts for the ability of *la parole* to transform the system of *la langue,* the second reversibility between language and the world accounts for the possibility of extra-referentiality. Not only does extra-referentiality suggest that words can be bound to transcendent objects, thus making words the consequence of expression of the perceptual world (such as an onomatopoeia), but also language through the process of sedimentation is able to affect the perceptual world. The gap of the *écart* that separates words and phonemes is also held open between language and perception, but this gap is not empty because it also pulls the two together (Dillon 1992, 136). As Merleau-Ponty writes: "When the silent vision falls into speech . . . when it metamorphoses the structures of the visible world and makes itself a gaze of the mind . . . this is always in virtue of the same fundamental phenomenon of reversibility which sustains both the mute perception and the speech" (VI, 154–55). The constant interplay and influence of language upon phenomena, and phenomena upon language, result in constant modification to both.

These two reversibilities are the depths from which architectural language emerges and provide the possibility of architectural language that is both immanent and transcendent. However, there seems to be a tension between these two reversibilities. In infra-referential reversibility language gets its meaning from difference—what it is not—and in the extra-referential reversibility language gets its meaning from what it signifies—what it is. Saussure recognized this tension: "Here is the paradox: on the one hand the concept seems to be the counterpart of the sound-image, and on the other hand the sign itself is in turn the counterpart of the other signs of language" (Saussure 1966, 114). He resolves this tension by suggesting that the extra-referential relationship is a completely arbitrary relationship (ibid., 113). Saussure says that "[t]here are no pre-existing ideas, and nothing is distinct before the appearance of language" (ibid., 112). The paradox is resolved by the introduction of arbitrariness, which is a correlative of difference (ibid., 118). Extra-referentiality is an arbitrary byproduct of infra-referentiality.

11. This dialectical relation of *parole* and *langue* also suggests an institutional reading of Merleau-Ponty's concept of the flesh that Evans and Lawlor refer to as "the geocentric view," in which flesh is the relation of interobjectivity (2000, 14–15). Interobjectivity sets up reflexive relations between all *signs* of presence. While intersubjectivity may only pertain to the meshing together of consciousnesses, interobjectivity results from, as Evans and Lawlor point out, the "production of subjects as signs" among other corporeal signs.

In contrast, Merleau-Ponty's ontology suggests that language is rooted in the wild meaning of the world—the possibilities of the flesh—which has us and speaks itself in us. In the working notes of *The Visible and the Invisible*, Merleau-Ponty says that "it is not we who speak, it is truth that speaks itself at the depths of speech" (VI, 185). However, Merleau-Ponty's hermeneutics of ambiguity is also one in which truth is not found, but *brought into being.*[12] "Truth is another name for sedimentation," he writes, it is "the presence of all presents in our own" (S, 96). Meaning is also present in the divergences of immanent language that are lifted out of the flesh. There is an intertwining of the infra-referentiality of sedimented language and extra-referentiality of signification of the transcendent world that resolves the tension. Language is born out of the flesh of the world—extra-referentiality makes the infra-referential language possible through an emergence of language out of the Gestalt of the flesh. However, infra-referentiality also makes extra-referential language possible by creating a mirrored condition of the visible: diacritical language mirrors the Gestalt of phenomena.

As we have already seen, reversibility provides for the possibility of a dialectical ontology in which neither the invisible nor the visible comes first, but Merleau-Ponty's preservation of the primacy of perception throughout his entire philosophy and his insistence that language emerges out of the flesh still seem to preserve some sort of foundationalism. If language is born at the depths of being, to understand the relationship of these two reversibilities, flesh-language and speech-language (with the correlate of percept-horizon), does it not make sense to try to go back to birth? More importantly, does it not make sense then to take architecture back to the condition of its birth, to a more primal, prelinguistic state, to create fleshy architecture? After all, architectural language as a series of reversibilities, just like spoken language, is born, emerging from the depths, of being.

The Birth of Architecture: The Gesture

Vitruvius—"The Architect," as he was once called (much in the same way Aristotle was "The Philosopher" to Aquinas and his scholastic peers)—tells a

12. "Philosophy is not the reflection of a pre-existing truth, but, like art, the act of bringing truth into being" (PhP, xxiii). See also Shaun Gallagher, "Introduction: The Hermeneutics of Ambiguity," in *Merleau-Ponty, Hermeneutics, and Postmodernism*, ed. Thomas W. Busch and Shaun Gallagher (Albany: State University of New York Press, 1992), 4.

story of the birth of language and the house, the first piece of architecture, in the same breath:

> The men of old were born like the wild beasts, in woods, caves, and groves, and lived on savage fare. As time went on, the thickly crowded trees in a certain place, tossed by storms and winds, and rubbing their branches against one another, caught fire, and so the inhabitants of the place were put to flight. . . . After it subsided, they drew near, and . . . while . . . keeping it alive, brought up other people to it, showing them by signs how much comfort they got from it. In that gathering of men, at a time when utterances of sound was purely individual, from daily habits they fixed upon articulate words just as these had happened to come; then, from indicating by name things in common use, the result was that in this chance way they began to talk, and thus originated conversation with one another. . . . And so, as they kept coming together in great numbers into one place . . . they began in that first assembly to construct shelters. (Vitruvius 1960, 38)

Regardless of its specious factuality, Vitruvius's story is one of the intertwined flesh of language, of the emergence of the sign from carnality and the emergence of architecture from a culture of signs. His story of birth places language in the flesh of the world as words emerged from gestures and sounds made by the individual and intersubjective community, things Merleau-Ponty also regards as necessary for the birth of language (Dillon 1997, 186–88). Words do refer to things as signifiers to signified things, but below this level there is a level of "affective tonality," which is contained in the words as a "patterned sound" (Edie 1973, xviii). This is the act of what Merleau-Ponty calls "singing the world," which is not a fully translatable system of communication, but is a carnally rooted form of deep communication that more closely connects the role of signifier and signified: "The meaning of words must be . . . induced by the words themselves, or more exactly, their conceptual meaning must be formed by a kind of deduction from *gestural meaning,* which is immanent in speech" (PhP, 208). Actual words that have similar meaning may bear little resemblance from language to language, and they do not need to. The important connection is that they emerged from carnality, from patterned sound.

Merleau-Ponty sets the origin of language in gestures, which are a bridge between natural signs (such as dark clouds being a sign for rain) and conventional signs (such as "cat" representing the idea of cat). A gesture departs from a situation in which the signifier and carnal event are the same (indexical, e.g., rain clouds), not to a point where the relationship between the signifier and carnal action is arbitrary (symbolic), but only to the point where, although the signifier is not the actual carnal event, it maintains some of its characteristics (iconic, e.g., doing the action of hammering to represent actually hammering). Thus, symbol, icon, and index can roughly be equivocated with conventional signs, gestures, and natural signs respectively. The connection of a symbol with its meaning is conventional, while the connection of an index with its meaning is natural. Gestures and icons are connected with their meaning by shared characteristics.

Natural sign ———— Gesture ———— Conventional Sign

The gestural theory of language argues that preconventional sign communication is not the result of representation but rather it is rooted in natural signs in which the signifier is identical with the signified. Gestures begin the process of moving signification away from indexical natural signs and open an incipient gap between signifier and signified. However, the process is never complete. As Dillon explains Merleau-Ponty's view, "There are no conventional signs, strictly speaking, because all conventional usage is grounded in an original expressive singing of the world" (Dillon 1997, 193). Poetry and other forms of nonrational writing return humanity to preconventional language because meaning is not only within the signifier, but also between it and the signified in nonsymbolic carnal expression. As Merleau-Ponty suggests: "It is well known that a poem, though it has a superficial meaning translatable into prose, leads, in the reader's mind, a further existence which makes it a poem. Just as the spoken word is significant not only through the medium of individual words, but also through that of accent, intonation, gesture and facial expression, and as these additional meanings no longer reveal the speaker's thoughts but the source of his thoughts and his fundamental manner of being, so poetry, which is accidentally narrative and in that way informative, is essentially a variety of existence" (PhP, 174).

Not surprisingly, much of prehistorical architecture appears to do much the same thing as poetry, but there is no need to return to Stonehenge or the primitive hut to find these gestures in architecture. Just as the poet is able to express with language something beyond the sedimented meaning of the words that she uses, the architect can express a meaning beyond the learned signification of architecture. For example, Frank Gehry, at the

Vontz Center in Cincinnati, uses windows and mullions to say something more than (and even contradictory to) the conventional and sedimented nature of these signs. By pushing the window and its mullions out and not stopping them at the edge of the opening in the wall, Gehry "objectifies" these signs. While still functioning as a sedimented sign of the window as an opening in the wall, the typical meaning is also contradicted by making the window stand out as a Gestalt figure on top of its ground. The gap between signifier and signified is almost closed by this architectural move because the windows become much greater than simply signifiers of a relationship between the inside and outside—they become elements that signify themselves. The glass and mullions are no longer talking about windows; they are talking about figures. In an alternative, although not necessarily contradictory, consideration, the gap could also be said to have been opened more because the connection between the signifier (the elements that make up window) and the signified (the actual window) has actually become more symbolic and less indexical.

If Gehry achieves the return to gestures by moving away from conventional signage by changing the denotation of the window elements, Frank Lloyd Wright achieved gesture in his houses by moving signifier and signified closer together with the hearth. The fireplace becomes the center of many of Wright's houses as a conventional sign, but also as a primordial experience. The hearth signifies warmth and is also actually the source of it. For example, in the Robie House in Chicago, Wright built the fireplace in the center of the house. The dense brick absorbs the heat of a burning fire and radiates throughout the house. Built-in seating around the fireplace both signifies and becomes the place for family to assemble.

As both of these examples show, although we are no longer born into a world of only the preconventional, neither is our world wholly conventional. Experiential access beyond the symbolic signs is still architecturally possible. Our world from birth is, as Merleau-Ponty suggests, full of conventional signs: "From his first waking moments the child hears someone speaking. . . . The child receives the 'sense' of language from his environment. . . . The child's relationship with his environment is what points him towards language" (CAL, 14). Architectural experiences are attached to sedimented meanings, but this does not mean we are bound up in a hermeneutic circle of diacritical language that is inescapable. The architect is not bound to an endless collage of self-referential signs, which Eisenman's Cannaregio project seems to want to suggest, nor is she completely in control of the meaning of what she speaks through design as the modernist may want, because language is born out of the world itself. Language, like depth, does not provide the possibility of a view from nowhere (or, more accurately, from everywhere) but rather the possibility of perspectivism of the flesh because language behaves like the flesh (it is another, "lighter flesh") and can never be fully separated from it.[13] As Merleau-Ponty suggests, ideas are always bound up in carnality: "Let us only say that the pure ideality is itself not without flesh nor freed from horizon structures: it lives of them, though they be another flesh and other horizons. It is as though the visibility that animates the sensible world were to emigrate, not outside of every body, but into another less heavy, more transparent body, as though it were to change flesh, abandoning the flesh of the body for that of language" (VI, 153). Language is bound up in, intertwined with, and never fully separable from the flesh. Architectural elements, although they act as language, are even less detachable than written language, and can return us to the preconventional and hold open the gap of experience before signified meaning is assigned. Architectural language, in contrast to spoken language, has a more difficult time separating itself from being.

Unfortunately, Merleau-Ponty has largely not been imported into architecture in a way that preserves the richness of both of these reversibilities. In attempts to react to the overindulgence in the self-gratifying language of postmodernism, recent phenomenological approaches to architecture have heavily rested on the ideas of perception and poetics with a tendency to downplay, if not dismiss, the infra-referential first-reversibility of language by focusing only on language's mirrored condition in perception. The fate of the second reversibility, because the first is dismissed, is a reduction that merely works the opposite of the semiological reduction. Instead of the chiasm allowing language to reconverge with and fold back onto the silent visible world, it is relegated to an emergent property. Language, while it may be given the autonomy of emergence, reduced to a surface quality whose aim to reference the visible world is impotent in its influence on architecture—an attitude toward language that tends toward correspondence theories of truth, a system in which truth can no longer be brought into being through new expressions.

---

13. PhP, 298. Duane Davis describes the relationship of language and the corporeal as follows: "Language is not merely a flawed copy, a representation that pales before its standard idea. Nor is language entire of itself, a standard somehow distanciated from humankind. It is a human event, made animate by this divergence between the ideal and the corporeal, the lack of coincidence within their interpenetration and intertwining" Martin C. Dillon, ed., *Merleau-Ponty Vivant* (Albany: State University of New York Press, 1991), 34–35.

For example, Alberto Pérez-Gómez, in an introduction to Steven Holl's *Intertwining*, writes that "phenomenological hermeneutics has recognized the *autonomy* of poetic language while demonstrating that its meaning hinges upon its capacity to speak about something 'other' that 'grounds' it and 'precedes' it, even if this 'other' is given *with* language" (Holl 1995, 10). Pérez-Gómez suggests that architecture must transcend architectural semiotics to ground itself and to avoid "irrelevant self-referential games" of postmodernism. He goes on to say that phenomenology can create more compassionate architecture that is culturally relevant by "operating at a level 'prior' to reductions, texts, and virtual reality" by allowing a diversity of meaning rather than denoting a single meaning. Language is, not unlike modernism, treated as something that can be made transparent in order to reveal what is real.

The troubling aspect of this usage of Merleau-Ponty and phenomenology is the suggestion that architecture should perform one-half of a reversibility without simultaneously doing another. That is to say, phenomenological architectural theory often emphasizes that the role of architectural design is to create space, experiential form, and worldly dwelling that are fleshy—providing many semiotic possibilities of interpretation and sedimentation—but not to create moments of overtly linguistic form (although this happens by accident) that fold back on to the flesh. Infra-referentiality is dismissed and extra-referentiality is only practiced as a creation of the visible. The result of this theoretical pressure is twofold: (1) the overexertion to make unnameability results in unintended symbolic and iconic form as infra-referential reversibility still occurs, and (2) the overt focus on phenomenological ideas such as intertwining or chiasm results in form and space that are symbolic of the philosophical concept as extra-referential reversibility turns language back on the visible.[14]

Steven Holl, no doubt one of the practicing figureheads of this movement, continually experiments with preconventional phenomena that are unnameable and therefore nonsymbolic in their meaning. Holl and other phenomenological architects such as Juhani Pallasmaa may design with an aesthetic that appears similar to modernism because of the shared mini-

14. One only needs to look at the sketchbooks of architects reading Merleau-Ponty or any contemporary philosopher to see the product of trying to produce architecture out of a philosophical concept (e.g., holey, intertwined, enmeshed, folded, chiasmatic). This is not to say the work produced is bad, but the illusion that the architecture is a direct embodiment of the philosophical concept needs to be dropped.

malism, but they are theoretically very far apart. Modernism focuses on the rational, ideal, primary qualities, while phenomenological architecture quite often focuses on the embodied experience of secondary qualities such as light and color. Holl's Bloch Building extension on the Nelson-Atkins Museum of Art in Kansas City is made up of multiple unnameable shapes and spaces. The control of light through translucent channel glass tubes gives an ethereal glow to spaces that returns participants to the preconventional, carnal experience of phenomena. However, Holl's solutions often still appear reductive in their attempts to eliminate the sedimented, symbolic nature of building. Intellectualism's retreat to immanence for meaning overemphasizes the internal process of sedimentation, but this does not mean the world should be built as if it is all preconventional.[15] In fact, Holl's buildings cannot escape semiotics—in the daytime, particularly to someone driving by, the exterior of the building, because of the spacing and articulation of the vertical lines recalls the image of metal sheds or shipping containers.[16]

In Vitruvius's story of the birth of language and architecture, communication begins from gestures resulting from visible fire, and language is born from the flesh of the world. In that sense the visible is undeniably "foundational" to the invisible, but Merleau-Ponty does not take this to mean the contemporary goal is to return to the birth condition, or even that this is possible. Just as the child is now born into a world inhabited by language, architecture is created in a world with sedimented meaning that is both immanent to the signifier and transcendent of the signified. The architect is not trying to get back to transcendent meaning, nor to avoid it, but is instead working in a reversible world. Language cannot introduce anything new back into the material world when it is reduced to merely a reflection of the visible. Architectural language has an extra-referential nature—an intertwined relationship with the flesh—but the flow of influence is omnidirectional. Architectural language modifies architectural

15. As with every other building, Holl did not truly design the Bloch building in a preconventional world. Building codes, circulation patterns and egress, structure, mechanical systems, and many other conventions define how architecture is formed. These are just some examples of the inability of an architect to fully escape sedimented meaning.

16. According to Suzanne Stevens, during the construction process Holl's building was often referred to as shipping containers (2007, 94). By bringing up these associations, I am not attempting to make a value judgment but to merely point out the fact that these signifying relationships will always be made, regardless of whether the architect intends them or not.

visibility, just as the visible modifies the invisible. It must be remembered, as Merleau-Ponty reminds us, that "there is a strict ideality in experiences that are experiences of the flesh" (VI, 152).

Reversible and Irreducible Architecture

Modernism in its extreme denies architecture its symbolic power and consequently its immanence; postmodernism's semiological reductionism denies architecture access to the transcendent world and relegates architectural language to an idea. On the one hand, the experience of architecture is an experience of space, geometry, material, phenomena, and other linguistically transcendent qualities. On the other, the world is full of conventional signs whose meaning is immanently derived from diacritical relationships with other signs, and architectural elements act as a form of signification. However, these signs are not simply an unwanted consequence of carnal experience, nor are they simply the result of ideational, nonmaterial, abstract thought. Language is not something that attempts to correspond with the flesh; it is born out of the flesh and intertwined with it in a relationship in which each is able to affect the other.

The ambiguity of the flesh and the carnality of architecture allow the participant to move past representations to an experience of phenomena that moves her closer to the carnal roots of language. Architecture is both an infra-referential play of signs throughout history and within each building, and it is also an extra-referential, lived-body experience of the world of phenomena. The language of architecture, much like that of a poem, not only holds meaning in a rational, conventional way but can be read for meaning between and beyond what the symbols literally say.

The concept of reversibility becomes the vital difference between Merleau-Ponty's conception of language and that of a semiological reductive postmodernism or of a purely extra-referential modernism. First, each instance of *la parole* is also able to affect *la langue,* just as *la langue* is the structure on which each act of *la parole* takes place. This reversibility of language and meaning results in a language that is neither controlled by the immanent speaker nor by the transcendent structure. The rules of the composition of architectural elements are not rigidly restricted by an inaccessible structure, but neither are they free of sedimented meaning that controls how they are read. A door will be (and arguably must be) read as a door, but every individual door modifies the rules of what a door is. Second, language is able to affect phenomena and phenomena are able to affect language. This reversibility leads to intercorporeity in which transcendence and immanence are both able to affect each other. Architectural signs are not only ideals, but part of carnality that is able to affect and change the structure of the visible. The language of architecture and the stuff of architecture are not two separate things, but are both elementally the same and different. That which is built is built-spoken and a witness to Being.

References

Banham, Reyner. 1960. *Theory and Design in the First Machine Age*. 2nd Edition. Cambridge: The MIT Press.

Broadbent, Geoffrey. 1978. "A Plain Man's Guide to the Theory of Signs in Architecture." *Architectural Design* 47, no. 7–8 (July/August): 474–82.

———, Richard Bunt, and Charles Jencks. 1980. *Signs, Symbols, and Architecture*. Chichester: John Wiley and Sons.

Busch, Thomas W., and Shaun Gallagher, eds. 1992. *Merleau-Ponty, Hermeneutics, and Postmodernism*. Albany: State University of New York Press.

Corbusier, Le. 2007. *Towards an Architecture*. Translated by John Goodman. Los Angeles: Getty Research Institute.

Dillon, Martin C. 1997. *Merleau-Ponty's Ontology*. Evanston: Northwestern University Press.

———, ed. 1991. *Merleau-Ponty Vivant*. Albany: State University of New York Press.

Eco, Umberto. 1972. "A Componential Analysis of the Architectural Sign */Column/*." *Semiotica* 5, Issue 2 (January): 97–117.

Edie, James. 1973. "Foreword." In Merleau-Ponty, CAL, xi–xxxii.

Evans, Fred, and Leonard Lawlor, eds. 2000. *Chiasms*. Albany: State University of New York Press.

Gandelsonas, Mario. 1976. "Neo-Functionalism." *Oppositions* no. 5 (Summer). Reprinted in K. Michael Hays, ed. 1998. *The Oppositions Reader*, 7–8. New York: Princeton Architectural Press.

———, and David Morton. 1972. "On Reading Architecture." *Progressive Architecture* no. 53 (March): 68–88.

Giedion, Sigfried. 1967. *Space, Time, and Architecture*. 5th Edition. Cambridge: Harvard University Press.

Hays, K. Michaels. 2010. *Architecture's Desire: Reading the Late Avant-Garde*. Cambridge: The MIT Press.

Holl, Steven. 1995. *Intertwining: Select Projects 1989–1995*. New York: Princeton Architectural Press.

Jencks, Charles. 1977. *The Language of Post-Modern Architecture*. New York: Rizzoli.

Loos, Adolf. 1997. *Ornament and Crime: Selected Essays*. Translated by Michael Mitchell. Riverside, CA: Ariadne Press.

de Saussure, Ferdinand. 1966. *Course in General Linguistics*. 3rd Edition. Edited by Charles Bally and Albert Sechehaye. Translated by Wade Baskin. New York: McGraw-Hill.

Schmidt, James. 1985. *Maurice Merleau-Ponty: Between Phenomenology and Structuralism*. New York: St. Martin's Press.

Stevens, Suzanne. 2007. "*Steven Holl* Architects Merges Architecture, Art, and Landscape into a Unified Experience for the Bloch Building at the Nelson-Atkins Museum of Art in Kansas City." *Architectural Record* 195, Issue 7 (July), 92–101, 124.

Summerson, John. 1963. *The Classical Language of Architecture*. Cambridge: The MIT Press.

Tafuri, Manfredo. 1976. *Architecture and Utopia*. Translated by Barbara Luigia La Penta. Cambridge: The MIT Press. Originally published in 1973 as *Progetto e Utopia*. Bari, Italy: Laterza and Figli.

Venturi, Robert, Denise Scott Brown, and Steven Izenour. 1977. *Learning from Las Vegas: The Forgotten Symbolism of Architectural Form*. Revised Edition. Cambridge: The MIT Press.

Vitruvius. 1960. *The Ten Books on Architecture*. Translated by Morris Hicky Morgan. New York: Dover Publication.

Zevi, Bruno. 1994. *The Modern Language of Architecture*. New York: Da Capo Press.

7

Architecture and Voices of Silence

Patricia M. Locke

In his essay "Indirect Language and the Voices of Silence," Maurice Merleau-Ponty questions the role of the museum, as described by André Malraux in his influential book *The Voices of Silence*. Malraux's *musée imaginaire,* a museum without walls, has been adopted beyond his wildest dreams, as virtual museum visits proliferate and artifacts from many cultures jostle each other for iconic status as reproductions.[1] In his critique of Malraux, Merleau-Ponty stands at the crossroads of structuralism and phenomenology as he thinks through the museum, memory, indirect language, and bodily gesture. My essay will take up these topics in a reading of his transitional 1952 article.[2] Merleau-Ponty states:

> Language signifies when instead of copying thought it lets itself be taken apart and put together again by thought. Language bears the meaning of thought as a footprint signifies the movement

1. Galen Johnson summarizes the various translations of "*musée imaginaire*" in his insightful essay "Structures and Painting: 'Indirect Language and the Voices of Silence,'" in *The Merleau-Ponty Aesthetics Reader, Philosophy and Painting*, ed. Galen A. Johnson, trans. ed. Michael B. Smith (Evanston: Northwestern University Press, 1993), 28. I intend to focus on the institution of the museum, rather than follow the path of various meanings of imagination in Merleau-Ponty and Sartre, thus the selection of "museum without walls." Johnson also notes (p. 24) that Malraux's virtual museum met bricks and mortar in a 1973 exhibition at Saint-Paul-de-Vence, "*André Malraux et le musée imaginaire.*"

2. Notice the "transitional" position of this essay, given a trajectory in thought from "Cézanne's Doubt" (1945), and "Eye and Mind," published in 1961. This spans the decades between *Phenomenology of Perception* to the conception of the posthumously published *Visible and the Invisible.*

> and effort of a body. . . . True speech . . . is only silence in respect to empirical usage. (S, 44/56)[3]

True originating speech is interlaced with silence: the unsaid, the unsayable. Poetry can express in an oblique manner the contours of the speechless. Through the voice, sound and rhetoric convey the shape of what lies between the words as content, what is latent in words as having a history. In short, what bodily gesture brings to true speech is depth. Nonetheless, Merleau-Ponty joins Hegel in observing that the "ductility" of speech allows for language about language. Architecture refers only tangentially to itself through symbolic forms or through self-conscious narrative. While not as flexibly self-referential as speech, architecture is more explicitly embodied, because it both takes into account and creates a spatial world.

Merleau-Ponty sets up this relation: poetic language is to thought as footprints are to bodily movement. The meaning of thought or movement is registered with the gestural qualities of intention traced in ink or sand. The turn in a sonnet, or the twisted marks of a walker who glances back or changes direction on the beach, shows the embodied being at work.

Architecture is like poetry, insofar as it incorporates silence, leaving a gap between what can be made present and what cannot. Architecture does not simply record what happened or is happening, but presents a future for embodied beings. Architecture makes an articulated place for bodily movement, without proscribing all of its possibilities.[4] Meaning in architecture shows up in the ways in which human beings align themselves with architecture's multidimensional organization of space-time. Thus, the meaning of their exploration is manifest in the footprints that sink in moist areas, skirt others, or confirm a destination. Architecture presents a

---

3. The editions cited here are, respectively, trans. Richard C. McCleary (Evanston: Northwestern University Press, 1964); and Paris: Gallimard, 1960.

4. A vivid example: *Broadway Dance Steps*, by Jack Mackie, Seattle WA. Spontaneously, people accept the invitation of the bronze footstep patterns in the sidewalk to tango, foxtrot or waltz. Mackie notes, "It's the people dancing who really complete the piece." One time as the steps were being installed, Mackie saw a man lying face down on one of them. He thought it was a drunk passed out in this "transitional" neighborhood, but it turned out to be a blind person feeling the steps. Another time, someone added hip spray-painted steps, titled "Break Dancing." See Kery Murakami, "The Story behind the Steps in the Sidewalk," *Seattle Post-Intelligencer*, April 4, 2006.

field of latent possibilities, and footprints represent the unfolding experience of that field.

When poetic speech likewise holds open new intentions for language and thought—what is between the words—it touches underlying structures, or "matrices of ideas," like architecture. Merleau-Ponty claims:

> Expressive speech does not simply choose a sign for an already defined signification, as one goes to look for a hammer in order to drive a nail or for a claw to pull it out. It gropes around a significative intention which is not guided by any text, and which is precisely in the process of writing the text. . . . We must consider the word before it is spoken, the background of silence which does not cease to surround it and without which it would say nothing. (S, 46/74)

This groping is thought at work, braiding the invisible into the visible, the future and past dimensions into what unfolds in the present. It is important to note the background of silence is both horizontally structured in space and vertically structured in time. It is as if the poet grasps with a kind of verbal body that which holds itself out in a shaped world. Poetic gesture mimics the human body's quiet movement, breath, and desire in a fully surrounding milieu.

Architecture has an intimate connection to the features of the world that depend upon physical and historical grounds, yet may bring out volume, light, or spatial and temporal experiences that haven't been articulated. It may make things more clear, but on the other hand, architecture may make it easier for us to appreciate what resides in folds or shadows. Merleau-Ponty's phenomenology respects what rests beneath the skin, acknowledging the resistance that certain aspects of reality have to being made to appear. This depth, or silence, is an integral dimension of that which does appear.

When Merleau-Ponty considers a child beginning to speak, he uses spatial terms: she crosses a threshold into language as a whole "domain." He understands each sign as "composed and organized in terms of itself"; thus, it "has an interior and ends up laying claim to a meaning" (S, 41/66). Architecture too has an interior, and the meaning of each building is likewise based on the whole ground of the built world. Merleau-Ponty here gives as an example Brunelleschi's dome for the Florentine cathedral, in its challenge to medieval spatial understanding. The startling newness of initiation into language as a child or into shaped space by the agency of radical architecture holds open a gap between what has gone before and what may emerge. Again, Merleau-Ponty speaks of language in spatial terms:

> Its opaqueness, its obstinate reference to itself, and its turning and folding back upon itself are precisely what make it a mental power; for it in turn becomes something like a universe, and it is capable of lodging things themselves in this universe—after it has transformed them into their meaning. (S, 43/70)

Architecture itself folds back upon its resources, and changes or brings out the meaning of earlier ways of perceiving space. Dwelling in its world means accepting opacity as necessary and as consonant with embodiment. Architectural latency, renewal, and openness to future structuring of space/time together show the location of artworks, in a surrounding field, both vertically and horizontally spread out. The human child is located in an analogous field of language when he or she begins, and continues, to speak.

In "Indirect Language and The Voices of Silence," Merleau-Ponty begins and ends with an assessment of language, but in the middle section he defines and gives examples of bodily gesture and its relationship to style in painting. He states that we must

> recognize that what is designated by the terms glance, hand, and in general body is a system of systems destined for the inspection of a world and capable of leaping over [*enjamber*] distances, piercing the perceptual future, and outlining the hollows and reliefs, distances and deviations [*écarts*]—a meaning [*un sens*]—in the inconceivable flatness of being. (S, 67/107–108)

Let us apply these terms, *glance, hand,* and *body* to architecture and see how they fulfill this description to bring our world into full color and three dimensions.

Glance/*Le Regard*

To experience the world as integrally connected to the self is to claim that we are embodied beings. We move through physical space, in time, and we know the world as it presents goals toward which we bring our attention or desire. The glance actively gathers different views of the entities in the field before us, and constitutes them as three-dimensional objects.[5] Merleau-Ponty states:

> It is not the mind which takes the place of the body and anticipates what we are going to see. No; it is my glances themselves—[their] synergy, their exploration, and their prospecting—which bring the imminent object into focus. (S, 66–67/107)

What is a glance as prospector? Old-time prospectors panning for gold rapidly distinguish its glinting from a background of sludge. They sense what to look for and have developed techniques of the hand to enable gold nuggets to show themselves. Prospection is a kind of forward looking, an anticipation of what might fit together, might make sense out of what presents itself to view. The glances of young girls at a dance, Jane Austen tells us, likewise explore the prospects before them, bachelors with assets held as hopefully as a hat in the hand. A built prospect itself stands out, gives us a wide or long vista, face to face with a receptive viewer, as in the Nevsky Prospekt in St. Petersburg, Russia. This mutuality between the active glance and the facing world is not simply an exchange of focused look and transparent openness.[6] The act of focusing attention brings the "imminent object" into being, and adjusts the viewer's field. With a glance, corrections to earlier profiles are made, until a fuller sense of the being before the viewer is held. These adjustments are due to the movement of the viewer, but also to the way the prospect shows itself. That figure retains a depth that resists complete clarity. The glance may "leap over" distances, respectful of the shadows and hollows that make distance itself perceptible. Prospection is a risk, a gesture toward an undetermined future that may or may not bear out what it has promised the glance.

---

5. Glance is a too casual translation for *le regard*, for it does not mean a cursory look that keeps one from bumping into the furniture or people in a crowd. See Jane Austen's heroine Elizabeth Bennet for instruction in how to sort through partial views, oblique glances that at first yield an overall Gestalt (perhaps too hasty), to come to genuine regard and mutual apprehension. See also Edward S. Casey's work, *The World at a Glance* (Bloomington and Indianapolis: Indiana University Press, 2007), for several senses of this important term.

6. The grand boulevards of St. Petersburg lined with freshly painted nineteenth-century brownstones give only one aspect of the life of the inhabitants. Walk around back, past the trash heap, broken cars, and skinny cats, and enter dwellings cut up into small apartments with high ceilings, flocked wallpaper and scarce hot water to see the juxtaposition of past grandeur and the shifted resources of current Russian society.

Merleau-Ponty compares "free perception," in which "objects spread out in depth" without a definite apparent size, to perspective, which "circumscribes my vision" (S, 49/78–79). Various geometrical systems give specific parameters to sight, adjusting the scale of objects in a uniform manner. In free perception, objects in space are related directly to the eye, not to one another. As an example, the moon can be as small as a coin or as large as a house in a child's drawing. The world invites *le regard* in an open, yet never exhaustive, way. The flexibility of this prereflective way of perceiving the world results in sensitivity to what is immediately before the viewer, who cannot grasp it as a whole in one glance. Those things closest to us present surfaces that draw the eye, competing for our attention. The glance shifts its hold from one aspect to another and the accretion we call object is now figure, now ground. Merleau-Ponty notes that, "Before, my glance, running freely over depth, height and width, was not subjected to any point of view, because it adopted them and rejected them in turn" (S, 49–50/80). Sight conforms to topological features in the immediacy of a here and now, while it retains a modest recognition of past terrain contiguous with this one.

On the other hand, Merleau-Ponty observes that perspective drawing flattens the depth of the perceptible world by instructing the eye to take in aspects of several objects as figure all at once. The gap between foreground figure and background is suppressed, as is the active role of the glance.[7] Immediate presence is ceded to an authorized perspective. Two-dimensional architectural representations, whether perspectival tropes of plan/section/elevation or axonometric views, cannot do justice to the phenomenal experience of being in a particular place, regardless of whether environmental conditions or material features are denoted. Thus, three-dimensional models continue to hold an appeal to our self-understanding as inevitably embodied beings within a moving horizon.

When designing, the architect must rely on his or her remembered experiences of kinesthesia, sight, touch, etc., rooted in a specific world. That world, which unfolded in collaboration with the architect-as-inhabitant, now calls on the architect's imagination to present new spatial and temporal possibilities. The overlapping of memory and imagination strengthens the architect's glance. This world is not a text to be read, nor a sight to be

7. One thinks of the different ways that Ptolemy and Newton consider the moon. Ptolemy's observations were of the "free" perceptual variety, in keeping with the different *nature* of lunar and sublunar bodies. Newton, on the other hand, found the moon rising right above earthly mountains and made of similar material. I feel the loss in such a transition.

surveyed from on high, but a place that presents itself to a sensing human being. The architect is uniquely capable of presenting the world as world. This Merleau-Pontian view contrasts sharply with Malraux's *musée imaginaire,* which imposes order on works with no inherent connection. Malraux's reproductions are not in a position to face one another, to regard and register responsiveness, unlike the embodied architect and the built world, however far-flung and temporally disparate. Malraux continues to assume a tacit Hegelian "spirit" of art that can link artworks outside of their context by the agency of a critical subject. Merleau-Ponty struggles to find the words here, but agrees with Paul Klee's experience of trees that look at him—the world is as much an agent as the artist. This is doubly true for an architect, whose responsive vision must be expressed in the three-dimensional given world, compared with a painter, whose vision opens onto its own world via the two-dimensional canvas.

The Isamu Noguchi Garden Museum in Long Island City, New York, is a responsive case study. Here, close to warehouses filled with stone, marble, and other building materials, the Japanese-American sculptor Noguchi (1904–1988) had his studio. In 1981, he began construction of a museum across the street on a triangular corner plot. It is a retrofitted chemical plant at its core, built with materials similar to his workshop, thus displaying continuity with the processes of production. The museum features studio-like flowing spaces and a garden with both Japanese and North American native plants, to be enjoyed by workers on their lunch hour as well as art lovers with the specific intention to experience Noguchi's sculpture.

One enters a modest door to a small antechamber, which juts out into the garden. Rooms for sculpture are larger in scale, with high ceilings to promote enough air around the tall stone artworks. In the first area, there is a roofless triangular corner that brings natural light and a softening suggestion of the earthly origin of stone into a rather industrial space. Walls are cinderblock, braced here and there with steel; floors are cement, and their grey colors are a harmonious ground for the large basalt and granite pieces Noguchi exhibits on the first floor. Factory-style mullioned windows look out onto the garden in a parallel set of rooms arranged with smaller or lighter sculptures in marble or colored stone. The sculptor himself helped to arrange his work, thus setting up dialogues between various pieces. Noguchi describes Area 4 as follows:

> One enters a door space. The shape of the room is defined by the walls, the floor, and the air. The ceiling retains the metal sheets of the original chemical plant. The window brings the

> outside inside, opening the room to the green of nature. There is a hint of spaces beyond corners. The disposition of sculptures in two opposite symmetries is in keeping with the shape of the room. These sculptures abet an infinitude of silence.[8]

This reflection on his work shows that Noguchi considers his sculptures not simply as separate objects but as woven with human habitation. The works "speak" one to another, in silence. One must walk around his sculptures, taking the hint of what is around the corner, allowing the wind outside or a glimpse of marble to draw one into an adjoining room. The metal ceiling continues to rust, the "door space" makes one aware of transitions, and the vertical elements straighten the human back. Alternately, one feels strong and treelike, or graceful and flowing.

Going out into the garden reinforces these feelings. It is familiar, like a back yard, with places to sit and birds to watch. There, Noguchi set a pink granite water holder, *Tsukubai* (1962), hollowed out as a tiny pond of sky amid the trees and plants. Gravel crunches beneath the feet, as one queries *Practice Rocks in Placement* (1982–83), an improvisation with smooth granite stones.[9] In some way, the sculptor himself seems just around the next corner, yet the meditative placement of his artworks has achieved a serene stability. The silence Merleau-Ponty ascribes to the depth of what lies between is demonstrated in Noguchi's sculpture and in its effects upon those who experience it. *Le regard* works as a system with overlapping of aspects of the facing world, whether reflections in water or the rough-hewn textures of stone. Noguchi's understanding of silence, and the interwoven dimensions of nature and artworks to be experienced simultaneously or sequentially, thus displays features of Merleau-Ponty's developing point of view. The artist thinking in the round deliberately takes features of the common world, such as air, into account. Even though familiar air is often "invisible" to us, unless motivated by wind or lit by shafts of sun, it is the medium that "fills" architecture and allows for our movement through it. Air is one of the worldly aspects that is undeniably, though silently, woven through our porous being. This way of speaking about it is perhaps anticipating Merleau-Ponty's later writing, but is evident in the work of Noguchi.

8. Isamu Noguchi, *The Isamu Noguchi Garden Museum* (New York: Harry N. Abrams, 1987), 76–77. The catalogue photos are records of original placements. Some of the features I describe have been altered by a recent renovation, or by rotating exhibitions.

9. *Tsukubai-Waterholder* (1962) Noguchi Museum. Material: Granite. Dimensions: 8⅜ × 27⅛ × 17½ in. (21.3 × 68.9 × 44.5 cm). *Practice Rocks in Placement* (1982–1983). Material: Aji granite.

The Isamu Noguchi Garden Museum resists the reduction of the museum to a bourgeois institution, by open display of its material sources, while at the same time refusing the romantic subjectivism implied in a notion of the artistic genius submitting everything to his "style." Isamu Noguchi presents himself as a collaborative worker, within a context of pause. Consider the artworks he has made with traces of effort and the materiality of granite, marble, paper, and metal. Many of the works have a monumental quality to them, or like the example of *Practice Rocks in Placement*, have an affinity with natural arrangements and shapes. I bring forth this description to highlight the overlapping of artist-worker and the made object in thoughtfully arranged space, intended to provoke the glance. Its provocation slows perception and breath in the collaboration of art and natural elements that remain silent.

Hand/*La Main*

How is the hand implied in the eye's perception of the world? Is seeing derived from touching, yet at a distance? The hand grasps things, writes letters, and points out nuances. Is it perhaps an extension of sight? Either way, contact with the world through the hand is more immediate. Running a hand across rough stone or a smooth metal railing evokes different feelings toward the surround, and summons different gestures. These gestures are already expressive, in a kind of excess over practical use.

Merleau-Ponty would draw attention to our felt sense of ourselves as kin to the materials we manipulate. He picks up on Husserl's example of clasping one's own hand, as the evidence of embodied yet self-aware being. The gap between the hand held and act of holding confirms that we are objects like other objects within our horizon, yet we have dimensions that remain opaque to sight or touch. Our contact with others through clasping their hands lets us infer their separateness yet similarity to us. Merleau-Ponty does not extend his analysis in "Indirect Language and Voices of Silence" to the implications for intersubjectivity, but Noguchi's sculpture and its arrangement in his museum supports this direction in Merleau-Ponty's thought. Noguchi's intentionally heightened "place" is set aside for experience of embodied perception and a crossing over of environment/perceiver.

The architect's hand in design displays a style, whether in small drawings, models, or large buildings. Yet architecture is fundamentally collaborative. Prosaic speech is implicated in architecture's collaborative nature. We have in common our human bodies; cultural, linguistic, and other differences register in our styles. Since we each have a style and can recognize each other as having a style, we can respond as complements to one another. Gestures can meet, with respect for different heritage and customs, as well as for variations in the natural environment. (Obviously, negative reactions to contrast in custom and style, and ignorance or violation of the environment are all too prevalent.)[10]

Here we see a significant difference from painting, at least. Both the working style and the lack of narrative tradition distinguish architecture from its two-dimensional cousin. Merleau-Ponty continues Hegel's priority of the singular genius, like Vermeer, who captures the sense of cloth or softly lit skin on canvas, and who sets out a "structure, a style and a meaning." This meaning has an expressive function beyond the objects represented, in the way that narrative poetry too acts as sign for a lived reality.

Merleau-Ponty notices that modern painting does not attempt to resemble things but, as in the case of Van Gogh, it "no longer indicates some reality one must go towards, but what still must be done in order to restore the encounter between his glance and the things which solicit it, the encounter between the man who has to be and what exists" (S, 57/92). This restoration shows itself in the work of art.

In Merleau-Ponty's view the encounter between the glance and the soliciting world is characterized by the vivid fluidity of a conversation as opposed to a written text. Yet he does not see architecture as a site of encounter. This is surprising, since architecture engages the whole human being rather than appealing to one or other of the senses.

Architecture aims at presentation of space, not representation of it. It may be that residual Hegelian influence prevents Merleau-Ponty from fully addressing the material arts of sculpture, dance, and architecture. When one considers air, or light and shadow, as materials for architecture, never mind the new uses of glass, cloth, and synthetic materials, Hegel's binary opposition between thought and matter falls away.

Architecture is poeisis, construed as a making, but it is not an attempt at mimesis, or imitation, of life, as Aristotle considers dramatic poetry or painting. We shall assert provisionally that architecture (and other building arts such as landscape architecture) is a framing or structuring poeisis that makes vivid human embodiment possible. Poetry aligns itself with

10. Isamu Noguchi met with lack of comprehension, racism, and political resistance, notably from Robert Moses and New York critics, about a playground he proposed for Riverside Park. See Masayo Duus, *Journey without Borders, The Life of Isamu Noguchi* (Princeton: Princeton University Press, 2004).

architecture when it makes the musicality of speech evident, and is more like painting when representation is prominent. Musicality brings out the qualities of the voice, including its pitch and timbre, reinforcing the participation of the body in speech. This is particularly effective in communicating emotions, which lie between the words. So here indirect language expresses itself, both in what is seen and what is felt. There is a genuine encounter between maker and perceiver of the made world.

In architecture, the hand is in touch with ideas, grasped through what the hand fashions. From a Merleau-Pontian viewpoint, the mind as embodied displays itself at work. Like the example of grasping one's own hand, there is a space between the human perceiver and the human-as-architect. The same person can experience both "sides" of the equation, and terms from one side can be shifted to the other. However, the act of translation from one role to the other relies on the distanced moments of memory and imagination. The architect responds imaginatively to vertical silences in memory of past experiences of place, in order to fashion new places with elements that invite the hand or eye, and that encourage various movements of the body.

Body/*Le Corps*

As the crossroads of perception and action, the body takes up space. The embodied being *is* somewhere, not merely as an object, but as an entity that haunts or inhabits its place. Merleau-Ponty considers action as well as perception expressive of a person's style of responsiveness to the surrounding world. Without commanding each muscle and nerve, the body desires to move and does so. He claims that "all perception, all action which presupposes it, and in short every human use of the body is already primordial expression" (S, 67/108). What does a "human use of the body" express? Style. One's upright posture and way of moving, for example, display a stylish meaning without speech. Merleau-Ponty borrows Paul Ricoeur's apt word, "advent" (*l'avènement*), to suggest an inauguration of meaning or shape that goes beyond what has existed before, yet depends upon its ground. Every gesture is comparable, as gesture, to those of different styles, thus indicating that we live with others in a common human world. Merleau-Ponty claims that "[e]ach [gesture] is both a beginning and a continuation which, insofar as it is not walled up in its singularity . . . points to . . . recommencements" (S, 68/109–10). In the expectation of a birth, human gestures accompany the anticipated yet unpredictable goal, which is not purely physical. Present activity is shaped by the promise of the future, even though it is more shadow than substance. Similarly, the whole person is involved in change of place and thereby in change of open horizon for meaningful activity. In a more complex example, an artist or architect sets into motion an expression of style and significance that goes beyond the initial intention.

We say of a new direction that it "shows promise." It is this promise that links present work with the ground of the past, while making genuine novelty possible. There is an integrative function at work in multiple directions: my body makes itself gesture to carry out intentions within a particular context, just as an architect's lifework shows stylistic developments that needn't be fixed in stone. Each move forward as an embodied being opens up new terrain for engagement, against the backdrop of personal and cultural history. We take up our place as inhabitants in the world, which connects times and places with one another. Thus, novelty is not simply discontinuous with the past, but is surrounded by it. Every human gesture is comparable *as* human, and *as* gesture. New works show us new aspects of being human, even as they align themselves with our common grounds.

Architecture faces the twin difficulties of fragmentation and global obliteration of differences. If we can assert that architecture has a claim on all of us, living and dead, we must find grounds for saying why what one culture produces can resonate with people of another culture or time. At the same time, I want to resist a relativistic stance, a danger of Malraux's approach, and the demotion of the art of architecture to a subset of language.

Prior to the step of translation or re-presentation, architecture connects beings with the same kinds of bodies. A museum, by design, shows us ourselves as beings that value material objects, marked by a maker's hand or blessed by a ritual action. Objects once worshipped as fetishes can retain a trace of the aura of their original use. Museum architecture that provides for a genuine encounter between human beings and artworks—rather than a "spurious reverence"—can be an occasion of meaning and engaged work. An actual building cannot be replaced authentically by virtual tours in cyberspace, nor have artworks been superseded by its rapidly morphing contents. Why? Whether we will or no, we remain irreducibly embodied beings, facing objects in a world of depth in space and time.

Consider the second-floor museum addition in the Noguchi museum. It has a hardwood floor laid directly on the corrugated steel ceiling of the space below. One enters up a few steps, which gives the impression of being at eye height ("earth level, as it were") with the beautiful floors. Noguchi observed that, "It still retains the sensation of floating—a special sensitivity which causes it to participate with whatever is placed upon it."[11] These hardwood floors act as a horizon, for one is invited to come close to sculptures just millimeters above it, or resting directly on it, as *Black Hills* (black granite, 1970) or *Floor Frame/Remembering India* (yellow Siena marble and Black Petit granite; 3 elements, 1970), each demanding a shift in perceptual scale. The spectator's sense of personal size shifts with these artworks. As with an experience of bonsai, we adjust our body sense to adapt to a miniature yet vast landscape. *This Earth, This Passage* (Bronze, 1962) was worked in wet clay on the floor, and bears the marks of Noguchi's feet, thus combining the tactile imprint of the true-to-scale body with an overall impression of a landscape. Noguchi states:

> Ultimately, the floor as a metaphor for earth is the basic base beyond all others. Gravity holds us there. The floor is our platform of humanity, as the Japanese well know. This floor in its entirety graces all who enter. They partake in the experience of being sculpture.[12]

Visitors become living sculptures, moving with a felt sense of three-dimensionality. The varying textures of stone and wood, seen against white walls or a surprising window looking back on Manhattan, call out human physicality. One feels Noguchi's effortful gestures of chisel against stone in one's own muscles. Because of the garden elements, and the models of Noguchi's designs for landscape, paper lanterns, theatre and dance productions, even because of the overlapping scent of coffee from the café, all of one's senses are engaged in a "system of systems." His work brings out the visitor's being in the world, which undermines the expectation of distanced aesthetic judgment. The experience of The Isamu Noguchi Garden Museum elicits a deep restfulness, but also a desire to dance, to bring space to life with one's own body. The architecture is an understated adaptation of an urban workspace, and as such fully supports the worked stone and engaged viewer.

It is relatively easy to have a sense of coherence in a museum filled with artworks by one person, arranged as the artist desires in a place he or she designs, like the Noguchi Garden Museum in Long Island City. Malraux's *The Voices of Silence* sought to juxtapose very different works in age, media,

11. Noguchi, *Garden* Museum, 113.

12. Ibid., 122.

and scale for a mass audience. In doing so, the works became images, flattened and altered through photography. Photographic distortions are far worse, as we know, in the case of architecture. Buildings can be designed with the camera's eye in mind, rather than with an articulated façade and sensitive interior for full sensory experience. This current tendency ignores one fundamental difference between painting and architecture. Architecture is non-transportable, and must be taken with its context.[13]

Merleau-Ponty acknowledges the problem with photographic access to artworks, but he notes further why we care about the works of the past: as data for our own expression. A past work of art undergoes alteration, or rehabilitation, and Merleau-Ponty insists "[I]t is not a question of a finite sum of signs, but of an open field or a new organ of human culture" (S, 58/96). This open field affirms what is in common among us, rather than denies through difference. Earlier works become that upon which we work, and so the present of the past is not identical with its presence in its own time. Our endeavors are supported and enriched by an interlacing with what has been made previously, and at the same time call out for a renewed interpretation of what earlier works of art mean.

Isamu Noguchi designed monuments and landscapes much in agreement with Merleau-Ponty's view; for example, the Billy Rose Sculpture Garden at the Israel Museum in Jerusalem. This garden, designed in 1960–65 to exhibit contemporary sculpture, draws on Noguchi's intersubjective attitude toward the arts. Neva Shaanan, or Place of Tranquility, as the hilly site is called, brought out his desire to "raise a song of praise to the place. The earth itself would be the means."[14] His ambition to make this a new kind of Acropolis, with the sculpture garden in relation to the Shrine of the Book, the adjoining Hebrew University, and the Knesset, addresses what Merleau-Ponty considers vertical depth in time. The project is large in scale and intends a conversation between political, intellectual, and artistic life practiced in kinship with the interwoven aspects of these areas in classical period Athens. Noguchi respected the ancient hill, while carving out platforms for the display of artworks. He designed five curved retaining walls,

13. Here, as throughout this essay, I do not mean to include prosaic building of replicable tract housing or shopping malls. I mean architecture as akin to true speech, that which opens us up to the experience of dwelling.

14. Isamu Noguchi, *Essays and Conversations*, ed. Diane Apostolos-Cappadona and Bruce Altshuler (New York: Harry Abrams, 1994), 68.

built of rocks from the site mounded like "silent prayers for the dead" for, as he said, "from the oldest forms we learn to build anew. These walls are, for me, prayers for the living, they make new land. Seen from the University they have the evocative power of great wings."[15] One can look out across the valley at the university and Knesset as well, seen as smaller and related to one another from this perspective.

Like the way the floor of the Isamu Noguchi Garden Museum becomes a visual horizon for a person climbing the stairs, the curved walls seen from inside the garden sometimes seem to touch the sky, thus heightening awareness of the swelling of earth. The garden is a sculpture on a grand scale, or "a piece of the earth itself, extending all the way to China." This is a challenge to curators, who must place many different kinds of sculpture on the site. Noguchi included right-angled symmetry in parts of the garden, and protective structures for more delicate sculptures. But he meant the "challenge implicit in the garden. What forms must sculpture aspire to, to conform to our new nuclear, non-Euclidean, non-base-lined, relativistic world?" he asked, and by extension, this is a question for architecture as well.[16] Noguchi places the urgency of our present questions within the context of the natural and historically shaped past. Here is a collection of contemporary sculpture, with its contrasting perspectives, within a context that acknowledges and confronts tradition. Noguchi's ideal sense of his terraced architectural work is based on the perceptual experience that "one may walk upon it and feel its solidity under foot and know that it belongs to all of us without limit and equally. That it is in Israel does not make it less a part of any of us. We are all Israelis who come here and walk its slopes."[17]

It is precisely through particularity that one can reach this universalizing conclusion. Noguchi's views are consonant with Merleau-Ponty's emphasis upon the role of the body in making a human world. That system of systems, which is already expressive in gestures toward the world, either in appreciation or in production, shares in its history. Contra Malraux, who emphasizes discontinuity, Merleau-Ponty affirms a history constituted by our "interest which bears us toward that which is not us and by that life which the past, in a continuous exchange, brings to us and finds in us"

15. Ibid.

16. Ibid., 69.

17. Ibid., 71.

(S, 60/97). Our active involvement renews the past in the present, and makes the task of looking at sculptures one of continuous exchange. Our perception restores yet transforms what a work of art once meant, but the work itself retains an aura that radiates toward us. When we walk in the Place of Tranquility, we sense through our bodies our likeness to one another. No words are necessary for this intersubjective connection, which displays the intertwining of silence with the inhabited world. Noguchi thinks of the aura through a mythological analogy when he states: "I wanted to discover anew the myth of Orpheus—up and down, inside and outside—a myth not bound to any space but attached to the stones from which it was born."[18]

Merleau-Ponty's "Indirect Language and The Voices of Silence" was written in 1951, and recast in 1952 for publication in *Les Temps Modernes*, the journal of arts and politics that he, along with Simone de Beauvoir and Sartre among others, began in 1945. Merleau-Ponty's essay shows concern for an ethical dimension in the search for a proportional relation between poetry and the silent arts. Merleau-Ponty claims that each of us, as an individual who must become aware of history, must add

> the obligation to understand situations other than my own and to create a path between my life and that of others, that is, to express myself. Through the action of culture, I take up my dwelling in lives that are not mine. I confront them, I make one known to the other, I make them co-possible in an order of truth, I make myself responsible for all of them, and I create a universal life, just as by the thick and living presence of my body, in one fell swoop I take up my dwelling in space. (S, 75/121)

It is architecture's responsibility to make this path, to draw out the fertility of the thick silence that surrounds human life and opens the possibility of true speech. Noguchi's museum structures counter the erosion of particularity in the flattening of Malraux's *musée imaginaire*. From the ground of embodied being, we can sustain the mutual support of architecture and poetic language for one another. They are distinct "actions of culture" that draw on the irreplaceable strengths of the voices of silence.

18. Isamu Noguchi in Ashton Dore, *Noguchi East and West* (Berkeley: University of California Press, 1992), 194.

References

Casey, Edward S. 2007. *The World at a Glance* (Bloomington and Indianapolis: Indiana University Press).

Dore, Ashton. 1992. *Noguchi East and West.* Berkeley: University of California Press.

Duus, Masayo. 2004. *Journey without Borders, The Life of Isamu Noguchi.* Princeton: Princeton University Press.

Johnson, Galen A., ed. 1993. *The Merleau-Ponty Aesthetics Reader. Philosophy and Painting.* Translation editor, Michael B. Smith. Evanston: Northwestern University Press.

Noguchi, Isamu. 1987. *The Isamu Noguchi Garden Museum* (New York: Harry N. Abrams).

———. 1994. *Essays and Conversations.* Edited by Diane Apostolos-Cappadona and Bruce Altshuler. New York: Harry Abrams.

8

The Philosopher of Modern Life*

Baudelaire, Merleau-Ponty, and the Art of Phenomenological Critique

Duane H. Davis

For Cynthia Willett and Tyrone Williams,
whose authentic criticism (philosophical and poetic)
continues to inspire

Phenomenology is a philosophy of lived experience. It offers a description that changes the experienced world from a standpoint situated within that world. Phenomenology owns up to being a part of the world it is accounting for—especially existential phenomenology, and most especially an aesthetic phenomenology. With that in mind, we begin with an account of the presentation of the phenomena as lived.

There is a specter haunting Europe—or Paris, at least. That is how I came to make the acquaintance of M. Charles Baudelaire in 1999.[1] While walking one afternoon in Paris, I found myself on the Île St Louis very

*I want to express my sincere gratitude to my friend, Richard Simanke, who generously offered to translate this essay at the Philosophy Congress in Curitiba, Brazil. An earlier version of this paper was presented at the *VI Congresso de Filosofia Contemporânea, Pontifícia Universidade Católica do Paraná—Brasil,* Curitiba, Brazil, August 5, 2008. I also presented an earlier version of this essay to the *Western North Carolina Continental Philosophy Group* in 2010.

1. Charles Baudelaire, 1821–1867.

close to his former residence. While sitting on a nearby bench, I took out my copy of *Les Fleurs du mal.* I remembered that Maurice Merleau-Ponty had taught one of his first courses at Lyon on the works of Proust and Baudelaire.[2] Mauro Carbone and Leonard Lawlor, among others, have rightly devoted serious study to the connections between Merleau-Ponty and Proust.[3] Obviously, Merleau-Ponty's published works are saturated with oblique and direct references to Proust. In the posthumously published *Le visible et l'invisible*, Merleau-Ponty even states that "no one has gone further than Proust in the fixation of the rapports between the visible and the invisible" (VI, 149/195)." (I will have more to say about this passage in the second section of this essay.) And anyone who has even glanced at Merleau-Ponty's unpublished notes has seen that he was inspired by Proust throughout most of his career to an even greater degree than his publications indicate.[4]

However, not nearly as much has been written about Baudelaire's influence on Merleau-Ponty. That is highly regrettable because *Les Fleurs du mal* even contains a poem titled *Réversibilité*.[5] And these amazing poems were teeming with so many of the metaphors that animate Merleau-Ponty's ontological writings in his later work. Therefore, the task of this paper is to call forth the Baudelairean spirit haunting Merleau-Ponty's thought, to beckon it to reveal itself and come into the light. This project has some

---

2. Hugh Silverman and James Edie each made rather cryptic reference to such courses in person and in print, though at this point it is not clear where the lecture notes to which they referred may be—if they still exist. Cf. Hugh J. Silverman and J. Barry Jr., eds., *Texts and Dialogues: Merleau-Ponty* (New Jersey: Humanities Press, 1992), xv; and James M. Edie, *Merleau-Ponty's Philosophy of Language: Structuralism and Dialectics* (Washington, DC: University Press of America,1987), 99. Merleau-Ponty did offer several remarks on Baudelaire in his 1953 course at the *Collège de France, Recherches sur l'usage littéraire du langage*, though here more often than not he is reacting to Sartre's account of Baudelaire as much as to the poet himself.

3. Leonard Lawlor has done some outstanding work on the different kinds of love in Proust and their manifestations in Merleau-Ponty's thought. Cf. also Mauro Carbone, *La visibilité de l'invisible* (Hildesheim: Olms Verlag, 2001). Carbone brilliantly shows how Merleau-Ponty's phenomenological attitude, as Merleau-Ponty explicitly states in the "Preface" to *Phénoménologie de la perception*, is one of astonishment before the world, and how Merleau-Ponty's interest in modern artists—especially Proust—has to do with the artist's similar attitude of astonishment with regard to cultivating the latency of meaning beyond the visible, beyond the literal, without appealing to a moment of interiority—"the breaking-up of the traditional notion of the subject" (Carbone 2001, 130).

4. It is also interesting that each time I visited Mme. Merleau-Ponty (now deceased), she had a copy of a journal of Proust studies on the table.

5. *Réversibilité* is one of the central concepts in Merleau-Ponty's later ontology.

intrinsic importance, since Baudelaire's critique of modernity reveals a depth to Merleau-Ponty's work that has received too little attention—a sociopolitical horizon to Merleau-Ponty's later work—and shows how we might take Merleau-Ponty's work a little farther today. The huge philosophical question lurking in the background is: What role or roles do philosophers and poets play in the critique of modernity?

These two great thinkers were separated by about one hundred years as well as by discipline. We will organize our restricted investigation along the axes of two key aspects of Merleau-Ponty's later thought, *réversibilité* and *écart* (actually, *correspondances* in Baudelaire), in the context of their antiromantic critiques of modernity. More specifically, I pose the following theses: (1) Baudelaire's antiromantic realism is a striking parallel to Merleau-Ponty's later thought. (2) Merleau-Ponty's later work can be read as an ontological appropriation of Baudelaire's antiromanticism in his development of *réversibilité* and *écart* in his later work. Finally, (3) recognizing the Baudelairean aspects of Merleau-Ponty's ontological thought reveals its critical (social and political) horizon and has implications for our own critical situation with respect to modernity.

The "Alchemy of Suffering" and the Art of "Secret Science"

Moesta et erranbunda[6] is more than the title of one of Baudelaire's poems—it describes both his own anguished role as a poet in modern urban life as well as his view of the existential state of nineteenth-century Europe.[7] His sorrow at the damned and decadent state of modern society flows from every page—his words surging forth in tearful torrents of rage and love. Baudelaire wandered through his Paris as he wandered through much of his life—driven to capture in his anguished verse the alienation he saw and felt

6. Charles Baudelaire, *Les fleurs du mal*, poem # 62, 1861 edition. I will cite Baudelaire from the bilingual edition that includes James McGowan's translation. However, as with all texts cited in this essay, all translations are my own unless noted otherwise. McGowan is more sensitive to poetic structure and rhyme than I prefer. For a philosophical appropriation of Baudelaire's work, I think that more emphasis should be placed upon the sense of the text while retaining the original metaphors whenever possible. Charles Baudelaire, *The Flowers of Evil*, with parallel French text, trans. James McGowan (Oxford: Oxford University Press, 1993), 128. This work will be cited as FM, with the poem # from the 1861 edition. *Moesta et erranbunda* means "sorrowful and wandering."

7. It would be interesting to contrast this state of wandering with Marcel's hopeful description of the human condition as *Homo Viator*.

so deeply—bemoaning the sickness his society suffered that destroyed his and so many other lives. Whistling past the graveyard, we are sanguine at our accomplishments as we remain obsessed with our petty tasks: "Our soul will be spent in subtle schemes."[8] Our state of being is so wretched that we have no recourse to God for help in dealing with what we have wrought. "O Satan, take pity on my prolonged misery."[9] Yet Baudelaire's love was expressed as passionately as his vitriolic disgust. His pride in his abilities figures into his role as a poet, and once again also reflects an existential state; for in his view we ought to love, so long as love remains possible. Perhaps there has never been a more profound and complicated account of alienation, ennui, and disgust at the modern human condition.[10]

We suffer the modern life we inflict upon ourselves. But perhaps Baudelaire shows that the expression of our suffering has a transformative effect, though it is quite distinct from the romantic self-pity of Shelley or Byron. Or at least, he grew out of that sort of romantic self-love. Baudelaire is clearly impressed with his own abilities—whether or not these abilities were recognized sufficiently by his mother, his half-brother, his teachers, his colleagues, his family's legal and financial advisor, his publishers, his critics, or his readers.[11] But he is also contemptuous of his own limitations, self-imposed afflictions, addictions, diseases, poverty, and perpetual professional and personal plight. And this dimension inspires a powerful antiromantic realism in his work. Baudelaire, having played the role of the dandy until his funds were cut off, was also always attracted to the sordid underbelly of urban Paris—

8. FM, "*La Mort des artistes*," # 123, 278: "*Nous userons notre âme en de subtils complots.*"

9. FM, 268ff. This is the refrain from the poem "Litanies of Satan," # 120: "*Ô Satan, prends pitié de ma longue misère.*"

10. Friedrich Nietzsche is a plausible exception to this claim. See especially his *Thus Spoke Zarathustra*, Third Part, ch. 5, "On Virtue That Makes Small."

11. Baudelaire's relationship with his mother is notorious in the secondary literature. His father died when he was only five years old, and his mother remarried the very next year. Baudelaire hated his stepfather throughout his life and never forgave his mother for remarrying, even though she married a very successful man. It is the general consensus that Baudelaire thought that his love for his mother should have been sufficient. At the same time, she was very, very possessive of him, refused to rein him in against the advice of her new husband, her stepson, and the family advisors. By 1844 he was spending his inheritance at an unreasonable rate, and she was persuaded to restrict his access to these funds. This disciplinary act notwithstanding, she remained overly protective of her boy even as he grew older, and he reacted by becoming more and more self-destructive. Cf. any of the copious biographies of Baudelaire, such as: Joanna Richardson, *Baudelaire* (New York: St. Martin's Press, 1994), esp. 3–219; Enid Starkie, *Baudelaire* (New York: New Directions, 1958), esp. 27–83, Jean-Paul Sartre's work on Baudelaire, etc.

prostitution, addiction, poverty, and the flouting of conventional morality. He regarded traditional morality as a comfortable hypocrisy, as did Nietzsche, but he also deplored the life of vice as much as the naive embrace of virtue. I commend to you any of the copious biographies, which often vary wildly in their speculative conclusions. Baudelaire is presented as everything from a bourgeois punk to a drug-addled Satanist, to an austere moralist. And each of these has a grain of truth, though none exhaustively captures his character.

Let us turn our attention from these general biographical issues to the philosophical implications of two remarkable poems from *Les Fleurs du mal* that I believe typify the style of antiromantic realism of some of Baudelaire's work that would later influence Merleau-Ponty: *Correspondances* and *Réversibilité.* Reading the poems for their philosophical implications is less tendentious than some philosophical appropriations of poetry, since Baudelaire apparently conceived of these implications as well. According to Enid Starkie, Baudelaire said at one point in his career that "philosophy seemed to him now the only thing worthy of the attention of a poet."[12]

Correspondances is a powerful poem that reacts to the idealism of Plato as well as the mysticism of Swedenborg.[13] For Baudelaire, whatever

12. Starkie, *Baudelaire*, 225. However, she implies that this reflects a turn toward mystical spiritualism as evidence of Baudelaire's maturation. I am not persuaded by this line of argument, as will be clear in a moment.

13. I prefer Jonathan Culler's interpretation of this poem to Starkie's, since I believe that she misses the irony. Cf. Jonathan Culler, *Baudelaire's "Correspondances": Intertextuality and Interpretation*, in *Nineteenth Century French Poetry* ed. Christopher Pendergast (Cambridge: Cambridge University Press, 1990). For the opposing interpretation, there is Starkie's reading of this poem as presaging Baudelaire's later conversion to a spiritual moralist at the direct influence of Swedenborg—though she makes a case for the gradual acquaintance with Swedenborg's symbolic mysticism even from Baudelaire's work on Poe. Cf. Starkie, 225–38. Though I profess no expertise here, it seems to me that Starkie is reading her own preferences for Baudelaire's later poems into his earlier work such that it either manifests a gradual acquaintance with Swedenborg's spirituality or else is proto-Swedenborgian. But much further study would be required to support that assertion. Indeed, the correspondences between senses seem as likely the product of Baudelaire's experiences with hashish as with Swedenborg's theology. Cf. Charles Baudelaire, *On Wine and Hashish*, trans. A. Brown (London: Hesperus Classics, 2002), 21: "External objects take on monstrous appearances. They reveal themselves to you in shapes hitherto unknown. Then they become distorted, transformed, and finally they enter into your very being, or you enter into them. The strangest equivocations, the most inexplicable transpositions of ideas take place. Sounds have their own colour, colours make music. Musical notes are numbers. . . . You are sitting down, smoking; you think that you are sitting in your pipe, and it's you that your pipe is smoking; it's you that you are breathing out in the form of blue-tinged clouds." Of course, experiences with hashish and Swedenborg need not be mutually exclusive.

correspondences there may be in life that lend life its sense and value are not those between a particular and a metaphysical ideal, nor are they concerned with perfect symbolization. The visible is no imperfect symbolic aperture upon a perfect and ideal invisible infinite. Their relation is not harmonious and symmetrical—some disguised ideal hidden to the many but revealed to the mystic. Baudelaire delighted in shocking and grotesque images in his poetry that are delicious examples of *dissonance* rather than harmony. For Baudelaire, the world yields "an irresistible allure of the horrible."[14] He stated that for humans, "the unique and supreme delight lies in the certainty of doing evil."[15] These words bespeak no mystical harmony, no moral world order, and no romantic idealism.

For Baudelaire, correspondences are not simply representations of ideals. They are instead matters of compromise and contingency wherein value appears. Correspondences often are accomplished by shocking, forceful juxtapositions that reveal a disturbing intramundane existence.

Mauro Carbone describes this very well:

> [Correspondences are] the repetition of an already lived situation, the rapport which is spontaneously established between different and analogous experiences, the bringing-together of things, beings, or signs that refer [*renvoient*] to other things, to other beings, to other signs, all that seems to bear witness to a "preobjective" accord between the individual and the sensible.[16]

Perhaps one ought to add that this accord is "presubjective" as well as "preobjective," and that the accord is dynamic and fragile. It is also unfortunate that Carbone's focus in this work is almost exclusively upon correspondences in Proust, even though he acknowledges in a few words immediately above this passage that "one can already find [them] in Baudelaire."[17] To be fair, Carbone is following Merleau-Ponty's explicit guide here in a passage I referred to above.

> No one has gone further than Proust in the fixation of the rapports between the visible and the invisible, in the description of

14. Ibid., 10.

15. Baudelaire quoted in Richardson, *Baudelaire,* 50.

16. Mauro Carbone, *La visibilité de l'invisible* (Hildesheim: Olms Verlag, 2001), 42.

17. Ibid.

> an idea that is not the contrary of the sensible, that is its double and its depth. (VI, 149/195)

If Proust went further than anyone, his inspiration, and hence Merleau-Ponty's, can be found in Baudelaire. It is worth a closer look at Baudelaire to see what can be revealed in Merleau-Ponty's thought.

Correspondances opens with what at first seems to be a romantic idealization of nature: "Nature is a temple." However, it soon becomes clear that human beings are part of the temple—its "living pillars"—they lend support yet they say some strange and confusing things. Humans are depicted as wandering in a "forest of symbols" which in turn observe us as symbols—peers. Apparently "*Sprache spricht*" in Baudelaire as well.

The unity that arises in this poem is not given or perfect, but is depicted through the metaphor of "echoes" that are heard from a long way off and hence interweave and interact in new ways. The unity is linked with a productive aural dissonance and immediately described in visual terms of a clarity that is to be found in darkness rather than in light. It is in these contingent terms that the senses interweave and interact—where "Scents, colors and sounds co-respond." The encroachment of these senses is expressed in the reflexive verb *se répondre*, rather than *répondre*: they respond together—co-respond—correspond. The unity of correspondence is creative and active rather than static or given a priori.

The activity of correspondences is further reflected in the term "*expansion* of infinite things"—where these things are in the process of creating and filling up the expanse, or spreading-out. And what is infinite about these things? Nothing more than the transcendence of embodied sensation—scents and sights and sounds and touches and tastes—that afford rapturous delights or heinous suffering. And ultimately, it is *perception* that grounds the relation of mind and body here: "Which sing the raptures of mind and senses." Baudelaire is a poet of the body every bit as much as a "spiritual" poet. It is this account of perception and its primacy that is quite similar to what Merleau-Ponty would call a ground in his earlier work, and what he would later call "the soil of the sensible."

I think that Merleau-Ponty's provocative notion of *écart*—divergence or the spread created by divergence—is prefigured in Baudelaire's correspondences. Merleau-Ponty begins the chapter on the chiasm in *Le visible et l'invisible* with his ubiquitous rejection of the subject/object dichotomy. For as soon as philosophy starts with a radical ontological distinction between subject and object, between inside and outside, between reflection and coincidence, "it prejudges what it will find" (130/172). So it is necessary to start anew so as to avoid these prejudices, which have become sedimented in the discourse of modern philosophy. Instead of an ontology presupposing a principle of identity, Merleau-Ponty began to develop a new direction in ontology that was based upon differences—differentiation—divergence—*écart*. This new direction in ontology stressed the encroachment (*empiétement*) and interactivity of things, senses, and beings as a process of differentiation very much like Baudelaire's correspondences.

> It is necessary for us to habituate ourselves to think that everything visible is cut from the tangible, all tactile being is in some manner promised to visibility, and that there is encroachment, impingement, not only between the touched and that which touches, but also between the tangible and the visible which is encrusted within it. (VI, 134/177)

It is through this encroachment and interference that the unity of the world is produced. It is as these series of differences that identity emerges—not as a static, given, harmonious unity, but as an implied horizon of differentiation. Indeed, the world *worlds* as an implied horizon of differentiation of horizons of differences.

> [One sees that] in general some visible thing is not an absolutely hard, indivisible being that is offered all nude to a vision which could only be total or null. Instead it is a kind of always gaping straits between interior horizons and exterior horizons, something that comes to touch lightly and make resound at a distance diverse regions of the colored or visible world, a certain differentiation . . . the difference between things and colors, a momentary crystallization of the world of color and the visibility. (VI, 132/175)

These gaping straits are the spread between emerging from one perspective as discrete identities differing from one another, and from another perspective the process of differentiation itself. Likewise, one word emphasizing the differentiation of these very Baudelairean correspondences in Merleau-Ponty's later work is *écart*. But it goes hand in hand with the word *réversibilité*, which emphasizes the horizon of differentiation—the *relations* of differences. Let us turn our attention to Baudelaire's poem *Réversibilité* to see how it informs Merleau-Ponty's later work.

Baudelaire writes this exquisite poem in the voice of a lover to another lover, whom he repeatedly characterizes as an "angel." And although the angel is certainly portrayed in positive terms—i.e., full of good-fated happiness, kindness, health, beauty, joy, and light—one must not jump to the conclusion that Baudelaire is guilty of romantic idealization of his lover.[18] There is a great irony in this poem. A quick look at other poems in *Les fleurs du mal* shows us that Baudelaire does not place angels in such high regard.[19] Furthermore, it is clear that Baudelaire has contempt for one who would be "full of happiness." In the previous poem, *À celle qui est trop gaie* (*To One Who Is Too Happy*), Baudelaire fantasizes vivisection and rape of the "angel."[20] Such purity of heart is unbecoming of the human condition.

The relationship is the focus here, along with the quite divergent perspectives of the lovers involved. While the "angel" is happy, healthy, etc., her lover indicts her for what her countenance has wrought in him and in others. While she is full of happiness, he is tossing and turning at night, sobbing, full of dread and remorse, with his heart crushed. While she is full of kindness, she seems oblivious to the hatred that corresponds to her kindness. While she is healthy, there are those who are feverous and driven mad by the conditions that produce her health. While she is beautiful, has she even considered what it will be like to be wrinkled, wretched, and despised? And even though she radiates her happiness, joy, and the light of her well-being, he asks only for her prayers—not to become her.

In the poem *Les Hiboux* (*The Owls*), Baudelaire describes the ambition of yearning to change place with those who are more fortunate as a useless distraction of those who are "drunk on shadows."[21] Reversibility is not an act of will, a yearning of the lover to become like his angel, or for her to become like him. It is instead a lesson on the divergent and different perspectives that emerge from this unhealthy relationship. Their experiences are interdependent in their divergence.

Nor is reversibility a cognitive exercise in reflective consciousness. For example, the remorse that Baudelaire contrasts to the happiness of the "angel" is a consuming existential state, quite visceral and no mere thought

18. Martin C. Dillon has brilliantly illustrated the dangers of romantic love, and shown how Merleau-Ponty's position can be developed to recognize this problem and avoid it, in *Beyond Romance* (Albany: State University of New York Press, 2004). He develops this approach in a more general way in the manuscript he was completing at the time of his death, *The Ethics of Particularity*.

19. Cf. *Les litanies de Satan*, where Satan is, of course, described as an angel. FM, poem# 120, 268–73.

20. Ibid., poem # 43a., 88.

21. Ibid., poem #67, 136.

process. In his striking poem, *Spleen (II)*, Baudelaire portrays his remorse with the image of worms "attending to the dearest of my dead."[22] They crawl, they gnaw, they consume, and the process is slow and inexorable—and a very physical phenomenon.

It hardly bears mentioning that this description of love as reversibility is antiromantic. Baudelaire points out what horrors come with this love. This is love for the sick alienated animals we have become in the modern age. Love as an ideal has surely fallen from the sky and been brought down to earth—not unlike what Merleau-Ponty intended in the "Preface" to *Phénoménologie de la perception*, where he promises to places essences "back into existence."

Baudelaire implicates the reader as being in a reversible relationship with him from the start of the book, in his poem *Au lecteur* (*To the Reader*). The reader suffers right alongside him, is suffering in the same age, is also limited by the ennui and alienation of the age.[23]

I contend that Merleau-Ponty appropriates Baudelaire's *réversibilité* as an ontological principle. Merleau-Ponty describes reversibility as "ultimate truth" (VI, 155/204). He contrasts it to the Sartrean dualistic dialectical opposition and instead emphasizes the reversible relation of differentiation. Reversibility is at the heart of Merleau-Ponty's ontology, alongside the *écart,* and expresses the way things achieve their divergent fragile identities through their differentiating actions intertwined with one another. Reversibility is the ability in principle—never complete—to be another being. It is a way of pointing out that the identity we have taken as the basis for modern thought is predicated upon the ability to share existence through differentiating actions.

This is also made clear in the essay *l'Oeil et l'esprit.*

> A human body is there when, between seeing and the visible, between touching and touched, between one eye and another, . . . between one hand and the other, between hand and hand a sort of crisscrossing [*recroisement*] takes place. (OE, 125/21)

22. Ibid., poem #76, 146.

23. Ibid., 4–6. Many Baudelairean metaphors animate *l'Oeil et l'esprit*. Merleau-Ponty is preoccupied with things mute, expressing the silent (122/13), the limpid (as flaw—Descartes's lament for consciousness to make all things clear) (130/36), "philtres" (130/35), haunting (122/13), fevers (128/30), shadow/twilight/dawn, phantoms (128/30, 129/33), *renversements* (125/19), dreams/nightmares, and embodiment throughout. In a longer work, each of these could be explored in greater detail.

And the emphasis here, once again, is on the *event*, the activity, and the process of differentiation. In fact, until the final version of this essay, Merleau-Ponty also included here "an encroachment, a transgression" immediately after this passage.[24] A nice parallel passage in *Le visible et l'invisible* occurs in the chiasm chapter: "By this crisscrossing within of the touching and the tangible, these very movements are incorporated within the universe that they interrogate" (VI, 155/176). This is how our divergent styles of being emerge. This is how we become who we are.

Merleau-Ponty's essay *l'Oeil et l'esprit* is a beautiful critique of modernity, especially the modern world as figured by science. Instead, Merleau-Ponty wants us to attend to a "secret science" of the artist (OE, 123/15). He does this by a phenomenological inquiry into the ways and means the artist is attuned to the "soil of the sensible world," which has been neglected in favor of the "worked-over" world of scientific knowledge (ibid., 122/10). And the themes of *réversibilité* and *écart,* developed from Baudelaire's *correspondances* and *réversibilité* are at the heart of Merleau-Ponty's secret science. So we can read M-P's account as he read the artists': the artist at work self-consciously reflecting upon his *praxis* as artist.

For Baudelaire, the praxis of the poet is to "lend grace to things most vile."[25] He also describes the poet as a "pious enemy of sleep" who takes to heart the indiscrete tears of the moon, "far from the sun."[26] So the poet here is an enemy of the Enlightenment—one who secrets things; yet the poet does this out of *love*.

Perhaps the most interesting analogy Baudelaire makes about the praxis of the poet is in his essay *On Wine and Hashish*, where he compares the poet to a garbage collector.[27]

24. Merleau-Ponty, notes, Vol XIII, cf. 2nd typed version.

25. FM, poem #87, 168.

26. Ibid., poem #65, 134.

27. It is interesting to contrast Baudelaire's antiromantic vision of the poet as the garbage collector of society with the romantic vision of Percy Bysshe Shelley. Cf. his "In Defense of Poetry," in *Norton Anthology of English Literature*, Volume D: *The Romantic Period*, ed. Stephen Greenblatt and M. C.Abrams. 8th ed. (New York: Norton, 2005), 850: "Poets are the unacknowledged legislators of the world." I want to express my gratitude to Mr. Jacob Riley for suggesting this passage to me to help express the contrast between Baudelaire's work and the older romantics. One of the greatest pleasures of teaching is in learning from outstanding students.

> Let's lower our sights a little. Let's contemplate one of those mysterious beings, living so to speak off the excrement of great cities; for there are some strange occupations around. There's a huge number of them. . . . Here is a man whose task it is to pick up all the rubbish produced on one day in the capital. All that the great city has thrown out, all it has lost, all it has disdained, all it has broken, he catalogues and collects. He consults the archives of debauchery. . . . He makes a selection, chooses astutely: he picks up, as a miser seizes on treasure, the refuse which, when chewed over by the divinity of Industry, will become objects of use or enjoyment. . . . He arrives, wagging his head and stumbling over the cobbles like those young poets who spend all their days wandering around in search of rhymes. He is talking to himself; he pours out his soul to the cold night air.[28]

The poet can create value amidst the alienation of modernity. What can the philosopher do?

Merleau-Ponty's ontology emerged from his political differences with Sartre. He began to try to develop a new philosophy of history, which led to his exploration of nature, which eventually developed into his nascent ontology, which he was unable to develop. I do not agree with Sartre that Merleau-Ponty's ontology was a theory set over against praxis. I think that by elaborating his ontology in situated terms of the work of the artist, Merleau-Ponty provides us a useful starting place for further thought about the relation between ontology and politics. In my own work, I have begun to explore how an ontology of differences provides the basis for a strong critique of Western liberalism. It may be useful to look to Baudelaire's inspiration to see how Merleau-Ponty's ontology differs from others in the phenomenological tradition, and thus why an ontology of differences is more promising for political thought.

Heidegger pointed out that every revealing is also a concealing. Nonetheless, for Heidegger phenomenology is concerned with bringing things to light.[29] Merleau-Ponty, drawing upon Baudelaire's gloomy leitmotif, allusively depicts phenomenology as more concerned with shadows,

28. Baudelaire, *On Wine and Hashish*, 8.

29. Ibid., §7, where Heidegger famously discloses the origins of phenomenology in *phō*—light.

chiaroscuro, and twilight. It is clear that phenomenology, and not only the philosopher, has a shadow. Merleau-Ponty transformed phenomenology to something much more radical.[30] In his working notes to *L'Oeil et l'esprit*, Merleau-Ponty wrote that it was essential to radicalize the notion of light "to make of the work of art a *Seinsgeschichte*."[31] It is the darkness that beckons us to wonder.

It is by moving away from the model of phenomenology as science of sciences that Merleau-Ponty engages in his critique of modernity. Or, to put it another way, his critique of science and valorization of the artist makes room for us to conceive of phenomenology as an *art* rather than as a science, thereby transplanting phenomenology back into the rich soil of the sensible world—the world of lived experience.

Phenomenology originally conceived of its wisdom as providing a science of the sciences. There can be no science of wisdom. There might be an *art* of wisdom; for certainly there is wisdom in art.

The Art of Phenomenological Critique

So: what would it cost political criticism if it were approached as an art rather than a science? We propose that there is a style of thinking that is very untimely—and therefore very timely in another sense. That is, we propose that one conceive of a political art rather than a political science—an art of political critique rather than a scientific critique. *We propose a political art that is intrinsically critical and distinctively phenomenological.*

The roles of the *epochē* and reduction in phenomenology would vary between phenomenology as science as opposed to phenomenology as art. In the *epochē,* there is a putting out of play, a parenthesizing, a bracketing whereby phenomenology takes a step back—but never a step away from the world of lived experience. Though Husserl repeatedly claimed that we do not forsake the world of lived experience in his vision of phenomenology

30. And it seems clear to me that he was conscious of this radicalization throughout his career. Perhaps this is most clear in the preface to *Phénoménologie de la perception*, where he contrasts his own direction to Husserl's; in the essay *l'Homme et l'adversité*, in *Signes*, where he contrasts phenomenology as *movement* to phenomenology as *method*; and in the working notes to *La visible et l'invisible*, where he contrasts his new insights with his earlier work.

31. Maurice Merleau-Ponty, notes OE, Vol. XIII, 148.

as a science of the sciences, I am not convinced he was successful. Contra Husserl, the understanding we gain of the world we live in through the phenomenological reduction cannot lay claim to any sense of purity or eidetic status. I think that we need to follow Merleau-Ponty's direction instead, where we see the task of phenomenology as seeking contingent knowledge through engagement rather than through an apodictic foundation.

Recall that Merleau-Ponty famously departs from Husserl in the "Preface" to his *Phenomenology of Perception* when he makes two bold proclamations: (1) "The one thing we can learn from the phenomenological reduction is that no complete reduction is possible" (lxvii/viii); and (2) his goal is to put "essences back into existence" (lxx/i). The first says that, since we can never complete the *epochē,* the corresponding phenomenological reduction will never be complete—and hence always call itself into question. This is the basis of political critique, since every interpretation is implicated as subject to critique. Not only is it impossible in practice, it ought not be even our ideal to stand clear of the vicissitudes of human experience and human existence. *For human existence purified of contingency is no longer human existence.* We are, as Merleau-Ponty insisted in that same text, "condemned to meaning" (PhP, lxxxiv/xiv) and that meaning is never pure. It is always open to interpretation, and hence it is always open to critique.

Merleau-Ponty did not explicitly describe his new direction in phenomenology as art, opposing it to science in the manner I am suggesting. But I think that it is appropriate to extend his thought in this way, and indeed I am drawing support from his analysis of art and science in his final essay, *L'oeil et l'esprit.* The point of the essay, in general, seems to be that art rather than science reveals fundamental truths about perception of the world. Science pretends to have objective truth of the world while art is relegated to a mere subjective imitation of that world. Merleau-Ponty clearly disagrees with this. The first line of the essay makes this clear: "Science understands the world at the cost of no longer living in it" (OE, 121/9). The enlightened scientist acknowledges that in any empirical scientific inquiry there is always contingency, but this is only seen as error that limits our quest for the objective ideal. The better way is to recognize that this "falling short" is not something to be overcome on the way to an objective ideal. Instead, it is this sort of contingency that is the means to *all* understanding of phenomena. Pure, objective knowledge of the world is not only impossible to attain, it is a goal that takes our attention away from the world we wish to understand—the world in which we live.

Science seeks pure objectivity by its theoretical "step back" from experience, whereas art offers another sort of transcendence altogether. Art disengages in order to allow us to engage in a new way. We cannot examine this in detail, but one can immediately think of many examples of this sort of *epochē* at work: attending to a film, a play, a painting, a piece of music, a dance, etc. But this sort of *epochē* is different from the theoretical step back of science. It involves physical discipline, not some abstract mental attitude that forsakes the body by trying to overcome its contingencies. There is a different kind of transcendence involved in an aesthetic *epochē*. Kurt Vonnegut describes this very well in the recent collection of short stories, *Bagombo Snuff Box*. Vonnegut describes the transcendence involved in reading a short story in a magazine when he was a boy.

> Imagine it is 1938 again. I am sixteen again. I come home again from yet another lousy day at Shortridge High School. Mother . . . says that there is a new *Saturday Evening Post* on the coffee table. It is raining outside, and I am unpopular. But I can't turn on a magazine like a TV set. I have to pick it up, or it will go on lying there, dead as a doornail. An unassisted magazine has no get-up-and-go.
>
> After I pick it up, I have to make all one hundred sixty pounds of male adolescent meat and bones comfortable in an easy chair. . . . But consider the incredible thing I myself have to do in turn. I turn my brains on!
>
> That isn't the half of it. With my brains all fired up, I do the nearly impossible thing that you are doing now, dear reader. I make sense of idiosyncratic arrangements, in horizontal lines, or nothing but twenty-six phonetic symbols, ten Arabic numerals, and perhaps eight punctuation marks, on a sheet of bleached and flattened wood pulp!
>
> But get this: While I am reading, my pulse and breathing slow down. My high school troubles drop away.[32]

Vonnegut goes on to playfully describe reading as a kind of meditation, and his own collection of short stories as a collection of "Buddhist catnaps."[33]

I would like to emphasize a few things from this account. First, that the process involves the body. The reader prepares himself or herself for the task by settling into a chair. Respiration and pulse slow down. An attitude

32. Kurt Vonnegut Jr., *Bagombo Snuff Box* (New York: Berkeley Books, 1999), 4.

33. Ibid., 5.

must be taken by the body, because it is the body that holds the story and which makes the sense of it. The *body* achieves transcendence in this aesthetic appreciation.

Second, there is a discipline involved in this preparation. It takes much practice to be able to achieve this kind of transcendence. It involves years of training in language skills, but also in the expectation that there is something of value in engaging in this process. Reading, like all aesthetic transcendence, is a cultivated skill—an acquired taste. This discipline has its own kind of rigor, and this rigor reveals new insights.

Finally, without appealing to any pure, objective meaning, there are better and worse ways to achieve this transcendence. Without foreclosing the variety of possible meanings, there are surely some that are more and less appropriate to the situation.

So: what would it cost us if we adopt an aesthetic model of phenomenology—and of a phenomenological political critique? Not insight, not depth, not truth, not discipline, and not rigor. For there is tremendous discipline in art—both in its production and its appreciation. *Art is disciplined creativity.*

The art of politics, then, must involve both discipline and creativity. Discipline provides the structure; creativity provides the potential for hope, for radical change. Critique must be disciplined if it is political. The *polis* disciplines critique as it manifests the spontaneous exercise of the general will. Indeed, the identity of the *polis* is implicated through its own *praxes*. Discipline leads to the intelligibility of the creativity, which is commensurate with the event of political judgment (the creative aspect of the praxis of political critique). Authentic political critique must be disciplined if it is to be recognizable as radical or creative. This is the paradox that lies at the heart of all genuine political critique. Thus, a phenomenological political critique of the sort I am suggesting affords disciplined creativity.

Merleau-Ponty's account of art in *L'oeil et l'esprit* manifests the aforementioned terms from his ontological work from the same period of his thought: *écart* and *réversibilité*. For the artist, the artwork, and the interpreter of the artwork are all inextricably linked in reversible relations. Their identities are never absolute or presupposed, but are recognizable only thorough their divergence. The painter paints with his or her body, which is implicated as *that* painter by the emergence of the artwork—just as the painting is identified as *that* painting as the artist becomes the artist who paints it. The painting has an infinite number of meanings that lie open before it. The interpreters who see the painting invest it with new meaning because they are implicated as who they are by their responses.[34] It is important to see the malleability of divergent identities in these relationships as manifestations of reversibility rather than as unfortunate equivocations of subject and object. Only by recognizing the divergence and reversibility of these situations can we disclose the practical implications. Reversibility bespeaks engagement such that things matter. And the contingency of the situation is, again, not something to be overcome, but the only means whereby things become meaningful. Phenomena call to be interpreted and implicate us as responsible for our interpretations.

The painter of modernity, or the writer of modernity, must never forsake his or her own concrete circumstances to attempt to seek some ideal. Ideality is manifest only in these contingent moments. These contingencies are not a stumbling block to be avoided; they are our only means of *creating* ideality. And the painter or the poet—or the philosopher—is distinguished as having artistic vision recognizing the ideal in the most decadent, the discarded, the refuse and ruins of modernity. One must engage in a critique with a watchful eye, caring for what society destroys.

Let us return briefly to Baudelaire—who, as we have seen, is not so far from Merleau-Ponty in many ways. His essay *The Painter of Modern Life* is at once homage to the artist, Constantin Guys, as well as an account of the role of the artist in decadent modern society—and hence is also indirectly autobiographical. Baudelaire's essay is not only an example of *praxis* but also of *parapraxis* insofar as his work involves a projection of his understanding of the virtues and vices related to the role of the modern artist. The analysis of Guys's work reveals Baudelaire's own understanding of the work as an artist *through his own artistic work*.

Baudelaire describes Guys as a "man of the world" who is not at home in the world. Guys "is an 'I' with an insatiable appetite for the 'non-I,' at

34. It is always interesting to compare Merleau-Ponty's early and later thought. One is reminded of an earlier essay, *Marxism and Philosophy*, from the 1940s, where Merleau-Ponty describes historical agents as "product-producers." Cf. *Sens et non-sens* (Paris: Gallimard, 1996): "For the first time since Hegel, militant philosophy reflects not on subjectivity, but on intersubjectivity" (134/163). Likewise, this explains how in the same passage Merleau-Ponty speaks of this intersubjectivity as the place where historical necessity "can turn into concrete liberty." One also recalls that in *Phenomenology of Perception*, Merleau-Ponty described how our actions transform contingency into necessity. The combination of these passages accounts for something like the reversible situation I am presenting here.

every instant rendering and explaining it in pictures more living than life itself."[35] Guys has a keen eye for relaying the vitality of circumstances, and thus conveying "the rights and privileges offered by the circumstance."[36] If it were not already clear that Baudelaire is reflecting upon his own position as an artist engaged in the critique of modernity, it is obvious when he praises Guys for being able "to extract from fashion whatever element it may contain of the *poetry* of history."[37] He praises Guys for being "bold and imaginative to seize upon nobility wherever it was to be found, even in the mire."[38] And he remarks that in art one finds "the special beauty of evil, the beautiful amid the horrible" and a "moral fecundity" that the modern artist creates to challenge the mores of his or her day.[39] One final passage from this fine essay will suffice to indicate the critical role Baudelaire sees Guys—and himself—to be playing in modern society.

> He has everywhere sought after the fugitive, fleeting beauty of present-day life, the distinguishing character of that quality we have called "modernity." Often weird, violent and excessive, he has contrived to concentrate in his drawings the acrid or heady bouquet of the wine of life.[40]

It might be interesting to do a thoroughgoing historical investigation into the direct influence of Baudelaire upon Merleau-Ponty's work. That would be another study. For our purposes, let us simply bracket the historical question of causality, and examine their cases as parallels. Consider Baudelaire's situation within the arts as he offered critique of the arts and of modern society. Likewise, consider Merleau-Ponty's situation within phenomenology as he offered a critique of phenomenology and of modern

---

35. Charles Baudelaire, *The Painter of Modern Life*, trans. J. Mayne (London: Phaidon Press, 1995), 10.

36. Ibid., 14. One is reminded here of Merleau-Ponty's criticism in a letter to Sartre of Sartre's rash political pronouncements on every event as if from the end of history—isolating the moment from history, and denying "the right to rectification intrinsic to each event."

37. Ibid., 12.

38. Ibid., 38.

39. Ibid.

40. Ibid., 41.

society.[41] The convergence of these parallel lines, as in a painting, is a matter of perspective. That is, the best way to indicate *depth* while portraying two infinitely parallel lines, like rails of a train track, is to present their convergence. So we cultivate the convergence of these parallels here and now in our own situation within modernity.

It is important to remember that, as Merleau-Ponty pointed out in his analysis of painting, depth is not subordinate or incidental, but the *primary* dimension. Likewise, the historical depth that emerges here and now for us regarding Baudelaire's and Merleau-Ponty's situations as critics is not the error of historicism, but lies at the heart of understanding, fundamentally evental, and the very hope we have to offer critique today. Merleau-Ponty offers us a hint of this *evental* dimension of history and its practical value, though he did not explore it in detail in *Eye and Mind.*

> There are, in the flesh of contingency, a structure of the event and a virtue peculiar to the scenario. These do not prevent the plurality of interpretations but, in fact, are the deepest reasons for this plurality. They make the event into a durable theme of historical life and have a right to philosophical status. (139/61–62)[42]

This historical depth, again, is in no way illusory, but the evental structure of historical phenomena. This depth is what allows history to *matter.* It is literally the making of differences that "makes a difference" to us. Furthermore, historical depth implicates us as historical agents who are responsible for the meaning of our historical situation, and who are responsible for creative responses within our historical situations. And these responses, like any interpretations, call for critique.

It is with this in mind that I condemn the close-minded dogmatism of my country's immediate past leaders. They strove to absolve themselves from critique for the safeguarding of their warped ideals. There is something fundamentally ironic that our president said, "Only history will judge my actions," as if history were a long way off. But the history that affords the

---

41. I have examined Merleau-Ponty's political philosophy and especially his relation to Marxism in several of my works. A discussion of this is quite relevant here, but it is impossible to enter into that discussion in the context of this essay.

42. Ibid., 61–62.

possibility of critique is alive, here and now—not that which that idealistic surd, President Bush, invoked—something like what Merleau-Ponty called a "Hegelian Monstrosity." Historical depth is intrinsic to genuine political critique.

But let us not be too happy in our condemnation. Our specific engagement within history implicates *us* as colonial. The very languages we use mark us as colonized and colonizers.[43] Our intentions to engage in genuine political critique fail to divest us of our imperial heritages. This pretense is the mistake liberals in the United States sometimes adopt to feel good about the very limited critical work they do, describing themselves as leftists when they are, alas, vulgar centrists—a political orientation that is less red than sanguine.

Today, we must avoid the allure of the false ideals of scientific political critique. We must engage in the *art* of political critique to achieve our freedom. Political freedom is freedom of the *polis* and can only be achieved through collaborative labor within the *polis*, no matter how vile or decadent it may be. We offer phenomenological descriptions of an inhumane world in the hope of transforming it. Our work and our hope lie nowhere else than in the critique of imperialism within the ruins of empires. This is the praxis of the philosopher of modern life.

References

Baudelaire, Charles. 1993. *The Flowers of Evil* [with parallel French text]. Translated by James McGowan. Oxford: Oxford University Press.

———. 1995. *The Painter of Modern Life.* Translated by J. Mayne. London: Phaidon Press.

———. 2002. *On Wine and Hashish.* Translated by A. Brown. London: Hesperus Classics.

Carbone, Mauro. 2001. *La visibilité de l'invisible.* Hildesheim: Olms Verlag.

Culler, Jonathan. 1990. "Baudelaire's '*Correspondances*': Intertextuality and Interpretation." In *Nineteenth Century French Poetry*, edited by Christopher Pendergast, 118–37. Cambridge: Cambridge University Press.

43. This phenomenological account is not an impertinent proclamation concerning Brazilian politics. I realize that these days one might tend to see it this way when someone from the United States starts talking about politics. Nor do I mean to imply that Brazilian politics must turn solely to French theorists for the possibility of genuine critique. Columbia might be turning to France for its leadership soon (Mme. Bettancourt), but Brazil has its own situation.

Derrida, Jacques. 2000. *Le Toucher, Jean-Luc Nancy.* Paris: Éditions Galiléi.
Dillon, Martin C. 2004. *Beyond Romance.* Albany: State University of New York Press.
Edie, James M. 1987. *Merleau-Ponty's Philosophy of Language: Structuralism and Dialectics.* Washington, DC: University Press of America.
Greenblatt, Stephen, and M. C. Abrams, eds. 2005. *Norton Anthology of English Literature, Volume D: The Romantic Period.* New York: W. W. Norton.
Merleau-Ponty, Maurice. 2013. *Recherches sur l'usage littéraire du langage: cours au Collège de France, 1953.* Genève: MētisPresses.
Pendergast, Christopher, ed. 1990. *Nineteenth Century French Poetry.* Cambridge: Cambridge University Press.
Richardson, Joanna. 1994. *Baudelaire.* New York: St. Martin's Press.
Silverman, Hugh J., and J. Barry Jr., eds. 1992. *Texts and Dialogues: Merleau-Ponty.* New Jersey: Humanities Press.
Starkie, Enid. 1958. *Baudelaire.* New York: New Directions Press.
Vonnegut, Kurt Jr. 1999. *Bagombo Snuff Box.* New York: Berkeley Books.

9

The Flesh Made Word*

As I Lay Dying and Being Incarnate

Cheryl A. Emerson

Speech is a gesture, and its signification is a world.

—Maurice Merleau-Ponty, *Phenomenology of Perception*

Introduction

In his 1951 lecture "Man and Adversity," Merleau-Ponty remarked that "we would have to present infinite explanations and commentaries, clear up a thousand misunderstandings, and translate quite different systems of concepts into one another in order to establish an objective relationship between, for example, Husserl's philosophy and Faulkner's works. And yet," he confirms, "within us readers they are connected" (S, 225/367).[1] In his notes from *Parcours deux* 1951–1961, Merleau-Ponty describes "the American literature of behavior" as turning away from "the most interior signification," as diffused "through gestures, behaviors," but gestures we must not

*Except where noted, the editions of *Phenomenology of Perception* cited in the epigraph and throughout the article are, respectively, revised edition, trans. Donald A. Landes (London and New York: Routledge, 2012); and Paris: Gallimard, 1945.

1. The editions cited here are, respectively, trans. Richard C. McCleary (Evanston: Northwestern University Press, 1964); and Paris: Gallimard, 1960.

reduce to mere behavioral coding (PC-II, 372).[2] In his notes on *"Littérature"* (*Notes de cours* 1959–1961), Merleau-Ponty groups *les Américains*—Faulkner, Caldwell, and Hemingway—with Marcel Proust and James Joyce as writers whose "mode of signification is indirect: myself-the other-the world deliberately mixed, implicat[ing] one in the other, expressed one by the other, in a lateral involvement" (NC, 49).[3] His description of the "*la brume,*" [the "mist"] of interior monologues "pierced by irruptions of others" in the novels of James Joyce is equally descriptive of "*la brume*" of interior voices the reader encounters in *As I Lay Dying.* In the close of his lecture upon "*Littérature,*" accompanying a reference to Faulkner, Merleau-Ponty notes a "surface destruction, dissociation—and search for a link, a solidity, more fundamental" among the writers he has grouped for discussion (NC, 50).[4]

In a 1995 essay, French critic André Bleikasten suggested the worth of examining Faulkner's novels "from a European perspective" beyond the context of United States Southern regional writing. Noting that Faulkner's novels won recognition in France "long before they were taken seriously in Faulkner's own country," Bleikasten realizes the importance of "Faulkner's Southernness" as a central concern of American literary criticism, but also notes that the magnitude of Faulkner's decidedly Southern writing extends well beyond U.S. borders and into the global South, having considerable influence upon such writers as Columbia's Gabriel García Márquez, Uruguay's Juan Carlos Onetti, and Peru's Mario Vargas Llosa (Bleikasten 1995, 76). While not all of Faulkner's work has established itself beyond the United States, Bleikasten offers dual citizenship to six select novels, stating that "*The Sound and the Fury, As I Lay Dying, Sanctuary, Light in August, Absalom, Absalom!,* and *The Wild Palms* belong as much to the history of the European novel as to that of American fiction" (ibid., 77). His estimate

2. *"La littérature américaine du comportement est une littérature qui renonce à s'intéresser à la signification la plus intérieure de ce comportement. Ce qu'il me semble, ou contraire, c'est qu'il y avait une voie d'accès à l'intérieur à partir des gestes, des conduites, à la seule condition que ces gestes, ces conduites ne soient pas notés simplement dans leurs détails"* (my translation).

3. *"Après Proust, Joyce, les Américains, le mode de signification est indirect: moi-autrui-le monde délibérément mélangés, impliqués l'un dans l'autre, exprimés l'un par l'autre, dans [un] rapport lateral"* (my translation).

4. *"Donc ni subjectif ni objectif, mais implication et rapport latéral des personnages l'un dans l'autre et dans le monde et de tous dans l'auteur, et par là signification indirecte. Ici, comme ci-dessus, il y a en surface destruction, dissociation,—et recherche d'un lien, d'une solidité, plus fondamentaux"* (my emphasis and translation).

of Faulkner's importance to international readers merits the inclusion of this lone American writer among Bleikasten's rather apostolic list of the twelve most significant modern European authors that "for all their differences, [have] much in common," noting that "indeed, their objectives strikingly resemble those of phenomenology, as defined by Merleau-Ponty: 'All its efforts are concentrated upon re-achieving a direct and primitive contact with the world' " (ibid., 78–80).[5]

Reading Faulkner *out* of an American regional context, for the purpose of this study, will revisit aspects of his writing that have ceased to be modern, in the sense of innovative or "new." *The Sound and the Fury* (1929) and *As I Lay Dying* (1930) were received as experimental, nearly indecipherable novels, and have been analyzed since then as studies in the failure of language, where "letters and words are left hanging in the void, *deprived of their place* of inscription" (Ferrer 1982, 22; my emphasis). Such readings articulate a prevailing view of the novel where Faulkner emerges as a transgressor breaking the rules of chronological principles necessary "for the novel to be read as a continuous text." Yet despite Faulkner's "transgressions of chronological order," (ibid., 29) or likely because of them, Bleikasten includes this one American author in his list of European modernists whose novels reflect "an abiding fascination with consciousness" (Bleikasten 1995, 81). Distanced from their original shock value, the stream of consciousness techniques which decades ago struck readers as destabilizing and unfamiliar now seem to be relatively navigable, with dissociating narratives of dissociative characters joining mainstream literary fiction.[6] In the more than eighty years since Faulkner's novels were embraced in France for their radical techniques by Sartre, Malraux, and de Beauvoir, readers have grown accustomed to navigating the fluid texts of unfiltered, often inarticulate interior monologues that wash through multiple voices of consciousness. I would like to examine Faulkner's second "experimental" novel from a distance removed from the initial shock over its apparent "deformations" of language and nar-

5. Bleikasten's personal list includes as Faulkner's peers "two Frenchmen, a German, two Austrians, two Irishmen, an Italian, an Englishwoman, a Russian émigré, and a Jew from Prague." Chronologically they are: Marcel Proust, Thomas Mann, Robert Musil, James Joyce, Virginia Woolf, Franz Kafka, Hermann Broch, Carlo Emilio Gadda, Louis-Ferdinand Céline, Vladimir Nabokov, and Samuel Beckett.

6. In the United States, for example, consider the familiar echoes of Faulkner's once "experimental" narratives in contemporary novelists as diverse in style and subject matter as Cormac McCarthy (*The Road*), Barbara Kingsolver (*The Poisonwood Bible*), and Toni Morrison (*A Mercy*).

rative. Reading Faulkner *out* of an American context in the present day, and apart from Southern regional and American historical concerns and from the gendered, racial, and sexualized readings vital to exploring the deep social and psychological issues raised through Faulkner's work, I wish to regard *As I Lay Dying*'s unadorned physicality as the raw soil of its meaning.

In light of the work of Merleau-Ponty, and because he himself was a reader of Faulkner's novels, I open with the premise that the characters of *As I Lay Dying* are "condemned to sense" because they are in a world (PhP, lxxxiv/xiv).[7] To read *As I Lay Dying* phenomenologically and in light of its form requires us to adopt a "perspective of consciousness—by which a world first arranges itself around me and begins to exist for me" (ibid., lxxii/iii). The world Faulkner conceived for his characters encompasses their often damaged or dying bodies, the land and its catastrophes of flood or drought, and the animal receivers of human conduct. Through the raw physicality of characters' relationships to the land, themselves, and each other, the novel draws our attention to "the site, the soil of the sensible and opened world such as it is in our life and for our body" (OE, 12–13).[8] To the degree to which it is possible, our task is "to return to the things themselves," to where they exist in "this world prior to knowledge, this world of which knowledge always "*speaks*" (PhP, lxxii/iii). Within the "mist" of interior monologues, consciousness is not ephemeral, but an embodiment of being. Detached yet intertwined, illustrating the concepts of *écart* and *réversibilité* so central to Merleau-Ponty's phenomenology, we see where "perspectives intersect, perceptions confirm each other, and a sense appears" (ibid., lxxxiv/xv). Beneath the noise and chatter of the characters' speech and thought (*logos proforikos*) is the original silence (*logos endiathetos*): carnal, amoral; neither cruel nor kind. In its mute presence, the Mississippi mud and dirt offer a grounding for values by which we make judgments of what it means to be "cruel" or "kind." For Merleau-Ponty, there is no "preconstituted world, a logic, except for having seen them arise from our experience of brute being, which is as it were the umbilical cord of our knowledge and the source of meaning for us" (VI, 157/209). Faulkner also draws upon natal imagery to ground his characters' being in the world. Throughout *As I Lay Dying*, the characters' relationship to the land itself is physical, primitive, and direct, where they begin and end as "wet seed[s] wild in the hot blind earth" (AILD, 64).[9]

---

7. In the French, "*nous sommes condamnés au sens*"; in Smith's translation, "condemned to meaning" (PhP, xiv/xix).

8. The edition cited here is "Eye and Mind," trans. Carleton Dallery, in PrP, 159–90.

9. *As I Lay Dying* will be abbreviated as AILD.

Surface Destruction of Narrative

The "surface destruction" of *As I Lay Dying* spans fifty-nine interior monologues dispersed unevenly among fifteen narrators that weave an anxious fabric of ill-fitting thought, interior realities diffused through exterior behaviors perceived and assimilated by others, misdirection and misinterpretations circling like the motionless buzzards that "hang in soaring circles, the clouds giving them an illusion of retrograde" (AILD, 95). The manner of telling casts doubt on the narrative movement of *As I Lay Dying*, analogous to the retrograde circling of buzzards. The framework conjures the essence of a sustained narrative through a "swarming of instants overlapped and enfolded," instead of a linear sequence of events.

In a brief overview of the plot, *As I Lay Dying* is the story of a funeral journey cursed by misfortune. Addie Bundren, wife to Anse and mother of five children, dies on a hot summer night just as a disastrous rain begins to fall. The rising flood and a broken wagon wheel delay her two older sons from returning with the wagon and mules, so that three days pass before the family can even begin the forty-mile ride to Jefferson, where Addie will be buried. Considering the Mississippi heat in July, the three days' wait for Darl and Jewel to return with the wagon, and the fact that the rural South rarely embalmed their dead in the 1920s, the funeral journey is a fool's mission from the start. Loading the coffin into the wagon three days after Addie's death, the family and neighbors keep their "faces averted, breathing through [their] teeth to keep [their] nostrils closed" (AILD, 98). Neighbors counsel Anse to bury Addie nearby, but he has given his oath "before God and man" that she'll be buried in Jefferson to "lie among her own people" (ibid., 23). Conveniently, fulfilling Addie's dying wish also allows the family to complete some personal errands on this rare trip into town: Anse will buy some new teeth, Cash will have a ride to his next carpentry job, Dewey Dell (who is secretly pregnant) will seek an abortion, and Vardaman hopes the toy train will still be for sale in the storefront window.

At the start of novel, World War I has recently ended. Cash, the oldest son, had been unfit for military service after falling off a church roof "twenty-eight foot, four and a half inches, about," (AILD, 90) a fall that crippled his leg. Darl has returned from the war exhibiting signs of detachment and disassociation, in behaviors that are a public embarrassment to the family. The funeral journey struggles on through a series of ridiculous misfortunes, and on the ninth night Darl sets fire to the barn where the family has stopped to rest for the night. Jewel rescues the burning coffin, the Bundrens arrive in Jefferson the next day, the burial is accomplished, and Darl is committed to an insane asylum. Before returning home, Anse buys the set of teeth he wanted and acquires a new Mrs. Bundren.

From start to finish, the sequence of events is framed by an exterior time span of only ten days, but the interior monologues reach back to Addie's memories from before she was married and forward to an indeterminate end, sometime after Darl is committed to the asylum. The ten days of the novel's exterior chronology are a drastic contrast to the forty or more years of interior time, not as wide a contrast as the twenty-four hours of James Joyce's *Ulysses* and its interior wanderings, but like *Ulysses*, *As I Lay Dying* slips freely through interior time unbounded by sequence, within a finite exterior chronological frame.[10]

Through its foldings of time and consciousness, as it layers through language, thought, and gestures from character to character, the surface destruction of narrative in *As I Lay Dying* opens to the reader the intimate relationships of a fully intercorporeal world, despite the interiority implied in these fragmented and apparently self-contained monologues. *As I Lay Dying* presents as a "collection of states of consciousness" uttered by characters who behave in ways that justify meaning, if only to themselves, but meanings lost in translation. "It is easy to strip language and actions of all meaning and to make them seem absurd, if only one looks at them from far enough away," writes Merleau-Ponty in *Metaphysics and the Novel*, but reminds us that "in an absurd world, language and behavior do have meaning for those who speak and act," cautioning against the temptation "to fall back into [an] 'isolating' analysis which breaks time up into unconnected instants and reduces life to a collection of states of consciousness" (SNS, 39/50). The surface destruction of *As I Lay Dying* presents as a "collection of states of consciousness," but with a mobile coherence that holds through the mist of monologues.

Addie Bundren: The Visible and the Invisible

In every way imaginable, Addie Bundren is the body of the text—where we see her, and where we don't. She is the literal corpse of the story, as well as the pivot point of the book's interior and exterior movements. After her death, the handling (and mishandling) of Addie's body stirs a dissonance between the comedy of misfortunes and the family's attempts to conduct

10. Cf. Patten, 30–32.

themselves in a manner befitting the social forms of loss and bereavement. Her body is the logistical center of the plot, and most importantly, the chiasmatic field and fold—where the visible and the invisible intertwine. Her essence infuses "*the mist*" of interior monologues, all fifty-nine. The physical presence of her corpse is undeniable, even concealed in a coffin, increasingly visible as the Mississippi summer accelerates the decay of her unembalmed flesh. Heralded by an increasing number of buzzards, the reader can "see" the smell of her, a smell either politely but uncomfortably ignored by onlookers or remarked upon in a way that stirs her son Jewel's anger, himself struggling to conceal his disgust at the rising stench of the corpse. Over the course of their journey, the text reeks of her presence.

Chercher l'Odeur

Addie has been dead eight days when the Bundrens arrive in the town of Mottson, "with the ladies all scattering up and down the street with handkerchiefs to their noses," where Moseley, a pharmacist, recounts the sight of the wagon in the town square: "It must have been like a piece of rotten cheese coming into an ant-hill, in that ramshackle wagon that Albert said folks were scared would fall all to pieces before they could get it out of town" (AILD, 203). Moseley's interior monologue closes with a residual smell still lingering the next day. "And the next day I met the marshal and I began to sniff and said, 'Smell anything?' " (ibid., 205). What lingers is the mere thought of the smell, a trace, causing Moseley to question whether it is real or imagined.

Several more characters in *As I Lay Dying* will share Moseley's confusion between real and imaginary sensations, touching upon what Merleau-Ponty identifies as "the most difficult point, that is, the bond between the flesh and the idea, between the visible and the interior armature which it manifests and which it conceals" (VI, 149/195). Intercorporeality rejects the idea of a clear, cause and effect relationship between a physical stimulus and the perceiver's response, since a stimulus-response model would fully sever the material world from human consciousness of being. What Merleau-Ponty says of Proust is also applicable to Faulkner, that "no one has gone further . . . in fixing the relations between the visible and the invisible, in describing an idea that is not the contrary of the sensible, that is its lining and its depth" (ibid., 149/195). Moseley's suspicion that the smell lingers after the funeral procession has moved on is "not the contrary of the sensible"—not just make-believe. The imaginary aspect gives "lining" and "depth"—in other words, meaning—to the strange spectacle and awkward social exchange Moseley and the townspeople are left to assimilate.

The family arrives at Armstid's the evening of the fifth day, with Cash strapped to the top of Addie's coffin to immobilize his newly broken leg. In this scene, Armstid anticipates Addie's smell before he returns to the house—and not only the smell, but also the curiosity of neighbors drawn to the spectacle. As he rides in from the field, Armstid sees the buzzards circling over his barn, but he is fortunately upwind from the smell. "Luckily the breeze was setting away from the house . . . but soon as I see them it was like I could smell it in the field a mile away from just watching them, and them circling and circling for everybody in the county to see what was in my barn" (AILD, 186–87). The sight of the buzzards invokes an odor that is not yet present, in a synesthetic communication between the visible buzzards and the suggested smell. Not only do vision and smell adhere in this scene, but an element of Armstid's future adheres to his factual present. Merleau-Ponty describes "the Proustian corporeity as guardian of the past," through a past-present containing "an intentional reference which is not only from the past to the factual, empirical present, but also and inversely from the factual present to a dimensional present or *Welt* or Being, where the past is "simultaneous" with the present in the narrow sense" (VI, 243–44/297).

By the same principle, the Faulknerian corporeity, in this scene, is guardian of the future.[11] Through embodiment, Armstid draws "an intentional reference" from the factual presence of buzzards to a dimensional presence of smells he has yet to smell. It is as if the sight of the buzzards allows Armstid to project his body ahead of himself in the field.[12] Understanding that buzzards are drawn to carrion, he displaces himself not only to where he can smell the carrion, but toward the eyes of his neighbors from their fields also watching the buzzards "circling for everybody in the county to

11. This scene illustrates that time is not a complete absurdity in Faulkner's work, despite Jean-Paul Sartre's famous claim that for Faulkner, "beyond this present, there is nothing, since the future does not exist" (Jean-Paul Sartre, "Time in Faulkner: *The Sound and the Fury*," in *William Faulkner: Three Decades of Criticism,* ed. Frederick J. Hoffman and Olga W. Vickery (East Lansing: Michigan State University Press, 1960), 225–32 (226) (originally published in *La Nouvelle Revue Française*, June and July, 1939).

12. Cf. Martin Heidegger, *Building, Dwelling, Thinking,* in *Basic Writings* ed. David Farrell Krell (San Francisco: Harper, 1993), 347–63. "When I go toward the door of the lecture hall, I am already there, and I could not go to it at all if I were not such that I am there. I am never here only, as this encapsulated body; rather, I am there, that is, I already pervade the space of the room, and only thus can I go through it" (ibid., 359).

see what was in my barn" (AILD, 187). When he's still half a mile from the house, Armstid hears Vardaman yelling and whips his horse into a run. In one of the most sadly comic scenes in the novel, Vardaman tries to stop the buzzards from landing on Addie's coffin, actualizing Armstid's projections. "There must have been a dozen of them setting along the ridge-pole of the barn, and that boy was chasing another one around the lot like it was a turkey and it just lifting enough to dodge him and go flopping back to the roof of the shed again where he had found it setting on the coffin" (ibid.). The buzzards have landed. Armstid's imaginary smells are now incarnate.

The most comic scenes of *As I Lay Dying* ultimately settle upon the smell of the corpse, the buzzards that follow the smell, and the humans who recoil and react. Merleau-Ponty's essay *The Chiasm*, in *The Visible and the Invisible*, helps to illustrate how much of Faulkner's humor in the novel plays upon the reversibility of subject-object relationships, the paradox of being "from one side a thing among things and otherwise what sees them and touches them" (VI, 137/180). Merleau-Ponty describes the "reciprocal insertion and intertwining" of the "seeing body" (subject) and the "visible body," (object) noting a "strange adhesion of the seer and the visible" (kibid., 138–39/183). Through the interior monologues of character after character in *As I Lay Dying*, we meet this "strange adhesion" not only through the physical "encroachment, infringement" of a rotting corpse upon the senses of the perceiving body, but also when the smell is reversed as a residual projection (or in Armstid's monologue, anticipatory projection). Each situation causes the perceiving subjects to imagine themselves as "seen" as they worry how their visible reactions to the smell will be perceived by others, who are socially prohibited from treating the Bundrens uncharitably in their time of grief. Despite how physically disgusted each onlooker is by the smell, each tempers his speech and conduct to conform to the exterior gestures of respect for the grieving.

When the marshal in Mottson argues with Anse to move the wagon out of town, he says, "It ain't that we're hard-hearted . . . but I reckon you can tell yourself how it is" (AILD, 205).[13] Concerned that the town's hostility and disgust will be perceived as uncharitable, the marshal appeals to Anse's sense of decency, hoping Anse "can tell [himself] how it is"; but that would necessitate Anse's recognizing the spectacle of the funeral procession from without—looking upon himself reflexively, as the family appears

13. Faulkner regularly omits the apostrophe in conjunctions to emphasize regional dialect. I will maintain his usage throughout this essay.

to the townspeople—instead of through Anse's self-abasing, "never aimed to bother nobody" tale of woe he recites to the marshal (ibid., 204). Anse comically refuses to detach from his interior self-narrative long enough to project the "double reference" needed to view the family spectacle from the townspeople's perspective.[14]

Another curious manifestation of the "strange adhesion" of seer to the visible is the way in which the Bundrens themselves cease to react to the smell after their initial response when carrying Addie's coffin from the house to the wagon. As the trip wears on, the family grows habituated to the odor, desensitized through close proximity with its gradual decay, which for them has ceased to shock their sense of smell. It is only through contact with others, exterior to the family's identification as a corporate "self," that Addie's smell reactivates in their awareness through encountering the visible responses of townspeople, helpful neighbors, and the circling buzzards, in a reversibility where "through other eyes we are for ourselves fully visible . . . for the first time I appear to myself completely turned inside out under my own eyes" (VI, 143/189). Merleau-Ponty describes this intercorporeal transfer of subject/object perceptions as "the paradox of expression:" "the unique occupation of floating in Being with another life, of making itself the outside its inside and the inside of its outside" (ibid., 144/189).[15]

When the family stops at Samson's farm for the night, his wife Rachel wants him to convince the Bundrens to sleep inside, away from the reek of the corpse in the barn. In clichés of courtesy, the Bundrens refuse Samson's invitation. Seeing that Vardaman, the youngest son, is already asleep where "they had done put him to bed in the trough in a empty stall," Samson "[leaves] them squatting there . . . [reckoning that] after four days they was used to it. But Rachel wasn't" (AILD, 117). The outrage against decency, decorum, and the rejection of her hospitality sparks her anger not against Anse Bundren specifically, but inclusive of her husband and all men, expressed in a truncated thought: "I just wish that you and him and all the men in the world that torture us alive and flout us dead, dragging us

14. "[The body's] double belongingness to the order of the "object" and to the order of the "subject" reveals to us quite unexpected relations between the two orders. It cannot be by incomprehensible accident. For if the body is a thing among things, it is so in a stronger and deeper sense than they: . . . and this means that it detaches itself upon them, and, accordingly, detaches itself from them" (VI, 137/180).

15. Cf. Martin Dillon, *Merleau-Ponty's Ontology*, (Bloomington: Indiana University Press, 1988). Dillon discusses the transfer of the body schema in detail.

up and down the country—" (ibid.), and here she breaks off into silence followed by sounds of weeping that will follow Samson well into the night.

If we consider the family unit as a "body," in the way that a family name identifies its members, then the encroachment of the Bundren family upon the Samson household is another example of embodied intersubjectivity, another "reciprocal insertion and intertwining of one in the other" (VI, 138/183). Reflecting on his fight with Rachel, Samson "imagined a lot of things coming up between us, but I be durn if I ever thought it would be a body four days dead and that a woman. But they make life hard on them, not taking it as it comes up, like a man does" (AILD, 118), suggesting, I suppose, that the reek of a male body "four days dead" would not have stirred such a fight. For Rachel to respond with outrage over Addie's smell on behalf of all women, before we consider the gendered expectations of female decorum as different from male social decorum (it is unladylike for women's bodies to reek, after all, whether alive or dead, especially in the American South), it is helpful to note that Rachel identifies with Addie's body in a self-object reversal, intertwining her personal identity as "wife" and "woman" with the female corpse in her barn. The reversibility of Addie (dead) to Rachel (living) allows Rachel to focus her outrage toward "the men in the world that torture us alive and flout us dead," implicating, unfortunately, her own husband in her critique. This is why I believe a phenomenological reading of *As I Lay Dying* is a useful foundation for studies exploring the book's gender and social implications, grounded in a phenomenological understanding of the body through what Duane Davis has termed, "reversible subjectivity" (Davis 1991, 31–45).

The concept of "reversible subjectivity" illuminates being as embodiment at the close of Samson's monologue, with the memory of his wife's tears echoing in his thoughts.

> So I laid there, hearing it commence to rain, thinking about them down there, squatting around the wagon and the rain on the roof, and thinking about Rachel crying there until after a while it was like I could still hear her crying even after she was asleep, *and smelling it even when I knowed I couldn't.* I couldn't decide even then whether I could or not, or if it wasn't just knowing it was what it was. (AILD, 118; my emphasis)

The "*it*" in "smelling *it*" references Addie's corpse, but in the wake of his wife's subjective reversal with Addie's body, "thinking about Rachel crying . . . *and smelling it even when I knowed I couldn't*" blurs the point of reference, permitting the echo of Rachel's tears to blur with the residual odor of the corpse, folding the sound of tears with the smell of decaying flesh. In *Phenomenology of Perception*, Merleau-Ponty presents synesthesia as a paradox in which "by opening up the structure of the thing, the senses communicate among themselves," allowing us to "see," for example, "the rigidity and the fragility of glass" (PhP, 238/265). Faulkner often allows unclear antecedents to blend into synesthesia, an aspect of his style cited as evidence that his novels are "inscrutable" and "opaque,"[16] as if clarity itself were the proper measure of truth and reality, while ambiguity merely poses an impediment to meaning. On the contrary, the blurred senses resulting from Faulkner's unclear antecedents "nonetheless all communicate through their meaningful core" (ibid., 239/266) when considered as a phenomenon of perception. The blurring does present as chaotic and irrational, but this is the way we make sense of the world and its myriad sensations, including the coherent deformations Faulkner creates within the text. "There is rationality," Merleau-Ponty writes in his preface, "that is, perspectives intersect, perceptions confirm each other, and a sense appears" (ibid., lxxxiv/xv).

Although Samson doubts whether what he smells is real or imagined, the communication of his senses assembles the evening's scattered events into a meaningful whole. While lying in the dark, he thinks of the Bundrens down in the barn "squatting around the wagon and the rain on the roof," thinks of Rachel crying "until after a while it was like I could still hear her crying even after she was asleep," and smells it "even when I knowed I couldn't." It is not a matter of sorting the real world from the imaginary world, but recognizing their interdependence.

> For if I am able to speak about "dreams" and "reality," to wonder about the distinction between the imaginary and the real, and to throw the "real" into doubt, this is because I have in fact drawn this distinction prior to the analysis, because I have an experience of the real as well as one of the imaginary. . . . Thus, we must not wonder if we truly perceive a world; rather, we must say: the world is what we perceive. (PhP, lxxx/xi)

16. Cf. Mark Edelman Boren, "The Southern Super Collider: William Faulkner Smashes Language into Reality in *As I Lay Dying*," which traces the ways in which the "narrative space" of the novel is obscured by "contaminations" of the text (24), but also supports the idea that "language consists of sensible phenomena just as much as eating or walking" (29).

The Bundrens pull out at daybreak, before Samson is able to invite them in to eat breakfast. On his way to the barn, he decides he only imagined the smell after all, "that it wasn't smelling it, but it was just knowing it was there, like you will get fooled now and then" (AILD, 118). But a souvenir buzzard resurrects the smell as real once again.

> But when I went to the barn I knew different. When I walked into the hallway I saw something. It kind of hunkered up when I come in and I thought at first it was one of them got left, then I saw what it was. It was a buzzard. It looked around and saw me and went on down the hall, spraddle-legged, with its wings kind of hunkered out, watching me first over one shoulder and then over the other, like a old baldheaded man. (AILD, 118–19)

Samson sees the buzzard, and it sees him as well, "watching [him] first over one shoulder and then over the other," making Samson an object of study by the buzzard. The double gaze in this mirror reflection allows Samson to confirm the smell—and himself—as fact, even though subjectively, "you will get fooled now and then."

Family as "Body"

Although the Bundren family maneuvers as a "body" of associated members on the road to Jefferson, especially as they engage the awareness and participation of onlookers, the exterior association of the family masks the interior discord of the Bundrens as a collection of separate beings. The interior monologues reveal the strain of characters asserting and defending their differences against encroachments upon their privacy of being, cohering as a "body" operationally, but not emotionally. Like their neighbors the Tulls, the Bundrens are dirt farmers living out seasons of toil and sweat, picking and planting side by side in the cotton field, where every egg counts, the cow must be milked, and the fish they catch is their supper. Family members have few personal possessions and operate within a communal expectation that the money they earn is not their own, and the labor of their bodies is owed to the family, not for personal gain.

Cash's tools are unique, in that regard, as identifiably his and therefore identifying "of" him as distinct from his family, although the money he earns from his carpentry jobs also supports the family. Cash's tools are not mere "things," the way the milking pail and kitchen skillet are things, but gathered into his sense of being. As he builds Addie's coffin, not even the rain interrupts the motion of his arm with the saw: "The rain rushes suddenly down, without thunder, without warning of any sort . . . in an instant Cash is wet to the skin. Yet the motion of the saw has not faltered, *as though it and the arm functioned in a tranquil conviction* that rain was an illusion of the mind" (AILD, 77; my emphasis). As an extension of Cash's arm and instrumental to his purpose, the saw translates his intent upon the wood, giving it shape and human form (it is a coffin, after all). Even in the rain, after Addie has died, Cash takes the time to bevel the boards "with the tedious and minute care of a jeweler" (ibid., 79). He works by lantern, in the rain, all through the night, then at dawn helps carry the coffin to Addie's room. Afterward, "he gathers up his tools and wipes them on a cloth carefully and puts them into the box with its leather sling to go over the shoulder" (ibid., 80). His tools are clean, ready, and near at hand.[17] After the family departs for the long ride to Jefferson, Jewel gallops past the wagon on his horse, spattering mud onto the coffin, which Cash hastens to clean. "A gout of mud, backflung, plops onto the box. Cash leans forward and takes a tool from his box and removes it carefully." When the wagon passes near enough to some willow trees, "he breaks off a branch and scours at the stain with the wet leaves" (ibid., 108–109). His gestures speak his intent: Cash has poured his labor into the wood, and whether it is his pride in craftsmanship, reverence for Addie's body, or one expressed in the other, we know his actions are meaningful. The gesture doesn't "*make me think*" of care—the gesture is the care itself.[18]

The only other character whose personal identity is invested in an object outside the family is Jewel, whose sense of self is so strongly bound to his horse that Darl tells Vardaman, "Jewel's mother is a horse" (AILD, 101) and taunts Jewel for his attachment to the animal. Cash purchased his carpentry tools openly, with (and for) the support of his family; Jewel,

---

17. Cf. Martin Heidegger's comments on "useful things" in *Being and Time*, trans. Joan Stambaugh (Albany: State University of New York Press, 2010), 68–69 (*Sein und Zeit*, 68–70). "The act of hammering itself discovers the specific 'handiness' [*Handlichkeit*] of the hammer. We shall call the useful thing's kind of being in which it reveals itself by itself *handiness* . . . they are handy in the broadest sense and are at our disposal" (ibid., 69/69).

18. "I do not perceive the anger or the threat as a psychological fact hidden behind the gesture, I read the anger in the gesture. The gesture does not *make me think* of anger, it is the anger itself" (PhP, 190/215).

however, earns his horse by stealth of night, clearing another farmer's land by lamplight in exchange for a half-wild stallion, "a descendant of those Texas ponies" Flem Snopes brought to town twenty-five years ago.[19] When Jewel "took a spell of sleeping" in the summer when he was fifteen, the family worries he is sick. After Cash and Darl discover he has been sneaking out at night, they speculate that Jewel is out "rutting" (ibid., 131) and cover his chores so Anse will not suspect. One morning, five months after his "sleeping spell" began, Jewel rides home on his horse, which Darl paints as a carnival scene. "Its mane and tail were going, as though in motion they were carrying out the splotchy pattern of its coat: he looked like he was riding on a big pinwheel, barebacked, with a rope bridle, and no hat on his head" (ibid., 134). Having been worried sick about Jewel, Addie bursts into tears, crying so hard that Darl intuits Addie's secret, that Jewel is illegitimate. "And then I knew that I knew. I knew that as plain on that day as I knew about Dewey Dell on that day" (ibid., 136). Meanwhile, Anse accuses Jewel of stealing labor from the family. "So you bought a horse. You went behind my back and bought a horse. You never consulted me; you know how tight it is for us to make by, yet you bought a horse for me to feed. Taken the work from your flesh and blood and bought a horse with it" (ibid.).

Jewel's ownership of the horse is significant because it announces him as an individual distinct from his family, because Cash and Darl collaborate to protect their brother's nocturnal activities, and because Darl's intuition that Anse is not Jewel's father informs our understanding of Darl's harsh treatment of Jewel later in the journey. In addition to the structural importance of Jewel's horse, Darl's description of the language of horse and rider is fascinating from a phenomenological perspective. Enveloped in Darl's vision, we see Jewel and the horse in movements expressive of love and hate, in a synchronous dance both violent and beautiful.

> When Jewel can almost touch him, the horse stands on his hind legs and slashes down at Jewel. Then Jewel is enclosed by a glittering maze of hooves as by an illusion of wings; among them, beneath the upreared chest, he moves with the flashing

19. "[And] auctioned off for two dollars a head and nobody but old Lon Quick ever caught his and still owned some of the blood because he could never give it away" (AILD, 134). For the history of Yoknapatawpha County's Texas ponies, see "Spotted Horses," in *Three Famous Short Novels* (1931); later included in *The Hamlet* (1940).

> limberness of a snake. For an instant before the jerk comes onto his arms he sees his whole body earth-free, horizontal, whipping snake-limber, until he finds the horse's nostrils and touches earth again. Then they are rigid, motionless, terrific, the horse back-thrust on stiffened, quivering legs, with lowered head; Jewel with dug heels, shutting off the horse's wind with one hand, with the other patting the horse's neck in short strokes myriad and caressing, cursing the horse with obscene ferocity. (AILD, 12)[20]

Jewel's mastery depends upon his agile anticipation of the horse's movements, in a relationship intuitive and intercorporeal, responsive and creative as human intimacy.[21] Mounting the horse, Jewel "flows upward in a stooping swirl like the lash of a whip, his body in midair shaped to the horse" (AILD, 13), anticipating not only the horse's resistance, but also the shape that his body will need to conform. Jewel rides his horse from the field to the barn, where they trade blows. "The horse kicks at him, slamming a single hoof into the wall with a pistol-like report. Jewel kicks him in the stomach; the horse arches his neck back, crop-toothed; Jewel strikes him across the face with his fist and slides on the trough and mounts upon it" (ibid.). He feeds his horse, cursing it in love and hate. "Eat. Get the goddamn stuff out of sight while you got a chance, you pussel-gutted bastard. You sweet son of a bitch" (ibid.). Jewel masters the horse as man over beast, reciprocating its power and rage. Jewel is keenly aware of both his and the horse's "postural" or "corporeal" schema, able to "appropriate the conducts given to [him] visually and make them [his] own" (PrP, 117/PC-I 176–77).[22]

---

20. On a visit to France prior to writing AILD, Faulkner had viewed paintings by Matisse, Picasso, and Cézanne, among others. I can imagine Picasso's horse paintings, especially "Boy Leading Horse" as backdrops to this scene.

21. Surprisingly, I have (so far) not encountered an analysis that exploits the scene in terms of homoerotic bestiality, which would be in keeping with much of the sexual reductivism I find among Faulkner studies. The scene does portray, after all, the grappling of two stallions.

22. Cf. *Child Psychology and Pedagogy* ("PPE"; bibliographical data in References below), notes on "concept of postural schema"—"If my body is no longer only known by a mass of strictly individual sensations, but as an object organized by relationship to its surroundings, the result is that the perception of my body can be transferred to the other and the other's image can be immediately "interpreted" by my body schema" (PPE, 247/311).

His movements with the horse intertwine, in a way Merleau-Ponty reflects upon in *The Visible and the Invisible.*

> Between the exploration and what it will teach me, between my movements and what I touch, there must exist some relationship by principle, some kinship, according to which they are not only, like the pseudopods of the amoeba, vague and ephemeral deformations of the corporeal space, but the initiation to and the opening upon a tactile world. . . . Through this crisscrossing within it of the touching and the tangible, its own movements incorporate themselves into the universe they interrogate, are recorded on the same map as it; *the two systems are applied upon one another,* as the two halves of an orange. (VI, 133/176; my emphasis)

After the family mules drown in the river crossing, Anse will trade Jewel's horse for a new team. In the flood, Jewel risked his life to recover every one of Cash's tools, only to lose his horse. The last we see of it is Jewel galloping away in anger to finish the trade, "the two of them looking like some kind of a spotted cyclone" (AILD, 191).

Gestural Language: Laughter and "Looks"

Of the forms of human expression, Merleau-Ponty grants primacy to gesture, so central as to be metaphoric, if not definitive of language itself. Speech, writing, painting, and music are gestural, in that each "sketches out its own sense," in communications "achieved through the reciprocity between my intentions and the other person's gestures, and between my gestures and the intentions which can be read in the other person's behavior" (PhP, 190–91/215). Gestures communicate intercorporeally, through a reversibility in which "everything happens as if the other person's intention inhabited my body, or as if my intentions inhabited his body," (ibid., 191/215) through a "transfer of the 'body schema' " (Davis 1991, 35). For Merleau-Ponty, "words or gestures" communicate with "an immanent signification" meanings that are immediately given through the shared experience of the speaker and listener, drawing upon "available significations" to communicate within a common world (PhP, 192/217). Our understanding of the other person's gesture is not "through an act of intellectual interpretation," any more than Cash needs to say the word *hammer* for his body to know to reach for that tool (ibid., 191/216). The meanings are available, within our shared experience, and ready for use. If the ability of gestures to communicate is grounded upon shared experience, however, what do gestures communicate beyond the shared, "available significations"? Darl, for example, left the family farmhouse for Europe, to fight in the war. When he returns, how is his family to understand his gestural language, if his (more than likely) graphic exposure to human carnage has colored his expected response to Addie's death? Is this the discrepancy that makes Darl laugh? For this study, I am less concerned with the possible significations of Darl's laughter than with its immediate affect within the family setting. Considering that in five days his family will commit him to an insane asylum, it is vital to examine the first scene in which Darl's laughter is wrongly perceived.

To trace the rise of Darl's laughter, we return an earlier monologue when he, Jewel, Cash, and Pa carry Addie's coffin from the house to the wagon, on the fourth day after her death. Her corpse has begun to ripen, but not to the point (yet) where social decorum is strained. Not so for Jewel, however, who is apparently more sensitive to smell than the rest of the family. On Jewel's face, "the blood goes in waves. In between them his flesh is greenish looking, about that smooth, thick, pale green of cow's cud; his face suffocated, furious, his lip lifted upon his teeth" (AILD, 97). As they carry it to the door, "Jewel's face goes completely green and [Darl] *can hear teeth in his breath*" (ibid., 98; my emphasis). Breath does not have teeth, and teeth cannot be heard, but a "transfer of the body schema" affords an "immanent signification" of the experience of wishing to breathe without smelling the air we breathe. They move the coffin cautiously, "as though it were something infinitely precious, [their] faces averted, breathing through our teeth to keep our nostrils closed" (ibid.). But Jewel rushes ahead until the coffin "coasts like a rushing straw upon the furious tide of Jewel's despair." He "sloughs it into the wagon bed" looking back at Darl, "his face suffused with fury and despair" (ibid., 98–99).

After loading the coffin, Jewel disappears into the barn and the family leaves without him, with buzzards "motionless in tall and soaring circles" already gathering overhead (AILD, 104). Jewel gallops after them on that "durn spotted critter wilder than a catymount," not as "a deliberate flouting of her and of me," as Anse believes, but as a way to keep his distance from the smell. The reader laughs openly at the humor of the scene because the reader inhabits a space beyond the text, but Darl may not, unless he too inhabits a space beyond the text, which (in a way) he does. His experiences in the war, though not detailed, return him to his family as a "reader" of events, within yet detached from the immediate moment, isolating him as a socially transcended being. Darl's world has widened in ways his family can only imagine, but returning from France to rural Mississippi undoubtedly increased his store of available significations. In addition to the shared experience of meanings, which helps the Bundrens maneuver as a unit, Darl's perceptions are now shaped by his war experience as well. Darl has a frame of reference for "corpse" that his family does not, which heightens the tensions between their conduct and his, emphasizing his "otherness" as the outcast within.

Jewel's horse had always been a source of contention between Anse and Jewel, but on the day of the flood, when Jewel refuses to ride to Jefferson in the family wagon, he directly defies an order from Anse, who "told him not to bring that horse out of respect for his dead ma, because it wouldn't look right, him prancing along on a durn circus animal and her wanting us all to be in the wagon with her that sprung from her flesh and blood." When Darl sees Jewel on the "durn circus animal," he erupts in laughter, humiliating Anse even further (AILD, 105). Once we place Darl's laughter within the language of embodiment, we may explore his gesture as an existential statement upon the cosmic absurdity of the human condition or as an early symptom of his psychosis, as other studies have done[23]—but now with a phenomenological foregrounding that certainly is essential.

Darl's laughter erupts just after they pass Tull's lane, where Tull waves at them from his yard. "He looks at us, lifts his hand" as they pass, a social gesture that also reveals the spectacle is on display (AILD, 107). Seeing himself through Tull's eyes, Anse's embarrassment illustrates what Merleau-Ponty describes as "a fundamental narcissism of all vision" in the reversibility of the seer and the seen, when "through other eyes we are for ourselves fully visible" (VI, 139, 143/183, 188). As the spectacle crosses Tull's vision, the family feels themselves "looked at" from without and within. When Darl bursts out laughing, Anse recalls all the times he's told him "it's doing such things as that that makes folks talk about him. I says I got some regard for what folks says about my flesh and blood even if you haven't" (AILD, 105–106). Anse transfers his narcissism to Addie, reasoning to himself that "when you fixes it so folks can say such about you, it's a reflection on your ma, not me: I am a man and I can stand it; it's on your womenfolks, your ma and sister that you should care for." Embarrassed on Addie's behalf, he "sees" Jewel following on that "durn circus animal" by watching Darl laugh.

23. See for example Joseph M. Garrison Jr., "Perception, Language, and Reality in AILD," in *William Faulkner's AILD: A Critical Casebook* (New York: Garland, 1985), 49–62.

"I don't have to be told who it is. I just looked back at Darl, setting there laughing" (ibid., 106). Made visible to himself by a neighbor's greeting, Anse asks God to pardon him for the conduct of his sons. "I done my best," he says aloud, "I tried to do as she would wish it. The Lord will pardon me and excuse the conduct of them He sent me," (ibid.) as if the sins of the sons have visited upon the father in a kind of spiritual reversibility.

The humor of the scene peaks as the wagon passes "a white signboard with faded lettering: New Hope Church 3 mi." which "wheels up like a motionless hand lifted above the profound desolation of the ocean" (AILD, 108). Dewey Dell looks back at Darl, "her eyes watchful and repudiant . . . for a smoldering while." Cash breaks the tension when he spits over the wheel and says, "In a couple of days now it'll be smelling" (ibid.). It must be this remark that finally triggers Darl's laughter, because he answers with a joke: "You might tell Jewel that." Addie's body already smells. The humor is in the understatement, and this is where the reader laughs aloud. The scene is a comedy of manners: Jewel's anger masks his inability to politely ignore the smell, and Darl's laughter reveals his ability to see beneath the surface conduct of his family.

Faulkner and "The Gaze"

If looks could kill, in *As I Lay Dying*, more characters than Addie would be dead. "If her eyes had a been pistols, I wouldn't be talking now. I be dog if they didn't blaze at me," Samson notes of Dewey Dell's hostile response to his offer of a night's lodging (AILD, 115). For all the hostility of her intent, however, Dewey Dell's fury merely fuels the bleak humor of the scene, as in so many scenes where what emerges from "the gaze" is a comic discrepancy between intention and affect. Dewey Dell's tendency to hyperbolize and literalize endows Darl's gaze with superhuman powers. "The land runs out of Darl's eyes; they swim to pin points. They begin at my feet and rise along my body to my face, and then my dress is gone: I sit naked on the seat above the unhurrying mules, above the travail" (ibid., 121). Even read as an incestual sibling fantasy, the level of exaggeration is ridiculous. Despite readings that draw a connection between *As I Lay Dying* and Sartre's *Being and Nothingness*,[24] Faulkner's incorporation of "the

24. Cf. Homer B. Pettey, "Perception and the Destruction of Being in *As I Lay Dying*," where Pettey draws such a thorough parallel between AILD (1929) and *Being and Nothingness* (1943) that he credits Faulkner as source material for Sartre. "Clearly, Sartre gained much from reading this novel" (30).

gaze" as a central comic element of the novel affirms the intersubjectivity of the characters who for all their interiority, illustrate how "consciousness that would be hidden in a piece of flesh and blood is the most absurd of occult qualities" (PhP, 365/406).

In his section on "Others and the Human World" in *Phenomenology of Perception*, Merleau-Ponty explores the difficulty of "coexistence with an indefinite number of consciousnesses," particularly "the paradox of a consciousness seen from the outside" (PhP, 364/406). By making the shift from a "constituting consciousness" to a "perceptual consciousness," Merleau-Ponty begins to resolve the "antinomies of objective thought" inherent in the *cogito* (ibid., 367/409). In *Phenomenology of Perception*, Merleau-Ponty makes no distinction between "vision," "seeing," and "the gaze" as intercorporeal relationships between self, others, and the social/natural world. Seeing is an aspect of embodiment.

> Through phenomenological reflection I find vision to be the gaze gearing into the visible world, and this is why another's gaze can exist for me and why that expressive instrument that we call a face can bear an existence just as my existence is borne by the knowing apparatus that is my body. (PhP, 367/409)

In contrast to Sartre's reading of Descartes, Merleau-Ponty makes clear that the other's visible body is never fully objectified.

> But if the other's body is not an object for me, nor my body an object for him, if they are rather behaviors, then the other's positing of me does not reduce me to the status of an object in his field, and my perception of the other does not reduce him to the status of an object in my field. (Ibid., 368/410)

Such an understanding of the gaze helps to account for why Dewey Dell's scalding looks, for all their hostile intent, comically fail to annihilate those around her. Her gestures of anger are nevertheless a social expression, a variation of "being in the world, undivided between body and consciousness," perceived and understood by others (PhP, 372/414).

Ironically, Dewey Dell's openly hostile looks spark less reaction than Darl's passive, land-filled gaze. It is not a result of Darl's visual containment or issue of power over others, but where he has been and what he has seen that turns others back toward themselves in an unsettling way. Darl's eyes are foreign, locked on the land rather than people, inscrutable and socially noncompliant. More than any other character, Darl's gaze is the most difficult for others to negotiate. Consider the contrast Vernon Tull notes in the gazes of Darl and Dewey Dell.

> He is looking at me. He dont say nothing; just looks at me with them queer eyes of hisn that makes folks talk. I always say it aint never been what he done so much or said or anything so much as how he looks at you. It's like he had got into the inside of you, someway. Like somehow you was looking at yourself and your doings outen his eyes. *Then I can feel that gal watching me like I had made to touch her.* (AILD, 125; my emphasis)

In both glances, Tull makes an embodied, perspectival shift. Although Dewey Dell's gaze is accusatory, Tull feels more implicated under the scrutiny of Darl's "queer eyes," touched by a strangeness that makes him foreign to himself. Tull's sense of strangeness under Darl's gaze is a matter of degree, however, not of kind. "Here again I have but the trace of a consciousness that escapes me in its actuality and, when my gaze crosses another, I reenact the foreign existence in a sort of reflection" (PhP, 367/409). Rather than negating social structures, Darl's strangeness makes them more apparent, hence more visibly awkward. His passive noncompliance strains and eventually exceeds the limits of human sympathy, building to a final rupture from the world when he's committed to an insane asylum. Merleau-Ponty would suggest that even there, Darl remains in dialogue with the social world "as the permanent field or dimension of existence," arguing that "I can certainly turn away from the social world, but I cannot cease to be situated in relation to it" (ibid., 379/420). If *As I Lay Dying* explores the boundaries of communication through the isolated subject, it also explores the boundaries of isolation by situating characters within an unavoidably social world.

It is at odds with the book's comic and communal elements to approach *As I Lay Dying* with a preconception of "the gaze" as a weapon of power enabling the seer to seize possession of the other's being, using vision to bind others in "frames" that represent "metaphors of confinement," to serve "as sites of death" (Pettey 2003, 27). "The gaze" is not "*fundamentally* an issue of power," (ibid., 29; my emphasis) although power, even cruelty, can subsequently rise. Within the comic structure of the novel, power is neither the essence of the gaze nor the result. Like other gestural expressions, the exchange of looks between characters further illustrates the body to body language of *As I Lay Dying*'s intercorporeality. Considering the prevalence of gestural language in *As I Lay Dying*, especially through the gaze, it is important not to frame *As I Lay Dying* into a series of duels to the death by looks that kill. Addie is not Medusa, and Darl's eyes are fixed on the whole world: land, horses, buzzards, and brothers, trading looks with them all. Language is in the eyes, in the exchange of looks; and there is more to language than containment and power. As Duane Davis notes, "Language is not a projectile, but a collaborative project of reversible subjectivity" (1991, 37).

Cruel Reversibility

Acknowledging that Merleau-Ponty sought a way to resolve the isolating dichotomy of Sartre's response to Descartes, let us turn to the emergent risks of his proposition in *Phenomenology of Perception* "that there is no private sphere of consciousness," (PhP, 395/435) and that "solitude and communication must not be two terms of an alternative, but rather two moments of a single phenomenon" (ibid., 376/417). When Merleau-Ponty speaks of "the price for there to be things and 'others' for us, not through some illusion, but rather *through a violent act that is perception itself,* he places "violence" and "perception" into a dangerous common context with ominous implications (ibid., 379/420; my emphasis). Even if by "a violent act" (*par un acte violent*) he meant only a metaphoric shattering of previously held images, the idea of violence in a fully intercorporeal world is a terrifying thought, opening a field of vulnerability relative to intent. If one's most privately held thoughts are subject to encroachment by others; if gestures betray our interiority, then existence itself is risky in uncomfortable ways. In "The Intertwining—The Chiasm," Merleau-Ponty's imagery is remarkably violent, with intercorporeality expressed in terms of "dehiscence," "fission," "encroachment," and "infringement" (VI, 146/192, 142/187, 134/177). Where cruelty is intended, it is viscerally cruel, intersubjectively, with the object of cruelty never fully objectified.

The starkest representation of cruel intercorporeality in *As I Lay Dying* appears in Addie's only interior monologue, in her account of physically abusing her students when she worked as a schoolteacher in Jefferson, before her marriage to Anse. She recalls her deep satisfaction in the corporal punishment of her students. "When the switch fell I could feel it upon my flesh; when it welted and ridged it was my blood that ran, and I would think with each blow of the switch: Now you are aware of me!" (AILD, 170). As the pain she inflicts on others registers upon her own flesh, she confirms that she exists by drawing blood on the skin of her students in a violent iteration of "reversibility" pushed to its limits. Even before her first pregnancy, Addie understood that flesh begets flesh, in both the procreative and physical sensual meaning—that we are beings incarnate: the body of the other solidifies the existence of her own. Such a relation occurs positively in a willingly shared embodiment, but reversibility also includes exchanges of pain. On one level, Addie, understands the bodies of her students are "other" than hers; on the other, *her* body feels the whip when she strikes *their* flesh—not her own, but flesh like her own. The beatings are a reverse self-flagellation that confirms her existence to herself and to the other. "Now you are aware of me! Now I am something in your secret and selfish life, who have marked your blood with my own for ever and ever" (ibid.).[25]

For Addie to look at them "day after day, each with his and her secret and selfish thought," she must have experienced "secret and selfish" thoughts of her own. She understood their bodies through similarities to hers yet different, as blood "strange to mine," illustrating the potential dangers and pain of *réversibilité*. Citing Wallon, Merleau-Ponty describes cruelty as a "suffering sympathy," reflecting sympathy with others as "other myselves." "When I hurt the other, therefore, I am hurting myself. Consequently to *like* to hurt the other is to *like* to hurt oneself," by which we arrive at "the psychoanalytic idea of sado-masochism" (PrP, 143/PC I, 213; PPE, 256/322). Addie's entire monologue is a study in "secret and selfish" thoughts in which she recalls her father's advice, "the reason for living was to get ready to stay dead a long time" (AILD, 169). She can "just remember" her father's statement, placing it as an early, possibly the only memory of her father. From her monologue, we don't know her age when he died; we have no reference at all to Addie's mother, who perhaps died in childbirth, but we do know all her relatives are dead at the time she meets Anse. She beats her students because "this seemed to be the only way I could get ready to stay dead," punishing herself (and them) for the sin of being alive, hating her father "for ever having planted [me]" (ibid., 170).

After beating her students, Addie "would go down the hill to the spring where [she] could be quiet and hate them. It would be quiet there then, with the water bubbling up and away and the sun slanting quiet in the trees and the quiet smelling of damp and rotting leaves and new earth; especially in the early spring, for it was worst then" (AILD, 169). The "it" of Addie's monologue has been interpreted predominantly as sexual

25. ". . . Amen." Addie didn't finish the litany phrase, perhaps because she recognizes the vacuity of litany phrases, hence her ridicule of her neighbor Cora Tull, who recites rather than speaks. The comic disparity between the two women's use of religious phrases merits further study.

desire—an animal itch satisfied by Anse, with no further mention of the quiet of the spring or the call of the wild geese that Addie hears in the night.[26] "Sometimes I thought that I could not bear it, lying in bed at night, with the wild geese going north and their honking coming faint and high and wild out of the wild darkness, and during the day it would seem as though I couldn't wait for the last one to go so I could go down to the spring" (ibid., 170). But must "it" reduce to sexual terms? Could Addie's yearning be a desire for life, which her only memory of her father forbids, or a longing for "home," a belonging which the call of wild geese seems able to represent in other, nonsexualized terms? Once again, a phenomenological reading affords a grounding in perceptual experience prior to the assignment of meaning.

Addie's cruelty to others ("other myselves") includes the mental annihilation of Anse and her two oldest sons, breaking the signification of their names from the beings their names signify, by repeating their names into absurdity. "And when I would think *Cash* and *Darl* that way until their names would die and solidify into a shape and then fade away, I would say, All right. It doesn't matter. It doesn't matter what they call them" (AILD, 173). She surveys her life, her yearnings, marriage, childbearing, and wrongdoings, how after avenging herself against Anse by having an adulterous affair with the Reverend Whitfield, she feels obligated to "[clean] up the house afterward" (ibid., 176). Her illogical "cleaning up" involves two more pregnancies to balance out Jewel, her illegitimate and favorite child, but by Addie's personal logic, invisible to her family, her house was "clean" when she died. "I hid nothing. I tried to deceive no one. I would not have cared," Addie says unconvincingly. Her monologue reveals what nobody in the family knows, that Addie extracted the promise from Anse to bury her in Jefferson as an act of revenge for impregnating ("planting") her not once, but twice, but in a way that "he would never know [she] was taking revenge" (ibid., 173). Addie is nowhere near death, at this point, and will hold the promise to be buried in Jefferson as a force of will over her husband and children for at least twenty-eight years. This is how she prepares "to stay dead for a long time."

Apart from its statement as a moral self-audit, Addie's interior monologue is a critique of words, but "words" as distinct from "language," which

26. For an overview of psychosexual studies of *As I Lay Dying*, see Doreen Fowler's chapter on "Psychological Criticism" in Peek and Hamblin's *Companion to Faulkner Studies*, 197–213.

is a difference overlooked by studies that approach the monologue through verbal syntax instead of embodied subjectivity.[27] Reading from a perspective of embodiment, it is clear that Addie holds an understanding of language as lived experience apart from "words" as vessels of meaning, hollow and used up. That bodies touch, but words do not, is clear in Addie's accounts of violence against her students.

> I knew that it had been, not that they had dirty noses, but that we had had to use one another by words like spiders dangling by their mouths from a beam, swinging and twisting and never touching, and that only through the blows of the switch could my blood and their blood flow as one stream. (AILD, 172)

The words *motherhood, sin, love,* and *fear,* for Addie, "are just sounds that people who never sinned nor loved nor feared have for what they never had and cannot have until they forget the words" (AILD, 173–74). Addie distinguishes the "dark voicelessness in which the words are the deeds" from "the other words that are not deeds . . . coming down like the cries of the geese out of the wild darkness in the old terrible nights, fumbling at the deeds like orphans to whom are pointed out in a crowd two faces and told, That is your father, your mother" (ibid., 174).

In *Nature and Logos*, William Hamrick and Jan Van der Veken explore how for Merleau-Ponty, "every speech act becomes an incarnation, words made flesh, and by the same token, in the expression of the ideas, *flesh is made words*."[28] Having been orphaned by social, institutionalized words, Addie grants primacy to lived experience, returning from "this perception fashioned by culture to the 'brute' or 'wild' perception" (VI, 212/266), which is the *logos endiathetos* "that pronounces itself silently in each sensible

27. Cf. Calvin Bedient's "Pride and Nakedness: *As I Lay Dying*," in *William Faulkner's* As I Lay Dying: *A Critical Casebook*, ed. Dianne Cox (New York: Garland, 1985), 95–110, at 96. (reference below), where Addie's monologue is described as "a marvel of dazzling unintelligibility." In *The Ink of Melancholy* (1990), André Bleikasten states that Addie's views on language "point to an irreducible chasm between word and world" (202), then beautifully extends his analysis of the relationship between language and silence far beyond verbal syntax, into the "stubborn silence of reality itself" (201), yet still using "words" and "language" interchangeably.

28. William Hamrick and Jan Van der Veken, *Nature and Logos, A Whiteheadian Key to Merleau-Ponty's Fundamental Thought* (Albany: State University of New York Press, 2011), 103 (referred to hereafter as "NL").

thing" (ibid., 208/261). This is the language of "emergence from the flesh of sound, color, the texture of the tactile" (ibid., 114/152), the "world of silence" which Addie finds in a chiasmatic reversibility through beating the blood of her students, then the spoken names of her husband and two older sons. (Remember she is carrying out a paternal command of preparing "to stay dead for a long time.") Where words are hollow and "dont ever fit even what they are trying to say at," her acts of savagery bespeak "a logos of *l'être sauvage*" (NL, 106) in gestures of cruelty and violence that are viscerally expressive. Addie dies in despair of words, but with an ancient sense of meaning intact.

Darl's Doubt

Addie's aggression in the family is passive, silent, and concealed. Darl, however, openly taunts Jewel and stirs him into fury. As Darl's monologues dominate the book (nineteen of the fifty-nine, or roughly one-third), a tremendous portion of *As I Lay Dying* is devoted to the strained relationship between Darl and Jewel, as the active translation of Addie's sin. Instead of punishing Addie directly for her adulterous affair, Darl cruelly attacks her issue, a half-brother ten years his junior, whom he paradoxically admires and protects. This is not a despotic relationship, by Merleau-Ponty's definition of "despotism," because Jewel in no way accepts the subjugation of self.[29] But like a despotic relationship, Darl and Jewel "find themselves founded in and by the situation" (PrP, 142/PC-I, 211).[30] Jewel's defiance of Darl appears in the novel's opening scene, as they walk in from the cotton field with Darl in front and Jewel trailing fifteen feet behind, until Jewel cuts through the cotton house to emerge ahead of Darl, who now trails behind

29. Cf. *The Primacy of Perception*, "What the master seeks, following Hegel's famous description of the relation between master and slave, is recognition [*Anerkennung*] by the slave, the consent of the slave to be a slave. The master is nothing without the humiliation of the slave; he would not feel alive without this abasement of the other" (PrP, 142/PC-I, 211); and *Child Psychology and Pedagogy*, "Above all, despotism is founded on the sentiment that the slave has in being a slave; it is not founded on the adversary's defeat. What the master searches for is recognition that he is the master, and he only finds it in debasing the slave" (PPE, 256/321).

30. Cf. *Child Psychology and Pedagogy:* "What characterizes this relationship is that the two children are in some manner merged in the situation. The contemplator only exists by identifying with the other" (PPE, 256/321).

Jewel (AILD, 3–4). Darl's opening monologue states distance and direction as facts void of embellishment or reaction: the scene announces their competitiveness indirectly, in the style Merleau-Ponty noted of Proust, Joyce, and "*les Américains*," Faulkner among them, in which "the mode of signification is indirect," where interior meanings are noted in the visible gestures and mannerisms of the characters (NC, 49). Darl's interior monologues often paint bare scenes in harsh, geometric perspectives resembling visual art, placing himself into his own scene from an outside perspective—from a double frame of reference that becomes significant in his final dissociation from his family and the world.[31]

Darl insists on bringing Jewel to deliver a load of lumber, not knowing if they would return in time to be present at their mother's death. While hauling the lumber, Darl taunts Jewel, "Do you know she is going to die, Jewel? . . . 'Jewel,' I say, 'do you know that Addie Bundren is going to die? Addie Bundren is going to die?' " (AILD, 39–40). He taunts him again as Jewel struggles to raise the wagon to fix a broken wheel. "Jewel, I say, she is dead, Jewel. Addie Bundren is dead" (52). The reader perceives taunting in Darl's words not because Faulkner elaborates on Darl's interior motives, but from shared understandings of what is customarily said (and not said) in times of death. The reader notes detachment in Darl's use of the formal name "Addie Bundren" in place of "Ma," but with no embellishment or interpretation within the text.

Darl's most vindictive treatment of Jewel occurs on the last night of the funeral journey, when the family has stopped at Gillespie's to rest. Darl and Jewel have put Addie's coffin under the apple tree, where "now and then she talks in little trickling bursts of secret and murmurous bubbling" (AILD, 212). As Addie's body bubbles and oozes, Darl asks Jewel, "Whose son are you? . . . Your mother was a horse, but who was your father, Jewel? . . . *Jewel, I say, Who was your father, Jewel?*" eliciting the expected response, "*Goddamn you. Goddamn you*" (ibid., 213; Faulkner's emphasis). Recalling Merleau-Ponty's comments that in relationships of cruelty, "When I hurt the other . . . I am hurting myself" (PrP, 143/PC-I, 213; PPE, 256/322), where is Darl's "suffering sympathy" with the pain he inflicts upon Jewel? Darl's cruelty to Jewel increases in severity as the funeral journey wears on, as does Darl's place as "other" in the family, which will soon culminate in an act of arson. He punishes the biological "other" of

31. For a fascinating examination of the influence of the European painters and Cubism on Faulkner's style, see Watson Branch, "Darl Bundren's Cubistic Vision," in Cox, 111–29.

the family, which is Jewel. In a cruel reversibility, his words hurt "another myself," similar to the way that when Addie whipped her students, she felt it upon her flesh.

Later that night, the wind shifts and they carry Addie down to the barn, which Darl sets ablaze as the family sleeps outside to escape the smell. After saving the livestock, Darl realizes that Jewel has run back into the fire to save the coffin. Darl tries to stop him, but Jewel is in the barn, looking out "through the rain of burning hay like a portière of flaming beads," and he can see Jewel's "mouth shape as he calls [Darl's] name" (AILD, 222). In an act of heroic fury, Jewel pulls the coffin from the flames. Later that night, Vardaman finds Darl crying on the coffin, which Vardaman describes as a play of shadows: "The moonlight dappled on him too. Oh her it was still, but on Darl it dappled up and down" (ibid., 225). Vardaman's observation is beautiful but sad, seeing his brother's sobbing defined by shadows in the moonlight. We are not told why Darl cries, only that he does. Despite the interiority of its monologues, the novel is gestural, not introspective, a literature of gestures where "instead of saying: my character is sad," will say, "my character cries" (PC, II 374).[32] We are not told why Jewel called out to Darl in the flames, only that his mouth shaped the word. We take in the scene as a painting, reading emotions and meaning through the shapes and shadows of surface detail. We understand Darl and Jewel's intentions toward each other through a mutual implication of "one in the other, expressed one by the other," in lateral involvements that open to meaning, but meanings that remain incomplete, the way Cézanne suggests a line by filling the available space without actually painting the line. The "mist" of interior monologues enters our understanding en masse, in the totality of intersubjective relationships where isolating one character for analysis drags along the whole entanglement.

Much has been made of Darl's ontological doubt in his monologue reflection on consciousness and sleep, but this well-analyzed passage about states of being still depends upon Jewel.[33]

> In a strange room you must empty yourself for sleep. And before you are emptied for sleep, what are you. And when you are emptied for sleep, you are not. And when you are filled with

32. *"Vous dites que c'est par pur artifice que le romancier américain, au lieu de dire: mon personnage est triste, dit: mon personnage pleure"* (my translation).

33. Cf. Colleen Donnelly (1990).

> sleep, you never were. I dont know what I am. I dont know if I am or not. (AILD, 80)

Darl contrasts his self-doubt with Jewel's certainty. "Jewel knows he is, because he does not know that he does not know whether he is or not. He cannot empty himself for sleep because he is not what he is and he is what he is not" (ibid.). Although the ontological doubt expressed in this monologue is its most prominent interest, I wish to draw attention to Darl's dependency upon Jewel's "otherness," their difference, to know himself, even as a self who doubts. Darl's doubt is placed, therefore, relative to his brother's lack of reflective self-consciousness. Darl also locates himself by their relationship to the wagon outside in the rain.

> Beyond the unlamped wall I can hear the rain shaping the wagon that is ours, the load that is no longer theirs that felled and sawed it nor yet theirs that bought it and which is not ours either, lie on our wagon though it does, since only the wind and the rain shape it only to Jewel and me, that are not asleep. (AILD, 80)

The wagon is real as "shaped" by the wind and the rain—that is, the wagon is real through an intercorporeal relationship with the elements of nature. Because he and Jewel are awake, the wagon is shaped "to Jewel and me," quieting his thoughts before sleep. His closing thoughts restore his sense of embodiment, after wandering in doubt. "How often have I lain beneath rain on a strange roof, thinking of home" (ibid., 81). Whether Darl lies *beneath* a strange roof or *on* a strange roof in the rain (the syntax is ambiguous), he is shaped by the rain—remembering, no doubt, his sense of displacement sleeping in strange rooms during the war, thinking of home.

Considering Jewel's importance as Addie's illegitimate son and that her coffin would never have made it safely to Jefferson without Jewel's sacrifice and risks, one would expect Jewel to be given more voice. Besides Addie herself, Jewel is the only Bundren with just a single interior monologue, and one considerably shorter than hers (one page to her six), casting the impression that Jewel's consciousness is the most concealed to the reader, since we have very brief access to his interior thoughts. Yet we do perceive his consciousness, in all its fury, because through Faulkner's portrayal of Jewel we see that consciousness is not expressed by interior thoughts alone, concealed within, but emanates throughout our being and habits of behavior. In "The Child's Relations with Others," Merleau-Ponty rejects the notion of the psyche as "a series of 'states of consciousness' that are rigorously closed in on themselves and inaccessible to anyone but me" (PrP, 116/PC-I, 176). This is because our consciousness "is above all a relation to the world," and "the other's consciousness as well is chiefly a certain way of comporting himself toward the world" (PrP, 117/PC-I, 176). In his earlier lectures, Merleau-Ponty notes that "*actions have a sense* [*les actions ont un sens*]" (PPE, 247/311). By this reasoning, the character's *exterior monologue* reveals interior consciousness (if I may coin a promising and useful expression to describe "comportment").[34] To think of comportment as an *exterior monologue* supports Merleau-Ponty's emphasis upon being as embodiment, and that thought and speech are not our only forms of language. The challenge in *As I Lay Dying* is that Jewel's *exterior monologue* is enveloped by Darl's *interior* monologues, leaving us uncertain whether it is Jewel or Darl's portrait of Jewel we read, painted by Darl's animosity.

The brothers are not always locked in emotional combat. Cash, Darl, and Jewel merge as a body with intuitive, wordless anticipation of the others' movements in life-or-death scenarios, in looks that "plunge unimpeded through one another's eyes . . . in all the old terror and the old foreboding, alert and secret and without shame" (AILD, 142). As they prepare to bring the wagon across the flooded river, Cash and Darl collaborate to keep Jewel out of danger, sending him across on his horse to secure a rope. As they discuss the logistics, Darl recalls how when Jewel was born "he had a bad time of it," how "Ma would sit in the lamp-light, holding him on a pillow on her lap. We would wake to find her so. There would be no sound from them" (ibid., 144). Note that this one of the few times in the novel where Darl says "Ma" instead of "Addie Bundren." Cash answers Darl's *thoughts,* not his speech, saying "that pillow was longer than him" "That's right," Darl answers, "neither his feet nor his head would reach the end of it." Cash berates himself for not coming down the week before to "sight" the old ford crossing, but Darl reassures him, "You couldn't have known" (ibid.). Throughout the dangerous scene, the brothers risk their safety for each other as Anse and Dewey Dell watch helplessly from across the river, where Vernon Tull holds Vardaman's hand. Even the mules communicate with their eyes, as "their gaze sweeps across us with in their eyes a wild,

34. If, in the most important sense, the word *monologue* remains applicable at all. In the traditional sense of the term, these are no longer "monologues," exclusively interior or exterior. If nothing else, *As I Lay Dying* problematizes the terms. I coin the term *exterior monologue* as merely a way to emphasize that the body also articulates.

sad, profound and despairing quality as though they had already seen in the thick water the shape of the disaster which they could not speak and we could not see" (ibid., 146–47).

The scene reminds us of the silent communion beneath the mask of cruelty Jewel and Darl wear for each other. The morning after the fire, as the family reaches Jefferson at last, Darl saves Jewel from a knife fight, when Jewel mistakenly turns on a white man instead of the negroes who had called out, "Great God, what they got in that wagon?" when they passed in the road (AILD, 229). In his rage, Jewel is blind to color and social class. Darl wrestles him back while talking the man into closing his knife, with Vardaman chiming in on behalf of brotherly pride, saying, "Jewel would a whipped him" as they drive off (ibid., 231). The wagon wheels into town past heads that turn "with that expression which we know," while Jewel holds to the side of the wagon "staring straight ahead, motionless, lean, wooden-backed, as though carved squatting out of the lean wood" (ibid.). It is a moment of shared understanding, as the family endures the humiliation of public racial scrutiny, forced to see themselves on parade.

While Addie doubts the ability of words to "ever fit even what they are trying to say at," Darl's doubt goes deeper, to the core of language itself. "How do our lives ravel out into the no-wind, no-sound, the weary gestures wearily recapitulant: echoes of old compulsions with no-and on no-strings: in sunset we fall into furious attitudes, dead gestures of dolls" (AILD, 207). As he mixes cement to pour a cast on Cash's broken leg, Darl wishes he could "just ravel out into time. That would be nice. It would be nice if you could just ravel out into time" (ibid., 208). Darl's journey, within the movements of his family, after returning from the war in France, has left him far removed from the taste of water "when it has set a while in a cedar bucket . . . with a faint taste like the hot July wind in cedar trees smells" (ibid., 10). At night, he used to return to the cedar bucket where "before I stirred it awake with the dipper, I could see maybe a star or two in the bucket, and maybe in the dipper a star or two before I drank" (ibid., 11). When he was older, he would lie with his shirttail up, "feeling myself without touching myself, feeling the cool silence blowing upon my parts and wonder if Cash was yonder in the darkness doing it too, had been doing it perhaps for the last two years before I could have wanted to or could have" (ibid.). What is missed, in moving immediately toward the sexual meaning, is that this is Darl's first moment of carnal awareness, and not only of his own flesh touched by the wind, but that his brother Cash is a feeling, sensual being similar to himself. It is a moment of complete attachment, with Darl fully aware of himself as a being in the world, fully aware of his embodiment in "the reversibility that defines the flesh" of himself, his brother Cash, and the world (VI, 144/189).

Other characters frequently notice how after the war, Darl's eyes are "full of the land," an attachment and openness to the earth that simultaneously detaches him from society. Dewey Dell describes how Darl "sits at the supper table with his eyes gone further than the food and the lamp, full of the land dug out of his skull and the holes filled with distance beyond the land" (AILD, 27). Here is the intertwining, the "the dehiscence of the seeing into the visible and of the visible into the seeing," (VI, 153/201) in a paradox of Being where Darl detaches himself upon the land, dissociating himself from others. In "Cézanne's Doubt," Merleau-Ponty's description of Cézanne's "devotion to the visible world" also describes Darl in his "flight from the human world, the alienation of his humanity," (SNS, 11/15) and becoming, in his detachment, "a stranger among men" (ibid., 23/20). Darl's final detachment is from himself, after Jewel tells the men from the asylum to "Kill him. Kill the son of a bitch," (AILD, 238) when Darl resists being bound. Jewel and Dewey Dell both physically attack Darl, and the men have to pull them off. When Darl realizes that even Cash has forsaken him, he laughs "Yes yes yes yes yes yes yes yes," a paradoxical affirmation that negates all sense, severing his connection to himself and to the world. The only redemption for Darl is his imaginative capacity to split off a detached observer within, disembodied but affirming, a quasi self—a Darl who isn't Darl, speaking to himself in the third person. "Darl is our brother, our brother Darl. Our brother Darl in a cage in Jackson where, his grimed hands lying light in the quiet interstices, looking out he foams. 'Yes yes yes yes yes yes yes yes' " (ibid., 254). He ends with his "double reference" of the body so fragmented that he is "other" to himself, though this is not "an incomprehensible accident" (VI, 137/181). Dissociation from self and society allows Darl a way to endure, which in Faulkner's world, might be all we can do. Cash's closing thoughts about Darl illustrate this double reference as an aspect of being common to every man, who nevertheless remains a social being.

> But I aint so sho that ere a man has the right to say what is crazy and what aint. It's like there was a fellow in every man that's done a-past the sanity or the insanity, that watches the sane and the insane doings of that man with the same horror and the same astonishment. (AILD, 238)

Closing Thoughts

Doc Peabody, the traveling rural physician, is seventy years old and ready to retire. He remembers "how when I was young I believed death to be a phenomenon of the body; now I know it to be merely a function of the mind—and that of the minds of the ones who suffer the bereavement" (AILD, 43–44), drawing a distinction between the death of Addie's body and the death of her being "in the minds" of her family. For Doc Peabody, death is not an end or a beginning, but a relocation—like vacating a house. "The nihilists say it is the end; the fundamentalists, the beginning; when in reality it is no more than a single tenant or family moving out of a tenement or a town" (ibid., 44). If death is a "function of the minds" of the bereaved, then the "tenement" or "town" to be vacated must be the mind. But Addie is still in residence, occupying her familiar place in the patterns of thought and behavior of Anse and the children. Habituated to her presence, the habits remain, the way we turn to speak to a person who is absent, either dead or distant. Language reaches for them, and the conversation continues. This is not an inability to distinguish the living from the dead, nor a mystical communion with spirits. It indicates the space a person occupies in our conversation with the world. We speak to our dead, as to someone who has moved away; we lend them our presence and reanimate their being, as they continue to show us who we are.

What, if anything, distinguishes our thoughts of the living from our thoughts of the dead, or for that matter, from the reader's thoughts of fictional characters? Our recollections begin with gestures: comportment, habits of being, timbre of voice, a facial expression, a smile—all through interior monologue, how Darl "sees" Jewel in the barn with his horse or "sees" Addie's last look at Vardaman as she dies. Consider the full weave of interiorities when we read *As I Lay Dying*: the characters mixed through the others' minds, all in the mind of Faulkner, and all within us, the readers. What we think of the book, then, is the last interior monologue. It is the reader at last, who closes the book and brings it away. It is not enough for these artists to have created their works, "they must also awaken the experiences which will make their idea take root in the consciousness of others" (SNS, 19/25). In "Cézanne's Doubt," Merleau-Ponty illustrates the interdependence of the artist and the viewer of art, and why the artist's effort is always incomplete: "The painter can do no more than construct an image; he must wait for this image to come to life for other people. . . . It will dwell undivided in several minds, with a claim on every possible mind *like a perennial acquisition*" (SNS, 20/26; my emphasis).

Merleau-Ponty teaches us that literature, as with all art, is intercorporeal, not only in the "involvement and lateral rapport of characters" (NC, 51) within the text, but through the reader's involvement as well, among "the mist" of interior monologues. As readers, our participation is also one of embodiment, where we perceive the interior consciousness of the characters through a transfer of our own "body schema" onto theirs, drawing our abject response to the stench of decomposition through our own associations of smells. The travail of women in birth and death, the public embarrassment of a family, the social incompatibilities of the rural farmer—every social, racial, and economic consideration raised by the book can be analyzed even more vividly, and with greater force, once we return to what lies "beneath the noise of words," (PhP, 190/214) where Addie Bundren will always lay dying.

References

Bedient, Calvin. 1985. "Pride and Nakedness: *As I Lay Dying*." In *William Faulkner's* As I Lay Dying*: A Critical Casebook*, edited by Dianne Cox, 95–110. New York: Garland.

Bleikasten, André. 1990. *The Ink of Melancholy: Faulkner's Novels from* The Sound and the Fury *to* Light in August. Indiana: Indiana University Press.

———. 1995. "Faulkner from a European Perspective." In *The Cambridge Companion to William Faulkner*, edited by Philip M. Weinstein, 75–95. Cambridge: Cambridge University Press.

Boren, Mark Edelman. 2002. "The Southern Super Collider: William Faulkner Smashes Language into Reality in *As I Lay Dying*." *Southern Quarterly* 40, no. 4: 21–38.

Branch, Watson. 1985. "Darl Bundren's Cubistic Vision." In *William Faulkner's* As I Lay Dying*: A Critical Casebook*, edited by Dianne Cox, 111—129. New York: Garland.

Cox, Dianne, ed. 1985. *William Faulkner's* As I Lay Dying*: A Critical Casebook*. New York: Garland.

Davis, Duane H. 1991. "Reversible Subjectivity: The Problem of Transcendence and Language." In *Merleau-Ponty Vivant*, edited by M. C. Dillon, 31–45. Albany: State University of New York Press.

Dillon, M. C., ed. 1991. *Merleau-Ponty Vivant*. Albany: State University of New York Press.

Donnelly, Colleen. 1990. "The Syntax of Perception in *As I Lay Dying*." *The CEA Critic* 53, no. 1 (Fall): 54–68.

Faulkner, William. 1985 (1930). *As I Lay Dying: The Corrected Text*. New York: Random House.

Ferrer, Daniel. 1982. "*In omnis iam vocabuli mortem*: Representation of Absence, the Subject of Representation and Absence of the Subject in William Faulkner's *As I Lay Dying*," *Oxford Literary Review* 5, no. 1–2: 21–36.

Fowler, Doreen. 2004. "Psychological Criticism." In *A Companion to Faulkner Studies*, edited by Charles A. Peek and Robert W. Hamblin, 197–213. Westport and London: Greenwood Press.

Hamrick, William S., and Jan Van der Veken. 2011. *Nature and Logos, A Whiteheadian Key to Merleau-Ponty's Fundamental Thought.* Albany: State University of New York Press.

Merleau-Ponty, Maurice. 2010. *Child Psychology and Pedagogy: The Sorbonne Lectures 1949–1952.* Translated by Talia Welsh. Evanston: Northwestern University Press. Published in 2001 as *Psychologie et pédagogie de l'enfant: Cours de Sorbonne 1949–1952.* Paris: Verdier.

Patten, Catherine. 1985. "The Chronology of *As I Lay Dying*." In *William Faulkner's* As I Lay Dying*: A Critical Casebook*, edited by Dianne Cox, 30–32. New York: Garland.

Peek, Charles A., and Robert W. Hamblin, eds. 2004. *A Companion to Faulkner Studies*. Westport and London: Greenwood Press.

Pettey, Homer B. 2003. "Perception and the Destruction of Being in *As I Lay Dying*." *The Faulkner Journal* (Fall): 27–46.

Weinstein, Philip M., ed. 1995. *The Cambridge Companion to William Faulkner.* Cambridge: Cambridge University Press.

10

Listening in Depth

Reading Merleau-Ponty Alongside Nancy

Galen A. Johnson

> We should have to return to this idea of proximity through distance, of intuition as auscultation or palpation in depth, of a view which is a view of the self, a torsion of self upon self, and which calls "coincidence" in question.
>
> —Maurice Merleau-Ponty, *The Visible and the Invisible*

I would like to explore the implications of this epigram taken from the third chapter of *The Visible and the Invisible* titled "Interrogation and Intuition" and to explore the thought of listening in depth. I want to do this alongside Jean-Luc Nancy's *Listening* (2002, 2007) and *Corpus* (2006, 2008). This placing achieves something like a counterpoint harmony between the voices of these two philosophers, but also certain provocations.

Hearing and Listening

Based on our opening epigram, Merleau-Ponty was reaching toward both a new but also ancient philosophical methodology for the thinking of Being when he proposed the thought of listening in depth—auscultation, also touching in depth—palpation. Against the grain of the tradition, our opening epigram puts listening together with touching while, since Aristotle's *De Anima*, touch has been classified along with taste as senses requiring contact.

Hearing, along with vision and smell, have been classified as senses "at a distance." Thus, at the methodological heart of Merleau-Ponty's late philosophy, we not only find the visibility of the invisible, but also touching the intangible and listening to the inaudible. We clearly have our hands full.[1]

"Auscultation" and "palpation" are new terms for a notion of intuition that does not seek or offer unity of thought with object, as is often attributed to the notion of intuition in Husserl and Bergson. These are both medical terms, or let us better say, terms with ancient roots that have been taken up within the history of modern medicine. The words are cognates in English and in French. "Palpation" refers to the physician's touch in manually examining the patient's body to assess the texture and tenderness of the body's internal organs and vertebrae. Palpation is also the mother's hand or father's wrist on the forehead of a feverish infant, and virtual palpation is the MRI machine and the tappings of its "echo-time" and "repetition-time." Based on the Latin verb, *auscultare,* "to listen," auscultation means listening to the inside of the body, particularly to the heart and lungs; the physician "reads" the heart sounds, later corroborated by echocardiogram. Merleau-Ponty's metaphors propose the image of philosopher-physician touching the outside and listening to the inside of body and world, speaking and writing their sound and un-sound, their rhythms, paces, and pulses.

Thus, we approach a first distinction between hearing and listening, in French between the verbs *entendre* (to hear) and *écouter* (to listen), and by this difference we mark the mere sound perception from the attentive, awake, alert state. This is Nancy's first distinction in *Listening*, and he tells us that hearing is like comprehending (*entendre—comprendre*), and is thus more of a cognitive experience, a state of knowledge bearing a certain isomorphism with the visual and the conceptual, while listening is more like feeling (*sentir*): making resonant what is heard, "touching" the other in a way that feels the accent, tone, and timbre of voice, an "acousmatics" (L, 3). Listening is a tension, an intention, "an intensification and a concern, a curiosity or an anxiety," and to listen is "to be straining toward a possible meaning, and consequently one that is not immediately accessible" (ibid., 5, 6). Sound and sense mix together and resonate in and through each other such that to be listening "is always to be on the edge of meaning, or in an

1. I grow more and more convinced of Derrida's assessment in *On Touching—Jean-Luc Nancy*: though Nancy does not cite Merleau-Ponty often, yet "their implicit affinities seem undeniable although sometimes difficult to outline or formalize" (Derrida, *OT*, 184).

edgy meaning of extremity, and as if the sound were precisely nothing else than this edge, this fringe, this margin" (ibid., 7).

Nancy joins with Merleau-Ponty in seeking to alter the figure of the philosopher from the seer to listener. Nancy asks: "Isn't the philosopher someone who always hears (and hears everything), but who cannot listen? (L, 1). And bringing phenomenology closer to himself than he normally would, he further asks: "If, from Kant to Heidegger, the major concern of philosophy has been found in the appearance or manifestation of being, in a 'phenomenology,' the ultimate truth of the phenomenon . . . shouldn't truth itself . . . be listened to rather than seen?" (ibid., 3–4). Both Nancy and Merleau-Ponty, together with Nietzsche, want to "prick up the philosophical ear" and Heidegger, too, should be brought into play. For he characterized the correspondence the philosopher seeks with Being as a co-respondence that is an attunement with the voice of Being (WP, 77) and which bears a close relation with poetic creation (ibid., 95).

We see in these passages a close transition from hearing to touching and from touching to a certain mode of seeing. We palpate the things "with our look" (VI, 131/173), Merleau-Ponty says, and in *Corpus*, Nancy explicitly writes that "vision does not penetrate. . . . It is a touching that does not absorb but moves along lines and recesses, inscribing and exscribing the body. A mobile, unstable caress . . ." (C, 47). What kind of look is this that does not penetrate but palpates and caresses? Certainly not the Sartrean hard gaze of conflict, mastery, and keyhole voyeurism, and certainly not the lascivious eye of Herod that undresses Salomé. Rather, it seems to be a vision that is both light as air and open to the world and at the same time a look of weight and gravity that takes in the fullness of things and draws things close together into, if not a unity, a certain closeness that Nancy dares call "fraternity." It is a look that caused Derrida to wonder if eyes looking at one another can actually touch and if they can, would it be day or night? (OT, 2), and to wonder as well about a kiss of the eyes (ibid., 301; cf. Randall Johnson, "Resisting the Kiss of a Dream of Reading").

Yet, having drawn hearing and seeing so close to one another in their touches, there remains a residue of differences between hearing and seeing that accord each of them its specificity and special gifts. For one thing, the judgments of hearing are not as acute in locating sound, whether behind or in front, to the left or right, close or far away. Hearing is also not as linear as seeing. We know that Merleau-Ponty has done more than anyone to revise the geometrical model of vision handed down from Descartes's *Optics* and the achievements of perspective drawing. Vision in depth is a play of differences in color and lighting and the art of Leonardo and Matisse and

Klee "frees the line" to let it muse and "go line," *d'aller ligne* (OE, 143/74).[2] Nevertheless, hearing can do what seeing cannot, namely hearing around corners, hearing and overhearing through walls and doors, all that goes with eavesdropping. And this wonderfully playful word—and dangerous word—"eavesdropping," with its history of roofs and buildings and Kings and Great Halls, also tells us that hearing is not as immediately reversible as seeing. It is entirely possible to hear and not be heard, to eavesdrop, to track, to snoop, to hunt, to listen in on the party line, to spy, to hack, to "electronic eavesdrop."

The differences between seeing and hearing can rise to the level of actual contradiction in the experience of listening to music: in order to attend acutely and anxiously to a piece of music, sometimes we must close our eyes and block out the visual sightscape in order to have before us only the soundscape. With eyes tight shut, we listen in the dark and are more available to being touched by sound. Like the blind who listen without sight, saturation by the soundscape swells like the ocean, and like the deaf who are without even the soundscape, the tacts, tangents, and tensions of the touchscape intensify like the textures of the bark of trees and the warmth of sunset. How could it be that Helen Keller gave us one of the most powerful writings on the beauty of nature? Keller wrote: "Only the deaf appreciate hearing, only the blind realize the manifold blessings that lie in sight."[3]

If we are not hasty but linger patiently with these differences, we will arrive at the question Nancy seeks: "How is it that sound has such a particular impact, a capacity to affect us, which is like nothing else, and is very different from what has to do with the visual and with touch?" (L, 10). Nancy himself has given us the hint of a partial answer in *Corpus*: "The sound that penetrates through the ear propagates throughout the entire body something of its effects, which could not be said to occur in the same way with the visual signal" (C, 14). This suggestion means that listening is close to the experience of being touched, held, and caressed; sound can stroke—as it can also strike—and penetrating through the ear, thus vibrates and communicates with the entire body.

2. The editions cited here are, respectively, "Eye and Mind," in *The Merleau-Ponty Aesthetics Reader*, edited with an introduction by Galen A. Johnson and Michael B. Smith, translation editor (Evanston: Northwestern University Press, 1993), 121–60; and Paris: Gallimard, 1964.

3. Helen Keller, "Three Days to See." *Atlantic Monthly*, January 1933, Part I.

Listening to the Depths of the Other

If we return to our opening epigram, at stake in listening in depth is also a relation between self and other. What is this deep listening that can heal and cure? Why is it that simply being listened to deeply, patiently, and silently, without judgment or interruption, is therapeutic? Why does the ear of the other so affect what is un-sound in the *psyche* and soul? For such difficult questions about the *psyche,* we have only glimpses. For one thing, there is hardly any clearer demonstration that the *psyche* is extended: there truly is "the body of the spirit," as Merleau-Ponty loved to cite Valéry's phrase. When we listen to others, Merleau-Ponty says, "words . . . have the extraordinary power to draw me out of my thoughts" and "suddenly swell with a meaning which overflows into the other person" (S, 235/298). Merleau-Ponty has read Freud, and it is with his help that he knows something of these things about overdetermination of sense and the body of the spirit. Nancy too knew Freud and says that Freud's most fascinating and decisive statement is found in a posthumous note: "The *psyche*'s extended; knows nothing about it [*Psyche ist ausgedehnt: weiss nichts davon*]." Nancy comments: "The 'psyche,' in other words, is *body.*" So it is "the body, or bodies, that we try to touch" (C, 21).

To listen deeply is to touch the body, that is to say, the spirit of the other. For another thing, listening is a certain way of being present, where being-present to the other is a presence that includes the nonverbal, the noncognitive, and a tacit knowledge borne from memory and history. Thus, listening is about time, about taking time, about knowing time. "Time is that 'body of the spirit' Valéry used to talk about," Merleau-Ponty writes. "Time and thought are mutually entangled" (S, 15/21).[4] Nancy offers a poignant description of the time of listening: "It is a present in waves on a swell, not in a point on a line; it is a time that opens up, that is hollowed out, that is enlarged or ramified, that envelops or separates, that becomes or is turned into a loop, that stretches out or contracts" (L, 13). And about this opening up, it is an openness that is unconstrained, for unlike the eyes, the ears have no eyelids (ibid., 14). Listening is presence without end, openness without ceasing.

Moreover, to listen is be silent, and not only to be silent and remain silent, it is the *promise of silence* (C, 51). Perhaps it is this above all that

4. The editions cited here are, respectively, trans. Richard C. McCleary (Evanston: Northwestern University Press, 1964); and Paris: Gallimard, 1960.

makes trouble for the philosopher as a listener. It is hard to listen without interrupting and without ceasing, yet doing so establishes a relationship and a bond. Here Nancy introduces language that is as unusual as it is precise. "The visual is tendentially mimetic," Nancy argues, while the sonorous is "tendentially methexic (that is, having to do with participation, sharing, or contagion)" (L, 10; E, 27). This means that the visual has a tendency toward the idea as representation while the sonorous has a different tendency toward participation and sharing. This foreign word, *methexis* (it is not found in the unabridged Oxford English Dictionary), is of Greek origin, the noun formed from the infinitive *metecho,* to participate, which makes the very nice pun in English of echoing across or back and forth. *Methexis* refers to "group sharing" and even audience participation in ancient Greek theater, and is the word Plato used in the *Parmenides* for the participation of sense particulars in the realm of Forms and the word Aristotle used in the *Logic* for the participation or classification of a species within a genus. These two, *mimesis* and *methexis,* formed the twin pillars of ancient Greek culture, *mimesis* correspondent with *logos* (speech, reason) and *methexis* correspondent with *muthos* (story, myth). It was *methexis* that had therapeutic benefits expressed in the Platonic dialogues not as the dialectic of argument but the situation, characters, and other dramatic elements.[5] Scene, sound, and voice tend toward participation. Thus, in listening is born the possibility of a relation to the other and a relation to a community of others that does not require mutual agreement on ideas, values, or principles but in which there can abide a genuine pluralism of voices that sound and re-sound.

The silence promised by the true listener ever expands over time into a voluminosity in space—thus, in space-time—that is the place, the placing and the logic, of the question. The silent intuition of listening grows interrogative, not the question that provokes, challenges, or defeats the other, but the thoughtful and feline question that draws the other out and creates elongations of meaning and sense. The question seeks a narrative or story or at least some broader temporal whole within which the particular has a place and a home. Perhaps, since this broader temporal whole will forever retain its gaps, empty spaces, and further questions, we could best designate it with Merleau-Ponty's term *lace-works.* He contrasts "lace-works" with the whole "bric-a-brac" of positive psychology: "perception, idea—affection, pleasure, desire, love, Eros" (VI, 270/318). "Lace-works" (*les dentelles*) give us the image of stitching or crossing that ties threads together without

5. Cf. Tullio Maranhao, *Therapeutic Discourse and Socratic Dialogue* (Madison: University of Wisconsin Press, 1986), ch. 6: "Mimesis vs. Methexis," especially 137ff.

closing things off, making room for an airiness in which we are not suffocated but are able to breathe. The image translates much of what we are seeking: temporal wholes that knot together touches, yet do not close off gaps. Listening is like an art of drawing, and in a double sense: drawing out the other at the same time as the listener is drawn in to the space of the question, and it means that listening to the other also becomes a listening to oneself and a relation to oneself.

In our opening epigram, Merleau-Ponty calls this relation of self upon oneself a "torsion" (*torsion*), from the Latin *torquere,* to twist, and this term too has a medical meaning referring to the twisting of an internal organ, such as the intestine. It would be an illusion to think that one could engage in a listening to the other in depth without being transformed oneself. Deep listening reverberates, resonates, and rebounds in the self in ways that twist, pressure, and even cause a loss of the phenomenological subject and a return to a self re-cast from the outside, which would be a self pieced together from the look and voice of the other. This is a self such as Merleau-Ponty speaks to in the next to last paragraph of *Eye and Mind,* "dense, open, rent beings [*peuplée d'êtres épais, ouverts, déchirés*]" (OE, 149/91). Nancy writes: "The subject of the listening or the subject who is listening . . . is not a phenomenological subject" (L, 22), but rather a "radicalization of the phenomenological voice" in which the self "is supported only in dehiscence" or in differential "from outside" (ibid., 28). This is a text and argument from Nancy, yet we all recognize the language of "dehiscence" as the borrowed language of Merleau-Ponty. We know that Merleau-Ponty's term for this exteriorized subjectivity is dimension or level but also "hollow" (*creux*) rather than the nothingness of Sartrean self as airy, absolute freedom: "The soul is the hollow of the body" (VI, 233/282), and "All those we have loved, detested, known, or simply glimpsed speak through our voice" (S, 19/28). My own voice absorbs the speaking, singing, laughing, and crying of others and listening is now become affect, affection, desire, and perhaps, love, for "love is the touch of the open" (C, 29).

In spite of such powers of auscultation, both philosophers emphasize that listening to the other falters and stumbles in efforts to achieve perfect concordance and understanding. Merleau-Ponty had already argued in *Phenomenology of Perception* that though solipsism per se is self-defeating because it assumes the existence of a community of speakers to address in articulating its claim (PhP, 360/414),[6] yet there remains a truth of solipsism

6. The editions cited here are, respectively, trans. Colin Smith (London: Routledge aand Kegan Paul, 1962); and Paris: Gallimard, 1945.

"rooted in living experience and quite insurmountable" (ibid., 358/411). Such are experiences in which a friend is suffering from grief or anger and insofar as I can, I want to share in that suffering but can do so only partially and one-sidedly, or the experience of a couple where there is more love felt on one side than on the other (ibid., 356, 357/409, 410). Nancy also writes: "I will never be able to speak from where you listen, nor will you be able to listen from where I speak" (BP, 189–90).

Therefore, we do not intend to overcredit the powers of listening and touching as if they are the keys to an occult wisdom or mystical *gnosis* capable of plumbing the secrets of the *psyche* all the way down. Though Merleau-Ponty stresses the differences among the superficial and the deep in his commentary on Freud's analysis of the case of Dora, he also stresses that there is "no absolutely deep and absolutely superficial." Rather, "the various layers of justifications have their truth" (IP, 184, 183/241, 239). In one of my favorite sections from *Corpus* titled "Mystery?" and one that Derrida also likes very much (OT, 307–308), Nancy cautions:

> We must not credit "touch" too quickly or, still less, suppose that we could eventually touch upon *the* sense of "touch" as a setting of limits for (the) sense(s). This tendency is very typical of the crudest and most robust ideologies (a vitalist-spiritualist fascism in the style of "muscled thought," or "sacred-heart thought"—with, undoubtedly, its real and secret horror of bodies). (C, 44–45)

There is not "the body," just as there is not "the touch" (C, 119), just as there is not "the true and absolute listening." There are bodies, there are soundings, there are touchings.

Listening to the Depths of the World

To this point, it has been possible to compose, as we have said, something like a counterpoint harmony between the voices of Merleau-Ponty and Nancy, but now it seems that Nancy will go no farther and Merleau-Ponty, as we know, wanted to go farther from body and spirit to the ontology of Flesh. Already for the phenomenological body-proper (*le corps propre*), the lived-body is the union of spirit and matter and any one of its bodily organs—hand, eye, ear—is a total part and expresses that thin membrane, that hinge, that inside-outside where body crosses over with spirit. No need for the ill-thought

Cartesian pineal gland, the mouth that speaks and sings is itself the union of spirit and matter, mind and body. It is of heaven as celestial song and thoroughly of earth as sonorous organ. The invisible, the inaudible, and the intangible, "is not the contrary of the sensible, but is its lining and its depth (VI, 149/195). Thus, the name for Merleau-Ponty's philosophy is "carnal spiritualism" or "oneiric naturalism." Derrida has written: "Without the mouth, one cannot conceive of the union of the soul and the body" (OT, 25).

For Nancy, the ontology of the body is already philosophy in *excess*: "In any language, it's the word in *excess*" (C, 21). Above all for Nancy, the signifying body means "one thing only: the absolute contradiction of not being able to be a *body* without being the body *of a spirit,* which disembodies it (ibid., 69). The phrase that needs emphasis is "absolute contradiction" that remains ever and always unmediated. This does not mean a new or even restored Cartesianism. There is no mind-substance ontologically distinct from body-substance; there is only body as flesh and body as spirit. Nancy could not be clearer:

> Sometimes this body is itself an "inside" where representation is formed or projected (sensation, perception, image, memory, idea, consciousness). . . . At other times, the body is the signifying "outside." . . . Thus the signifying body never stops exchanging inside and outside. . . . Particular philosophical perspectives don't greatly alter things: the dualism of "body" and "soul," the monism of "flesh," cultural and psychoanalytic symbolisms of bodies. . . . It's an instance par excellence of contradiction. (C, 69)

This text means there is the body of matter, gravity, and weight and there is the "glorious body" of spirit and between them is no third term. "What body means and provides for thought, is only this, that there's no mediation *here*. The finite and infinite do not *pass* into one another, they do not dialecticize each other. . . . This is why a 'thought' about the body should really *ponder* the body, be a feeling of its weight" (C, 43). This is what Nancy means by lingering with *areality,* the hard strangeness of this *body*" with its "un-thinking, unthinkable exteriority" (ibid., 17). Between body-matter and body-spirit there is temporal oscillation back and forth and there are spacings and placings, but truly thinking the body is to touch upon the limit of thought. Here Nancy enters into explicit opposition to Merleau-Ponty: the body is unnameable like God, "unnameable also as the intimate self-texture toward which a philosophy of the 'body-proper' struggles. ("What we call flesh, this inwardly worked mass, has no name in any philosophy"—Merleau-Ponty.) God, Death, Flesh: the three-fold name of the entire body of onto-theology . . . these three impossible names" (ibid., 75).

For Nancy, onto-theology means that he finds Merleau-Ponty's philosophy of Flesh infected with the legacy of the Christian doctrines of incarnation (the Word made Flesh) and the cross (chiasm) insufficiently deconstructed in the age of the death of God. Nancy is content to dwell with contradiction rather than incarnation and with the areality of the body, this faint reality, strangeness, and opacity of embodiment. There is much to disagree with in what we would have to regard as Nancy's overly hasty reading of Merleau-Ponty's ontology as a "monism of the flesh" (C, 69) without crediting Merleau-Ponty's careful attention to noncoincidence. Of Françoise Dastur in contrast with Nancy, Derrida has recognized that she sets afoot a reading that "is more accurate, which is to say generous, with regard to the Merleau-Ponty who is more attentive to distancing and non-coincidence" (OT, 203). Yet it is true that what Merleau-Ponty ultimately does hear in the auscultation of Being is a silence that is fullness, and listening in depth, Merleau-Ponty says, is "called forth by the voices of silence" (VI, 127/168). This is the voluminous silence of the forest at dawn or at dusk, of the vortex of a windless canyon at sunset, of the calm and quiet sea at daybreak. *The Visible and the Invisible* concludes with the voice of Being as "the voice of no one, since it is the very voice of the things, the waves, and the forests" (ibid., 155/204). Though the philosopher does not tell us so, this phrase is taken from the ending of Valéry's poem, *La Pythie* ("The Pythoness"). In it we can also hear the echo of the inspiration Merleau-Ponty took from the *Poetic Art* of Paul Claudel, that "the world is a poem" and a "total harmony" whispered "in adoration in the ear of *Sigé* the Abyss (Sigé) (S, 317/395).

Nancy does not want this ontology of fullness, harmony, and adoration; he seeks to live and think a philosophy of bodily "intrusion" (cardiomyopathy, lymphoma). He lives and writes the body as medical and technological, as suffering and survival, an exscription of Being—body written and imprinted from the outside rather than, or at least in addition to, signifying inscriptions written from the inside. Thus, he states a different challenge: "Unless we ponder without reservation the ecotechnical creation of bodies as the truth of *our* world, and a truth *just as valid* as those that myths, religions, and humanisms were able to represent, we won't have begun to think *this* very world" (C, 89). If we wanted a *rapprochement* of lived-body with body-techne as sacrifice and suffering we would perhaps begin from the expansion of what Merleau-Ponty means by "anonymous body" and his ways of taking seriously illness and disease. Nancy abides in this unmediated contradiction between lived-body and anonymous body that Merleau-Ponty would have called "ambiguity."

To assess properly Nancy's objection to Merleau-Ponty that *Flesh* is infected with onto-theology is beyond what we can properly begin, let alone finish, here. Any proper assessment would have to take into account Merleau-Ponty's own critique of "explicative theology" and his interpretation of the meaning of the death of God and "faith and good faith." Indeed, Nancy has his own problems with onto-theology for he takes as his opening and central motif throughout *Corpus* the invocation from the Christian Mass: "This is my body" (*Hoc est enim corpus meum*). Nevertheless, what he wants from this liturgical text is a "deconstruction of Christianity," not incarnation or a "sublimated paganism" of bread and wine (C, 3), but body as wound, as sacrifice. He does not want a religious meaning of resurrection either, only its "nonreligious meaning" (*Noli*, 15), as he makes clear in *Noli me tangere: On the Raising of the Body*. These words, *noli me tangere* ("Do not touch me") were spoken to Mary Magdalene at the Gospel scene outside the empty tomb. Originally spoken in Aramaic, Nancy prefers the Latin because the negative infinitive, *noli*, implies "do not wish, do not even desire, to touch me" (*Noli*, 37). What does Mary hear in this command? What does true listening touch upon in the depths of these words? They are the opposite of what Jesus speaks to the doubting disciple, Thomas, whom he commands to touch his side. But Thomas was the disciple of doubt and Mary Magdalene hears these words from within a relationship, a love, a bond, and a faith; it was she who anointed his feet with perfume, she the sister of Lazarus whom he had raised from the dead. She has already entered into the proper listening to these words (*Noli*, 9) and she is not one of those other disciples who "hearing, hear not" (ibid., 5). Nancy reads Mary's understanding and feelings this way: she hears both a withdrawal and a promise. Do not seek not to hold or detain me and do not believe there is a proof of the kind Thomas wanted (ibid., 47). The withdrawal is precisely what Mary must love and know. "Love what escapes you. Love the one who goes. Love that he goes" (ibid., 37). And in the withdrawal, yet there is the promise, for the command is addressed to the singular "Mary," and in the voice of that command she hears her name. Nancy writes: "To say the name is to say that which both dies and does not die. . . . The name leaves without leaving, for it bears the revelation of everyone's infinite finitude" (ibid., 46). Thus, two bodies in the garden at the tomb, one of glory and the other of flesh, and they belong mutually to each other.

This is the provocation Nancy presents for Merleau-Ponty's thinking of Flesh, Time, and Silence: the ontology of the body is already philosophy in excess, and, like God and Death, Flesh is also unnamable. The true name is that of immemorial singular existence, "Mary." The preliminary lesson I draw from Nancy's provocation is that Flesh itself as an ultimate ontological notion needs to be thought less in unity and more in multiples, even to the extremity that we speak of "fleshes" with their differences and hesitate before the one Flesh.[7] This would be to emphasize those Working Notes in which Merleau-Ponty speaks of flesh as "differentiations" (December 1960: "Body and Flesh—Eros—Philosophy of Freudianism," VI, 270/318), as "divergence" (*l'écart*), and especially as time: "Then past and present are *Ineinander,* each enveloping-enveloped—and that itself is the flesh" (VI, 268/315). And with respect to onto-theology, this would push the ontology of "fleshes" more toward pantheism,[8] or even at the extreme, polytheism, and at the very least, toward the notion of a divine that does not escape a certain finitude, immanence, and impotence,[9] all of which mean openness and a relation with the open (sky, *le ciel*), whether one says justice, love, or mercy (*Noli,* 80–83). But these are all quite preliminary thoughts that require much further study and meditation.

---

7. Cf. Bryan Bannon, "In the Space of the Garden," 5–8, unpublished manuscript, as well as chapter 3 of his doctoral dissertation, "Developing a Theoretical Framework for an Ethical Understanding of Nature through the Phenomenologies of Heidegger and Merleau-Ponty," The University of Memphis, 2008.

8. Pantheism as the theological meaning of Flesh is the suggestion made by Fred Evans and Leonard Lawlor in their Introduction to *Chiasms: Merleau-Ponty's Notion of Flesh,* ed. Fred Evans and Leonard Lawlor (Albany: State University of New York Press, 2000), 14–15.

9. Speaking of Schelling in the *Nature* course, Merleau-Ponty says: "The introduction of the relation of expression is at the origin of a conception of the finality of the actual world, a finality that includes internal entanglements, incompossibilities—that is, evil—and so finality by an almighty power, but weighed down and hampered" (*Nature,* trans. Robert Vallier, 41). In "Indirect Language and the Voices of Silence," Merleau-Ponty expresses his own view more directly: "The Christian God wants nothing to do with a vertical relation of subordination. He is not simply a principle of which we are the consequence, a will whose instruments we are, or even a model of which human values are only the reflection. There is a sort of impotence of God without us, and Christ attests that God would not be fully God without becoming fully human" ("Indirect Language and the Voices of Silence," in *The Merleau-Ponty Aesthetics Reader*, 107–108).

Abbreviations

Jacques Derrida

OT *On Touching—Jean-Luc Nancy* Translated by Christine Irizarry. Stanford: Stanford University Press, 2005.

Martin Heidegger

WP *What Is Philosophy?* Translated by Jean T. Wilde and William Kluback. New Haven: Twayne Publishers, New College and University Press, 1956.

Jean-Luc Nancy

BP *The Birth to Presence.* Translated by Brian Holmes and others. Stanford: Stanford University Press, 1993.

C *Corpus.* Translated by Richard A. Rand. New York: Fordham University Press, 2008.

D *Dis-Enclosure: The Deconstruction of Christianity.* Translated by Bettina Bergo, Gabriel Malenfant, and Michael B. Smith. New York: Fordham University Press, 2008.

E *À l'écoute.* Paris: Éditions Galilée, 2002.

L *Listening.* Translated by Charlotte Mandell. New York: Fordham University Press, 2007.

Noli *Noli me tangere: On the Raising of the Body.* Translated by Sarah Clift, Pascale-Anne Brault, and Michael Naas. New York: Fordham University Press, 2008.

References

Augoyard, Jean-François, and Henry Torgue, eds. 2006. *Sonic Experience: A Guide to Everyday Sounds.* Montreal: McGill-Queen's University Press.

Blesser, Barry, and Linda-Ruth Salter. 2009. *Spaces Speak, Are You Listening? Experiencing Aural Architecture.* Cambridge: The MIT Press.

Cage, John. 1961. *Silence: Lectures and Writings.* Middletown, CT: Wesleyan University Press.

Casey, Edward S. 2009. "On Finding (One's Own) Philosophical Voice." Presidential Address, American Philosophical Association, December 29.

Evans, Fred. 2008. *The Multivoiced Body: Society and Communication in the Age of Diversity*. New York: Columbia University Press.

Ihde, Don. 2007. *Listening and Voice: Phenomenologies of Sound*. 2nd Edition. Albany: State University of New York Press.

Johnson, Randall. "Resisting the Kiss of a Dream of Reading." Unpublished manuscript.

Johnstone, Christopher Lyle. 2009. *Listening to the Logos: Speech and the Coming of Wisdom in Ancient Greece*. Columbia: The University of South Carolina Press.

Keller, Helen. 1933. "Three Days to See." *Atlantic Monthly*, January.

Sacks, Oliver. 2007. *Musicophilia: Tales of Music and the Brain*. New York: Alfred A. Knopf.

Schafer, R. Murray. 1993. *The Soundscape*. Rochester, VT: Destiny Books.

Szendy, Peter. 2007. *Listen: A History of our Ears*. Translated by Charlotte Mandell, Foreword by Jean-Luc Nancy. New York: Fordham University Press.

11

Art and the Overcoming of the Discourse of Modernity

William S. Hamrick

Much of the thought of Maurice Merleau-Ponty is dedicated to overcoming the legacy of another European thinker who was born a little over four hundred and fifty years ago, and whose life and work have had a profound impact on European history and culture. This remarkable individual was Galileo Galilei. His views developed across the next three centuries into differing conceptions of nature and our place within it, almost all of which conceptions subscribe to three basic, mistaken beliefs that still exist, and against which Merleau-Ponty began to formulate an alternative ontology (see RC, 67/97 and N, ch. 2). Because these beliefs are so well known, the briefest possible summary will suffice here.[1]

The Discourse of Modernity

The first belief, formed in counterpoise to the "wild overstressing"[2] of final causes in the Middle Ages, is that the intelligibility of the externally real—matter, substance, measurable spatial extension—is exclusively quantitative and therefore limited to mathematics and its practical applications.

1. For a further discussion of this subject, see William S. Hamrick and Jan Van der Veken, *Nature and Logos* (Albany: State University of New York Press, 2011), ch. I and II.

2. Alfred North Whitehead, *Process and Reality*, corrected edition, ed. David Ray Griffin and Donald W. Sherburne (New York: The Free Press, 1978), 84 (hereafter abbreviated as PR). In the same vein, Galileo quoted Cardinal Baronius (1598) that the Bible teaches us how to go to heaven, not how the heavens go.

The second belief, which flows from the first, consists of the forced exile from nature of all purposes and values, including the good. They, along with everything else that Locke termed "secondary" qualities,[3] are purely nominal. In Galileo's words, they are "nothing else but mere names."[4] All such qualities become what Alfred North Whitehead complains of as "psychic additions" that are "only the mind's way of perceiving nature."[5] Hence Whitehead's protest against "the bifurcation of nature" into "nature apprehended in awareness and the nature which is the cause of awareness," "two systems of reality" (CN, 30, 31) in which what we see is not the real, and what is real we do not see.

As a result, Galileo's and, later, Descartes's *mathesis* of nature had the effect of breaking the seamless whole of humanity—with its purposes, values, and feelings—and its environing nature. This "mechanistic despiritualization of nature"[6] also survives today in many ways in the biotechnology

3. John Locke, *An Essay Concerning Human Understanding*, abridged and ed. A. S. Pringle-Pattison (Oxford: Clarendon Press, 1969), II, 8, § 23, 71ff.

4. Galileo Galilei, *Il Saggiatore*, cited in E. A. Burtt, *The Metaphysical Foundations of Modern Science* (New York: Anchor Books, 1954), 85.

5. Whitehead, *The Concept of Nature* (Cambridge: Cambridge University Press, 1964 [1920]), 42 (hereafter CN). Galileo, curiously enough, defined "heaviness" as an objective property of objects instead of referring to a percipient for whom a body is heavy. See his *On Mechanics*, trans. with intro. and notes by Stillman Drake (Madison: University of Wisconsin Press, 1960), 151, 170–71. Anything mental for Galileo was, in Whitehead's language, a "psychic addition." As Whitehead pointed out, with the development of transmission theories of light and sound, seventeenth- and eighteenth-century philosophers such as Descartes and Locke argued that a secondary quality such as color emerged from the transmitted waves of light, and so was not itself in the object or the light waves projected from it, whereas inertia, "heaviness," and "pushiness" were primary qualities that were so transmitted. As Whitehead notes, this distinction inconsistently privileges touch because, "Perceptions of push are just as much the outcome of transmission as are perceptions of colour" (CN, 42). Thus, if color is not in nature, neither should inertia be.

6. Wilhelm Windelband, *A History of Philosophy*, trans. James H. Tufts (New York and London: Macmillan, 1926), 403. Compare Rupert Sheldrake: "Both animistic and mechanistic thinking are metaphorical. But whereas mythic and animistic thinking (earth as mother, mother nature, etc.) depends on organic metaphors drawn from the processes of life, mechanistic thinking depends on metaphors drawn from man-made machines." *The Rebirth of Nature, the Greening of Science and God* (London: Random Century Group, 1990), 6. The view of nature as mechanistic, objective plenum of matter is what Whitehead labeled "scientific materialism." In this doctrine, nature appears as "senseless, valueless, purposeless. It just does what it does do, following a fixed routine imposed by external relations which do not spring from the nature of its being." *Science and the Modern World* (New York: The Free Press, 1967 [1925]) (hereafter SMW), 17.

industry. Writing in *The New York Times* following the death of Ingmar Bergman, Stephen Holden underscored one dimension of this mode of thought in a manner that is central to this paper. He wrote:

> Today the religion of high art that dominated the 1950s and '60s seems increasingly quaint and provincial. The longstanding belief that humans are born with singular psyches and souls is being superseded by an emerging new ideal: the human as technologically perfect machine. The culture of the soul—of Freud and Marx and, yes, Bergman—has been overtaken by the culture of the body. Biotechnology leads the shaky way into the future, and pseudo-immortality, through cloning, is in sight. Who needs a soul if the self is technologically mutable? For that matter, who needs art? That may be why Mr. Bergman's spiritual malaise seems less relevant than his flesh-and-blood experience. No filmmaker has explored relationships between men and women with such depth and passion.[7]

The "mechanistic despiritualization" of nature leads directly to the third mistaken belief shared by modern philosophers and scientists—with the exception of Spinoza—namely, that nature is an object standing over against us as subjects, or spectators. E. A. Burtt touches on this when he observes that Galileo's "new metaphysics" is one in which human beings are shoved apart as unimportant spectators and a semi-real effect of the great mathematical drama outside.[8] This view is, as noted in Part One, what Merleau-Ponty labels the "ontology of the object" with its corresponding "overlooking thought" ("*pensée de survol*"). However, Burtt slides too quickly over this decisive change of human beings from active participants within the nature they study to a view of a subject as an onlooker disengaged from that nature. Whether in the form of a Cartesian ego or Kantian transcendental consciousness separated from unknowable things in themselves, thought about nature became essentially disengaged from it. How else can we explain why it took so long to develop an ecological consciousness, to make people aware that they are not disconnected from their environment? As Whitehead noted correctly in *Science and the Modern World*, we are so much habituated to seeing the world materialistically that we have trouble

---

7. "In Art's Old Sanctuary, a High Priest of Film." *The New York Times*, July 31, 2007, B4.

8. Burtt, 104.

comprehending "the possibility of another mode of approach to the problems of nature" (Whitehead 1967, 42).

The Aesthetic Critique: Schelling

In this paper, I want to advance an *aesthetic* critique of all three of these modernist beliefs—that our understanding of nature is purely quantitative, that there is no room in nature for purposes, values, and "secondary qualities," and that nature is an object for us as spectators. This critique is based on two main sources, the first of which is German Romanticism, especially the work of F. W. J. Schelling. I will then appeal to Merleau-Ponty's discussions of art, chiefly painting, which he employs to illustrate his ontology of flesh.

Schelling's work had a substantial influence on Merleau-Ponty as well as on Whitehead, about whom I have already written concerning a process interpretation of Merleau-Ponty's ontology of flesh.[9] Thinking after Schelling, both twentieth-century thinkers reject all three modernist beliefs, and they do so for reasons that are aesthetic in both the senses of feeling and of art. All three thinkers hold, correctly, that the universe overflows with meaning that, among other things, transcends quantification. They also agree that purposes, values, and the good cannot be excluded from nature and that the ontology of the object, in any of its forms, stems from detached, "high altitude" thinking which the aesthetic feeling of our flesh-and-blood experiences refutes. Schelling can speak for all three thinkers when he says that nature is visible spirit and spirit is invisible nature.[10] Experience shows us that, as John Compton has indicated, "nature is through and through fluid, active, generative, expressive, inter-weaving and inter-corporeal and, indeed, inter-sensory."[11] Nature is, therefore, inherently and affectively linked to values, including the good and the beautiful. Admittedly, this is a huge

9. William S. Hamrick, "A Process View of the Flesh: Whitehead and Merleau-Ponty," *Process Studies*, 28, no. 1–2 (Spring–Summer 1999): 117–29, and "Whitehead and Merleau-Ponty: Healing the Bifurcation of Nature," in *Whitehead's Philosophy: Points of Connection*, ed. Janusz A. Polanowski and Donald W. Sherburne (Albany: State University of New York Press, 2004), 127–42.

10. F. W. J. Schelling, *Ideas for a Philosophy of Nature*, trans. Errol E. Harris and Peter Heath (Cambridge: Cambridge University Press, 1988 [1797], 42.

11. Personal correspondence, October 13, 2007. Epistemologically, this is an "unbreakable circle," a phrase I owe to Jocelyn Dunphy-Blomfield.

claim and I can hardly "prove" it. The best that I can do here is to use Schelling's and Merleau-Ponty's accounts of our bodily indivisibility from the world and their remarks about art to provide reasons for it.

Schelling, as well as his Tübingen seminary roommates, Hölderlin and Hegel, worked in the shadow of the Kantian cleft between the good and the true, which includes the real. They took up the challenge of finding, as against Kant, a *knowable* connection between the good and the true, conceived as what could be known through the application of the categories of pure understanding to the manifold of sensory intuition.

This is apparent even in Hegel's early fragment, "The Oldest System-Program," written from June to August 1796, and which certainly reflected the thinking of both of his former Tübingen roommates as well. The fragment begins immediately with the theme of ethics and then quickly proceeds to the claim that "the idea which unites all [of the] previous ones is the idea of beauty."[12] The "highest act of reason [is that in] which—in that it comprises all ideas—is an aesthetic act, and . . . *truth and goodness* are united as sisters *only in beauty*. The philosopher must possess as much aesthetic capacity as the poet. The people without an aesthetic sensibility are our philosophical literalists [*Buchstabenphilosophen*]. Philosophy of the spirit is an aesthetic philosophy."[13]

In five short paragraphs, Hegel joins together ethics and metaphysics, goodness and truth, and links both to freedom and then to beauty as the one flesh that unites truth and goodness. Jason Wirth is correct to say of this fragment that there must be a sense in which the good would have to be prior to the true because we would not be motivated to seek the latter unless we saw something of the former in it.[14] Similarly, Whitehead's oft-quoted claim that "[i]t is more important that a proposition be interesting than it be true"[15] is likewise grounded in the priority of the good because unless some goodness were perceived, interest in the proposition would not arise.

Although Hegel refers in his fragment to poetry, which is also Schelling's preferred artistic medium, eighteen years later Schelling made

12. G. W. F. Hegel, "The Oldest System-Program of German Idealism," in *Friedrich Hölderlin, Essays and Letters on Theory*, trans. and ed. Thomas Pfau (Albany: State University of New York Press, 1987), 155.

13. Ibid.

14. Jason Wirth, *The Conspiracy of Life, Meditations on Schelling and His Time* (Albany: State University of New York Press, 2003), 7.

15. Whitehead, *Adventures of Ideas* (New York: The Free Press, 1967 [1933]), 244.

similar claims about music. Where Hegel wrote about "aesthetic capacity," Schelling offers the example of the "divine and holy madness"[16] of Dionysian rites. "For nothing," he tells us, "is more similar to that inner madness than music, which, through the incessant eccentric relinquishing and re-attracting of tones, most clearly imitates that primordial movement." That "primordial movement" is one of nature: "Music itself is a turning wheel that, going out from a single point, always, through all excesses, spins back again to the beginning" (AW, 103).

Hegel unjustly criticized Schelling for advocating an undifferentiated universality—the "night in which, as we say, all cows are black—that is the very *naïveté* of knowledge."[17] Schelling, in fact, was deeply immersed in the study of chemistry and medicine and, were he alive today, he would certainly turn his attention to the emerging science of neuromusicology, which studies the connections between music and the brain. For, as Schelling knew well, music both solicits and nourishes our connections with nature through emotions. He would not have been surprised by the discoveries of neuromusicologists about the links between music and natural rhythms controlled by the brain: circadian rhythms and those of breathing and heartbeats. Likewise, he would not have taken the ubiquity of music in cultures throughout the world to be a matter of chance.

Schelling's own appeal to art in order to bridge the Kantian cleft between the good and the true reached its apogee in the *System of Transcendental Idealism* (1800).[18] In the *System*, art and philosophy are intertwined without being identical, and art is portrayed as the highest spiritual development because of its ability to incarnate and express the primordial identity of nature and spirit, the unconscious and the conscious. In the *Ideas for a Philosophy of Nature* three years earlier, he had written, "So long as I myself am *identical* with Nature, I understand what a living nature is as well as I understand my own life. . . . As soon, however, as I separate myself, and with me everything ideal, from nature, nothing remains to me but a dead object, and I cease to comprehend how a *life outside* me can be possible."[19] In the *System*, he tells us that art is "the only true and

16. Schelling, *The Ages of the World (Fragment)* from the handwritten remains, Third Version (c. 1815), trans. with intro. Jason M. Wirth (Albany: State University of New York Press, 2000) (hereafter AW), 102, 103.

17. Hegel, *The Phenomenology of Spirit*, trans. with intro. and notes by J. B. Baillie (London: George Allen and Unwin, 1964), 79.

18. Schelling, *System of Transcendental Idealism* (1800), trans. Peter Heath, intro. Michael Vater (Charlottesville: University of Virginia Press, 1978) (hereafter *System*).

19. *Ideas for a Philosophy of Nature*, 36.

eternal organ and document of philosophy, which ever and again continues to speak to us of what philosophy cannot depict in external form, namely the unconscious element in acting and producing, and its original identity with the conscious" (System, 231). Consequently, "The objective world is simply the original, as yet unconscious, poetry of the spirit; the universal organon of philosophy—and the keystone of its entire arch—*is the philosophy of art*" (ibid., 12).

Being is to be interrogated from within human experience through the experience of artistic creation that reaches the identity of consciousness and nature. The artist therefore parallels the expressivity of the freedom of nature and our identity with it. As Patrick Burke nicely expresses it, for Schelling the artist "must raise himself up to the level of the creative power of nature in order to gain vision and expression of the therein-dwelling spirit of nature. The artist achieves the level of the creative power of the indwelling spirit of nature through a deep and rich communion which is aesthetic intuition itself."[20] Further, one key aspect of artistic creation is the "irresistible impulse" that impels artists to create, and Schelling identifies this impulse with inspiration, "the actual taking in of the spirit which is unconsciously creative within nature."[21]

Nine years later, in his *Freedom* essay[22] of 1809, Schelling expanded on the priority of the good to the true when he speaks of understanding, knowledge of the true, as a search for light that arises out of the dark and incomprehensible "yearning" (*Sehnsucht*) for "the unknown and nameless good" (*Freedom*, 29–30). As opposed to "rule, order and form" (the true), this good is a principle of "the incomprehensible base of reality in things," a principle of anarchical freedom, a principle of darkness that drives us "to strive for the light" (ibid., 29).

The priority of the good to the true is also such that Schelling agreed with Franz von Baader's claim that "the drive to know is most analogous with the reproductive drive" (*Freedom*, 75).[23] Therefore, it is the yearning

20. "Creativity and the Unconscious in Merleau-Ponty and Schelling," in *Framing a Vision of the World, Essays in Philosophy, Science, and Religion*, ed. André Cloots and Santiago Sia (Leuven: Leuven University Press, 1999), 289–90.

21. Ibid.

22. Schelling, *Philosophical Investigations into the Essence of Human Freedom*, trans. with intro. and notes by Jeff Love and Johannes Schmidt (Albany: State University of New York Press, 2006) (hereafter *Freedom*).

23. Therefore, in male-dominated culture and history, it is not surprising that we speak of the "thrust" of an argument or use "penetrating" as a synonym for "illuminating" and its cognates.

for the nameless good that gives birth to the truth, and Schelling uses von Baader's analogy to lash pedantic philosophers ("philosophical literalists") even more than Hegel did in "The Oldest System-Program." They are "the uncreative people incapable of procreation, the ones that call themselves sober spirits. These are the so-called intellectuals [*Verstandesmenschen*] whose works and deeds are nothing but cold intellectual works and intellectual deeds. . . . [There is] no proper, active, living intellect (and consequently there is just the dead intellect, dead intellectuals)" (AW, 103).

Schelling argues correctly that there can be "no proper, active, living intellect," as well as no connection with the good, if we accept a Cartesian dualism and also reduce living nature to a mechanism. Both lines of argument would have a substantial impact on Whitehead and Merleau-Ponty. For Schelling, Descartes's dualism is the "fundamental error" that infected all subsequent philosophy that descended from it (AW, 50). It is the basic mistake because it disengages the self-grounded subject from the "living basis" of nature (*Freedom*, 26),[24] and this attempted rift in the unitary fabric of matter and spirit also leads to the sterility of philosophy itself. For Schelling, the only way to explain correctly the "circulation between the corporeal and the spiritual" is to say that

> [t]he whole life process is founded on this bipartite quality of that which we call matter and of that inner side, averted from our senses, that we intimate but do not discern. An image or inner spirit of life constantly emerges out of the corporeal and it always again becomes embodied through a reverse process. (AW, 62)

Such language looks forward in time to Merleau-Ponty's key terms, the visible and the invisible. It also looks into the past because, as Schelling points out, this fundamental unity of the corporeal and the spiritual was the object of ancient and long-standing belief, which was "abandoned as soon as matter and spirit were brought into that unholy (incurable) Cartesian conflict [*Zwiespalt*]" (AW, 62). In addition, his defense of this unity led him

24. Compare AW, 105: "Descartes, the founder of modern philosophy, lacerated the world into body and spirit and hence, the unity was lost in favor of duality. Spinoza had unified them into a single, albeit dead, substance and had lost duality in favor of unity." Earlier Schelling had written, "So long as I myself am *identical* with Nature, I understand what a living nature is as well as I understand my own life." *Ideas for a Philosophy of Nature*, 36.

to criticize Spinoza's account of the attributes of substance. Whereas for the latter, all particular modes of substance are manifestations of the distinct attributes of either matter or spirit, for Schelling, any given phenomenon of Nature contains both "reality" and "ideality." Schelling attempted to satisfy a "felt need of a living content of Nature."[25] Inspired by this desire, Goethe held that the reality of nature behind "the charming play of colours [is] not a vibration of atoms, but a something that is originally qualitative. . . . This is the philosophical meaning of Goethe's 'Theory of Colours,' "[26] and it is a conclusion that Whitehead and Merleau-Ponty also endorse (with the latter citing Goethe explicitly).

Accordingly, Schelling is right to reject mechanism as a complete account of nature, although nature does work mechanically, as he knew from his immersion in chemistry and medicine. However, since all of nature is alive, *both* real and ideal, material and spiritual, mechanism as a doctrine is an abstraction from the whole. As a result, Schelling reversed the modernist view that, if one begins with some type of mechanical motion, life can be best understood as a supplemental animating principle added on. There is a strong echo of Schelling's view in some contemporary attempts to avoid "additive" theories of mind, as well as in Henri Bergson's protest against privileging "inert" matter to which "life" would be added.[27]

When Schelling refers to "that unholy (incurable) Cartesian conflict," as Wirth points out, he is "playing on the relationship between *heilen,* to heal, and *heilig,* holy. The Cartesian . . . conflict is both *heillos,* literally, unholy, but hinting at an absence of *heilen,* and *unheilbar,* not admitting of healing, [being] incurable, terminable. The unholy is a terminal illness. Holiness is the font of health" (AW, 143, n. 69). Schelling might be playing

25. Windelband, 599.

26. Ibid.

27. See, for example, John McDowell, *Mind and World* (Cambridge: Harvard University Press, 1998). Schelling also rejects mechanism on a divine scale as well. He adds that "God is not a god of the dead but of the living. It is not comprehensible how the most perfect being could find pleasure even in the most perfect machine possible. However one may conceive of the way in which beings proceed from God, the way can never be mechanical, not mere production or installation whereby the product is nothing for itself" (*Freedom,* 18). For Bergson, see among other places, *La pensée et le mouvant* (Paris: Presses Universitaires de France, 2005 [1938]), 101: "De quel droit met-on l'inert d'abord? [By contrast] Les anciens avaient imaginé une Ame du Monde qui assurerait la continuité d'existence de l'univers matériel." Bergson apparently did not read Schelling, but he was substantially influenced by Ravaisson, who did.

on a linguistic relationship here, but he is clearly right that it is an index to an essential truth. The loss of nature in this unhealthy disconnection entails the loss of the good as regards the experience of beauty—the "joyful amazement that consummate beauty posits to the cultivated perhaps has its main basis in the feeling that beauty brings matter before our eyes in its divine and, so to speak, primordial state" (ibid., 62). The "unholy conflict" also entails the loss of the good at the level of the ethical by making the latter an object of inquiry, something requiring justification. As Wirth notes, having to ask why we should be moral already implies a loss of the ethical. For Schelling, as for Emmanuel Levinas in our own time, if such a choice is possible, the questioner is "already detached from the good" (Wirth 2003, 90).

We can also see this unhealthy detachment in the connection between the ontology of the object and the phenomenon of narcissism. As David Levin points out, "Because it was in the *Meditations* that Descartes began the philosophical discourse of modernity, writing from the position of a self-grounding subjectivity, this correspondence suggests that our late modern culture of narcissism is very deeply rooted, its elements already at work in the subjectivism proclaimed by philosophical reason at the beginning of the modern age."[28]

Merleau-Ponty's Response

For Merleau-Ponty, disconnection from nature and the good is prevented by the reversibilities of flesh. In his last ontological writings, "flesh" (*la chair*) expressed his final attempt to overcome the ontology of the object and reintegrate all the dualities in modern philosophy into something more primary. "Flesh" is an equivocal notion that refers to one's own flesh and the flesh of the world, and as a metaphysical category. As regards the latter, flesh is not a fact or collection of facts, mind, or mental representations. It is, rather, "the formative medium of the object and the subject" that "has no name in any philosophy" (VI, 147/193). Flesh is "the concrete emblem of a general manner of being (ibid.). "To designate it," Merleau-Ponty writes, "we should need the old term 'element,' in the sense it was used to speak of water, air, earth, and fire, that is, in the sense of a *general thing,* midway

28. David Michael Levin, "Visions of Narcissism: Intersubjectivity and the Reversals of Reflection," in *Merleau-Ponty Vivant,* ed. M. C. Dillon (Albany: State University of New York Press, 1991), 54.

between the spatio-temporal individual and the idea, a sort of incarnate principle that brings a style of being wherever there is a fragment of being. The flesh is in this sense an 'element' of Being" (ibid., 139/184).

The principal characteristic of flesh is its chiasmic nature of reversibility. There is a "strange adhesion of the seer and the visible" (VI, 139/183) because every act of touching is doubled by being touched and seeing by being seen, such that the body is inseparably sentient and sensible (ibid., 136/180). The "seer and the visible reciprocate one another and we no longer know which sees and which is seen" (ibid., 139/183).

Intercorporeity is also implied in this ontology because the schema of relationships possible between us is already inscribed in our flesh. As Merleau-Ponty put it in his 1960 lecture course at the Collège de France on "Nature and Logos: The Human Body,"

> If I am capable of feeling by means of a sort of interweaving of the lived body and the sensible, I am also able to see and recognize other bodies and other men. The schema of the lived body, because I see myself, is open to participation by all the other bodies that I see. It is a lexicon of corporeity in general, a system of equivalences between the interior and the exterior, which prescribes to the one to fulfill itself in the other. (RC, 129/178)

Merleau-Ponty's consideration of modern art—discussions that illuminate vital connections between the good, the real, and the intelligible—helps us to understand his ontology of flesh. In the first place, he holds that the world of classical science, based as it is on Euclidean geometry, should be decentered and recentered as a less than ultimate explanation of nature. He points out that non-Euclidean geometries, in which space is curved, show that there are changes in things from the sole fact that they are displaced. They do not remain unchanged despite a change of place. Thus, "form and content are as blurred and mixed up with each other. . . . It becomes impossible to distinguish rigorously space and the things in space, the pure idea of space and the concrete spectacle that our senses provide" (C, 39/18–19). "Curiously," he says, "the efforts of modern painting . . . agree with those of science" (ibid.). Here also, form and content cannot be strictly distinguished from each other, in which blending color plays a signal role. So far from color being a "secondary" quality, "Cézanne," he tells us, "wants to engender the contour and the form of objects as nature engenders them before our eyes: by the arrangement of colors" (ibid.).

This attempt to recover the world as we live it overturns the methods of "classical art" that are founded on the flat projection of perspectival space and that encourage adherence to the ontology of the object. The painter thus trained would not paint what he sees, but "a compromise," "the common denominator" (C, 40/20) of perspectives adjusted for each item included in the painting according to distances established from the viewer. The sizes would be what would be presented to a look oriented toward the line of a horizon. The landscapes of such paintings would be disengaged from the viewer, "at a distance without the spectator being involved with them. But it is not thus that the world presents itself to us in the contact we have with it that perception gives us" (ibid.). From Cézanne onward, for Merleau-Ponty, many painters have defied "the law of geometrical perspective" because they wanted "to render the very birth of the landscape before our eyes" as well as its "vibration and life" (ibid., 41/21). Rather than being what is available for inspection to a detached spectator, "the space of modern painting . . . [is] organically linked to us," "a space with its familiar milieu" (ibid., 41/22).

Part of this organic linkage, what is not accurately expressed in classical painting, is a crucial part of perception that contests the ontology of the object: depth.[29] Giacometti stated his belief that "Cézanne sought for depth all his life,"[30] and for Merleau-Ponty we all have the same task. Seeing things that overlap and conceal each other in my vision shows me "their exteriority known in their envelopment and their mutual dependence in their autonomy. . . . [Depth is] the experience . . . of a voluminosity that one expresses in a word in saying that a thing is there" (OE, 140/65).[31]

Color, as Cézanne knew well, also plays a key role in the experience of depth. Color brings us "closer to the 'heart of things,'" as Paul Klee put it (OE, 141/67).[32] In color, space, line, and form we "plunge into" Being, to use the Bergsonian image so often employed by Merleau-Ponty, such that the painter's vision "is no longer a look on an *outside*, only a

---

29. However, one wonders what Merleau-Ponty would have said about the dark, haunting, nightmarish world of Pirenese's prison drawings.

30. Georges Charbonnier, *Le Monologue du peintre* (Paris: Julliard, 1959), 176. Cited at OE, 140/64.

31. The editions cited here are, respectively, "Eye and Mind," in *The Merleau-Ponty Aesthetics Reader*, ed. with intro. Galen A. Johnson and Michael B. Smith, translation ed., 121–60 (Evanston: Northwestern University Press, 1993); and Paris: Gallimard, 1964.

32. On this topic, see Galen A. Johnson, *The Retrieval of the Beautiful* (Evanston: Northwestern University Press, 2010), 45–70.

'physical-optical' relation (Klee) with the world. The world is no longer before him through representation: it is rather the painter who is born in things as through concentration and a coming to itself of the visible" (ibid., 141/69). As against flat projections of perspectival space, when modern art stresses the depth of something, it appeals to "an ontological incompletion that also creates its capacity for solicitation, its strange power to tear us out of ourselves as it does to plunge us into it."[33]

Color is not a replacement for the line in a painting, but it does contest the line "as a positive attribute and property of the object in itself" (OE, 142/72). Line is not to be abolished, as with the Impressionists, but liberated, as in the works of Klee and Matisse (ibid., 143/74). In fact, although Merleau-Ponty does not mention it, Matisse struggled for years with the relationship of line and color, and his last cutouts were his final attempt to enable form (line) to emerge from color.

Color is also implicated in the role of art in the experience of values. Like Schelling and Whitehead, Merleau-Ponty rejects the notion of valueless fact. He holds that meaning permeates the universe anterior to the constitutive activities of consciousness. Values appear in and through our bodily engagement with the world and with others. Following Goethe's theory of colors, he maintains that every quality of a thing, "far from being strictly isolated, possesses an affective meaning" (C, 46/25) that establishes a certain relationship with us, "a certain behavior that it suggests or imposes on us, a certain manner that it has to seduce, attract, fascinate the free subject who finds himself confronted with it. . . . Cézanne said that one should be able to paint the odor of the trees" (ibid., 48/27).

In this way, art can illustrate the essential *empiétement,* an encroaching or overlapping of my body and the world in the reversibilities of flesh: "Man is invested in things and things are invested in him" (ibid., 49/29). This is, in fact, the ultimate metaphysical significance of painting for Merleau-Ponty: it illustrates the chiasmatic nature of flesh, its reversibilities of seeing and being seen, touching and being touched. Thus, our tastes that reflect our character and personality can be detected in the things we buy, our favorite colors, our choices of environments for leisure activities, etc., and conversely, they are inscribed in us. Hence also, "it is impossible to separate things and their manner of appearing" (ibid., 70/54), and the same is true in modern paintings. It is not so much the content, classically judged according to

33. Emmanuel de Saint Aubert, *Du lien des êtres aux éléments de l'être, Merleau-Ponty au tournant des années 1945–1951* (Paris: J. Vrin, 2004), 120.

representational accuracy, which interests us. The aim of these paintings is not to be either a photograph[34] or a *trompe l'oeil* experience; the meaning of the painting does not lie beyond it.

Painters have consciously rejected this meaning of a painting; they do not attempt to give us "an imitation of the world, but a world for itself" (C, 71/56). For example, "Matisse's women, (let us keep in mind his contemporaries' sarcasm) were not immediately women; they became women. It is Matisse who taught us to see their contours not in a 'physical-optical' way but rather as structural filaments [*des nervures*], as the axes of a system of carnal activity and passivity. In any case, figurative or not, the line is no longer imitation of things or a thing" (OE, 144/76).[35]

This unity of form and content not only brings together fact and value, but also our investment in the artwork—its values in which we participate—and its investment in us. For instance, certain people apparently complained to Picasso that his picture of Gertrude Stein seriously failed to look like her. He replied, "Everybody thinks she is not at all like her portrait, but never mind, in the end she will manage to look just like it." And indeed, in after years the portrait later was widely praised as a remarkable likeness.[36] There is a fundamental *empiétement* in all these examples because we are implicated in the artworks and they in us. This is to say that they have the capacity to speak meaningfully to us, to engage us bodily, and through it with others as well.

This capacity is also present in other media as well, such as films, sculpture, music, and poetry. For example, Gaston Bachelard shows how the experience of poetry illustrates exactly what Merleau-Ponty refers to as the reversibilities of flesh. When a "poem possesses us entirely," when "a single poetic image" reverberates in our souls, Bachelard says rightly that it "takes root in us . . . expressing us by making us what it expresses; in other words, it is at once a becoming of expression, and a becoming of

34. "Matisse said that the camera was a great boon to painters, since it relieved them from any apparent necessity of copying objects." John Dewey, *Art as Experience* (New York: Minton, Balch, 1934), 83. However, if this implied passivity in photography was ever true, it has long since been false, and Matisse, Dewey, and Merleau-Ponty all had the means to know it.

35. Compare John Dewey: "When some one complained to him [Matisse] that she had never seen a woman who looked like the one in his painting, he replied: 'Madam, that is not a woman; that is a picture.'" Ibid., 113.

36. Roland Penrose, *Picasso: His Life and Work* (Berkeley and Los Angeles: University of California Press, 1981), 118.

our being. Here expression creates being."[37] Therefore, poetry, like paintings such as the previous examples by Matisse and Picasso, also has the ability to mediate the real and the intelligible by opening us up to unsuspected dimensions of Being.

For Merleau-Ponty, modern art also has a revelatory power by preventing our normal gazes taking the world for granted in order to recover the perceived world beneath the sedimentations of social life and knowledge. Such artworks "put to the test the pact of coexistence that we have concluded with the world through our body" (PM, 152/211). For example, the "lemons, mandolins, bunches of grapes, [and] packets of tobacco" painted by Cézanne, Juan Gris, Braque, and Picasso, "in different ways . . . arrest and interrogate [our gaze]. Thus painting leads us back to the vision of things themselves" (C, 69/53).

Merleau-Ponty also discusses the activities of the artist herself in addition to the perspective of the spectator as regards the power of art to illuminate the reversibilities of flesh. While he is painting, "he practices a magical theory of vision" (OE, 127/27–28) in that, as Valéry put it, "the painter lends his body" to the world and in so doing, "changes the world into painting" (ibid., 123/16). Merleau-Ponty even uses the religious term "transubstantiations" (ibid., 124/16) to express this action and, at one point, in the context of discussing Schelling's "brute" natural being, he describes painting as *natura naturans* because it gives us "what nature means and does not say: the 'generative principle' that brings things and the world into being."[38] In other words, in the act of painting, the painter *performs* the chiasm of touching and being touched, seeing and being seen, and that is why, as Merleau-Ponty points out, so many painters speak of the objects they paint returning their gaze. Referring to Klee's remark that the trees he was painting were looking at him, Merleau-Ponty writes, "What one calls inspiration should be taken literally: there is really inspiration and expiration of Being, respiration in Being, action and passion so little discernible that one no longer knows who sees and who is seen. . . . The vision of the painter is a continued birth" (ibid., 129/31–32).[39]

Hence also, painters' fascination with mirrors and their penchant for painting themselves painting (OE, 129–30/33–34). Given the "indivision of

37. *The Poetics of Space*, (Boston: Beacon Press, 1964), ix, xviii.

38. Merleau-Ponty, "La Philosophie aujourd'hui," (1958–59), in NC, 56.

39. Merleau-Ponty's claim owes a substantial debt to Paul Claudel's notion of sensation as "co-naissance," knowledge and co-birth. See de Saint Aubert, op. cit., 243 ff.

feeling and being felt" (ibid., 125/20), and the "strange system of exchanges" (ibid., 125/21) between them, "all the problems of painting are there. They illustrate the enigma of the body and the body justifies them. . . . Quality, light, color, depth, which are there before us, are only there because they awaken an echo in our body, because it welcomes them" (ibid., 125/21, 22).

These reversibilities also function from the perspective of the spectator as well, and over a temporal duration. For example, Holland Carter, writing about his decades-long experiences of, and meditations on, the Cloisters in New York City, concludes, "You grow into art; or it grows into you. This takes immersion and time."[40] Merleau-Ponty knew that these possibilities are not disjuncts, for both can be true.

Thus far, I have tried to show how, for Merleau-Ponty, we live in a universe overflowing with values, to which we gain access via art with its power that engages us in a bodily chiasm with nature, and which resonates in us to enable our recovery of a more fundamental reality concealed beneath culturally sedimented meanings. To conclude, I would now like to sketch some ways that, for Merleau-Ponty, art reveals values in general and the good in particular. Whether in literature, poetry, painting, other artistic media, or in any other context in the social world, values present themselves to us like "resistant kernels in a diffuse milieu. They only define and circumscribe themselves, as perceptual objects do, through the complicity of a background, and they suppose as much shadow as light" (PM, 112/159). This is to say that values appear in Gestalt structures, as focal points against backgrounds that contribute to their identity and are intrinsic to the way that they are perceived.

This view has four important implications. First, values are always presented in a context of historical fact; there is no Platonic heaven of ideas. Values lose their meaning apart from reference to facts. They become, in Galileo's terms, "mere names." As Whitehead puts it, "Value refers to Fact, and Fact refers to Value. [This statement is a direct contradiction to Plato, and to the theological tradition derived from him.]"[41]

40. "Epiphanies in a Medieval Courtyard," *The New York Times*, December 21, 2007, B37.

41. "Immortality," in *The Philosophy of Alfred North Whitehead*, ed. Paul Arthur Schillp, 2nd ed. (New York: Tudor, 1951), 684. The bracketed words are in the cited text. Compare Merleau-Ponty's statement that "[t]he war and the occupation have only taught us that values remain nominal, and do not even count, without an economic and political infrastructure that makes them begin to exist." *"La guerre a eu lieu,"* in SNS, 152/268.

The second implication is that there are no moral absolutes. In discussing the ways that materialism and idealism competed for an account of human beings and values at the beginning of the twentieth century, he underscores the way that idealists construed values as absolutes revealed either through a supernatural source or through human nature. "The epoch was full of these absolutes," he writes, including "a moral gold standard: family and marriage were the good, even if they secreted hatred and rebellion" (S, 226/287).[42] It is here that Ingmar Bergman's films such as *Scenes from a Marriage* and *Fanny and Alexander* have considerable power to oppose such absolutism, and precisely in terms of the flesh-and-blood relationships between men and women described earlier on. They show vividly that our relationships with others are always nuanced, ambiguous, indeterminate, and open to interrogation.

The third implication of Merleau-Ponty's conception of values is the unavoidable overlapping (*empiétement*) of myself and others. We are "enmeshed in the to-and-fro of being for self and being for others that produces the tragic element of love in Proust's works and what is perhaps the most striking element in Gide's *Journal*" (S, 231/293). Still more, it produces them in Greek tragedies, and Merleau-Ponty wrote in his review of Jean-Paul Sartre's play "*Les Mouches*" that "Greek myths are the best scenario there could be for a drama of liberty"[43] that entangles self and others. It becomes clearer and clearer that, as Bergman knew well, "incarnation and the other person are the labyrinth of reflection and feeling" (ibid., 232/294).

Finally, the factual contextualization of values implies the inevitable contingency of the good. I think that Merleau-Ponty could have agreed with Schelling about our yearning for a nameless good concretized in expressions of freedom and creativity in nature. Instances of such freedom and creativity figure prominently in his last lectures on nature at the Collège de France. Yet, he would also maintain that whether the good prevails in any given instance is always contingent. In "Man and Adversity," for example, he states, "Progress is not necessary. . . . We cannot even exclude in principle that humanity, like a sentence that does not succeed in ending, fails

42. The editions cited here are, respectively, Evanston: Northwestern University Press, 1964; and Paris: Gallimard, 1960.

43. "*Les Mouches*," *Confluences*, Year 3, no. 25 (septembre-octobre 1943): 514–16. Reprinted and cited in *Maurice Merleau-Ponty Parcours 1935–1951* (Paris: Éditions Verdier, 1997), 62.

along the way" (S, 239/304). Nothing is guaranteed, and if we read into the achievement of some goodness its preordained necessity, this would be to give way to "retrospective illusion" (ibid., 240/304) that Bergson termed the "retrograde movement of the true."[44] It would be to fail to grasp "the human moment *par excellence* in which a life woven out of chance events turns back upon, regrasps, and expresses itself" (ibid., 240/305).

In this regard, it is regrettable that Merleau-Ponty never read Whitehead's *Adventures of Ideas*, particularly chapter XVII, "Beauty." For there, the author discusses not only the capacity of art to reveal "intimate, absolute Truth regarding the Nature of Things" (AI, 272),[45] but also *degrees* of progress, higher and lower perfections, and discord as a necessary condition for progress in instantiating as much goodness as possible, a spur to higher forms of perfection. As he indicated in *Process and Reality*, "chaos is not to be identified with evil; for harmony requires the due coordination of chaos, vagueness, narrowness, and width" (PR, 112). Also, Whitehead would stress the phrase "as much goodness as possible," for he also thinks that goodness is contingent, even in the subjective aims for each occasion of experience that are provided by God's conceptual vision. The best possible aim can be bad, yet "if the best be bad, then the ruthlessness of God can be personified as Atè, the goddess of mischief. The chaff is burnt" (ibid., 244). As against Dante and Pope Benedict XVI, love does not necessarily steer the stars.

Even so, Whitehead is right to insist that "Adventure . . . the search for new perfections" (AI, 263) is indispensable. As he indicates in *Science and the Modern World*, "When man ceases to wander, he will cease to ascend in the scale of being. Physical wandering is still important, but greater still is the power of man's spiritual adventures—adventures of thought, adventures of passionate feeling, adventures of aesthetic experience. . . . Other nations of different habits are not enemies: they are godsends" (ibid., 207).

44. See *La pensée et le mouvant* (Paris: F. Alcan, 1934), ch. I.

45. Curiously, though, Whitehead denies that goodness is one of "the aims of art. For Goodness is a qualification belonging to the constitution of reality, which in any of its individual actualizations is better or worse. Good and evil lie in depths and distances below and beyond appearance. They solely concern inter-relations within the real world. The real world is good when it is beautiful. Art has essentially to do with perfections attainable by purposeful adaptation of appearance" (AI, 268). If art can reveal the "absolute Truth of Things," and "Good and evil lie in depths and distances below and beyond appearance," why cannot art reveal the good *and* the evil? In the absence of any explanation, Whitehead apparently does not see a contradiction here.

(However, the evils of the second half of the twentieth century and our current one have taught us that Whitehead should have said that other nations are not *necessarily* enemies or godsends.)

The spontaneity and freedom required for such adventures brings us back to Schelling's yearning for the "nameless good" and its anarchical freedom in a constant dialectic with order. "In Discord there is always frustration," Whitehead goes on to say, but as Schelling would surely agree, "even Discord may be preferable to a feeling of slow relapse into general anæsthesia, or into tameness which is its prelude [Remember the *Verstandesmenschen*!]. Perfection at a low level ranks below Imperfection with higher aim. A mere qualitative Harmony within an experience comparatively barren of objects of high significance is a debased type of Harmony, tame, vague, deficient in outline and intention" (AI, 263–64).

The type of humanism defended by Merleau-Ponty finds its point of departure in an awareness of contingency. On the other hand, he admits, "fear of contingency is everywhere, even in the doctrines that helped reveal it [Marxism and Catholicism]" (S, 242/307). "Sometimes," he says ruefully, "one starts to dream about what culture, literary life, and teaching could be if all those who participate, having for once rejected idols, would give themselves up to the happiness of reflecting together" (S, 242/308). It remains true that, as Sophocles pointed out, "Stubbornness and stupidity are twins."[46] Yet one can still subscribe to practical ideals without idols, and live the philosophical life without arrogance, self-worship, and the will to dominate others. More generally, as Merleau-Ponty knew well, there is radical evil in the world, but there is, despite all, some reason to hope. That is why, as the last sentence of *Sense and Nonsense* states, "The contemporary hero is not Lucifer, nor even Prometheus; he is man" (SNS, 187/331).

References

Bachelard, Gaston. 1964. *The Poetics of Space*. Boston: Beacon Press.

Bergson, Henri. 2005. *La pensée et le mouvant*. Paris: Presses Universitaires de France.

Burke, Patrick. 1999. "Creativity and the Unconscious in Merleau-Ponty and Schelling." In *Framing a Vision of the World, Essays in Philosophy, Science, and Religion*, edited by André Cloots and Santiago Sia, 183–208. Leuven: Leuven University Press.

46. *Antigone*, trans. Elizabeth Wyckoff, in *The Complete Greek Tragedies*, Vol. II *Sophocles* (Chicago: University of Chicago Press, 1959), line 1028, 193.

Burtt, E. A. 1954. *The Metaphysical Foundations of Modern Science.* New York: Anchor Books.

Carter, Holland. 2007. "Epiphanies in a Medieval Courtyard." *The New York Times*, December 21, B37.

Charbonnier, Georges. 1959. *Le Monologue du peintre.* Paris: Julliard.

Cloots, André, and Santiago Sia, eds. 1999. *Framing a Vision of the World, Essays in Philosophy, Science, and Religion.* Leuven: Leuven University Press.

Dewey, John. 1934. *Art as Experience.* New York: Minton, Balch.

Dillon, Martin C., ed. 1991. *Merleau-Ponty Vivant.* Albany: State University of New York Press.

Galilei, Galileo. 1960. *On Mechanics.* Translated with Introduction and Notes by Stillman Drake. Madison: University of Wisconsin Press.

Grene, David, and Richmond Lattimore. 1959. *The Complete Greek Tragedies.* Vol. II: *Sophocles.* Chicago: University of Chicago Press.

Hamrick, William S. 1999. "A Process View of the Flesh: Whitehead and Merleau-Ponty." *Process Studies* 28, no. 1–2 (Spring-Summer): 117–29.

———. 2004. "Whitehead and Merleau-Ponty: Healing the Bifurcation of Nature." In *Whitehead's Philosophy: Points of Connection*, edited by Janusz A. Polanowski and Donald W. Sherburne, 127–42. Albany: State University of New York Press.

———, and Jan Van der Veken. 2011. *Nature and Logos, A Whiteheadian Key to Merleau-Ponty's Fundamental Thought.* Albany: State University of New York Press.

Hegel, G. W. F. 1987. "The Oldest System-Program of German Idealism." In *Friedrich Hölderlin, Essays and Letters on Theory*, edited and translated by Thomas Pfau, 154–56. Albany: State University of New York Press.

Holden, Stephen. 2007. "In Art's Old Sanctuary, a High Priest of Film." *The New York Times*, July 31, B4.

Hume, David. 1969. *An Essay Concerning Human Understanding.* Abridged and Edited by A. S. Pringle-Pattison. Oxford: Clarendon Press.

Johnson, Galen A., ed. 1993. *The Merleau-Ponty Aesthetics Reader, Philosophy and Painting.* Translation editor, Michael B. Smith. Evanston: Northwestern University Press.

———. 2010. *The Retrieval of the Beautiful.* Evanston: Northwestern University Press.

Levin, David Michael. 1991. "Visions of Narcissism: Intersubjectivity and the Reversals of Reflection." In *Merleau-Ponty Vivant*, edited by Martin C. Dillon, 47–90. Albany: State University of New York Press.

McDowell, John. 1998. *Mind and World.* Cambridge: Harvard University Press.

Penrose, Roland. 1981. *Picasso: His Life and Work.* Berkeley and Los Angeles: University of California Press.

Pfau, Thomas, trans. and ed. 1987. *Friedrich Hölderlin, Essays and Letters on Theory.* Albany: State University of New York Press.

Polanowski, Janusz A., and Donald W. Sherburne, eds. 2004. *Whitehead's Philosophy: Points of Connection.* Albany: State University of New York Press.

Saint Aubert, Emmanuel de. 2004. *Du lien des êtres aux éléments de l'être, Merleau-Ponty au tournant des années 1945–1951.* Paris: J. Vrin.

Schelling, F. W. J. 1978. *System of Transcendental Idealism.* Translated by Peter Heath, with an Introduction by Michael Vater. Charlottesville: University of Virginia Press.

———. 1988. *Ideas for a Philosophy of Nature.* Translated by Errol E. Harris and Peter Heath, with an Introduction by Robert Stern. Cambridge: Cambridge University Press.

———. 2000. *The Ages of the World (Fragment)* from the handwritten remains, Third Version (c. 1815). Translated with an Introduction by Jason M. Wirth. Albany: State University of New York Press.

———. 2006. *Philosophical Investigations into the Essence of Human Freedom.* Translated with an Introduction and Notes by Jeff Love and Johannes Schmidt. Albany: State University of New York Press.

Schillp, Paul Arthur, ed. 1951. *The Philosophy of Alfred North Whitehead.* 2nd Ed. New York: Tudor.

Sheldrake, Rupert. 1990. *The Rebirth of Nature, The Greening of Science and God.* London: Random Century Group.

Sophocles. 1959. *Antigone.* Translated by Elizabeth Wyckoff. In David Grene and Richmond Lattimore, *The Complete Greek Tragedies.* Vol. II: *Sophocles,* 159–207. Chicago: University of Chicago Press.

Whitehead, Alfred North. 1951. "Immortality." In *The Philosophy of Alfred North Whitehead,* 2nd ed., edited by Paul Arthur Schillp, 682–700 New York: Tudor.

———. 1964 [1920]. *The Concept of Nature.* Cambridge: Cambridge University Press.

———. 1967 [1925]. *Science and the Modern World.* New York: The Free Press.

———. 1967 [1933]. *Adventures of Ideas.* New York: The Free Press.

———. 1978 [1929]. *Process and Reality,* Corrected Edition. Edited by David Ray Griffin and Donald W. Sherburne. New York: The Free Press.

Windelband, Wilhelm. 1926. *A History of Philosophy.* Translated by James H. Tufts. New York and London: Macmillan.

Wirth, Jason. 2003. *The Conspiracy of Life, Meditations on Schelling and His Time.* Albany: State University of New York Press.

12

Tactile Cogito

Horizons of Corporeity, Animality, and Affect in Merleau-Ponty

Robert Switzer

From its beginnings, and with increasing fervor in the Modern period, philosophy has developed a program of reflection on mind and reality based on the distinctness and elevation of the former over the latter, of the seeing "I" over all it surveys—and above all, of the soul over the body, of pure timeless thought over that aspect of us that moves and breathes, and so can cease, and die. In art, the body is seen as a means to—or, in dance and in song for example, itself becomes—a medium of expression; the body holds the artist's tools, or is itself a tool, an instrument on which the soul plays, from above. Indeed, in Plato's account, the height of the soul telescopes to an even greater height: the soul is outside of itself, medium of the muses, possessed by a divine madness; in the ecstasy of "*enthusiasmos*," the artist becomes an instrument or conduit of the gods.

The origins and persistence of the myth of a disembodied cogito, even in the understanding of art, is itself a topic of some interest, and I will touch on these matters briefly by way of introduction. But my main concern here is to outline Merleau-Ponty's contributions in decisively smashing this philosophical idol (to invoke the long shadow of Nietzsche), and in redeeming the place of the body at the heart of both truth and art—which is to say, as we'll now consider, in beginning to mend the "metaphysical fissure" at the heart of the "human animal."

The rootedness of this polar opposition—depth of the fissure—is remarkable; it is, seemingly, among the founding tropes of philosophy itself.

In Plato's *Phaedo,* for example, the dying Socrates not only effectively indicts life itself as a kind of disease, but asserts that "no thought of any kind ever comes to us from the body," which he famously characterizes as evil, a prison for the soul (118a, 66c, 82e et passim). These are themes developed by Medieval and Modern thinkers, from Maimonides to Descartes, who castigate the "shamefully" feeling, passionate, sensible (and visible) body. Already with Aristotle's *De Anima* the caesura, the line of demarcation and so contestation between human and nonhuman life, had been drawn within "man himself" as the "rational animal" (414b17; see also *Politics* 1253a9 and 1332b3f). The relentless privileging of disembodied rationality in this "composite" being—from *nous* to cogito—has entailed a number of tenacious philosophical problems: philosophers have posited a pure inner seeing, outside of time and space, and over against it an "external" reality understood as an array, within "objective" spatiality, of extended bodies, including one's own body, constituted before the synoptic gaze of an impossible but firmly attested-to "view from nowhere"—so that finally, as a result, they have fallen into perplexity as to how these dualisms could ever achieve contact, communication, or unity: not only self with world, but mind with body. Yet, through it all, the sense persists of an ineliminable bond with the natural world around us—its texture and feel, the resonant sonority of its surfaces and depths—and with the animals with which, in our own animal being, we share, as Heidegger wrote, a fundamental "kinship."

As suggested, this elemental materiality and animality is at the center of essentially all artwork, from the shaping of earthy material with our hands, to the gestures that apply pigments to surfaces, to the creaturely cries and trills and howls that, transformed, have become our poetry and song and—extended through the dance of careful gestures, releasing the sonority of wood and reed, of metal, canvas, and stretched strings—our music. Yet even here, there has been a relentless drive to deny the obvious rootedness of the aesthetic in the corporeal. Philosophy in many ways began in the profound wonder of Pythagoras at the concord between the physical experience of musical harmony, as heard, and the abstract ratios between the lengths of harmoniously vibrating strings. But by the time of Plato, philosophy had largely disowned its rootedness in the sensuous, and turned from attentive listening to the "seeing as" of *theoria.* In the *Republic,* for example; Plato mocks those who strain to hear relationships among actual tones; the task of the true philosopher is to examine only "which *numbers* are consonant and which are not, and what is the reason in each case" (530d–531d; emphasis added). Two millennia later, Kant's *Critique of Judgment* strikes a similar note, dismissing the sensuous enjoyment of tones as "mere sensible impressions"—and in doing so reinscribes the core dichotomy of body and soul: "The *matter* of sensation," Kant writes, "has only to do with enjoyment; this leaves behind nothing in the idea, and it makes the spirit dull"; instead, "in all beautiful art the essential thing is the *form*," which means, he explains, pure structure liable to formal-mathematical comprehension. As he adds, "only pleasantness, and not beauty of composition, is bound up with colors and tones" (169–70; emphasis added).

Heidegger, in contrast, attentively elicits the "earthly," physical aspect of artworks in his "Origin of the Work of Art." In a temple, for example, the rock, "bearing and resting," first becomes rock—and so also colors first glow, the word first speaks or names, and the tone first "clangs" or sings, as they are set forth in specific sorts of art (46). But it is not the artist—who disappears into the work as a kind of passageway or conduit—but the artwork itself that brings together, in their dissonant proximity, the self-concealing earth and the "clearing" (visible, one might dare say "formal") open of world, such that, in the "jutting through" of this fecund juncture, new possibilities of being emerge, new pathways of decision "in the destiny of a historical people" (48). On this account, art seems to become, as in Hegel, a product of disembodied Spirit; where Heidegger seems to preserve the trope of a descent of truth "from above," Merleau-Ponty finds in art's emergence something far more autochthonous, arising from a visceral confrontation—or carnal embrace—between artist and world, united in their corporeity, their flesh: a union realized precisely in the work.

Not only did Heidegger fail to take up a truly philosophical engagement with the body, in his account of the origin of art and elsewhere in his work, he seemed at times to actively reinscribe the basic metaphysical diremption of the human (as "rational animal"). This can be seen, for example, when he writes in "The Letter on Humanism" of an "abyssal bodily kinship" ("*abgründige leiblich Verwandtschaft*") with the animal that can "scarcely be fathomed" (326/230).[1] Rather than turning away from

1. Heidegger explored, and problematized, the "man-animal" relationship in a number of places, most notably in the 1929 lecture course on "The Fundamental Concepts of Metaphysics" (1983/1995)—which, significantly from my point of view, combines a lengthy discussion of how animals are "poor in world" with a detailed engagement with affectivity (*Stimmungen*)—and his later lectures on "What Calls for Thinking" (1961/1968). These texts have formed part of the basis for detailed discussions on human nature and animality in Agamben (2004) and Derrida (1993, 2008a, 2008b), which in turn have been taken up in two important recent treatments by Matthew Calarco (2008) and Leonard Lawler (2007).

this abyss as unfathomable, Maurice Merleau-Ponty strove to situate his thought very much within the mystery of the human as incarnate, affective, animal—and saw in this fecund tension the origins both of artworks and of aesthetic experience. That, is, for Merleau-Ponty, the "kinships" in question are not "abyssal" but chiasmic: the bond between human and animal, as between soul and body, form and matter, the visible and the invisible, is a fecund intertwining, a tensional divide that also unites, that brings into closeness even what it holds apart.

I believe that a core aim of Merleau-Ponty's philosophy, from first to last, was not to "bridge" such metaphysical divides, but to unmask them as trope or myth, to deconstruct the very conception of such barriers, oppositions, and discontinuities—and, while also avoiding reductionism or biologism, to affirm instead the restless ambiguity of mutual reflection, interchange, and chiasm, which is literally embodied by the physical insertion of the human animal into, and carnal implication with, the environing natural world.[2]

Throughout his work, Merleau-Ponty draws into question the privileged standpoint—and indeed the very project—of philosophical reflection as traditionally understood. Casting aside the illusion of an apodictically self-certain self-awareness, he set out on a program of post- or (as he terms it in *The Visible and the Invisible*) "hyper-reflection." That is, in place of a disembodied transcendental ego that conditions the "pure" contents of infallible inner sense, Merleau-Ponty articulated a portrait of the self as field-phenomenon, as horizon of corporeity—but as such also exteriority, engagement, an adhesion in and on the world, a Gestalt, a style; pregnant, in short, with "*sens,*" that wonderful French word that invokes both meaning and directionality. These insights are extended and deepened in Merleau-Ponty's later work in the conception of the "flesh," and its dehiscence, the chiasmic cohabitation of self-world-others, alongside what he terms, in the Working Notes of *The Visible and the Invisible*, "man-animal *intertwining*" (VI, 274).

2. It is worth stressing how pervasive a theme this is: already in 1935, in an article on Max Scheler's notion of *ressentiment,* Merleau-Ponty had written disapprovingly of what he called "Promethean" humanism, which strips Nature of its value "since man is only worth as much as he separates himself from it and withdraws from it." "Christianity and *Ressentiment*" (1935), cited in Hugh J. Silverman and James Barry Jr., eds., *Texts and Dialogues, Maurice Merleau-Ponty,* trans. Michael B. Smith et al. (Atlantic Highlands, NJ: Humanities Press International, 1992), 96 (referred to hereafter as TD).

It is this last theme that I hope at least to adumbrate in the present paper. For if affectivity comes to the fore as primordially revelatory of our basic being-in-the world, as Heidegger had already begun to show, and if the body and its motility, in its capacities and vulnerabilities, is implicated in every act of perception and even in the genesis of our most abstract conceptions, as Husserl had begun to see—and as it was always Merleau-Ponty's particular project to elucidate—then the traditional conception of the human, in contradistinction to the natural and the animal, will have undergone a radical transformation: in brief, the chasm of separateness and superiority will have given way to chiasmic intertwining. The implications of this—in terms of aesthetics, but also ontology and ethics as well—are only now beginning to become manifest for us.

If we are right in seeing in Merleau-Ponty a robust effort to reimagine the human, we must seek the foundations of that redemption from the "abyssal" in his analysis, deconstruction, and reconstruction of the cogito, including his own early struggles to break free from the residues of Cartesian subjectivity and Sartrean negativism. What emerges already in this breaking-free is the trajectory of Merleau-Ponty's later thought, in which he reincorporates or "re-members" the cogito, returns to it its web of involvements and its tactile sensitivities, resituates it as always outside itself: an interleaving in the world, a tensional dehiscence on and in the things themselves. In laying out his new ontology of depths, vectors, and levels, of a world not so much seen as felt—a world of perturbations, protuberances, textural contours, of terrain demarcated in elevations and relief, by warmth as much as light—Merleau-Ponty's philosophical project returns us, through what I will call a *tactile* cogito, to "the very pulp of the sensible"; he brings us to a rediscovery of our implication with and in the natural world, as the passivity-in-action and the vulnerability summed up in the realization that all touching is also a being-touched; he makes possible a new philosophy of nature inclusive of the human, and of art founded not on ideality but on our corporeal insertion into the real, in a mutually dependent dance.

What Merleau-Ponty rejected in and as the philosophy of reflection is the Cartesian and Kantian insistence on finding for philosophy an absolute grounding in subjectivity—in the transcendental ego cogito that will be synonymous with, and provide an apodictic ground for, timeless, unassailable truth and which, in contradistinction from the body's flesh, positionality, weakness, and mortality, comes to represent, at once beyond and foundational to experience, the truly human. Chapter 1 of Part Three of *The Phenomenology of Perception* sets out to demolish this "intellectualist" view of the cogito as pure self-presence—indeed, to unseat the sovereign myth within philosophy of a self-identical, self-certifying, fully adequate and indubitable realm of pure immanence. It then works through a series of dense arguments concerning fallibility—in perception, inner feelings, emotions and the will—and abstract ideas, before turning to three specific "idealities": language, eternity (time), and the question of evidence. The chapter concludes with the famous account of the "tacit cogito." While all this material is of interest, I will begin with Merleau-Ponty's discussion of abstract ideas—specifically, the example of the "construction" that lays bare the "essential" or "disembodied truth" concerning the internal angles of a triangle; although brief, it is fact a vitally important frontal attack on the idealistic valorization of the supra-sensible, and a pivot toward the ineluctable centrality of the physical, and the inexpungible animality in all human thought and artistic creation. I will then turn to two other foci for analysis: the example of love used to explore the issue of fallibility, and finally the tacit cogito itself. These stops along our way will be important in different ways: the first as it illustrates the kinesthetic component of even abstract geometric construction, the second as it discloses the affective, and ambiguous, horizon of self-disclosure; bringing us finally to the dispersal of what had been imagined as a point of pure self-presence into a halo or echo, an "ambient" cogito, liable only to "tacit" understanding at best, pure sensitivity of flesh that touches itself only in the act—or, as I will call it, the "tactile cogito."

As Merleau-Ponty points out, even Kant saw that the localization of objects in space is not "purely" intellectual, but always and necessarily involves kinesthetic motility; the geometer "knows the relationships with which he is concerned only by describing them, at least potentially, with his body." Hence, as Merleau-Ponty puts it succinctly, "the subject of geometry is a motor subject" (PhP, 387).[3] That is, even in such a seemingly abstract and "purely" eidetic example as a geometric construction, the putative "transcendental ego" succumbs to its shadow. Synthesis is not "pure," but rather always situated, finite—and performed, as Merleau-Ponty writes, "by means of my body."[4] Hence, the triangle can by no means be construed as a time-

3. The edition cited here is London and New York: Routledge and Kegan Paul, 1962.

4. Merleau-Ponty makes no direct reference to Kant here, but only to Lachièze-Rey, specifically his *Utilisation possible du schématisme kantien pour une théorie de la perception* (7) and his *Réflexions sur l'activité spirituelle constituante* (132). The relevant discussion is found in Kant's anthropology, most especially his work *Was Heist: Sich im Denken orientieren?* Interestingly, Heidegger had discussed the same key passages from this text of Kant's in section 23 of *Being and Time*, on "the spatiality of being-in-the-world"—a discussion in which Heidegger raises, and then passes over with strange silence, the very problem of Dasein's "bodily nature" so key to Merleau-Ponty's deconstruction of the philosophy of reflection.

less eidetic "essence" constructed via the syntheses of a pure, disembodied ego cogito, any more than a painting can be said to exist as a pure thought, outside of muscular intentionality and gesture Rather, it is "a formula of an attitude, a certain modality of my hold on the world," a "structure" in Merleau-Ponty's sense of the word: less a noun than a verb; not timeless, but an event; a dynamic Gestalt, inextricably bound up with bodily motility, pregnant with possibilities and "lines of force" (PhP, 386).

But how is this hold on things—the synthesis of what had been taken to be "pure essences"—possible at the bodily level that is so clearly implicated in it? It is so only if the body is "itself an original intentionality, a manner of relating itself to the distinct object of knowledge." The surrounding world is not, therefore, as in the early Husserl, for example, "a system of objects which we synthesize"; rather, it is an indeterminate determining ground, which Merleau-Ponty will come to speak of in terms of vectors and levels, and which already here in *The Phenomenology of Perception* he writes of as "open to us, towards which we project ourselves" (PhP, 387).

Even Husserl, however, had rejected the folly of a pure "inner realm" of auto-affection, the Cartesian "thoughts of sensing or feeling," posited in opposition to the so-called external reality that such thoughts are "judged" to resemble or represent. "Perception," Merleau-Ponty writes here, in sharp contrast to such a view, is "precisely that kind of act in which there can be no question of setting the act itself apart from the end to which it is directed." Hence, the impossibility, he insists, of a pristine "sphere of immanence," a "realm in which my consciousness is fully at home and secure against all risk of error." Instead, he asserts, "the acts of the I" continually "outstrip themselves;" consciousness is active transcendence "through and through" (PhP, 376). All perception, as action in the world, must be recognized to be "an operation which fulfils more than it promises" and is "inwardly prepared only by my primordial opening upon a field of transcendence, that is . . . by an *ek-stase*." In fulfilling itself, sight does indeed "take a hold upon itself"—but it does so in a manner that is fundamentally "ambiguous and obscure"; it is a hold without self-possession but rather a continual slipping away, an escape "from itself into the thing seen." It is precisely in this way that Merleau-Ponty reimagines the cogito, in words that prefigure his later work: "It is the deep-seated momentum of transcendence which is my very being, the simultaneous contact with my own being and with the world's being" (PhP, 377). It is precisely in this "adhesion which preserves difference" that the possibility emerges for the original work of art.

For Merleau-Ponty, perception is the model not only of my being, but of being itself; an upsurge "into" the world, understood as opening up a background phenomenon always already pregnant with "sense," and always ambiguous, resistant, elusive. For the "perceptual 'synthesis' " is always necessarily incomplete; "it cannot present me with a 'reality' otherwise than by running the risk of error." Inevitably, things remain partly veiled, turning from me sides not now seen, and blocking my access to what lies behind. And yet, these hidden sides and covered views remain, importantly, accessible in principle, and serve indeed to invoke "the others"—the living, perceiving beings alongside me—even in their absence, in the sides and aspects things offer to them and not to me. It is precisely this depth, this texture, and this reserve of endless dis-covery beyond the given, that defines reality for Merleau-Ponty: a perceptual plenitude that is, inevitably and manifestly, shared. And it is precisely for his sensitivity to this plentitude, this latency, and this depth, that Merleau-Ponty so admires the work of Cézanne.

But do not hallucinations, for example, lack just this depth, this texture of the real? And do not "psychic facts" in general have a status of pure possession and pure lucidity, of absolute transparency, privacy, and self-presence? Certainly, this has been the view dominant in the tradition since Descartes. Merleau-Ponty explores this theme in an interesting context: he bids me imagine thinking I am in love when I am not, and, conversely, being in love and not knowing it.

"True love," we read, "summons all the subject's resources"; it is something that concerns me in my "entire being, whereas mistaken love touches on only one persona" and a "return to my own self" reveals it as misguided. The tantalizing ideal of "authenticity" arises here; but already in this early work, Merleau-Ponty sees it chimerical. For ambiguity always remains—not least, in this case, because "in order to discern its mistaken nature I require a knowledge of myself which I can gain only through disillusionment" (PhP, 379). In brief, we are not in fact in possession of ourselves, "in our whole reality"—but this does not mean that this life or this "total being" is on that account "unconscious." Rather, it is accessible in principle, if always elusive: "It is simply a question of what we are doing," he writes. It is by my acts, in other words, that I best know myself—just as an artwork is realized only in the *work,* the physical engagement with the materiality of the medium.

Suppose, though, that "I make the discovery" that I am in love. The "facts" of the case were there all along, in some sense, unrecognized; but "I now discover that I can no longer conceive my life without this love." Going back over the preceding days and months, "I am made aware that my thoughts and actions were polarized, I pick out the course of a process of organization," the formation of a Gestalt, not a *constitution* of sense and meaning by noetic spontaneity, but an *emergence,* as it were, autochthonously, from the margins. Yet this love is not hidden, unconscious; it is mine, and I can retrospectively trace the path of its growth and crystallization. This love was there, before I owned it, as "the impulse carrying me towards someone, the transmutation of my thoughts and behavior." I cannot say I was unaware of it "since it was I who endured the hours of boredom preceding a meeting, and who felt elation when she approached"; but from the start it was "lived, not known" (PhP, 380–81). Again the parallel is clear: an artistic creation, too, emerges not from conscious decision so much as from an impulse that gathers itself, as it were, of its own volition, from out of the margins—and is recognizable in its import only retrospectively. In these moments—such as those of inspired improvisation—one is tempted to believe in a force "from above," but, as Nietzsche wrote in *The Gay Science*, "the wisest providence could not think up a more beautiful music than that which our foolish hand produces then" (§277).

As lover, as artist, I interpret myself. I draw out the unthematized that grounds the thematic. I open my awareness to the implicit sense of direction that pervades experience like a "general atmosphere" of which we are "unconscious" only as we are unconscious of the sound of an air conditioner that is always on—which is to say, not because it is sealed from us and inaccessible in principle, but because it is ubiquitous and pervasive. But unlike such a sound, this background phenomenon is pregnant with meaning, with intention; its work, I believe, lies in focusing attention, drawing out patterns of salience, highlighting or diminishing features of experience; indeed, it *is* just such a structuring, such a Gestalt—as temporalized, unfolding, as always already underway. If I ask "What am I?" or "What is artistic inspiration?" perhaps just this Gestalt—an emergent pattern, a stylistic impulse, rich with possibility—is as close to an answer as we can come. We inhabit our lives and our projects always, deeply, at a mythic level; things beckon or forbid, radiate and absorb warmth as much as light, stand out for us not just as objects nameable by way of abstract categories, not just as symbols, but for and as their "affective values"—with the inevitability that the painter feels when she adds a necessary color to the canvas, or in the manner that, on Merleau-Ponty's account, "fire" functions in the dream-work (PhP, 381). "For the lover whose experience it is, love is nameless." It is not "a thing capable of being circumscribed and designated," not "the love spoken of in books," but an "existential situation": the manner or style in which one relates to the world. Again, it is really only in my acts and my commitments that I know myself; for I am not a placeless, timeless ego cogito, pure spontaneity or unity of apperceptions, but an incarnate projection weighted with the sedimentations of history and language and the sheer physicality of my being, as horizons out of which I emerge and in terms of which I situate myself, and from which I cannot be separated. To be is always to be more or less caught up in a "situation," to be surrounded by it and to surrender ourselves to it, such that we can never be wholly transparent to ourselves, such that "our contact with ourselves is necessarily achieved only in the sphere of ambiguity" (PhP, 381). And it is out of this sphere, once again—in the latency of the silences between words, in the interstices that recede behind the commonplace hold on things—that art appears as an emergent phenomenon.

It is precisely at and as this "sphere of ambiguity" that the key notion of "tacit cogito" emerges in *The Phenomenology of Perception*; though it is only named as such a few pages farther on, as Merleau-Ponty develops a response to a specific problem addressed, significantly, by way of language. In my view, though the problem itself and, more fundamentally, the view of language here espoused will later be rejected or surpassed, many of the insights remain central—particularly the emphasis on affectivity, horizonality, and embodiment.

Although, as we'll discuss in a moment, the debt to Sartre here is considerable, Merleau-Ponty situates his account of the tacit cogito in the context of the work of Husserl, who had seen that "the body is 'never completely constituted,' does not require, and even rules out, a constituting subject," such that there must be, corresponding to the "open unity of the world," an "open and indefinite unity of subjectivity" as "the background against which" the "effulgent forms" I perceive "stand out" (PhP, 406).

> In so far as, when I reflect on the essence of subjectivity, I find it bound up with that of the body and that of the world, this is because my existence as subjectivity is merely one with my existence as a body and with the existence of the world, and because the subject that I am, when taken concretely, is inseparable from this body and this world. (PhP, 408)

Merleau-Ponty agrees with those who, like Hume, have come to see that the self is no "thing," and most assuredly not some "acosmic subject." Rather, it is emergent, an always-running-ahead-of-itself that responsively confers the "form of things" in the nascent order of the perceptual field; there is, he writes, "an autochthonous significance of the world which is constituted in the dealings which our incarnate existence has with it" (PhP, 441); a patterning of the real that takes place, not through the synthesizing acts of an indifferent Kantian spectator, but through an engaged improvisational interplay.

The problem that emerged for Merleau-Ponty at the time was this: How can I be the "constituting agent" of my thought generally, as mine, "noticed" by me and hence properly spoken of as "thought" at all—"without ever being that agent of my particular thoughts," since (as we have seen) "I never see them come into being in the full light of day, but merely know myself through them"? The puzzle of subjectivity, in short, is: how thought can be at once mine and yet never fully owned by me—or, in Merleau-Ponty's words, how it is "dependent yet indeclinable" (PhP, 400).[5]

Merleau-Ponty's response is, importantly, by way of language: "The cogito at which we arrive by reading Descartes" is, he says, "a spoken cogito"; and talk of "the cogito" easily devolves into mere words: statements about relations among significations that have been "sedimented" in expressive acts, as he writes in 1959 (VI, 170). And just for this reason, such talk again and again finds itself failing in its objective, "since that part of our existence which is engaged in fixing our life in conceptual forms, and thinking of it as indubitable" is "escaping focus and thought" (PhP, 402). As Merleau-Ponty summarizes his view in 1959, what this presupposes is a nonreflective or non-thetic "contact of self with self." Or, as he puts it in an oft-quoted passage from *The Phenomenology of Perception*,

> Behind the spoken cogito, the one which is converted into discourse and into essential truth, there lies a tacit cogito, myself experienced by myself. But this subjectivity, indeclinable, has upon itself and upon the world only a precarious hold. It does not constitute the world, it divines the world's presence round about it as a field not provided by itself; nor does it constitute the word, but speaks as we sing when we are happy. . . . The tacit cogito, the presence of oneself to oneself, being no less than existence, is anterior to any philosophy. . . . What is believed to be thought about thought, as pure feeling of the self, cannot yet be thought and needs to be revealed. (PhP, 403–404)

One cannot fail to see, in the reference to the spontaneity of song, the suggestion that the artistic impulse manifests itself precisely out of the non-thetic self-apprehension of the tacit cogito. A few pages later, impor-

5. For the later Merleau-Ponty, this formulation is itself problematic, remaining attached as it does to a basic bifurcation between a pure constituting spontaneity on the one hand, and dispersal among beings on the other—an issue I take up in more detail, below.

tantly, Merleau-Ponty poses the key question as to the nature of the tacit cogito and the possibility—and limits—of our access to it: "What remains," he asks, "on the hither side of my particular thoughts, to constitute the tacit cogito and the original project towards the world, and what, ultimately, am I in so far as I can catch a glimpse of myself independently of any particular act? I am a field, an experience" (PhP, 406).

When he reexamines these passages in 1959, in one of the first of the Working Notes published in *The Visible and the Invisible*, Merleau-Ponty proclaims, "What I call the tacit cogito is impossible." Before rushing to embrace in this a wholesale rejection of his earlier thought, however, we need to attend to the specifics, which highlight lingering Cartesian, Husserlian, and above all Sartrean commitments. To meditate in the manner of Descartes, "thoughts about thoughts and feelings . . ." or to apply the reduction and so access the realm of immanence and the intentional structures of consciousness, he now argues, "it is necessary to have words." Only in and with language do I "*form* the transcendental attitude . . . *constitute* the constitutive consciousness" (VI, 171). What Merleau-Ponty comes to reject most strenuously, in short, is the positivism implicit in either ignoring the need for words, and so falling into a kind of direct intuitionism, or in valorizing them to the point of postulating a realm of univocal ideality. What he does not address in this passage, however, is the middle ground of artistic expression, which opens up not the established system of signification that is a language, but its ground.

The general point remains, however: for Merleau-Ponty, our encounters with reality and with ourselves are always mediated, always caught up and contextualized within a "web" of difference (that is, differentiated significations), such as, for example, a living language. And yet he does recognize, in this 1959 note, that there is a realm of silence, of nonlinguistic signification—the very soil from which important art emerges. There is no simple, unmediated access either to the sensorial field in which I am engaged as a body, or to the field of significations in which I am engaged in speech, as an articulate being. What is rightly the interrogative focus is the way I find myself within both these zones of engagement: the visible and the invisible, as at once "wholly spiritual and wholly corporeal" (TD, 6). Hence, in his last work, Merleau-Ponty calls for an originary return into language, a poetic recasting of words "against the grain," using their established significations to undercut themselves, as it were, "to express, beyond themselves, our mute contact with the things, when they are not yet things said" (VI, 38). Language is not a closed system but rather, like art, "lives only from silence"; indeed, philosophy itself is language, he writes here, while also "open upon the things, called forth by the voices of silence," and continuing "an effort of articulation which is the Being of every being" (ibid., 126–27).

Alongside the issue of language, Merleau-Ponty is also ambivalent toward his early account of the tacit cogito because of the strong Sartrean influence manifest in it. "If there must be consciousness, if something must appear to someone," he wrote in the "Cogito" chapter, for example, "it is necessary that behind all our particular thoughts there should lie a retreat of not-being" (PhP, 400). Merleau-Ponty's relations with Sartre and his "philosophy of negativity," as it is discussed exhaustively in chapter 2 of *The Visible and the Invisible*, are notoriously complex. Here I can but sketch some of the affinities and divergences, specifically on the issue of the embodied-horizonal or, as I am dubbing it here, the tactile cogito—as a means to better lay out the emergence and trajectory of Merleau-Ponty's mature reimagining of the perceiving self, the self integrated with its "animal" physicality, the self capable of artistic insight.

A central goal behind the discussion of the tacit cogito is, not unlike Sartre's in *The Transcendence of the Ego*, to elicit a pre-positional, non-thetic, preobjective level of self-awareness, on or as a situated "horizon of corporeity." The methodological problems, however, are daunting: as Husserl wrote in *Ideas I*,[6] the advertence of consciousness is normally understood as "a kind of spotlight," or "ray of regard" (section 27, section 92 et passim). To interrogate something, to analyze, simply to "envision" it as object of enquiry, is to focus this light of mental regard on it, to draw out an object against a background. But in this case, that is to destroy the thing sought—for this is, I am suggesting, nothing but horizonality itself, which recedes always behind the thetic "object," into the shadows. There are, nonetheless, possibilities for access—as we have seen already, for example, in Merleau-Ponty's account of love. Sartre approached the issue somewhat differently: By reliving a remembered experience, for example, of reading—and "by joining in a sort of conspiracy with it"—I can remember not only "external details," but also, out of the corner of the eye, as it were, "a certain density [*épaisseur*] of unreflected consciousness, since the objects revived could only have been perceived by this consciousness, and remain relative to it."[7] Thus, in addition

6. Edmund Husserl, *Ideas Pertaining to a Pure Phenomenology and to a Phenomenological Philosophy*, First Book, trans. Fred Kersten (The Hague: Martinus Nijhoff), 1982.

7. Jean-Paul Sartre, *The Transcendence of the Ego*, trans. Forrest Williams and Robert Kirkpatrick (New York: Farrar, Straus, and Giroux, 1957), 46.

to a nonreflective consciousness of the book, and a possible second-order reflective advertence to "myself-reading-the-book," there is always, as it were "penumbrally," a third level of consciousness, in which the first is glimpsed from within itself as part of the background of the intended-to object's appearing.[8] There are clearly congruencies between this view of Sartre's and Merleau-Ponty's own—though the latter aims to take things much farther: the field of experience that I am is not merely an affective density, but also pulsional, shot through with vectors of movement, articulated by axes and levels that sketch out in advance pathways of compossible directionalities, and so delimit the "field of (perceptual) engagement" in advance. As Merleau-Ponty writes of the tacit cogito, in language that again anticipates his later work: "The act which draws together at the same time takes away and holds at a distance, so that I touch myself only by escaping from myself" (PhP, 408).

Although Sartre did speak here of the "density" of recollected experience, and did, in his striking account of the encounter in the park in *Being and Nothingness*, employ vivid metaphors of blood, of "internal hemorrhage," where "capture" by the gaze of the other is depicted as a "flow without limit" in which "the world flows out of the world and I flow outside myself" (257, 261), for Merleau-Ponty it is precisely the living flesh of reality—its density, its weight—that is lost within the starkly dichotomous machinery of Sartrean theory. For Sartre, as Merleau-Ponty writes in *The Visible and the Invisible*, "I am unaware of myself as nothingness, I believe only in the things" (VI, 56). Yet this is not so much a gift of priority as, ultimately, a negation of what was to have been positive: the world becomes merely a prolongation of "me," of my body; I "am the world." In sum, the vital difference is lost; Sartre's unmediated opposition of being and nothingness leads inevitably to the collapse of both; "as absolutely opposed, Being and Nothingness are indiscernible" (ibid., 66).

What we need to note in contrast is the very different language used by Merleau-Ponty in *The Visible and the Invisible*, which expands on the insights tentatively laid out already in his early work: "By position, and before all

8. Since consciousness is always consciousness of an "object," it would appear consciousness can only grasp itself through a self-objectifying "reflective" consciousness. But, as Sartre here sees—and as Husserl had already hinted at in his pioneering work on passive synthesis—access to a deeper, more primordial level is possible; consciousness need not stand apart from itself and "posit" itself as object (as in Sartre's "second order" consciousness) to be (let us say) "mindfully" self-aware (though, as Sartre rightly insists, in a non-positional, non-thetic or, as I might say, "ambient" way).

reflection, I touch myself through my situation" (VI, 56). What I touch is a touching of the world, as flesh upon flesh, which maintains the difference precisely in the adhesion, complicity, interchange and preserved distance within the contact. Sartre's truncated dialectic, in contrast—his stark opposition between being and nothingness, between "fullness and void" (ibid., 77)—elevates vision over everything, into total disclosure without depth, grain, relief or resistance. As a philosophy of vision, it falls into the aerial view, into totalizing "high-altitude" thinking (cf. ibid., 69, 88 et passim) where "the look dominates, and it can dominate only things," as Merleau-Ponty writes. To this he adds, if this look "falls upon men it transforms them into puppets which move only by strings" (ibid., 77). Here one cannot help but be reminded: this is exactly the Cartesian view of animals. But it is more than merely a Cartesian question when he then asks, "How would we ever find a mind, an invisible, at the end of our look?" (ibid., 78). The danger is that, under an objectifying regard, the Other—whether human or nonhuman animal—will remains simply a "thing," which, as such, can never truly touch me: "Just as 'being is' *adds* nothing to 'nothingness is not' and the recognition of Being as absolute plenitude and positivity changes nothing in the negintuition of nothingness," Merleau-Ponty writes, "so also the other's gaze which suddenly congeals me adds to my universe no new dimension" (ibid., 71).

For all the problems arising from ontological commitments and "truncated dialectic," there is undeniable richness and vigor in Sartre's examples and descriptions. One of the key discussions in *Being and Nothingness*[9]—in Part Three, chapter 1, section IV, "The Look," after an invocation of the very Cartesian "puppet" we were just discussing (254)—could be very productively recast as an encounter in a park not with "a man" but with, for example, a dog. For the dog too sees the lawn, the statue, the tree, and between the dog and these things too there is a "relation without distance" that "creates distance," which also, arguably, sets up a "total space" that is at the same time a disintegration of "my space," a "regrouping" and "decentralization" of the world I thought was "mine."

Similarly, in Sartre's account of soldiers "during an attack" who experience the look to be avoided in terms of the white farmhouse on the hill, one could easily add it is also the many-sensed alertness of the farmer's dog that lights up or dims with aversion certain quadrants, contours, or

9. Jean-Paul Sartre, *Being and Nothingness, An Essay on Phenomenological Ontology*, trans. with an intro. by Hazel E. Barnes (New York: Philosophical Library, 1956) (hereafter BN).

axes of the field of engagement (cf. BN, 257–58). Sartre himself seems to acknowledge these possible readings, even as he makes the point criticized by Merleau-Ponty: "The look which the eyes manifest, *no matter what kind of eyes they are,* is a pure reference to myself" . . . merely "an intermediary which refers from me to myself" (ibid., 259; emphasis added). How can we slip this noose of solipsism, move from what Sartre highlights, the experience of my own vulnerability as visible, to encompass also the vulnerability of the perceiving others, whether human or not—encompassing, indeed, precisely their stand in excess of all encompassing, in their capacity and eminence as sensing, feeling, and suffering? To take this question seriously is not only to acknowledge that I share this world with other animals who are not human, but with whom I must acknowledge a "kinship"; it is also to openly confront my own residual commitment to a supra-sensible stance within the world, and to follow Merleau-Ponty not only toward redeeming my own ineluctable animality, but toward embracing it as the fecund source of creative vitality, precisely in its carnal hold upon the real.

For Merleau-Ponty, such encompassing of the non-encompassable, which arises out of a recognition of encroachment and implication in a shared world, becomes realizable in and as the flesh. The debt to Sartre is not insignificant: in his early work, especially, as we've seen, Merleau-Ponty shared with Sartre a desire to unearth a field-being or horizonal self engaged affectively and carnally in its perceptual situation. But the essence of the break with Sartre, in my view, is in Merleau-Ponty's eschewing of the dominance of the appropriating gaze and Sartre's "high-altitude" thinking in favor of a deepening of affectivity, an openness to our insertion into the real as chiasmic, the touching of touch itself. It is not merely that the gaze of the other, whether man or dog, with "*no matter what kind of eyes,*" superimposes on my world an alien matrix of distances and proximities, and so enacts a flowing out, an "internal hemorrhage" on my horizon. Instead, for Merleau-Ponty, the very notion of the "horizon" has to be redrawn. As he comes to see in his later work, it is

> a new type of being, a being by porosity, pregnancy, or generality, and he before whom the horizon opens is caught up, included within it. His body and the distances participate in one same corporeity or visibility in general, which reigns between them and it, and even beyond the horizon, beneath his skin, unto the depths of being. (VI, 149)

Where Sartre's philosophy of negativity simply reinscribed the basic opposition between the mind or soul and body, and hence did nothing to repair the wound or caesura at the heart of the "human animal," Merleau-Ponty's aim was to return us into the living tissue of nature and the real, in the leap of perceptual faith. That reality withdraws, veils itself even as it reveals itself, had already been central to the thought of Nietzsche and Heidegger; even as he deepens our awareness of this, Merleau-Ponty adds that the same ambiguity exists also upon the side of the "self," at once losing and finding itself in its perceptual life. Here too, in this opening-to that takes up what is given, we find a play of hiddenness and depth, clarity and opacity both, affect and history, "an ideality that is not alien to the flesh, that gives it its axes, its depth, its dimensions" (VI, 152)—in short, visibility and the invisible, incarnate in a tensional (dis)union, and at play on and as the levels, vectors, and dimensions of the horizon of corporeity that I am, as my bodily insertion into and complicity with the very flesh of the world.

What Merleau-Ponty aimed at throughout his work was a philosophy of perception freed from the confines of the ego cogito, but which also turns back from a complete emptying out of the self, its complete dispersal over "what is" as mere translucence, a patina of nonbeing. Both views, as he argues at length in *The Visible and the Invisible*, merely mirror the positivity of the other; both "render impossible that *openness upon being* which is the perceptual faith" (VI, 88). In addition, both these views forget the distance between reflecting and the unreflected, the irreducible ambiguities we saw, for example, in Merleau-Ponty's early discussion of the emergence of love. Finally, both, on my reading, also represent almost desperate attempts to reinscribe the abyssal *difference* of man from animal, of "soul" from thing, of mind from world. Merleau-Ponty sees, though, that *that things matter* requires of me a prior insertion in and complicity with the material world, in and through my body; it is only for such a one that things can come forth, and be taken up into my projects, with all the richness, elusiveness, pregnancy, and ambiguity that is being in its mysterious (un)veiling. And it only out of such an open-handed grasp that artistic creation emerges as a possibility.

Here we have traced Merleau-Ponty's elaboration of a new understanding of the "self" of perception, and the emergence of what we have been calling the tactile cogito. We have emphasized this reimagining in part because it is the cogito that has traditionally been the privileged locus and ground of the elevation of man over animal, as of form over matter, of spirit over body, and of the "essence" of an artwork over its mere instrumental execution in sensuous media. The direction of Merleau-Ponty's thought, we have seen, has been toward a healing of the rift, the mythic "abyss" that is at once at the core of the human, as "rational animal," and of our relation to the environing natural world. The key to the impossible possibility of overcoming this divide and this wound is the intertwining of affective corporeity; the felt insertion into the world. It is in inhabiting the tactile moment, the touching that is also touched, that we can return to the affective natal bond with the real, lived in and as the interstices and ligaments of the perceptual field, an intertwining that cuts from the lowest to the most exalted regions of the human experience: a chiasmic intertwining. As Merleau-Ponty writes in a working note from 1960, what is entailed in recognizing the irreducibility of the chiasm is a rejection of the traditional notion of "the subject" in favor of "defining [it] as a field, as a hierarchized system of structures opened by an inaugural there is." As a result, he continues, we see that

> the structures of affectivity are constitutive with the same right as the others, for the simple reasons that they are already the structures of knowledge, being those of language. We must no longer ask why we have affections in addition to "representative sensations," since the representative sensation also . . . is affection, being a presence to the world through the body and to the body through the world, being flesh, and language is also. (VI, 239)[10]

As Merleau-Ponty suggested in a 1960 interview, the key question is, "How can the human being be at once wholly spiritual and wholly corporeal?" (TD, 6). The hope of the impossible-possibility lies in recognizing "an ideality that is not alien to the flesh, that gives it its axes, its depth, its dimensions" (VI, 152)—embracing, in short, a chiasmic intertwining of animality and man, of body or earth and world, as of the visible and the invisible. While he does not himself enact an abyssal healing, Merleau-Ponty's expli-

10. We must not underestimate the importance of those last few words, though there is no room at present to explore them in detail. Language, the traditional view insists, is distinctly human, *definitively* human. But as Merleau-Ponty began more and more to see, in all speaking there resound also the voices of silence; language, like art (indeed, in a profound sense, as art) emerges from and rests always within the elements of sonority and visibility as such, the mews and howls, grimaces and scowls, which "find voice" in everything from the simplest blessings and cursing to our most refined utterances and creations. Here too one could perhaps speak of a kind of "animal faith" that opens the place of interchange, of promise, of language—the "element of speech" that we are always already within, as Derrida discusses in *Of Spirit* (129, n. 5; also see Lawlor's interesting discussion of this text and the Heideggerian notion of *Zusage*, 82–85).

cation of what I've called the "tactile cogito," alongside his explorations of incarnate artistic realization in the work of Cézanne and others, reveals his thought as above all the thought of "kinship," which bids us take up again the task of perception uncorrupted by dualistic metaphysical myths, in an ever-renewed, carnal innocence.

References

Agamben, Giorgio. 2004. *The Open: Man and Animal.* Translated by Kevin Artell. Stanford: Stanford University Press.

Calarco, Matthew. 2008. *Zoographies.* New York: Columbia University Press.

Derrida, Jacques. 1989. *Of Spirit.* Translated by Geoff Bennington and Rachel Bowlby. Chicago: University of Chicago Press.

———. 1993. *Aporias.* Translated byThomas Dutoit. Stanford: Stanford University Press.

———. 2008a. *The Animal That Therefore I Am.* Edited by Marie-Louise Mallert. Translated by David Wills. New York: Fordham University Press.

———. 2008b. "Geschlecht II: Heidegger's Hand." In *Psyche: Inventions of the Other*, edited by Peggy Kamuf and Elizebeth Rottenberg. Vol. 2, 27–63. Stanford: Stanford University Press.

Heidegger, Martin. 1953. *Sein und Zeit.* Tűbingen: Max Niemeyer. English translation, 1962. *Being and Time.* Translated by Macquarrie and E. Robinson. New York: Harper and Row.

———. 1961. *Was Heist Denken?* Tűbingen: Max Niemeyer. English translation, 1968. *What Is Called Thinking?* Translated by J. Glen Gray. New York: Harper and Row.

———. 1967 "Brief über den 'Humanismus.'" In *Wegmarken.* Frankfurt: Vittorio Klostermann. English translation, 1977. "The Letter on Humanism." Translated by D. F. Krell. In *Basic Writings*edited by D. F. Krell. New York: Harper and Row.

———. 1971. "The Origin of the Work of Art." In *Poetry, Language, Thought*, translated by A. Hofstadter. New York: Harper and Row.

———. 1983. *Die Grundbegriffe der Metaphysik. Welt—Endlichkeit—Einsamkeit. Gesamtausgabe*, vol. 29. Frankfurt a. M.: Klostermann. English translation, 1995. *The Fundamental Concepts of Metaphysics: World, Finititude, Solitiude.* Translated by William McNeill and Nicholas Walker. Bloomington: Indiana University Press.

Husserl, Edmund. 1982. *Ideas Pertaining to a Pure Phenomenology and to a Phenomenological Philosophy.* First Book. Translated by Fred Kersten. The Hague: Martinus Nijhoff.

Kant, Immanuel. 1951. *Critique of Judgment.* Translated by J. H. Bernard. New York: Hafner.

Lawlor, Leonard. 2007. *This Is Not Sufficient: An Essay on Animality and Human Nature in Derrida.* New York, Columbia University Press.

Nietzsche, Friedrich. 1974. *The Gay Science.* Translated by Walter Kaufmann. New York: Vintage.

Plato. 1961. *Collected Dialogues.* Edited by E. Hamilton and H. Cairns. Princeton: Princeton University Press.

Sartre, Jean-Paul. 1956. *Being and Nothingness.* Translated by Hazel Barnes. New York: Philosophical Library.

———. 1957. *The Transcendence of the Ego.* Translated by Forrest Williams and Robert Kirkpatrick. New York: Farrar, Straus, and Giroux.

Silverman, Hugh J., and James Barry Jr., eds. 1992. *Texts and Dialogues, Maurice Merleau-Ponty.* Translated by Michael B. Smith et al. Atlantic Highlands, NJ: Humanities Press.

13

The Chiasm as a Virtual

A Non-concept in Merleau-Ponty's Work (with a Coda on Theatre)

Marcello Vitali Rosati

Introduction

Although numerous concepts of contemporary philosophy such as "the flesh," "interweaving," and "dehiscence" now bear the indelible seal of Merleau-Ponty, the concept of the *virtual* barely belongs with them. This is rightly the case because although Merleau-Ponty employs the *virtual* now and again, as every faithful Bergson reader should, one searches in vain for Merleau-Ponty to use the virtual in a concrete way.[1] Yet in this article we suggest reading Merleau-Ponty precisely as a thinker of the virtual, not so much in his explicit remarks about the virtual as in the articulation of the chiasm in his later thinking. This often escapes our attention as the unhappy alternative between ability and action that haunts philosophy from Aristotle to the present day. Our hypothesis is, therefore, that certain notions developed by Merleau-Ponty, in particular that of the chiasm, can resolve a theoretical problem raised by the Aristotelian concept of *dunaton* (the possible). We also want to demonstrate that this problem is at the heart of

1. This paper owes a lot to a discussion I had with Emmanuel Alloa who helped me in finding the occurrences of the word *virtual* in Merleau-Ponty's work. I wish to thank him here. He recently published the results of his own analysis in "Le Théâtre du virtuel," in *Du sensible à l'oeuvre. Esthétiques de Merleau-Ponty*, La Lettre Volée, 2012, 317–34.

the modern notion of the possible and above all at the heart of the class of the virtual, used increasingly frequently in different domains.

The Aristotelian question can be thus formulated: Is the *dunaton* an autonomous element, existent before all actualization (or realization), or can it only exist in relation with an action? In this article, we will speak of a pre-actualization *possible* and a post-actualization *possible.* The intrinsic polarity of the *dunaton* is not resolved in Aristotle's work. Instead, he maintains a certain ambiguity in this respect, sometimes being almost contradictory in his remarks. Another outworking of the problem, and the most traditional one, is the issue of the principle of plenitude: Can the possible ever not be realized? According to the principle of plenitude, everything that is possible is realized one day; Aristotle's position as regards plenitude is not clear and remains a subject of debate for his scholars. Indeed, Greek philosophy seemingly sees problems in both rejecting and accepting the concept of plenitude.[2]

In order to understand the theoretical issues surrounding these two arguments, based on Aristotle's point of view, it is necessary to clarify that we want to reduce the *dunaton* to two fundamental concepts.[3] First of all, *dunaton* is something that possesses a principle of movement, meaning something that has the capacity to do something. In this ontological sense, *dunaton* is often translated in to Latin as *potentialis* or *virtualis.*[4] Secondly, *dunaton* means what is not necessarily false; this is the purely

2. Interpreting Aristotle's position as regards "principle of plenitude" is controversial. According to Lovejoy, who introduced the concept, Plato would accept the principle whereas Aristotle would reject it. Contrastingly, Hintikka considers the principle of plenitude to be at the very foundation of Aristotle's thinking. See Arthur O. Lovejoy, *The Great Chain of Being, A Study of the History of an Idea* (Cambridge: Harvard University Press, 1936); Jakko Hintikka, *Time and Necessity: Studies in Aristotle's Theory of Modality* (Oxford: Clarendon Press, 1975); and Jakko Hintikka, *Aristotle on Modality and Determinism* (Amsterdam: North-Holland, Acta philosophica fennica, 1977). Richard Gaskin provides a good reconstruction of the different interpretations of this theme in Aristotle's work: Richard Gaskin, *Sea Battle and the Master Argument: Aristotle and Diodorus Cronus on the Metaphysics of the Future* (Berlin: W. de Gruyter, Quellen und Studien zur Philosophie, 1995).

3. More precisely, Aristotle highlights three meanings of the *dunaton* in his volumes 5 and 9 of *Metaphysics,* and one other in his books on logic, in particular in *Peri hermeneia* 8, but it seems that for the purposes of this essay we can consider the word as having two meanings.

4. Although we also use the term *possibilis.*

logical sense of the word that Aristotle uses in *Peri hermeneia* 13 as a synonym of *endechomenon.*[5]

In the light of these two meanings, we are able to analyze the problems that Aristotle raises in the respective positions of those who accept and reject the principle of plenitude. If we subscribe to the idea that there exists a possible that can never be realized—in Aristotelian terms, if we want to imagine a *dunaton* that never reaches *entelechy*—we arrive at assertions of the type: x is a painter who has never created a painting. In the *Metaphysics,* Aristotle maintains that *dunamis,* or the ability to do something, must be actualized. If the *dunaton* is a principle of movement, then it must have produced a movement or must produce one one day. If the contrary is true, it cannot be said to be a principle as, by definition, it must be a principle of something. We are thus led to interpret the *dunaton* based on the *entelechy* that results from it, to judge the painter's ability to paint based on what he or she has actually painted or will paint.

On the other hand, if every *dunaton* is destined to become an action, there are a few problems in thinking of it as contingent, such as the Diodorus's objection in his Master Argument: nothing is contingent, everything is necessary. Aristotle cannot accept Diodorus's determinism, nor that of other Megarics. In *Peri hermeneia* he tries to appropriate the notion of contingency in speaking of the coat that could be tailored but will never be because it disappears beforehand. It would therefore seem fundamental to be able to think of a *dunaton* as independent from its actualization, that is to say a *dunaton* in the *pre-actualization.*

To summarize, if the principle of plenitude is not valid, we are dealing with a *dunaton* that is independent from the action, a *pre-actualization dunaton,* but this concept runs the risk of being invalid. If the principle of plenitude is valid, we will consider the *dunaton* as being *post-actualization,* as dependent on the action, but that prevents us from considering it as contingent. Diverse approaches to the notion of the possible were born and have developed throughout the history of thought based on these two positions, between which Aristotle seems not to have decided. Every idea of the possible risks being affected by one of the aforementioned problems.

5. The logical definition can be more or less precise: sometimes Aristotle restricts the meaning to being something that is neither necessarily true nor necessarily false. In relation to this, see Jakko Hintikka, *Time and Necessity*, 41–61.

In the following pages, I will try to analyze briefly the two conflicting notions of the possible in order to suggest a solution to this opposition through having recourse to the idea of the virtual.

The Possible in the Pre-actualization

In order to properly understand the idea of a possible that exists in an autonomous way before any realization, we can refer to the idea of the possible world as described by Saul Kripke in *Naming and Necessity.*[6] According to Kripke, possible worlds are like possibilities of states in a probability calculation. The example suggested by the logician is one of rolling two dice. Before the roll, there are thirty-six combinations, thirty-six states of affairs, and thirty-six possible worlds. These possible worlds are perfectly conceivable before the roll: we know exactly how each of the worlds is structured and what its characteristics are. This is why realization is not necessary: the possibilities are already there and the realization is nothing other than the choice between a determined series existing of alternatives. This argument renders the relationship between the possible and its realization problematic. The real does not differ at all from the possible, it is exactly the same. In no way can we distinguish the two poles; the real does not add anything new. The difficulty of distinguishing between the possible and the real engenders four theoretical issues.

Firstly, the notion of the *possible in the pre-actualization* implies the existence of an omniscient exterior outlook that can grasp every alternative, from an external perspective as in a predefined plan. Obviously, this does not create any problems when calculating probabilities since the combinations that give rise to a state of affairs are purely logical. But the notion is more difficult to accept when dealing with ontological combinations.

The second difficulty stems from the fact that this idea of the possible completely prevents novelty: in the transition to becoming an action, nothing new arises, everything already existed beforehand and is realized as foreseen. There is no difference between the number six resulting from a roll of the dice and the possible number six.[7]

6. Saul A. Kripke, *Naming and Necessity* (Cambridge: Harvard University Press, 1999), 167 ff.

7. This idea, as we will see in looking closer, is criticized by Bergson in "The Possible and the Real," in *The Creative Mind: An Introduction to Metaphysics*, trans. Mabelle L. Andison (New York: The Citadel Press, 1992), 91–106.

In order to resolve these problems, we could try to think of possibility as existent before realization, but unknowable. However, this solution would have unacceptable consequences: we would be dealing with a completely invalid idea of the possible; everything could be possible, we could add an infinite number of possibilities, and thus stumble into what Hegel calls bad infinity. This danger undoubtedly motivated Aristotle to adhere to the principle of plenitude: the possible must have a very strict relationship with its realization; otherwise we run the risk of considering possibility as a hollow. This is the case with the *dunamis* of being a painter but never realizing a painting.

The fourth difficulty is that if the real does not differ at all from the possible, how is it possible to explain the choice between alternatives? How is it possible to account for the fact that among thirty-six combinations, only one will become real? Kripke, as a result of his purely logical intentions, does not seem to be interested in this question, whereas Leibniz bases himself on the question to construct his conception of possible worlds. There must be a reason that justifies the realization of one possible rather than another, which is, of course, the principle of sufficient reason.

The Leibnizian idea of the possible world is not very different from that appropriated by Kripke. Every world is a combination of things that does not provoke a contradiction. There is thus a limited series of alternative states of affairs. Yet, clearly, it is impossible for a human being to know all these worlds, but this impossibility is just a material characteristic. It would take too long for a human being to calculate all combinations, but they remain logically conceivable even so and therefore known only by God.

The role of the principle of sufficient reason is to justify why just one of these worlds comes to be. According to Leibniz, as we know, the best world possible is realized. But the fact that one world is better than another is not random: we can easily establish which the best world is. Given that all possibilities tend towards existence and that existence is preferable to nonexistence, the best world is the one in which the highest number of possibilities exists. Since there are contradictory possibilities, the world in which there is the lowest number of contradictions has to be chosen. God, who knows all possibilities, can therefore calculate all the combinations and see in which world the highest number of compossibles exist.[8]

8. See Louis Couturat, *La logique de Leibniz* (Hildesheim: Georg Olms, 1985 [1901]), 214 ff., and Joseph Moreau, *L'univers leibnizien* (Hildesheim: Georg Olms, 1987 [1956]), 191 ff.

In this way, Leibniz distinguishes the principle of sufficient reason from the principle of identity, and his thinking therefore realizes contingency. But, to overcome the problem of the relationship between the possible and the real, Leibniz runs the risk of lapsing into the principle of plenitude in dealing with a *necessary* contingency. Indeed, in affirming that all compossibles exist, Leibniz aligns himself more closely with the principle of plenitude in spite of himself, a principle according to which all possibles exist.[9]

The Possible in the Post-actualization

We can therefore say that there are at least two reasons to accept the principle of plenitude and to opt for a possible that stems from and is dependent on an action: firstly, the difficulty of considering a possible as abstract, and also of the need to have a reason that accounts for the process of realization. But too narrow a relationship between the possible and the real runs the risk of reducing one as dependent on the other. If the possible is just a word, just the name of the real, it implies the disappearance of the contingency, and in particular the impossibility of difference. This is the paradox of the Megarics' school of thought as described by Aristotle in *Metaphysics* 9: something is only possible when it is in action.[10] According to this principle, someone not in the process of painting does not have the ability to paint: that person only has the ability to paint when he is doing so. Clearly, it is the theoretical difficulty of explaining the journey from immobility to movement that gives rise to this position. We could thus outline the difficulty: if there is a cause of movement, the cause has always existed—unless we imagine that the cause was generated by another cause, which only serves to displace the argument. Yet if this cause has always existed, then immobility never existed. If, on the contrary, there is no cause, then there is no movement and therefore everything is immobile. Thus, we face the following polarity: in one reasoning there is too powerful a cause and in the other there is no cause.

In the concept of the possible, the problem is the same. If there is a reason that explains the transition from the possible to the real, then the possible has to become a reality. Leibniz believes there is a logical reason

9. We will see that the critique of the principle of sufficient reason in Leibniz's work is based on this point. It is developed by Gilles Deleuze in *Difference and Repetition* (London: Athlone, 1994), 275.

10. *Metaphysics*, 1046b30.

that determines the existence of one world rather than another. His position therefore coincides with that of Spinoza, for whom all possibles exist. If everything that exists is justified by a reason, there is no contingency.[11] If, however, there is no reason that determines the transition from the possible to the real, then we cannot at all understand why the possible comes to be.

Although Aristotle rejects the Megarics' argument in *Metaphysics* 9 in order to get away from determinism, he seems to subscribe to the principle of plenitude in the same text, exactly to avoid an invalid idea of ability.[12] What is more, this position is perfectly in line with the Aristotelian principle whereby ability follows the action ontologically. The action is nothing other than the perfection of ability. It is therefore anterior to ability both in ontological and in gnoseological terms. In order to understand ability we must first comprehend what it relates to, namely, the action.[13]

The anteriority of the action is what Bergson describes in *the possible and the real.*[14] The reason that Bergson wants to consider the possible as post-real is because what we called the possible in the pre-actualization would imply the absence of all novelty. If the possible has always been there, ready to be realized, there is nothing new at the moment of realization.

Bergson explains that when we imagine a meeting, we see things exactly as they will take place, where the protagonists will sit, how they will be dressed, etc. But when the event is realized, we will be dealing with something else entirely. When a journalist asked him about the future of art, Bergson replied that it is not possible to imagine now what will be in the future. There are no possibilities already existent that will not be realized. What, therefore, is the possible? The possible is just the real combined with an action of the mind that rejects the image in the past once it has happened.[15] The possible is an after-event to the real: there is nothing possible now. But what is not possible now will have been possible tomorrow.

The aim of the philosopher is to completely invalidate the meaning of the concept of the possible. The possible is neutralized and no longer has any strength. We are faced with the failure of the possible. The question remains as to how what happens happens. But this question is displaced because we no longer we have to look for the response in the concept of the possible.

11. See proposition 29 of *Ethics*, for example.

12. *Metaphysics*, 1047b3.

13. Ibid., 1049b5.

14. Bergson, *The Creative Mind*, ch. III.

15. Ibid., 110.

The Middle Way

We thus come back to the plurivocity of the word *dunaton* in Aristotle's work to try to find a meaning that avoids the logical concept of the possible. The *dunaton* is primarily a principle of movement, not found in the pre- or the post-actualization. It is precisely the tension that links the two poles. As Hintikka says, the *dunaton* can be interpreted based on its end point, and therefore based on what it is the potential to do, or as a movement that aims to produce something.[16]

This is the notion of *kinesis* as the middle course. *Kinesis* is the realization of an ability.[17] We therefore consider the *dunaton* as a middle course characterized by its tension, strength, and transition from before to after. The *dunaton* is exactly what explains the transition from past to present, from what is not yet existent to what is. Thus, it is no longer a case of seeing whether the possible existent before realization becomes reality or not; rather, we have to try to understand the concept of the transition that leads to the creation of a pre-actualization before a completely novel post-actualization.

So we can no longer equate the *dunaton* to the possible, we must use another term: virtual. In this way we can interpret the work of Deleuze. In appropriating the Bergsonian critique of the concept of the possible, Deleuze affirms that the virtual does not conflict with the real, but rather with what is actual. In terms of the virtual, we are no longer dealing with a polar structure where we have a before and an after. The virtual and the actual constitute both parts of the real object. The virtual is an interstitial principle from which existence is produced. Virtuality is therefore not found in the before, because it belongs to the real object, or in the after. Indeed, actual situations never resemble the virtuality that they actualize.[18] The virtual is the tension that gives rise to differentiation in the now, meaning multiplicity, which while being behind everything present forms the structure of the real.

According to Deleuze, in order to understand the virtual we need to consider it separately from its reality. In this way we can interpret his critique of Leibniz's thinking. As we have seen, the Leibnizian idea consisted of thinking of a possible in the before, as separate from what will be produced. Deleuze says that Ideas are virtual multiplicities in Leibniz's work. But as soon as we have to speak of the transition to action, Leibniz ends up referring back to the structure of a possible that comes to be, precisely

16. Hintikka, "Aristotle on Modality and Determinism," 59.

17. Phys, 201a 10–11.

18. Deleuze, *Difference and Repetition*, 273.

because of too rigid a principle of sufficient reason.[19] To get away from the risk of having a possible that is nothing other than an after-event of the real, we have to think of the virtual as always present in every realization: multiplicity guarantees this differentiation.

The Deleuzian virtual is therefore real without being actual. It belongs to the real as a structure of reality. However, it remains to understand what happens at the virtual moment of actualization. In order to avoid following the actualist model, copied from the possible-real module that he contests, Deleuze tries to rescue the virtual in introducing the term *drama*. This term was inspired by Raymond Ruyer's organology, the essential inspiration behind *Difference and Repetition*. According to Ruyer, life provides a "theme," as it were, which sets itself apart not in the actual, but in a "role." Deleuze radicalizes this idea in bringing a philosophy of life and theatre nearer together. Rather than just being a transition to the action, actualization is a "dramatization," the game of a "role" in which actor takes a back seat: "The world is an egg, but the egg itself is a theatre: a staged theatre in which the roles dominate the actors."[20] Something virtual is *staged* as though it is actual, and presented *as* actual, but the virtual is still behind everything actual like dynamic tension that gives rise to other actualities. In these transitions, we measure the difficulty of the Deleuzian attempt to materialize the virtual. He claimed never to be satisfied with his attempts,[21] yet he was seldom so close to his aim. At the same time, the example that would seem to help him achieve his aim, the theatre, threatened to lead him back to one of the two poles from which he was trying to depart. Because, if the role takes priority over the actor, if it precedes the actualization in the body of an actor, it is that the role was *written* and therefore *possible* before. The "method of dramatization" described in the conference of the same name in 1967[22] reveals itself as the *pharmakon* of the virtual. Although

19. Ibid., 275.

20. Ibid., 279.

21. Cf. David Lapoujade's note reminding us that *L'immanence: une vie,* published in *Philosophie* immediately before he died on November 4, 1995 and "The Actual and the Virtual," published in the appendices of *Dialogues* (with Claire Parnet), (Paris: Flammarion, 1996), should have belonged to a more extensive book, the title of which should be *Ensemble et multiplicités*: "Deleuze wanted to reinforce the concept of the virtual as he felt that he had not been widely understood." Gilles Deleuze, *Deux régimes de fous, textes et entretiens 1975–1995*; édition préparée par David Lapoujade (Paris: Minuit, 2003), 359.

22. Gilles Deleuze, "The Method of Dramatization" in *Desert Islands: and Other Texts*, ed. David Lapoujade, trans. Mike Taormina (Paris, Minuit, 2002), 131–62.

actualization is only *playing* at being actual, without being so, the virtual is intact, but everything remains in the most complete possibilism.

In order to attempt to consider the existence of a virtual and an actual that belong to each other, and of an actualization which belongs to the virtual[23] and of a strictly correlative virtuality of the actual,[24] while still being able to cite the example of the body of the actor, we suggest departing from Deleuze's thinking to examine that of the late Merleau-Ponty.

The Chiasm

Although some commentators such as Renauld Barbaras have underlined the centrality of the virtual,[25] the notion is never taken into account in a systematic way in the work of Merleau-Ponty, as we have said. It even seems that the critical distinction between the possible and the virtual, introduced by Bergson, is not appropriated by Merleau-Ponty, because he indifferently uses the two interchangeably.

In *Phenomenology of Perception,* however, the term *virtual* appears several times, and James Steeves was able to show that the term here is used primarily to overcome the strict Sartrean opposition between the real and the imaginary.[26] Merleau-Ponty refers notably to Wertheimer's experiment (PhP, 248),[27] which consists of letting an individual see the room he/she is in only through the medium of a mirror that reflects with an incline of 45 degrees. One's own body is therefore repeated in a virtual body found in the space of action. The virtual body replaces the real body: the individual is found where the virtual body is found. The virtual can therefore be considered as the projection of the actual in another state, which will then also become actualized.

Numerous similar examples are also analyzed in *Child Psychology and Pedagogy*, notably in relation to body schema, children's drawings, and cybernetics. Merleau-Ponty even goes so far as to construct an anthropological

23. Gilles Deleuze, *Dialogues* (Paris: Flammarion, 1996), 181.

24. Ibid., 184.

25. Cf. Renaud Barbaras, "Merleau-Ponty aux limites de la phénoménologie," *Chiasmi International* 1: 199–212, esp. 206 ff.

26. James Steeves, "The Virtual Body: Merleau-Ponty's Early Philosophy of Imagination," *Philosophy Today* 45, no. 1 (2001): 370–80.

27. The edition cited here is *Phenomenology of Perception*, trans. Colin Smith (New York: The Humanities Press, 1962).

argument out of the notion of the virtual: the ability to indicate a particular point in space with your finger presupposes being "already present in the virtual" (PC-II, 43). This is an ability that is inaccessible to most animals and people with apraxia. The virtual space is a "centrifugal or cultural space" (ibid).

Each of these examples deserves an in-depth analysis, which is beyond the confines of this essay. We do, however, remain convinced that the notion of the virtual cannot develop every ability in the context of a philosophy of subjectivity, of which Merleau-Ponty still remains a prisoner.

Indeed, if we stayed with Merleau-Ponty's first writings, we would have the impression that the virtual is nothing other than a pre-actualization awaiting actualization in the post-actualization that is represented by the body. In other words, there would be a virtualizing structure, which materializes in one way or another in the actuality of a body, in an incarnation. This idea would not account for the innovative strength of the Merleau-Pontian notion of the body. Merleau-Ponty's thinking truly achieves a way of thinking about the virtual that overcomes this difficulty. This is true of his later writings, which are based on a new ontology that, importantly, still draws on many of his early concepts of psychology. These early concepts now influence cosmo-ontology. We therefore suggest verifying how the transformation of Gestaltists' terms such as Wertheimer's perceptive overlapping into ontological "impingement" opens up the possibility of a subtle philosophy of the virtual.

The virtual can lead one to think of the "chiasm" (we are following Fabrice Bourlez's proposal)[28] in which it forms. Indeed, the chiasm is a nothing-being in which the inside and the outside collide. It is therefore the surface of contact between the inside and the outside: this nothing-being is virtual because it remains above and below every actualization. The chiasm of the visible and the invisible cannot be considered as a substantial and stable unit; rather, it is a virtual intertwining of movements of differentiation; the flesh is the unit of noncoincidence, the intertwining of inassimilable elements that can only be thought of together thanks to the virtuality of their chiasm.

We are therefore dealing with a polar structure where the virtual plays the role of the middle ground. It seems clear that the relationship that the chiasm creates between the visible and the invisible and the way in which

28. Fabrice Bourlez, "Deleuze/Merleau-Ponty: propositions pour une rencontre a-parallel," in *Gilles Deleuze* (Series: Concepts. Hors série) (Mons: Sils Maria, 2002), 231–57.

the two poles are thought of can resolve the recurrent problem of the relationship between the pre- and post-actualization. Indeed, the chiasm is a tension between two poles that affects both poles by altering their meaning. In other words, if the chiasm is virtual and is found in the middle of the two elements as a principle, it virtualizes these two elements and we can no longer speak of one as the actualization of the other.

The chiasm is a virtual point where a visible that becomes virtually invisible and an invisible that becomes virtually visible are intertwined. Let us begin to explain the first element of this intertwining: the invisible, the before, becomes virtually visible in the virtual environment of the chiasm. Merleau-Ponty uses terminology that refers directly to the idea of the virtual when he defines the invisible as what is not currently visible but what could be (VI, 257/310): the invisible is therefore virtually visible.

In other words, the invisible is not only the hidden part of the visible. There is a tension, put into action by the virtual, that always puts the invisible in the position of being able to become visible. In the perspective structure, it is enough for example to change position to make the invisible visible and vice versa. In continuing the analysis we notice that invisibility in the chiasm constitutes every visibility. When we see a table we do not say that we see a part of the table, even if two feet are hidden. Invisibility is therefore virtually visible because invisibility forms the basis of what we *see*. We could therefore think that the invisible is incarnated precisely as a visible. The invisible could be considered as a virtual that is found after the actualization in the visibility of a body, in an incarnation. Thus, we would come back to the idea of the virtual in the pre-event, already existent before the actualization, restricted to appear during the transition to the action. But this is not the case, since the visible is also virtualized in its turn. It does not emerge as a crystallized actualization. Indeed, the visible in contact with the virtual becomes virtually invisible; the visibility of what is before us, the opening of a space before us, cannot be interpreted as an actual objectuality. The visible is only visible in relation with the invisible that structures it. The idea of depth further explains the meaning of a visible that becomes virtually invisible in the chiasm: depth is overlapping. In other words, it is latency, which is not possibility in the sense of another actuality of observation, of another actual simply matched to our own, but possibility in the sense of pregnancy, envelopment of an inaccessible actual in the accessible actual (NC, 167). In the chiasm, the visible, the accessible actual, acquires a different sense because it overlaps something else, an inaccessible actual, an invisible. Merleau-Ponty, in this transition, criticizes the idea of possibility as actuality preceding realization and seeks to imagine a unity between virtual latency and actuality.

The operation brought about by the virtuality of the chiasm consists of taking something visible, which according to our terminology could correspond to the after-event, and virtualizing its meaning. After the actualization the meaning would have nothing but unitary function and a sense, while the meaning is multiplied in coming into contact with the virtual. The visible virtually presupposes the multiplicity of the invisible.

In the idea that we have just laid out, one difficulty immediately arises: we do not seem to be able to distinguish the invisible as something virtual from the visible as something virtual. In other words, the two poles which we departed from can no longer be thought of separately. But, indeed, this means that we never deal with a pre- or post-actualization, but with the tension that links them. Every actualization is nothing but a pole of a virtualizing structure; we can only think of the actual in relation with the virtual. This is how we come to understand the ontological primacy of the virtual over the actual that Deleuze wanted to affirm.

The Metaphor of the Theatre

Yet, if we want to understand this structure better, it is useful to refer to a metaphor which, while seemingly marginal in Merleau-Ponty's work, assumes a completely unexpected value compared with some theoretical reasonings: the metaphor of theatre. Bizarrely, the theatre metaphor also appears in passing in Deleuze's discourse on the virtual, when he discusses drama—without linking this notion too much to that of the world of theatre.

In his *Phenomenology of Perception*, quoting Proust's *Le côté des Guermantes*, Merleau-Ponty refers to the actress Berma playing the role of Phèdre. The analysis he proposes is a critique of the idea of the theatre as a representation. The theatre experience therefore consists of renewing the presence of an event that is no longer there. The actor is therefore a representative of the character in a structure of strong opposition between subject and object: a represented object and a representing subject. In Merleau-Ponty's notion, however, theatre gives rise to nothing other than a representative structure. The relationship between actor and character can be considered an explicative example of what is produced in the chiasm between the visible and the invisible.

We are not faced with a visible pole, once Phèdre, that is reproduced and represented here and now thanks to the action of an actor. Rather, we are dealing with an invisible, an invisible that structures everything visible; Phèdre is this invisible. What is produced on stage is a sort of incarnation: the actor becomes the visibility of the invisible; therefore, it's Phèdre on stage and not Berma. Here we are close to Deleuze's affirmation whereby "[t]he roles dominate the actors"; but, after consideration, the notion elaborated by Merleau-Ponty is more complex.

According to the classical structure, the spectator would be in a tension between two poles: he would wonder whether he is seeing Phèdre (the before) or Berma (the after), whether Berma simply serves to give existence to Phèdre or whether Phèdre is just an after-event of Berma. In the latter case, we would only be able to think of Phèdre in relation to Berma.

But in this experience of the theatre we do not sense this tension or this polarity at all. We observe, however, a chiasm, an overlapping of Phèdre and Berma. The spectator is not conditioned to see Berma knowing that she is acting the role of Phèdre; the spectator perceives a unity between role and actor.[29] It is not possible to see Phèdre without Berma on stage, but neither is it possible to observe Berma without Phèdre.

Proust studied the role of Phèdre in advance (in principle, Phèdre's role is common to all actresses who play her). Proust believed that one could eliminate this common aspect from Berma's performance and therefore finally identify what was unique to Berma: her talent. However, he realized that this was not possible and that it is not possible to distinguish between the role and what the actor brings to it. The actor's talent is intertwined with the role.

In *Child Psychology and Pedagogy*, Merleau-Ponty highlights that it is impossible to consider role and actor separately. He states, "The role is in no way given in advance" (PPE, 560).[30] This means that we cannot mention the actor who plays the role before he/she plays it. The theatre experience teaches us that both role and actor appear when they overlap.

We are therefore departing from Deleuze since the roles do not dominate the actors, or the invisible the visible. However, the actors do not dominate the roles: there are no roles without actors and no actors without

29. We can find the same structure in the language. See Emmanuel Alloa, *La résistance du sensible. Merleau-Ponty critique de la transparence* (Paris: Kimé, 2008), 63.

30. Maurice Merleau-Ponty, *Psychologie et pédagogie de l'enfant: Cours de Sorbonne 1949–1952* (Paris: Lagrasse, Éditions Verdier, collection "Philosophie," 2001), 560 (hereafter PPE).

roles. The Deleuzian conception, if we are to keep to this metaphor, will result in matching the virtual with one of the two poles, the invisible. In this case, we would have an invisible virtual that is actualized visible body in the post-actualization. But this is not the idea that Merleau-Ponty puts forward.

On stage we are dealing with a unity between the invisible and the visible, which is exactly how we described the virtual. A middle ground between two poles that changes the meaning of each of these poles and prevents us from thinking of them separately. What we see on stage is the virtualization of an invisible that becomes virtually visible and, at the same time, the virtualization of a visible that becomes virtually invisible.

It is no longer a matter of a pre- and post-actualization; the visible, the post-actualization, Berma, is virtualized and is only there as a result of the relationship with the invisible. The virtual plunges the visible into the invisible. We cannot see a pure visible. We can therefore no longer think of the body of the actor as an actualization of a virtual, his role. On the other hand, the invisible is virtualized, Phèdre is visible. In short, Phèdre is virtually Berma and Berma is virtually Phèdre, which means that the two poles disappear in the virtual.

The virtual decreases the function of the pre-actualization; tritely, Phèdre can be played by different actresses. The virtually also decreases the function of the post-actualization; Berma can incarnate different characters.

It is very significant that the term *virtual*, so rarely employed by Merleau-Ponty, appears in his discourse on theatre in *Child Psychology and Pedagogy*. "The meaning that he [the actor] conveys . . . is virtual at heart in its movements, which is precisely what we call 'drama' " (PPE, 562). We find the Deleuzian term used in another sense: drama is the virtual meeting of the movements of a character and a role, and the movements of the actor. The movements of the character become virtualities for the actor and the drama is the virtual home where role and actor overlap.

And what about the actual? We are obliged at this point to think of it as one of the two poles brought into tension by virtualization. Would Berma on stage as an actress be the actualization of the virtuality of the meeting between character and actor? Obviously, every solution to this question runs the risk of quashing our line of argument and of returning to the opposition between the pre- and post-actualization that we are trying to overcome. We therefore propose thinking of the actual as a post-actualization of the virtual by reverting to the Bergsonian idea. The actual is inconceivable separately from the virtual; the virtual precedes it ontologically and conditions its conceivability. In this way, the actual would only be the downfall of the virtual in its post-event.

To use an expression of Levinas, the actual would be the said of the saying that the virtual continually unsays. The actual would be the after-event where we crystallize the dynamism of the virtual, with a posthumous judgment. The actual would be what is left from the meeting between Berma and Phèdre after the play has finished and the audience has gone home.

The fact that the chosen metaphor is the theatre helps us to understand the link that exists between the study of the virtual and the attempt to overcome the opposition between subject and object, central to Merleau-Ponty's philosophy and that of many of his contemporaries. Indeed, the notion of subject, was born precisely in the aesthetic domain, since, as we know, this notion was used for the first time by Baumgarten. The classical idea of the theatre as a representation constitutes the archetypal metaphor of the oppositional relationship between a perceiving subject and a perceived object. The suggestion of a concept of theatre that is no longer a representation but a virtual tension between a visible and an invisible is therefore the key to moving beyond the modern conception of the subject.[31]

Far from being an arbitrary and fortuitous metaphor, the theatre could be considered as a fundamental to understanding one of the major issues of twentieth-century thought. The theoretical thinking of Merleau-Ponty on theatre could not be said to be marginal, but should be considered as a way of resolving the issue that arose with Baumgarten and of permanently departing from the problems raised by the opposition between subject and object. And the concept of the virtual would actually be the middle ground structure to facilitate this new conception.

Conclusion

In the light of this middle ground structure, let us come back to the questions that we asked ourselves at the beginning of this article: is the *dunaton,* that can now be translated by virtual, an autonomous element that is already existent before every actualization (or realization) or can it only exist in relation with an action? Clearly, neither the first nor the second response accounts for the problem; we can no longer wonder about one or the other of these two poles separately, precisely because we can only think of them based on the middle ground where they meet.

31. This idea, which deserves a much more exhaustive analysis, was proposed several times during the meeting of the Groupes de Recherche théoriques (Paris 4—Pompidou Centre) led by Dénis Guénoun, to whom I owe thanks for this suggestion.

To cite Kripke's example again, we cannot imagine a series of pre-prepared possibilities, and the realization of one of these alternatives. The fact that there are thirty-six possible alternatives in rolling two dice only has meaning when we observe what happens in the interstice that the tension between these possibilities and the situation that will come to be creates. And the situation that comes to pass can only be considered if we position ourselves in the virtuality that relates it to a pre-actualization. In this virtuality the thirty-six possibilities overlap (to use a Merleau-Pontian term) in the unity of actualization. In this overlapping, the thirty-six possibilities are multiplied and in the same way the unity of actualization is multiplied. Once again, the pre- and post-actualizations only make sense in their virtualization. This idea implies the impossibility of considering a continuity between the pre- and post-actualization, precisely because they are two distinct units, since they are separated by something that also links them.

To cite an example dear to Aristotle, the house in the head of the architect is only related to the built house as a middle ground that creates a link between the two. And the virtual is not found in either one but in the very environment that exists as the point of contact between the two poles. The poles are each the virtualization of the other in this interstice.

A question remains that will have to be the subject of future study: Is this middle ground the place of coexistence of the pre- and the post-actualization, and is it therefore the moment of contradiction, or rather must it be considered as a non-place, a utopia formed from the absence of each of the two poles?[32]

References

Alloa, Emmanuel. 2008. *La résistance du sensible. Merleau-Ponty critique de la transparence*. Paris: Kimé.

Bergson, Henri. 1992 [1934]. *The Creative Mind: An Introduction to Metaphysics*. Translated by Mabelle L. Andison (New York: The Citadel Press, 1992). Originally published as *La Pensée et le mouvant*.

Bourlez, Fabrice. 2002. "Deleuze/Merleau-Ponty: propositions pour une rencontre a-parallel." In Stéfan Leclercq, *Gilles Deleuze*, 231–57. Mons: Éditions Sils Maria.

Couturat, Louis. 1985. *La logique de Leibniz*. Hildesheim: Georg Olms.

Deleuze, Gilles. 1994. *Difference and Repetition*. London: Athlone.

32. This problem is raised for the first time by Plato in the second part of the second inference of *Parménide*, 155e4–157b5.

———. 1996. *Dialogues*. Paris: Flammarion.

———. 2003. *Deux régimes de fous, textes et entretiens 1975–1995*. Édition préparée par David Lapoujade. Paris: Minuit.

Gaskin Richard. 1995. *The Sea Battle and the Master Argument: Aristotle and Diodorus Cronus on the Metaphysics of the Future*. Berlin: W. de Gruyter.

Hintikka, Jakko. 1975. *Time and Necessity: Studies in Aristotle's Theory of Modality*. Oxford: At the Clarendon Press.

———. 1977. *Aristotle on Modality and Determinism*. Amsterdam: North-Holland, Acta philosophica fennic.

Kripke, Saul A. 1999. *Naming and Necessity*. Cambridge: Harvard University Press.

Leclercq, Stéfan. 2002. *Gilles Deleuze*. Mons: Éditions Sils Maria.

Lovejoy, Arthur O. 1936. *The Great Chain of Being, A Study of the History of an Idea*. Cambridge: Harvard University Press.

Moreau, Joseph. 1987. *L'univers leibnizien*. Hildesheim: Georg Olms.

Steeves, James. 2001. "The Virtual Body: Merleau-Ponty's Early Philosophy of Imagination." *Philosophy Today* 45, no. 1: 370–80.

Contributors

Duane H. Davis is a professor of philosophy at The University of North Carolina at Asheville. He was 2011 Distinguished Scholar in Residence, Pontificia Universidade Católica do Paraná, Curitiba, Brasil. He edited *Merleau-Ponty's Later Works and Their Practical Implications: The Dehiscence of Responsibility* (Albany: Humanity Press, 2001) and is the author of numerous publications on philosophical and interdisciplinary projects concerning recent French thought—especially Merleau-Ponty, phenomenology, and French Marxism. He has lectured extensively in many countries of Europe, South America, and North America. He has directed or co-directed four international conferences on Merleau-Ponty's thought.

Cheryl A. Emerson is a doctoral student in comparative literature at SUNY Buffalo, with interests in William Faulkner, Merleau-Ponty, modern and postmodern aesthetics, and narrative theory. She has published essays on Henri Bergson and Robert Penn Warren's *All the King's Men*, the imagery of Ovid's *Metamorphosis* as present in Thomas Wolfe's *Look Homeward, Angel*, and presented conference papers on the aesthetics of modernism in Katherine Anne Porter's *Ship of Fools* as well as language of race in Porter's short story collection *The Old Order*. Her current projects include a study of "Ambiguities of Appearance in Hannah Arendt and Merleau-Ponty," and "In the Language of Departure: Erín Moure's *Insecession* of Chus Pato's *Secession*."

William S. Hamrick is professor emeritus of philosophy at Southern Illinois University Edwardsville. He is the author of numerous articles and presentations to national and international philosophical groups. His specialties include Merleau-Ponty and process philosophies, mainly that of Alfred North Whitehead. He is the author of *An Existential Phenomenology of Law* (Dordrecht: Martinus Nijhoff Publishers, 1987), *Kindness and the Good Society* (Albany: State University of New York Press, 2002), co-editor of *Merleau-Ponty and Environmental Philosophy* (Albany: State University of New York Press, 2007); and, most recently, the author, with Jan Van der Veken, of *Nature and Logos, A Whiteheadian Key to Merleau-Ponty's Fundamental Thought* (Albany: State University of New York Press, 2011).

Galen A. Johnson is professor of philosophy at the University of Rhode Island and general secretary (executive director) of the International Merleau-Ponty Circle. He received his PhD from Boston University and has studied additionally in France, Switzerland, Belgium, and the UK. He has been a recent recipient of fellowships from the National Endowment for the Humanities (NEH) and American Philosophical Society (APS). Most recently, he is editor of *The Merleau-Ponty Aesthetics Reader: Philosophy and Painting* (1993, 2008), and author of *The Retrieval of the Beautiful: Thinking Through Merleau-Ponty's Aesthetics* (2010). He has presented his research across North America, in Europe, and Africa, especially in France at *École Normale Supérieure* in Paris and the University of Paris—Sorbonne. His current research interests include the art and writings of Paul Klee, a co-authored book-length study of Merleau-Ponty's poetics, and a study of the sublime and the baroque in Merleau-Ponty's late writings.

Patricia M. Locke is a tutor at St. John's College, Annapolis, Md., where she teaches across the curriculum. Most recently she edited *Merleau-Ponty: Space, Place, Architecture*, with Rachel McCann (Ohio University Press, 2015). Current manuscript in progress: *The Nighttime World of Marcel Proust*. Locke is also a painter.

Marta Nijhuis is an Italian-Dutch visual artist based in Lyon, France. Due to her philosophical background, she is lecturer at the Université Jean Moulin Lyon 3 and at the EAC Lyon, School of Engineering in Culture, Art and Luxury, where she teaches aesthetics and theory of images. Her artworks have been on show in several galleries, cultural associations, foundations, and institutions in Italy and France; among these, the Cappelletti Gallery and the Ponte Rosso Gallery in Milan, the Giorgio Correggiari Foundation in Bari, and the historical venue of the Manufacture des Tabacs in Lyon. Many of her works are part of private collections in Italy, France, England, Switzerland, China, and the United States.

Sara J. Northerner has a Bachelor of Fine Arts degree from Washington University in St. Louis, Missouri, and a Master of Fine Arts degree from

Cranbrook Academy of Art in Bloomfield Hills, Michigan. A former professor of art, Sara graduated from the University of Louisville with her doctorate in interdisciplinary humanities with a specialization in phenomenological aesthetics. To continue her interests in contemporary art, she maintains an active studio practice and works collaboratively with other artists, designers, and writers. Currently, Dr. Northerner is an independent scholar and oversees creative communication as an administrator in the Information Technology department at the University of Louisville.

Bryan E. Norwood is a PhD candidate in the history and theory of architecture at Harvard University working on the intersection of philosophy and architectural thought. His dissertation is an investigation of the conceptual and historiographical developments in architectural history that accompanied the formation of university-based architectural education in the late nineteenth and early twentieth century. He received a BA in philosophy and a bachelor of architecture from Mississippi State University, an MA in philosophy from Boston University, and an AM in architecture from Harvard.

Marcello Vitali Rosati is an assistant professor in literature and digital culture in the Department of French Literature of the University of Montreal. He studied philosophy and literature, and holds a PhD from the University of Pisa (Italy) and the University of Paris IV La Sorbonne. Previous publications include several articles and four books: *Riflessione e trascendenza, Itinerari a partire da Lévinas* (Pisa: ETS, 2003), *Corps et virtuel. Itinéraires à partir de Merleau-Ponty* (Paris: Harmattan, 2009), *S'orienter dans le virtuel* (Paris: Hermann, 2012), and *Égarements. Amour, mort et identités numériques* (Paris: Hermann, 2014).

Robert Switzer has been teaching philosophy at The American University in Cairo since 1991; currently, he is dean of undergraduate studies and the university's Academy of Liberal Arts. He received his BA and MA from the University of Toronto (1982, 1983), and his PhD from The Pennsylvania State University (1989). Switzer's research interests are mainly centered in the history of philosophy and recent continental thought, but also range from the ethics of economic development to the philosophy of music. Recent publications include "Ambient Soundscapes: Towards a Phenomenology of Musical Space," in *The Journal of Phenomenological Inquiry,* " 'Raging Discordance': Heidegger-Nietzsche on Truth and Art," in Babich, Denker, and Zaboroski, eds, *Neu Interpretation Zu Heidegger's Auseinandersetzung mit Nietzsche* (Amsterdam: Rodopi Press), and "The Resonance of the Sacred:

Body, Dimensionality and Place," in *Humanistic Perspectives on Sacred Space* (Cairo Papers in Social Science).

Jessica Wiskus conducts interdisciplinary research that explores the intersection between phenomenology and artistic expression. She is the author of *The Rhythm of Thought: Art, Literature, and Music after Merleau-Ponty* (Chicago: University of Chicago Press, 2013) and serves as an associate professor of music at Duquesne University, where she is also the director of the Center for the Study of Music and Philosophy.

Index

www.ingramcontent.com/pod-product-compliance
Lightning Source LLC
La Vergne TN
LVHW040757070826
844660LV00025B/1176

* 9 7 8 1 4 3 8 4 5 9 5 8 5 *